PENGUIN BOOKS ·

RUSSIA'S WAR

Richard Overy is Professor of Modern History at King's College, London. He is the author of thirteen books on the Third Reich and the history of World War II, including, most recently, *Why the Allies Won*. He is currently at work on the *Oxford History of the Second World War* and completing a history of the Nazi economy.

Bomber Command, 1939–45

The Nazi Economic Recovery, 1932–1938

Origins of the Second World War

Penguin Historical Atlas of the Third Reich

'Times' Atlas of the Twentieth Century

Why the Allies Won

The Inter-War Crisis, 1919–1939

The Air War, 1939–1945

Goering: The 'Iron Man'

The Road to War (with A. Wheatcroft)

War and Economy in the Third Reich

RICHARD OVERY

Russia's War

PENGUIN BOOKS

PENGUIN BOOKS
Published by the Penguin Group
Penguin Group (USA) Inc., 375 Hudson Street, New York, New York 10014, U.S.A.
Penguin Books Ltd, 80 Strand, London WC2R 0RL, England
Penguin Books Australia Ltd, 250 Camberwell Road, Camberwell, Victoria 3124, Australia
Penguin Books Canada Ltd, 10 Alcorn Avenue, Toronto, Ontario, Canada M4V 3B2
Penguin Books India (P) Ltd, 11 Community Centre, Panchsheel Park, New Delhi – 110 017, India
Penguin Books (N.Z.) Ltd, Cnr Rosedale and Airborne Roads, Albany, Auckland, New Zealand
Penguin Books (South Africa) (Pty) Ltd, 24 Sturdee Avenue,
Rosebank, Johannesburg 2196, South Africa

Penguin Books Ltd, Registered Offices: 80 Strand, London WC2R 0RL, England

First published in the United States of America by TV Books, Inc. 1997
Published in Penguin Books 1998

9   10

Copyright © IBP Films Distribution, Ltd., 1997
All rights reserved
Photo illustrations courtesy of IBP Films Distribution, Ltd.

THE LIBRARY OF CONGRESS HAS CATALOGUED THE HARDCOVER AS FOLLOWS:
Overy, R.J.
Russia's war: blood upon the snow/Richard Overy—1st ed.
p.   cm.
Includes bibliographical references and index.
ISBN 1-57500-051-2 (hc.)
ISBN 0 14 02.7169 4 (pbk.)
1. World War, 1939–1945—Russia (Federation)
2. Russia (Federation)—History.   I. Title.
D765.O84   1997
940.54′0947   QBI97–40837

Printed in the United States of America
Set in Monotype Sabon
Designed by Joe Gannon
Maps courtesy of Richard Overy

Contents

Illustrations

List of Maps and Tables

Preface

The story of the Soviet war effort between 1941 and 1945 is one of the most remarkable, not just in the modern age, but in any age. For a long time it was a story shrouded in secrecy, little known or understood in the West. Over the past decade or so that situation has changed. Few would now contest the view that the Soviet war effort was the most important factor, though not the only one, in the defeat of Germany. The focus of the debate has now shifted to how the Soviet Union achieved that victory, and on this issue there is still no scholarly consensus. There is now a wealth of evidence not available twenty years ago to help to answer that question. Much of *Russia's War* draws on that evidence, which is now widely available in the West. It shows both sides of the war: the war against Germany and the war against Soviet society; the military conflict and the terror.

This book was produced to accompany a television series that has succeeded triumphantly in bringing the Soviet war effort to life. 'Russia's War', a series of ten fifty-two minute documentaries produced and financed by IBP Films in London in association with Victory Series in Russia, was inspired by the changing history of the war. The documentaries show all sides of the war, from military defeat and incompetence to military triumph, from simple Soviet patriotism to the terror of the regime against its own people. The films were made using materials made available from hitherto-closed film sources in the former Soviet Union. They are intercut with testimony from survivors of the war. The interviews were conducted in Russia in 1995, with the exception of a number which were made much earlier for Soviet films.

The inspiration behind the project lay with the executive producer, Judith De Paul, who succeeded in winning the co-operation of five senior Russian film directors and a co-executive producer in Moscow, Alexander Surikov. The films were produced in collaboration over a two-year period in 1994 and 1995. The book was written in 1997 and incorporates further material that became available from Russia in the two preceding years. I am particularly grateful for all the unstinting encouragement that Judith De Paul has given me. I would also like to thank the supervising editor of 'Russia's War', Nick Barnard, who has been unfailingly helpful over the six months it took to produce the book. Vladimir Bouilov has translated at a moment's notice anything in Russian that I needed, for which I am more than thankful. My publisher, Peter B. Kaufman, has been patient and long-suffering enough. The usual pre-emptive confession of responsibility for errors and misinterpretations is more than necessary here as I trespass into less familiar territory. A final thanks, as ever, to my family.

Richard Overy
London, May 1997

Introduction

This book is the direct offspring of a remarkable series of television documentaries that were made in London during 1995 with the co-operation of a number of distinguished Russian film-makers. The film records used in making the series were made available from the KGB film collection and the Presidential Archive, and they are unique in their range and historical quality. The very fact that 'Russia's War', the name given to the television series, could be made outside Russia at all reflects the greater openness between Russia and the West following the collapse of the Soviet Union in 1991. The objective of the films is to give Western audiences for the first time as full a visual account of the Soviet war effort as the film sources will allow.

The book follows closely the structure and substance of the films and takes its title from the series. Like the films, the purpose of the book is to bring to a non-Russian readership a history of the Soviet war effort based on the extensive revelations made during the decade after Mikhail Gorbachev declared the age of *glasnost*. It does not pretend to offer startling new discoveries. It is a summary of the present state of the debate in what has become an extraordinarily unstable historical landscape. Every month brings new discoveries and new publications. The history of the former Soviet Union is in ferment. In twenty years' time it may be possible at last to write something approaching a definitive history. Current writing has a provisional air to it, and this book is no exception. Nonetheless, the history of the Soviet war effort between 1941 and 1945 is well worth writing. The spate of new material has not failed to make the subject more exhilarating and more vivid. None of the human drama has been lost. In many ways the revelations have fortified it.

The established story of the Soviet war effort, of the 'Great Patriotic War', as it came to be called, was allowed to solidify in the decade after 1945 and remained remarkably intact down to the 1980s. In official circles the tale of heroic socialist struggle against the fascist demon remained intact down to 1991. Soviet writing on the war was carefully censored, and the central archives of the conflict remained closed or were restricted to only the most privileged of officially favoured historians. To give but one example: in the 1960s Marshal Zhukov, Stalin's Deputy Commander in Chief for much of the war, wrote two volumes of memoirs. They were heavily doctored. The first edition took three years to prepare and was shown, briefly, to Leonid Brezhnev, the Soviet leader, for final approval. Zhukov was told to include the fiction that Brezhnev took part in an incident on the southern front. When the first edition was published Zhukov complained, 'That book, it is not mine.' Even the smallest changes were insisted upon. Where Zhukov wanted to call the failure in the summer of 1941 a 'rout', he was made to write 'retreat' instead.[1]

Zhukov's memoirs finally appeared in a tenth, and full, version in 1990. Other memoirs have been released for the first time or have been freed from the censor's red pencil. The full version of Khrushchev's taped interviews, many of which were suppressed in the 1960s when his sanitized memoir was published, has now become available.[2] Much of the testimony on which it was necessary to rely even ten years ago has turned out to be misleading and distorted, even mendacious. When Zhukov challenged Marshal Yeremenko face-to-face about why he had lied in his memoirs about the role he and Zhukov had played at Stalingrad, Yeremenko replied that Khrushchev had asked him to.[3] It may never be possible to penetrate entirely this veil of half-truths and distortions, but there is a genuine will in modern Russia to set the record straight. We now know much more than we did, and we can be more confident that what we do know is closer to historical reality.

There remain serious gaps, however. Wartime Foreign Ministry archives and the records of the main political and administrative organs remain closed, as do the records of the KGB/NKVD security apparatus and military or technical records regarded as still too sensitive to reveal. Even where greater candour has prevailed – the publication of official casualty statistics, for example – there remain frustrating gaps. The figures published in 1993 by General G. F. Krivosheyev give the fullest account yet available, but they omit three operations that were clear failures. The official figures themselves must be viewed critically, given the difficulty of knowing in the chaos of 1941 and 1942 exactly who had been killed, wounded or even conscripted.[4] If the words 'alleged' or 'suggested' or 'approximately' appear with disarming regularity in what follows, this is testament to how much work still needs to be done to provide even an agreed-upon narrative for the war years.

Stalin remains almost as elusive as ever. The crude popular image of Stalin, the triumphant and omnicompetent warlord, disappeared in 1956 when de-Stalinization began in earnest in the Soviet Union. But the absence of a full private archive, or even one based upon Stalin's extensive public activities, forces historians to speculate on a great many aspects of his wartime leadership. Much more testimony is available now from Stalin's political associates or from his military leaders than ever before, but the inner thoughts, hard to decipher even for those who knew him, remain shrouded. Even the circumstances of his death, discussed at greater length in Chapter 10, cannot be agreed upon among those who claim to have been witnesses.

This is not the only problem when discussing Stalin. The revelations of the wartime terror and the early military failures make Stalin an easy target in the search for culprits. Yet the concentration of fire on the dictator not only makes it difficult to understand how a man so apparently corrupt and brutalized could have led his country to victory at all, but also fails to take account of the wider system in which Stalin was lodged. The war effort was not the product of one man, nor could it be made to bend entirely to his will. The role of the Party in sustaining popular mobilization, of the apparatus of terror under the grotesque Beria or of the Red Army itself, the largest military force ever assembled, is as much a part of the history of the war as Stalin's personal dictatorship. The mood of *glasnost* history has been one of recrimination and anger. When the dust has settled there will be time to assess Stalin and the system anew, both strengths and weaknesses. Stalin is an easy figure to hate but more difficult to understand, as history must.

Writing the story of the Soviet war has been a humbling experience. The debt that is owed to the many historians of the conflict, Russian and non-Russian, will quickly be evident. Soviet studies now provide a wealth of imaginative and exciting scholarship, much of it carried out at the very coalface of the subject, where the material is being dug out and shipped to the sunlight for the first time. Two veritable Stakhanovites deserve particular mention. Professor John Erickson and Colonel David Glantz have done more than any other Western scholars to communicate to the non-Russian world the fruits of Soviet and post-Soviet research. The account of the military struggle that follows would have been impossible without the careful reconstruction of the battle history carried out by both historians over the last twenty years.

The story of the Soviet war is humbling in another sense, too. The conflict was fought on such a gigantic scale and with such an intensity of feeling that conventional historical discourse seems ill-equipped to convey either very satisfactorily. The human cost, now estimated by some Soviet scholars to be as high as 43–47 million people, can only poorly be conveyed by statistics.[5] It is surely no accident that poetry meant so much to ordinary Russians and that through poetry, not a mere recital of numbers, the awful reality of war could be expressed: 'Tired with the last fatigue/ Seized by the death-before-death,/ His great hands limply spread,/ The soldier lies.'[6] Even Marshal Zhukov, remembered by those who served him as a coarse and brutal commander, read poetry in the midst of the carnage. A Tolstoy, a Nietzsche, perhaps might convey the essence of the suffering of the vast, tragic canvas on which that suffering was daubed. Little, perhaps nothing, of the experience of most Western historians will have prepared them to account for what they find in the history of Russia's war.

The key to understanding that war lies with an understanding of Russia herself. It was not, of course, just 'Russia's war'. The Russian empire, and after it the Soviet Union, embraced a complex ethnic geography. In 1940 Russians made up only 58 per cent of the population. There were at least twenty other major nationalities, most prominent among them the Ukrainians and Belorussians, on whose territories in the western Soviet Union most of the war was fought out. The nationalities, though dominated by the Russian heartland, provided a rich and diverse set of cultures, steeped in an ancient history. These differences were also shaped by topography. The Soviet Union spanned the whole of northern and central Asia, from almost permanently frozen tundra wasteland in the north to the luxuriant farmlands of Transcaucasia in the south. The Soviet Union inherited a state that was as Asian as it was European.

It is essential to grasp this diversity to understand what it is that made Russia, and the Soviet Union, different from the Western world. That difference has often been ignored. It is still underestimated by many in the West, who see the region as a backward version of modern industrial society, just as it was played down by Communists and fellow-travellers of the 1930s and 1940s, who thought that Stalin had created a form of the modern Western state that was both more socially efficient and more just. That difference was greater still in the 1940s. 'Few Western Europeans,' wrote the German SS General Max Simon, 'have any idea of the actual habits and mode of life of the Russians . . .'[7] The German attackers were already predisposed to assume that Soviet society was primitive, and, by the standards of the developed economies of the West, much of it was, at least in the countryside. But this was to misunderstand Russian society. It was not so much primitive as alien. The Soviet Union was not like Western Europe, and there is no reason why it should have been.

The war exposed many of the enduring features of Russian and Soviet culture. Soldiers were brutal because much of their experience of life was brutal and harsh. Their resilience and stubbornness, the toughness of both men and women, were the product of a bitter climate and extreme conditions of work. The coarser side of Russian life was evident in the routine of the labour camps or the discipline of the regiment or the factory. Yet ordinary people could also display a traditional sentimentality, founded in a powerful sense of both history and place. Some idea of how universal was that respect for the past, the feeling of rootedness, of belonging, can be gleaned from one among many stories of the war years told by the writer Ilya Ehrenburg. In the retreat of 1941 before the German onslaught, the curator of the Turgenev Museum in the city of Orel packed up the contents and placed them in a railcar. The centrepiece was a worn sofa upon which the famous writer had thought great thoughts. At every station the curator was faced with an angry crowd of refugees struggling to find space on the train to take them eastward. Each time he explained that the jumble belonged to the great Turgenev, and each time the mob relented.[8]

This is a story that can be understood only in the wider context of a popular attachment to art that cuts entirely across boundaries of class or education. It fits ill with any idea of primitiveness. Locked away in the horrors of the Gulag camps, Aleksandr Solzhenitsyn could still recall a man who sang to him snatches of Schubert.[9] The almost universal love of poetry has already been remarked. People were sentimental about the place they came from, about their way of life, even when conditions were grim. Soviet society was still, by the war, shot through with traditional modes of association, through tribe or clan or commune. The modernization imposed by the Communist Party in the 1930s had already begun to break down those ancient patterns of belonging, but not entirely so. The feeling can scarcely be described as nationalism, for there were too many nationalities for that to be coherent. Patriotism conveys it better, but not entirely, for the feeling which brought forth a remarkable endurance from the Soviet people is almost passive, fatalistic. One of the most famous verses to come out of the 'Great Patriotic War', from a poem about the comic hero Vasya Tyorkin, exactly captures the mixture of dull stoicism and historical awareness:

> Tiorkin snores. There's no more to it.
> He just takes things as they come.
> 'I belong, and well I know it.
> Russia needs me. Here I am.'[10]

The history of the war cannot be understood if these elements in Soviet life are ignored. Material explanations of Soviet victory are never quite convincing. It is difficult to write the history of the war without recognizing that some idea of a Russian 'soul' or 'spirit' mattered too much to ordinary people to be written off as mere sentimentality, however mundane or banal or brutalizing was the real day-to-day experience of war.

Other striking aspects of the Soviet war effort are the continuities with an older past, which Stalinist modernization did not eliminate. Much of what is taken to be a product of the Stalinist system was part of Russian tradition, modified, enlarged or transposed, but still recognizable. Some of those continuities are more trivial. The famous Potemkin villages of Catherine the Great's Russia, which were painted and cleaned up for important visitors to demonstrate the cheerful progressiveness of the autocracy, have more-than-faint echoes in the model farms and factories decked out to show Western well-wishers the smiling face of Communism. When the American politician Henry A. Wallace visited the gold-mining centre at Magadan in the Soviet far east in 1944, he saw nothing of the brutal forced-labour regime that kept the mines going. In Irkutsk Wallace gave a speech laden with a terrible irony: 'Men born in wide, free spaces will not brook injustice and tyranny. They will not live even temporarily in slavery.'[11]

Other continuities are more striking and more significant. The regime of forced prison labour, deportations and exile was not a Stalinist invention, not even a Soviet one. For 300 years imperial Russia exploited slave labour. The state used criminals, rebels, even tax-dodgers, to build roads and railways, to man mines in the harsh climate of the northern empire, to construct cities and fortifications. During the nineteenth century thousands were exiled to the sparsely populated reaches of Siberia, where they were left with nothing and died in their thousands. In the early twentieth century political dissidents began to join the criminals in large numbers. Between 1905 and 1914 the numbers sentenced to hard labour (*katorga*) rose fivefold as the political authority of the Tsarist regime began to crumble.[12] The world of the secret policeman and the *zek*, the hapless slave labourer, long predated the coming of revolution in 1917. Stalin did to his people what Russia's rulers had always done.

This does not make it any easier to forgive the terror and the atrocities of the 1930s and the 1940s, but it does help to make more comprehensible what otherwise seems inexplicable. Perhaps Western opinion has been more shocked by the revelations of Stalinist oppression because it contrasted so sharply with the romantic image of a young proletarian state struggling to impose social justice, a view that seduced western Communists before the war. Stalin did fight a war against his own people, but not simply because he was a Bolshevik. It would not be an exaggeration to say that every Russian ruler has been at war with the people, partly because the Russian empire was a multinational empire built on conquest, partly because governing Russian society always required some element of terror to hold the vast, peasant-based, anarchic community together.

The situation was no different in war. The final publication in 1988, after almost half a century of official silence, of Stalin's notorious wartime Orders 270 and 227 (which authorized savage reprisals against those who fell into captivity, and their families, and against those who retreated rather than fight) evoked outrage as a manifestation of Stalinist tyranny at its most irrational and vicious. Yet military life had always been harsh in Russia. Discipline was arbitrary and bloody. The Tsarist war effort between 1914 and 1917 ushered in 'penal battalions', punishment units for deserters and criminals which were sent on the worst missions. The army was kept at the front in the First World War with what came to be called 'blocking units' in the Second, whose job was to prevent desertion and banditry. During the civil war that followed the revolution in 1917, military discipline was so difficult to maintain for both sides that methods were adopted which easily stand comparison with Stalin's. A harsh regime produced a brutalized soldiery. The atrocities of the civil war did not cause the atrocities of the later conflict, but many of the Red Army officers who rose to command positions after 1941 had been junior officers in the civil war and had witnessed or perpetrated horrors, against the enemy, against peasant rebels, even against their own men.

Most of this story lies outside the scope of *Russia's War*. It is recalled here only in order to put Stalin, Stalinism and the 'Great Patriotic War' into the context of Russia's past. The revolutionaries of 1917 inherited that complex legacy, and the state they constructed on the ruins of Tsarism owed more to that inheritance than they would have wished. Modernization continued during the 1920s and 1930s; indeed, without it the war with Germany would have gone very differently. Russia's war between 1941 and 1945 was a rich amalgam of the modern and the ancient. Stalin chose to fight the war not as a simple expression of socialist patriotism. The propaganda war was fought using heroes of the past viewed through red-tinted spectacles. Aleksandr Nevsky, the thirteenth-century Muscovite prince who defeated invasion by the Teutonic Knights, was made at the end of Sergei Eisenstein's film to say words which were reproduced throughout the war: 'He who comes to us with the sword, shall perish by the sword. On that the Russian land has stood and will stand.'[13]

I

The Darkness Descends:
1919–1937

He is the new Genghis Khan. He will slaughter us all.

Nikolai Bukharin, 1928

It is October in Russia. Three Army Groups are forcing their way against weak defences towards Petrograd and Moscow. They treat the local population with brutality, burning villages, slaughtering the inhabitants. They capture one city after another: Kiev, Odessa, Voronezh, Orel. By mid-October one Army Group is within striking distance of Moscow, approaching Tula; another is encircling Petrograd, preparing to seize the city. They are harassed by partisan bands. In Moscow the Government panics. Plans are laid to move eastward to a safer haven in the Ural mountains. Local workers are forced into labour battalions to dig trenches and barricades to keep the enemy at bay. In Tula local Communists force the city's population at the point of a gun to prepare primitive fortifications, while their families are held hostage. Improvised forces are gathered together for a last-ditch defence. A successful counter-offensive saves Moscow. The fighting is murderous, high casualties on both sides, little quarter given. The Government stays on in Moscow; the Red Army of workers and peasants, bullied by Communist commissars and security police, finally triumphs over the forces of reaction.

This is a thoroughly familiar story, but it is not 1941. The year is 1919, and the threat comes not from the three German Army Groups that powered across the Soviet Union after the attack launched on 22 June 1941, but from the armies of the counter-revolutionaries in the long and sanguinary civil war that followed the Bolshevik

Revolution of October 1917. The story is retold here because the civil war was central not only for the establishment of the Soviet state, but in shaping the attitude to war of Soviet leaders and the future commanders of the Red Army that fought Hitler. Fighting among the troops that drove back the threat to Moscow in 1919 was the young Georgi Zhukov, who became the most celebrated soldier of the Second World War. He was a cavalryman in the 1st Red Cavalry Corps, which supplied not only Zhukov, but Marshal Kliment Voroshilov, the Commissar of Defence for fifteen years under Stalin; Marshal Semyon Timoshenko, his successor in 1940; and the colourful but incompetent cavalryman, Semyon Budyenny, who became the commander of Soviet cavalry in 1943.[1]

Stalin himself was a representative of the Central Committee, the leading organ of the Bolshevik Party and of the fledgling revolutionary state, in the threatened city of Petrograd. Survivors remembered a soft-spoken but arrogant man who was used to getting his own way and who treated his colleagues and subordinates with unusual harshness. He was adept at inventing conspiracies and hunting out treachery. He unearthed a plot in the Western Front command at Petrograd, and the plotters were removed. He helped to organize the defence of the city with threats and force. He had no scruples about punishing deserters or slackers or the hated bourgeoisie, the enemy of the new proletarian order, demonized by Bolshevik propaganda. For his work in Petrograd he shared with Leon Trotsky, Commissar of Defence, the honour of receiving the first award of the Order of the Red Banner. Stalin won a reputation for being both blunt and uncompromising. He characteristically ordered vigorous counter-attacks, whatever the cost in lives, and urged the Central Committee to sack hesitant or more scrupulous commanders. It would be rash to argue that Stalin's behaviour during the civil war anticipated exactly the role he would play as Supreme Commander during the German-Soviet war between 1941 and 1945, but the resemblances are remarkable.

The civil war played a major part in defining the character of the new Communist state, for the success of the revolution of October 1917 had to be won through three years of cruel and desperate conflict.

The civil war defined the enemies that the new society faced and continued to face in Communist demonology thereafter: the club of imperialist capitalist powers, which sent troops and supplies to help the counter-revolutionary forces; the counter-revolutionaries themselves, reactionary 'bourgeois' agents who were the mortal class enemies of the worker–peasant alliance; nationalist movements in the many non-Russian areas of the new state, which threatened to undermine the new proletarian commonwealth by promoting a narrow chauvinism. Stalin fought against them all with vigour in 1919 and continued to fight them with relentless terror until his death in 1953.

He was not alone in seeing the civil war not as a simple military conflict but as a clash of ideologies and social forces. The civil war placed Soviet Communism on a war footing. The new party became an agent of mobilization, in the towns, where workers were forced to join militia or dig defences, and in the villages, where food was seized with a savage disregard for peasant survival and farmers were drafted, often against their will, into the tough regime of the young Red Army. The language of the Party was spiced with military vocabulary; Party activists wore simple military-style uniforms (Stalin retained the habit throughout his life); thousands of new recruits into the Party in 1919 and 1920 came from the ranks of the Red Army. Military service and service to the Communist cause merged as one. The campaigns were undertaken in many cases by former officers of the Tsarist army, but control over strategy and operational decisions lay with local Military Committees or Soviets run by civilian revolutionaries, acting on the orders of the Central Committee. The army came to be viewed not as a professional force with its own institutions and commanders but as an arm of the broad social movement which was building Communism. The ideal of many revolutionaries was to do away with an army altogether and in its place to erect a popular militia of worker-peasant soldiers, the kind of revolutionary *levée* that Lenin, the architect of Bolshevik success in 1917, had described in *State and Revolution*, written the same year.

The effect of the Communist military struggle, which was finally won in 1920, was to create what one historian has described as a 'militarized socialism'.[2] Most of the Soviet élite of the 1920s and 1930s had either fought in or directed the civil war; those who had done neither found themselves at a disadvantage. The veteran mentality of the Party pervaded all areas of its activity. In the 1930s and during the war Stalin promoted to high office numerous men who had worked beside him in the civil war struggles, and also remembered those who had crossed him. That veteran loyalty kept in office many Stalinists who were manifestly inept. What they all shared was a profound belief that war and struggle was part of the order of things, a central characteristic of that stage of historical development in which the crumbling imperialist-capitalist order would give way to movements of social emancipation. They expected further foreign wars because it was in the nature of imperialism, as Lenin had also argued. They anticipated ceaseless struggles against the domestic enemies of revolution, whether peasant-capitalists or foreign spies. The result was a society that was kept in an almost perennial state of mobilization.

The cult of 'struggle' was not confined to the Soviet Union. It was central to the world-view of Adolf Hitler, who became during the war the greatest of the many enemies that Soviet Communism confronted. The widely shared belief in the necessity of conflict drew its substance from a generation of *fin-de-siècle* writing whose pessimistic forebodings of cataclysmic war and cultural decline were apparently borne out by the Great War of 1914–1918. The conflict provoked revolutionary upheaval in Russia and laid the foundations for German radical nationalism. The Communist belief that war was the locomotive of history, shunting old societies aside from the line to Utopia, was triumphantly demonstrated in 1917. Hitler's view that war was the proper school of national reawakening and sociobiological reconstruction was predicated on the German defeat. The two versions of struggle were not pre-ordained to meet on the battlefield in 1941, but given Hitler's view, expressed to his inner circle in the autumn of 1936, that since the eighteenth century the world had been rushing headlong towards a final historical reckoning with the tradition of the French Revolution and its bastard offspring, Bolshevism, such an outcome was always likely.[3]

The ending of the civil war in 1920 left the Soviet Union – a name not formally adopted until 1923 – a nominal federation of national

4

republics controlled in practice from the new Russian capital at Moscow. The cost of the civil war was the impoverishment of the country, the decline of industry, a famine that claimed millions of victims in the formerly grain-rich areas of the Ukraine and the loss of a fringe of territories which had belonged to the Tsarist empire – Finland, the Baltic states, Bessarabia (ceded to Romania) and half of Poland. As a result of these losses the new Soviet state was less European and more Asian than its predecessor. Its exclusion from Eastern Europe had been sealed in 1920 during a brief war with Poland, a state recently re-created by the post-war settlement. Polish leaders eager to take advantage of what they perceived to be the exhaustion of the Red Army invaded the Ukraine and occupied Kiev that May. Hatred of the Poles united Soviet society. Mikhail Tukhachevsky, one of the most successful of the younger civil war generals, handsome, forthright and personally courageous, led five armies against the main Polish forces and drove them back into Poland accompanied by some of the most savage fighting of the civil war. Poorly supplied and with tired troops, Tukhachevsky was finally halted in front of Warsaw. A treaty signed at Riga in March 1921 gave Poland a slice of the western Ukraine and pushed the Soviet frontier a hundred miles further to the east.

The Soviet leaders never forgot the war with Poland. Twenty years later the area was reoccupied amidst an orgy of reprisals. The defeat of 1920 showed that despite victory in the civil war the new state was weakly defended and insecure. Throughout the 1920s there were regular war scares, often based on the most trivial pretext – in 1923 when the Frenchman Marshal Foch visited Warsaw, in 1925 after the signing of the Treaty of Locarno ('preparation for war against the USSR', as the Soviet newspaper *Pravda* put it), in 1927 following the British decision to break off diplomatic relations.[4] It is customary to see these fears as a product of domestic politics, a device to focus popular attention on the external enemy and to unify the Party, but Russia's recent history, which included invasion by Germany and the Habsburg empire in 1914, intervention by fourteen states in the civil war and invasion by Poland in 1920, was enough in itself to encourage a constant vigilance and helps to explain the almost paranoid fear of attack or subversion that distinguished the Stalinist dictatorship.

The question of Soviet security was central to the development of the Soviet system. The Soviet state found itself, in Lenin's famous mixed metaphor, 'an oasis in the middle of the raging imperialist sea'.[5] Lenin counted on the Bolshevik example to provoke social revolution in the rest of Europe, so that the isolation would be overcome. In March 1919 an international Communist organization, the Comintern, was set up in Moscow. Its first task was to call on workers everywhere 'to wipe out the boundaries between states, transform the whole world into one co-operative commonwealth'. Lenin promised the first assembly of the International that the victory of Communism throughout the world was only a matter of time.[6] By the time of his death, in January 1924, that confidence had evaporated. The Soviet state was not in the vanguard of world revolution, but was an international pariah, perpetually on the defensive. Lenin's successors could not agree among themselves whether security lay in the hope that imperialist competition would engulf capitalism and usher in world revolution or in the mobilization of the Soviet Union's own resources to defend its own revolution. The former carried impossible risks. In 1925 the General Secretary of the Party, Josef Stalin, announced to Party leaders what was to become the chosen strategy for the regime, the building of 'socialism in one country'.[7]

The strategy of socialist self-defence made it imperative that the Soviet Union be adequately protected by military force. The position of the Red Army after the civil war was an uncertain one. It was regularly referred to as the Worker-Peasant Red Army to reflect its popular social base. Much of the civil war force melted away with the end of hostilities. Trotsky, who led the Red forces as head of the Revolutionary Military Council, established in April 1918, lost interest in military developments once the war was won. There was popular hostility to the officer corps on the grounds that the military élite constituted a threat of Bonapartist dictatorship, composed as it was of a great many officers unsympathetic to Bolshevism. Conditions in the armed forces were poor, with low pay, inadequate housing and limited career prospects. The place of the armed forces in a socialist society was poorly defined, their status insecure.

In January 1924, shortly after Lenin's death, the Central Committee established a commission to review the whole question of the future of the military in the Soviet state. The findings represented a powerful indictment of Trotsky's fading leadership. Many units had only half their officers. Out of 87,000 men trained to officer standard during the civil war, only 25,000 remained in service. Of the rest 30,000 were dead and approximately the same number demobilized.[8] The supply situation was found to be anything but adequate, with insufficient weapons and poor levels of food and equipment. The rank and file were regarded as demoralized; their officers were condemned as ill-trained and unprofessional. Trotsky's role was usurped by his deputy, Mikhail Frunze, a veteran civil war commander, who was to play a central part in shaping the development of the modern Red Army and Soviet military strategy. In January 1925 Trotsky was removed from his position as Chairman of the Military Council and Commissar for the Army and Navy, and Frunze took his place.

Though he held office for only ten months, until his death in October, Frunze achieved a great deal. Frunze's view of the armed forces represented a compromise between those who saw them as an instrument of revolution, to be led by Communists and composed of a proletarian militia, and those like Tukhachevsky who favoured large professional armed forces equipped with modern weapons and free from political supervision. Frunze started from the point of view that war with any capitalist enemy would be a total war, drawing on all the social and economic reserves of the state as the civil war had done. He favoured the development of an offensive army, rooted in the proletariat. But to achieve forces capable of protecting the revolution required, he believed, large-scale industrialization, with a commitment to a major defence sector, and a programme of military education to turn workers into professional soldiers with a Communist outlook. Professionalism combined with revolutionary zeal was to be assured by organizing both a regular army, with enhanced status and powers for its officer corps, and a territorial militia of workers and peasants.[9]

The organization was launched in 1924, but the first full call-up was achieved only in 1925 with a comprehensive military service law which laid down the foundation for the remarkable record of military mobilization achieved after 1941. For the regular soldiers the role of the political commissar, who had dominated the military system since the civil war, was downgraded, and full command responsibility was granted to officers. To counter the numerous complaints from Communist functionaries about the political unreliability of the officer corps, the proportion of Communists among the corps was increased. In 1925 over 40 per cent of the 76,000 officers and military officials were members of the Party.[10] Frunze also tackled one of the major problems exposed by the 1924 review: low morale and poor discipline. For officers there were immediate improvements. A distinctive uniform was introduced to set them apart from the rank and file. They were given a generous pay rise and better living quarters. Above all, they were given the right to tell their men what to do. This was the most contentious issue of all, for under Order Number 1, issued by the Petrograd Soviet in the memorable spring of 1917, officers could be challenged by those they led. The object had been to make the army democratic, but it led, as might have been expected, to ordinary soldiers arguing for hours about whether to obey a particular order. Discipline was impossible under such conditions. Scant attention was paid to the regular routine of military life; observers found Red Army soldiers shabby and unkempt. In 1925 Frunze introduced a new disciplinary code. Though strongly opposed by Communists, who saw this as a return to the bad old habits of the imperial army, it was gradually implemented, restoring the right of officers both to order and to punish.[11]

Frunze laid the foundation of the armed forces that fought the war against Germany, but he died before he saw the fruits of his reform programme in circumstances that remain obscure. He suffered from a chronic stomach complaint that doctors insisted required surgery, despite his protests. Stalin visited him in the hospital, where he pressured the surgeon to operate. Frunze died shortly afterwards. Foul play has never been proved.[12] Frunze's place was taken by one of Stalin's closest political allies, Kliment Voroshilov. A former metalworker from the southern Ukraine, he was a military amateur, with little formal education and no military training. Most of his forty-four years had been spent as a terrorist and, first in 1905 then 1917, as a revolutionary. During the civil war he became a political soldier, like Stalin. He was an unprepossessing personality. Short and pig-nosed, he had nothing of the military dash of other civil war heroes. He was an intimate of Stalin's from the civil war and remained part of the inner circle around the dictator for more than twenty years, a remarkable achievement in itself. He became Commissar of the Army and Navy (later changed to Commissar of Defence) in 1925 and kept the post until 1940. America's wartime ambassador doubly damned him as a man who was 'incompetent, but not dangerous'.[13]

Voroshilov's manifest ineptitude was compensated for by a second appointment in 1925. At the young age of thirty-two, Mikhail Tukhachevsky became chief of staff. A colonel in the Tsarist army, he had spent most of the Great War in a German prison camp. On his return he joined the Red Army and became an enthusiastic revolutionary and outstanding commander. He fought the campaign against the Poles in 1920 with Stalin as his political officer. His appointment was an inspired choice. What Voroshilov lacked in energy and experience was supplied by Tukhachevsky, a contrast that permanently soured relations between the two men. The chief of staff had one overriding ambition: to create a modern professional armed force fired with revolutionary élan. As did almost all the leading figures in the military establishment, Tukhachevsky saw the mass offensive as the strategy most appropriate to a revolutionary state. In 1926 he ordered a complete review of the armed forces and Soviet military doctrine. The fruit of that review, unambiguously titled *The Future War*, was published in May 1928. In it Tukhachevsky first laid out the idea that the grand offensive must be supported by thousands of tanks and armoured vehicles and thousands more aircraft, pouring forward at great speed to deliver to any enemy a knock-out blow of annihilating power.[14]

It was no accident that such a description almost perfectly matched the German attack launched on the Soviet Union thirteen years later. Tukhachevsky was a firm advocate of military westernization. *The Future War* owed not a little to a burgeoning programme of military collaboration in the 1920s between two most unlikely partners, the Red Army and the German Reichswehr. Links were first established between them in 1921. In August 1922 a firm agreement on military co-operation was signed, with a second and more extensive programme agreed to in March 1926 in Berlin. They were drawn together by their shared status as international pariahs in the early 1920s, the Soviet Union for its Communism, Germany for its alleged responsibility for the war of 1914.[15] Each had something the other badly wanted: the Soviet Union wanted access to advanced military technology and military thinking; Germany needed somewhere to develop the weapons and tactical experience it was denied under the disarmament terms of the Treaty of Versailles.

So it was that German officers, who were separated from their Communist collaborators by a yawning ideological chasm, found themselves operating together in secret three major military installations and a handful of industrial enterprises. At the spa town of Lipetsk, 300 miles south-west of Moscow, an airfield was set up where German pilots were trained and new aircraft were put through their paces. At Kama on the Volga a tank school was founded, where German soldiers first tried out the ideas that bore rich fruit in 1939. At Tomka a chemical warfare centre was built, where Soviet observers watched the German staff experiment with gas attack and gas protection. The entire collaboration was kept as secret as possible. Trainees travelled to the Soviet Union on false passports, in civilian dress. Those that died in training accidents were put in coffins in large crates described as 'aircraft parts', and shipped by sea back to the Baltic port of Stettin.[16] There also existed a more public exchange. Red Army officers were invited to German manoeuvres from 1925 on. Under Tukhachevsky's guidance Soviet military leaders spent months or years in Germany absorbing German strategic thinking, German tactical doctrine and German ideas on the military economy and logistical support. In 1931 German officers were sent to Moscow on training courses. The roll-call of Germans involved in the exchanges included names that became famous a decade later – Model, Brauchitsch, Keitel, Manstein, Guderian. But a decade later almost all their Red Army counterparts were dead.[17]

The lessons Tukhachevsky drew from the German side were central to the conception of modern war that emerged from the modernization of Red forces in the late 1920s. The primacy of the offensive became dogma. Revolutionary spirit may have been its justification, but the idea drew its real rationale from the nature of modern military technology – primarily the tank and the airplane. Tukhachevsky assumed that an offensive force, using these in combination and in large quantities, could, once it was mobilized, power forward at speed, penetrate the enemy lines of defence and then envelop the main enemy force in large, sweeping operations.[18] The concept of 'deep operations', so very different from the static trench warfare and the primacy of the machine-gun in the Great War, was bound up with modernity. The armed forces Tukhachevsky inherited were almost all horse-drawn; mobility was more likely to be supplied by a bicycle than a truck. The equipment was obsolete and badly made. He recognized that the offensive strategy could work only in the context of a more general modernization of Soviet society. He accepted the views of his German acquaintances that modern war meant total war, the mobilization of economic resources as a fundament for successful military campaigns. The Soviet Union lacked those resources. There thus existed a profound gap between the operational plans for the fast-moving armoured offensive and the reality of economic underdevelopment, which could be bridged only by a radical transformation of the Soviet economy.

Tukhachevsky's proposals for a military revolution were premature. His plans for aircraft and tank production were dismissed as quite unrealistic. His independent mind and authoritarian leadership earned him political enemies. In 1928 Stalin and Voroshilov had him removed as chief of staff. But in 1930, from a more modest post in Leningrad, Tukhachevsky forwarded a memorandum to the Kremlin, pressing the case for 40,000 aircraft and 50,000 tanks. Stalin accused him of 'Red militarism' and hinted that the idea smacked of economic ruin and counter-revolutionary sabotage.[19] Nonetheless the core of Tukhachevsky's reforms survived. By the early 1930s the Military Council and the General Staff had rejected any idea of defence in depth as an answer to Soviet backwardness. Under the guiding hand of Tukhachevsky's successor, the former Tsarist staff officer Boris Shaposhnikov, a strategy was elaborated which remained in force until its weaknesses were abruptly exposed in 1941. Future war was deemed to be a two-stage affair. The preliminaries would be fought out at or near the frontier by strong covering forces operating behind fixed fortified areas, while the slow process of mobilizing the mass peasant-worker army went on at a prudent distance from the front until it was ready to rain shattering blows on the enemy on the other side of the border. The mass offensive had more of the steamroller about it than Tukhachevsky's fast-moving juggernaut, but the shape of the strategy was not dissimilar. The difference lay with the idea of 'deep operations'. A powerful mobile strike force able to manoeuvre at will in the rear of the enemy line was regarded as incompatible with the current state of industrial development and the largely peasant soldiery at the army's disposal. The reforms of Frunze and Tukhachevsky supplied a more professional armed force. Standards of training and equipment were raised. The officers were given a status more consistent with their function. But the force was still primitively armed and poorly supplied, with an unsatisfactory level of morale.[20]

After ten years the Soviet state was little more secure than it had been at the end of the civil war. In 1927 there developed a war scare more alarming than anything Soviet leaders had seen since 1919, when forces from more than a dozen countries fought briefly side by side with the counter-revolutionaries. The war scare had a number of separate components, each by itself only mildly threatening but in combination full of menace. In late May in London the Soviet trade delegation was closed down following pressure from the 'Clear Out the Reds' campaign, organized by a group of Conservative Members of Parliament. The British Government broke off diplomatic relations.[21] In April the Soviet mission to China was closed down, and Chinese nationalists launched a bloody campaign against the Chinese Communists. In June the Soviet chargé d'affaires in Warsaw was assassinated. That month in *Pravda* Stalin announced that there was now 'the real and actual threat of a new war', though none came. The whiff of imperialist conspiracy begged for scapegoats. In May, twenty former Tsarist nobles who worked in government offices were arrested. On the day following the Warsaw assassination they were all executed without trial. Over the following weeks war-scare fever gripped Moscow.[22]

A few months later the Soviet Union embarked on a programme of large-scale industrialization, the first step in what came to be seen as a 'Second Revolution'. The timing perhaps owed something to the war scare or to the pressures to modernize the armed forces, but ultimately the industrial drive was brought about by the growing recognition among the Party faithful that their revolution was stumbling over the reality of a society largely composed of peasants, craftsmen and petty traders. At the end of the civil war little could be done to reverse the social reality of old Russia. In 1921 Lenin introduced the 'New Economic Policy', which permitted private trade and private ownership of land, and the grip on economic life held during the war loosened. By 1927 industrial output was back to approximately the levels of the pre-war Tsarist state, but the proletariat, in whose name the revolution to create a workers' state had been launched, was small, impoverished and socially isolated. Among the vast mass of the Soviet peasantry fewer than 0.7 per cent of households boasted a Communist Party member. The apparatus of state and industry relied on large numbers of what came to be called 'bourgeois experts', whose enthusiasm for the new regime believed to be muted.

The 'Second Revolution' has always been identified with the name of Josef Stalin, but it was the consequence not just of Stalin, who for much of the 1920s had been uncertain about how to approach issues of economic expansion and social reconstruction, but of pressure from thousands in the Party who wanted more aggressive modernization. They were intolerant of the backwardness of the peasant masses; they disliked their reliance on older experts who had served the Tsarist regime. Stalin came to identify with the radical element in the Party because he saw in the strategy of forced economic change the only way of strengthening the Soviet state, and with it his own position in the Party hierarchy, which had not yet reached the scale of full-fledged dictatorship. By the end of the first Five-Year Plan, launched in October 1927, that position had changed. He successfully isolated and eclipsed potential rivals in the Party. By the late 1920s Party organs began to address him by the simple term *vozhd*, or leader.

Stalin's rise to supreme power in the Soviet Union was slow and unobtrusive. Trotsky dismissed him as a political simpleton; Lenin condemned him in his final testament, written in December 1922, as a man too rude and impatient to be trusted with power. To outward appearances he was obliging, even-handed and modest, a dull official. His secretary recalled that Stalin would often sit for hours at meetings, at the side of the room, puffing on his pipe, asking the occasional question, proffering few opinions. His 'gift for silence' made him unique 'in a country where everybody talked too much'.[23] The contrast between the image of placid ordinariness and the historical picture of Stalin as the enslaver and butcher of his people has no easy explanation. It may never be fully explained, for Stalin left no secret diary and seldom revealed his inner thoughts. The official letters and speeches cannot be taken at face value, though they should not be discarded out of hand. The inner motives, the demons that drove Stalin on, are still the stuff of speculation. More than any other modern historical giant, Stalin remains an enigma. The story of his life is composed of effects as much as of causes. Why he chose to play the dictator's part is open to wide and conflicting interpretation.

The details of his life are well known. Stalin was born in 1879 in the small Georgian town of Gori. He had a squalid and brutalized upbringing. Regular beatings by his father, a failed and drunken cobbler, produced a personality that in the view of a boyhood friend was 'grim and heartless'.[24] He caught smallpox when he was six, which left him with the tell-tale marks on his sallow complexion. One arm was slightly withered from an infected ulcer. He escaped from penniless obscurity thanks to the exceptional memory that turned him into a star pupil at the local school. He was sent to a seminary school in Tiflis, where he made contact with the local social democrats. He was immediately attracted to Marxism in its Russian guise, with its emphasis on violent confrontation with the Tsarist state and an uncompromising terrorism. He carried with him all his life a hatred of privilege. He became a revolutionary activist, robbing banks to fund his politics. He was in and out of jail, fortunate to avoid execution. He emerged in 1917, at thirty-seven a revolutionary of wide experience, an agitator and terrorist by profession.

In 1917 Stalin was catapulted onto the national stage. He became one of the inner circle of Bolshevik leaders. In October he was rewarded by Lenin with the job of Commissar for the Russian Nationalities. As a Georgian, Stalin was thought to understand the problems of the smaller non-Russian peoples more than the westernized Bolshevik intellectuals. It could be said that he understood that mentality too well. He stamped hard on the drift towards autonomy, even on his own Georgian people. His second appointment, as Commissar for the Workers' and Peasants' Inspectorate, came in 1919. The office was created by Lenin to ensure that the Party could monitor what the sprawling bureaucratic apparatus was doing. Stalin used the position as a lever to examine the whole apparatus of state. He understood the machinery of government and its wide-flung personnel better than any other Communist leader. In 1922 his administrative skills and wide knowledge of the apparatus brought him the post of General Secretary of the Party, a position which he used to create his own power base and his only official role until he assumed high political office in 1941. There is no dispute that he had considerable political skills. He was not a dilettante dictator like Hitler. He worked long hours, late into the night. He paid extraordinary attention to detail.[25] He became adept in the art of dissimulation, so much so that he was usually able to get others to take the blame for unpopular decisions or political errors. He sheltered behind a carefully crafted myth of infallibility.

Those who knew Stalin well were only too aware that behind the austere and modest exterior there lurked another, coarser side to his personality. He was rude, cruel and vindictive. He bore grudges, thanks perhaps to his remarkable memory, for years. He was capable of displaying a ferocious temper; he treated those around him with a peremptory disdain. With a bullying sarcasm he could reduce those he summoned to stuttering confusion. He induced fear, not because people knew what he was capable of, but because there was no way of knowing. He was capricious – Lenin's word – and devious.[26] He had a deep, almost obsessive distrust of everyone around him, learned from his revolutionary youth lived in a world of police spies and *agents provocateurs*. He had no scruples whatsoever about the use of violence nor about the betrayal of trust. He was amoral, rather than immoral. In 1931 he told the biographer Emil Ludwig that he had learned from experience that 'the only way to deal with enemies is to apply the most ruthless policy of suppression.'[27] For one so personally self-effacing – Stalin, as we have seen, always chose to sit to one side in meetings, never to preside – he displayed a powerful vanity. His habits were modest enough. He dressed simply, worked in his unostentatious lodgings in the Kremlin, drank sparingly of vodka and Georgian wines and ate traditional Russian food. He liked to remain sober on most occasions, but encouraged a repulsive licence amongst those he invited to his conventional late-night feasting. The vanity was about power and its trappings. At some point in the early 1920s, in his new career as a revolutionary statesman, Stalin became an avid seeker after power.

Power is what Stalin got, more of it than he could ever have imagined in the Party squabbles that followed Lenin's death in 1924. Was it power for himself? His Russian biographer, Dmitri Volkogonov, has argued that power became an end in itself: 'the more power he had, the more power he accumulated and kept in his hands, the more power he wanted.'[28] The view of Stalin first as power-hungry, then power-crazed, has a long and respectable pedigree. But it is not entirely convincing. Stalin sought not simply power, but revolutionary power. His own advance, the survival of his personal power, depended upon the course of the revolution. No one doubts the sincerity of his revolutionary zeal before 1917. Lenin expressed open doubts in his testament as to whether Stalin could use 'power with sufficient caution', but he does not seem to have hesitated over Stalin's commitment to the cause. Stalin's bodyguard recalled his master's words, uttered in the civil war during the defence of the city of Tsaritsyn: 'I shall ruthlessly sacrifice 49 per cent, if by doing so I can save the 51 per cent, that is, save the Revolution.'[29] Stalin was unashamedly ruthless all his life; his egotism persuaded him that he was indispensable to the survival of Lenin's revolution. Power for himself was power to pursue his own narrow vision of what that revolution constituted.

Stalin was the driving force behind the 'Second Revolution'. His ambition was to turn a backward and inefficient state into a modern industrial society in ten years. It was a uniquely revolutionary ambition, which shaped the Soviet state and the Soviet peoples down to the collapse of the system in the 1990s. Together with the Five-Year Plans for industrial modernization the Party radicals recognized that the countryside – the prime cause of Soviet backwardness in the Communist view – had to undergo its own social revolution. In place of the millions of small private communes which had been formed since the revolution, as peasants seized the land for themselves, the state began to impose collectivization (the substitution of large state-owned farms run by Communist managers) and a new rural wage-labour force. The assault on peasant independence began in 1927 and was completed almost five years later. Millions were moved from the villages to the cities, where they were compelled to adopt an utterly different life. Millions refused or resisted and were taken as forced labour to build the infrastructure of the new economic system under the harshest conditions of work. The damage done to peasant life produced wide unrest in what was largely a peasant-based army. The collectivization programme was enforced not by the military, whose loyalty was doubtful, but by the special troops of the NKVD, the Internal Affairs Commissariat. In a little over ten years Soviet cities swelled by more than 30 million people; in 1926, four-fifths of Soviet society had lived and worked on the land; in 1939 the figure was down to just half. The industrial and agricultural policies of the 1930s produced the social revolution that Lenin could not produce in 1917.

Despite formidable obstacles to the provision of skilled labour, capital equipment and finance, the industrial revolution was pushed through. Behind the revolutionary rhetoric and dubious statistics there lay real achievement. The latest Western estimates of Soviet production in the 1930s still tell a remarkable story: steel output rose from 4.3 million tons in 1928 to 18.1 million a decade later; coal production more than trebled, from 35 million tons to 133 million; truck production, an insignificant 700 at the start of the plans, reached 182,000 in 1938.[30] The programme of industrialization was presented as a second civil war against the enemies of social change, chief among them the rich peasant or *kulak*, the saboteur and hooligan who held back economic progress, and the ideological deviationist who undermined popular commitment to change. The military language of 'struggle', 'battle', 'victory' and 'enemy' was not accidental. The regime saw counter-revolutionaries as the shock troops of foreign imperialism. The campaign for modernization was not simply about the survival of Communism in a backward society, but about the survival of the Soviet Union in a world of hostile capitalist powers.

Amidst the poverty and violence of working-class life in the Soviet Union under the three Five-Year Plans which spanned the period from 1927 to the outbreak of war, there surfaced a genuine popular enthusiasm for the tasks set by the Party. It was expressed in a country-wide culture of 'socialist emulation', exemplified by the young peasant-turned-miner from the Donbas region, Aleksandr Stakhanov. On 30 August 1935, Stakhanov, already deemed to be a model worker for regularly exceeding the modest norm of 6.5 tons per five-hour shift, worked non-stop through the night to produce 102 tons of coal. This was double the amount normally produced by the whole squad of eight miners working at the coalface, and it earned Stakhanov 200 roubles instead of the usual 30. At six in the morning the mine manager, Konstantin Petrov, called an emergency meeting of the Party committee of the enterprise. The early hour was explained by the news Petrov had to announce: a new world record for mining productivity. Not to be outdone, Stakhanov's comrades rushed to exceed his achievement: three days later the record tumbled. On 7 September a miner at the Karl Marx mine hewed 125 tons. A day later the editors of *Pravda*, keen to make what capital they could out of a man they nicknamed 'the Soviet Hercules', reported that a Red Army soldier on leave had dug 240 tons in six hours. The results were in fact achieved with a good deal of assistance from other workers, but the new soldiers of the industrial front won instant recognition. The 'shock workers', as they were called, were rewarded with extra pay and rations and better housing. By 1939 there were over 3 million exceptional workers, laden with medals for industrial heroism. When Stakhanov died at a ripe age in 1977, his home town was renamed in his honour, the only Soviet city to bear the name of a humble worker.[31]

The military strengthening of the Soviet Union was the most significant consequence of the 'Second Revolution'. The first Five-Year Plan gave priority to heavy industry and machine engineering, as Lenin's theory of economic development dictated. But from the early 1930s the industrial system began to turn out large quantities of weapons. At the beginning of 1928 the Red Army had 92 tanks; by January 1935 there were 10,180. In 1928 the air force had 1,394 aircraft of all kinds; in 1935 6,672. Fighter output increased fivefold between 1930 and 1934, bomber output by a factor of four. The significant figure was the proportion of the national product devoted to the defence sector. In 1913 it was 5.2 per cent; in 1932 it was already 9 per cent, more than double the figure at the outset of the plans; by 1940 it was 19 per cent. By 1932 one-quarter of all capital investment in heavy industry and engineering was in defence-related areas.[32] These figures represented an exceptional level of commitment to defence in peace-time. Arms were bought at the expense of living standards. Under the economic regime of the Five-Year Plans consumer goods were suppressed in favour of military output and the heavy industrial sectors vital to future war-making. The turning point in the military effort came in 1931. In February of that year Stalin addressed the first All-Union Congress of Managers, where he emphasized the priority of Soviet security in what became one of the few memorable speeches of his career:

One feature of the old Russia was the continual beatings she suffered for falling behind, for backwardness. She was beaten by the Mongol khans. She was beaten by the Turkish beys. She was beaten by the Swedish feudal lords. She was beaten by the Polish and Lithuanian gentry. She was beaten by the British and French capitalists. She was beaten by the Japanese barons. All beat her – for her backwardness. . . . We are fifty or a hundred years behind the advanced countries. We must make good this distance in ten years. Either we do it or they crush us.[33]

This was Stalin's most important statement on the relation-ship between military power and economic modernization. It was followed by a sharp acceleration in military output and the military budget.

One of the first results of Stalin's new military course was the rehabilitation of Tukhachevsky. In May 1931 he was brought back from exile in the Leningrad Military District to become Chief of Armaments; he was chief of staff again by 1934. Stalin and Voroshilov were now inclined to accept the Tukhachevsky strategic vision of massed tanks and aircraft, even to endorse the strategy of deep penetration, now that tanks and military vehicles were pouring off the assembly line. The Tukhachevsky plan called for 15,000 operational aircraft. In 1930 there were just over 1,000. By 1935 there were between 4,000 and 5,000, vastly greater than the air force of any other power. The mechanization plan called for a total of 90,000 tanks on mobilization. Tukhachevsky favoured bridging the gap between the modest tank force available in the mid-1930s and the giant tank armies of the future by utilizing 40,000 tractors from the factories supplying the collective farms, protected with armour plate and each carrying a heavy machine-gun. The development of fast tanks with large-calibre guns was made a priority, producing by the late 1930s the prototype of the famous T-34, the chief Soviet battle tank of the Second World War.[34]

From a policy of economic caution, Stalin moved to a strategy of massive stockpiling. The purpose was to provide the Red Army with the striking force necessary to destroy the putative enemy in a battle of annihilation, but the effect was to saddle the Soviet Union with a defence sector far larger than current international dangers justified and the armed forces with *matériel* that would soon be obsolescent. Nor, until the necessary personnel training was completed, could effective use be made of the strategy of 'deep operations' and the extensive stocks of current weapons. These issues were gradually addressed as Tukhachevsky took up the torch of professionalization once again. By 1932 two-thirds of the officer corps had been formally trained in military academies. Two years later the political officers were removed from all field formations, and their remaining influence at higher levels was much reduced. In 1935 the rank of Marshal of the Soviet Union was introduced, giving the military leadership a status it had not enjoyed since Tsarist times. The five new marshals included Voroshilov and Tukhachevsky and the former Tsarist general, Aleksandr Yegerov.[35] By the mid-1930s the military had become a part of the new Soviet élite. That achievement alone may explain the paradox of its downfall. For at the very moment that Tukhachevsky had begun to build up large, modern armed forces, freer than ever before of narrow political interference, the military leadership was swept away in a violent, nation-wide purge.

The crisis that destroyed the military establishment in 1937 can be understood only against the wider background of the state terror practised from the first weeks of the infant Bolshevik regime in 1917. One of Lenin's first acts was to re-form Russia's political police force, the Cheka, an organization that may have been responsible for the violent deaths of at least 250,000 people during the civil war. The Cheka conditioned Communist leaders to the brutalization of the revolution. They were brought up to believe that class war was to be fought with a merciless ferocity against anyone, enemy and erstwhile friend alike, who threatened to undermine the revolutionary achievement or challenge the authority of the Party, the vanguard of the proletarian movement. During the civil war there was real resistance, but the term 'class enemy' was applied without discrimination against whole groups whose social position or national loyalty defined them as counter-revolutionaries. The nature of the terror changed from a savage reaction to civil conflict to an instrument for sustaining popular mobilization and allegiance. The creation of imagined enemies, and the constant fear of conspiracy, foreign spies and sabotage to which it gave rise, became a central feature of Soviet political culture. It encouraged a popular vigilance, whose darker face was revealed in the hysterical climate of denunciation and betrayal by which Soviet society, like other revolutionary societies before and since, was periodically engulfed.

The end-product of the system of terror was either refined and soul-breaking torture and a bullet in the back of the neck, or a long spell in a prison camp. The first Soviet forced-labour camps were set up in the early 1920s. Like their Tsarist predecessors they housed a mixture of regular criminals and political dissidents, the latter preyed upon by the former. Those deemed to be hardened enemies of the revolution were transported to the first Soviet concentration camp for political opponents, on the island of Solovki in the White Sea. Housed in a sixteenth-century monastery, the camp was opened in 1923. It was run by the organization that succeeded the Cheka, the State Political Directorate (OGPU), established the same year. The euphemistic title shielded the identity of the state security police who ran the system from the Internal Affairs Commissariat (NKVD). Long before the Stalinist terror of the 1930s, the regime imprisoned or executed thousands in the name of political conformity. OGPU officials, working in the notorious Lubyanka prison in Moscow, beat, tortured, raped and blackmailed their victims, in order to extract fanciful confessions of counter-revolutionary crimes. Even genuine dissidents were made to own up to grotesque conspiracies and 'deviationism' quite unrelated to the usually banal pretext for their arrest. Confessions earned a mandatory twenty-five-year sentence, which only the hardiest or the luckiest survived.[36]

Two things combined to turn the revolutionary terror of the 1920s into the frantic blood-lettings of the 1930s. First came the drive for forced modernization, the 'Second Revolution'. The embattled Party found itself facing widespread opposition from the peasants (and from peasants in uniform, who made up 70 per cent of the army rank and file) as the reforms were pushed through.[37] The social crisis revived the atmosphere of the civil war, and, as in that earlier conflict, the Party conjured up counter-revolutionary phantoms to secure wider support for radical change. A collective paranoia increasingly permeated every level of the state, down to individual factories or collective farms, where every broken machine or tractor was attributed to counter-revolutionary 'hooligans'. More often than not the hapless victims were ill-educated, technically illiterate peasant-workers whose only crime was ignorance, drunkenness or poor timekeeping. But they were also plant managers who undershot their monthly quota or engineers who wrestled to install sophisticated foreign machinery in crude, cold and ill-lit workshops. The modernization drive provoked a national witch-hunt, for which there was no rational foundation. As in the witch-hunts of an earlier age, there was no defence. It was sufficient to point the finger of blame; local kangaroo courts did the rest. There was no appeal. Thousands of peasants and workers found themselves shipped to the growing empire of camps stretched across the Soviet Union, understanding neither their crime nor their persecutors.

Most of the victims of the 1930s were peasants, whose way of life was violently overturned in order to modernize Soviet society. The chaotic conditions of 1932 and 1933, when collectivization was at its height, generated the worst famine of the century. In the grain-rich regions of the Ukraine, the northern Caucasus and Kazakhstan, peasant resistance brought on the full fury of the Party. The farmers' own food was seized, even the seed for the following year's planting. Stalin ordered the security police to seal off the whole of the Ukraine from the rest of the Soviet Union to prevent anyone from leaving or food from getting in. It was almost certainly Stalin's single most murderous act. The most recent Russian estimates indicate a death toll of 4.2 million in the Ukraine alone in 1933. Whole villages starved to death or were dispatched by epidemics to which there was scant bodily resistance.[38] In Kazakhstan the mainly nomadic farmers were forced into crude camps and left to die. An estimated 1.7 million, almost half the population of the republic, perished in the most wretched conditions.[39] Thousands fled across the Soviet border to escape the death camps. In total an estimated 7 million fell victim to the class war launched in the countryside. Stalin told a critic in 1933 that it was the fault of the peasantry, for waging 'silent war' against the Soviet state.

The second factor that transformed the nature of the terror in the 1930s was the personality of Stalin. It is hard to judge whether he himself believed the Jacobin statements about the defence of the revolution or the Leninist heritage with which he publicly justified the war on the peasants and the elimination of political enemies. They were useful rallying cries in the internal Party struggles of the 1920s, when Stalin successively rid himself of his most powerful rivals among the old Bolshevik élite – Trotsky and Grigory Zinoviev in 1927, Nikolai Bukharin in 1929 – but Stalin's opportunism in these cases was self-evident. The campaigns of the 1930s against the rich peasant or the industrial saboteur can be explained, though hardly excused, as the product of a deliberate manipulation of popular opinion to secure the Party's goals. Stalinist demonology made the whole system paranoid, but it was not necessary for the leader to share those fears.

Stalin may not have been paranoid in this sense, but he was consumed throughout his dictatorial career by a profound fear of assassination. His personal security was notoriously extravagant. He travelled in heavily armour-plated cars, surrounded by personal bodyguards supplied by the NKVD. He never drove the same route twice in succession. He ordered curtains to be cropped so that assassins could not hide behind them. He was guarded twenty-four hours a day. By the end of his life the defensive perimeter around his *dacha* [country retreat] at Kuntsevo on the outskirts of Moscow resembled a prison camp. These might all be regarded as the precautions of any tyrant whose career was littered with men and women with reason enough to murder him. In the Soviet Union they were more than usually necessary, for there was a long tradition of assassination in Russian life. Before the war of 1914 thousands of state officials, from minor bureaucrats to the prime minister himself, Petr Stolypin, were assassinated. Political murder was central to the Russian terrorist tradition that helped to shape the political tactics of Bolshevism. Once in power those traditions were turned against the new masters. Lenin narrowly survived an assassination attempt in August 1920 by a woman who had already spent eleven years hard labour in a Tsarist prison camp for an earlier attempt to murder an imperial official in Kiev. Stalin's personal security, tight though it was, could not guarantee immunity from what was widely regarded (and is still so viewed in Russia today) as a conventional way to settle scores. Stalin never scrupled to resort to assassination himself when he perceived a threat great enough to warrant it.

What made Stalin's terror different was not merely the scale of arrests and executions – by 1939 there were, in recent estimates, approximately 3.5 million prisoners in the various categories of camps – but the fact that this fearful and vindictive man turned the terror on the very heart of the Soviet system, the Party and the armed forces, even on the NKVD, itself the apparatus of terror.[40] The political terror began in 1933 with the expulsion of 790,000 Party members on charges of corruption and careerism, not all of them fabricated.[41] In 1934, following the murder of the popular Party leader in Leningrad, Sergei Kirov (probably, but not certainly, on Stalin's orders), draconian powers were granted to the state to arrest, try and execute political conspirators summarily, without due process of law.

Within weeks of Kirov's death thousands were rounded up in

Moscow and Leningrad, accused of a plot to overturn Stalin. At the Leningrad headquarters of the NKVD, 200 suspects a day were shot.[42] The outcome of the investigation was the first of the major 'show trials', which opened on 15 August 1936 with the trial of the Zinoviev circle. The fabricated plots, linking Communist leaders with foreign imperialists or renegade socialists, above all with that exiled and disgraced apostate, Leon Trotsky, were fed as truth to the public at home and abroad. Many Soviet citizens, with access only to the mass media controlled by the regime, believed the accusations. The show trials held between 1936 and 1938 produced one confession after another of counter-revolutionary crimes, beaten and extorted from the defendants. Stalin is said to have undertaken occasional interrogations, though it is almost beyond credibility that he could have believed the web of deceit that was spun at his own ordaining. His real political skill, and a feature of his behaviour throughout the dictatorship, was to be perceived by the public as the incorruptible statesman who had saved the revolution from the machinations of countless fifth-columnists. On occasion he turned the terror on the secret policemen themselves to give the calculated impression that they, not he, were to blame for the orgy of violence – a political practice that he later persistently used to mask his military failures during the war.[43]

Stalin was assisted at the height of the terror by two able accomplices, the lawyer Andrei Vyshinsky, who was made Procurator General in 1935, and later became the Soviet Union's first ambassador to the United Nations, and Nikolai Yezhov, who was appointed to head the NKVD in 1936. Together they cut swathes through the Party élite. Of the 1,966 delegates at the 17th Party Congress in 1934, 1,108 were shot as enemies of the people. The two years of the 'Yezhovshchina' saw the execution, according to the latest Russian figures, of 680,000 people.[44] Almost no area of state or Party was immune from the spiral of terror. There remained not a single base for opposition to Stalin. The fear induced by the terror promoted the most grotesque expressions of loyalty, which in turn laid the foundation for the widespread 'cult of personality'.

The Soviet armed forces appeared to be the only major area of state to avoid the terror, until on the morning of 11 June 1937

Voroshilov announced the sudden arrest of the country's top generals and the unearthing of a treacherous plot whose tentacles reached out to Germany. It was alleged that no less a figure than Tukhachevsky himself was responsible for planning to overthrow the state at the head of a German army of invasion. The precise motives for the purge remain obscure, for the accusations themselves were entirely without foundation. Tukhachevsky was a popular and outspoken man who disliked Voroshilov and the military amateurs in the Party. He crossed Stalin over the issue of political propaganda in the armed forces, which he wanted to reduce. Neither attitude provides a convincing explanation for Stalin's sudden change of heart about the army or for the speed and violence of the purge. The explanation least likely to an outside observer may well be nearest the truth: Stalin's suspicious mind may have been sufficiently aroused by the flimsy rumours of army unreliability currently circulating abroad to take the story of the conspiracy seriously.

According to one version, German counter-intelligence deliberately planted in Prague a document with Tukhachevsky's forged signature on it suggesting a German–Red Army conspiracy. President Edvard Beneš of Czechoslovakia passed the information on when it was discovered, and the NKVD simply extrapolated the plot from the German deception.[45] A second version suggests that the NKVD, in order to boost the reputation of its leader, not only encouraged the circulation of foreign rumours and opinions suggesting the unreliability of the army, but may also have had a hand in encouraging the German misinformation. Since Stalin may not even have seen the documents sent from Czechoslovakia, and since the fears of army dissent were already in circulation before they arrived, this version seems the more likely. Yezhov's deputy, Frinovsky, was alleged to have told a Moscow NKVD investigator in the spring of 1937 that he should 'develop a line about an important, deep-seated plot in the Red Army'. He was instructed to make it clear that Yezhov's own role in unmasking it 'must appear enormous'.[46]

However the purge was plotted, the effect was to persuade the habitually distrustful Stalin that there was some substance to the idea of army disloyalty. The NKVD had in their cells a brigade commander named Medvedev who was chosen as the unfortunate instrument to betray his seniors. He was tortured into confessing the necessary evidence, then recanted and was tortured again until the confessions stuck.[47] The details were passed on to Stalin. Mikhail Shpigelglaz, head of foreign intelligence in the NKVD, remembered that the news was treated as 'a real conspiracy'. In the Kremlin he observed a genuine panic. All Kremlin passes were declared invalid, and NKVD troops were put on a state of alert.[48] Stalin did not order Tukhachevsky's immediate arrest but played cat and mouse with him. He had been tailed for some time, as Yezhov searched for incriminating behaviour. He was due to represent the Soviet Union at the coronation of the British King, George VI, in May 1937. His attendance was suddenly cancelled on the grounds that another plot had been unearthed, one to murder Tukhachevsky on his way through Warsaw to London. He was then ordered to take up command of the Volga Military District, a dizzying demotion.[49] He must have sensed something worse. To those around him he appeared nervous and depressed. His hair reportedly turned grey in two months.

Shortly after his arrival to take command he was summoned to a meeting of local political officers. He never returned to his new home. His wife heard of his arrest and rushed to Moscow to intercede. She was promptly arrested along with the whole of Tukhachevsky's family, as was usually the case with alleged traitors. She was eventually killed, together with two of Tukhachevsky's brothers. His sisters were sent to a labour camp, and when his young daughter came of age, she was sent, too. The first military victims were eight senior Red Army commanders, headed by Tukhachevsky. They were taken to Moscow's Lefortovo Prison, set up for special prisoners, and further confessions were beaten out of them. In most cases the only real evidence of sympathy for Germany came from the many visits of Soviet military men to that country during the late 1920s and early 1930s, during the period of close German–Soviet collaboration. Every effort was made to find anything else, however preposterous, as evidence of ill-intent. The first victim interrogated, a corps commander named Feldman, was handed over to one of the NKVD's notorious sadists, who worked on him behind a locked door. He confessed that the conspiracy was true. A day later Tukhachevsky was given the same brutal treatment and confessed to his own treachery; repeated torture forced him to reveal a wider circle of names. Each victim dragged in friends and colleagues to try to end his own maltreatment. To his interrogator's delight, Tukhachevsky continued to furnish him with names right up to the day of the trial.[50]

While the plot was constructed and the lists of victims lengthened, Stalin played out a charade of revolutionary justice. At the Central Committee meeting on May 24 he told the Party leaders of the military plot and passed around voting papers for them to sign, approving the proceedings. The papers were signed by some of Tukhachevsky's closest collaborators, including Semyon Budyenny, who had been promoted to Marshal at the same time as the man on whose fate he was now asked to decide. Budyenny wrote: 'Definitely yes. These scoundrels must be punished.'[51] A week later, on June 1, Stalin staged a remarkable two-week long conference in which he sat with Voroshilov and Yezhov listening to soldiers who had been invited to the Kremlin profess loyalty to Stalin and a forceful rejection of the conspirators. Each of them was searched at the door for arms and then given a blue folder containing details of the charges, drawn up by Vyshinsky as news of each fresh crime was rushed hot from the interrogation room. As they read, some of them found their own names on the list of accomplices. At intervals NKVD men would make their way through the crowd, taking officers away with them. The following day another group of conspirators was detailed on the testimony of the hapless victims of the day before.[52] The military purge developed a momentum that took it far beyond the handful of commanders seized in May.

Stalin was in a hurry to complete the process. On June 9 the indictment was complete. Eight marshals and generals were chosen to sit on the tribunal to try the eight military defendants, all of whom they knew well. The night before the trial, set for June 11, the interrogators extracted a flurry of further confessions which incriminated the very men who would sit in judgment on the morrow. Five of the soldiers sitting on the tribunal bench were executed over the following months. (Marshal Budyenny, who was to be among them, was saved from death when he resisted arrest by force and telephoned

Stalin directly.) The trial lasted a day. Tukhachevsky and his co-defendants, once free of their torturers, refused to ratify their confessions until they were bullied by the prosecutor to confess again that some of it was true. Just after midnight sentence was pronounced.[53] All eight were shot that day. Tukhachevsky and Jonah Yakir, commander of the Kiev Military District, died expressing their continued loyalty to Stalin, the man who only a few hours before had given his personal approval for their death.[54]

After the death of its chief victims, the purge rolled on over the rest of the senior officer corps. Marshal Yegerov was liquidated in March 1938, after his wife was forced to confess her part as a Polish spy; Marshal Blyukher, the son of a peasant, and the most famous of the civil war generals, who was a judge in the Tukhachevsky case, was arrested in October 1938. Alone of the top military commanders he refused to confess anything. He was beaten to a pulp, and one eye was torn out. On November 9, the anniversary of the Bolshevik Revolution, he was killed in an office of the Lubyanka as he attacked his torturers. During the purge, 45 per cent of the senior officers and political officials of the army and navy were executed or sacked, including 720 out of the 837 commanders, from colonel to marshal, appointed under the new table of ranks established in 1935. Out of eighty-five senior officers on the Military Council, seventy-one were dead by 1941; only nine avoided the purges entirely, including no fewer than seven who served in the 1st Cavalry Army, which Stalin helped to direct in the civil war.[55] Surprisingly untouched was the former Tsarist General Staff officer, the only one to survive into the 1930s, Boris Shaposhnikov. He was one of the three judges in the Tukhachevsky trial not murdered. Stalin was said to show a genuine respect, even awe, in his presence. His Tsarist roots were not enough to condemn him and he lived on, in poor health, until the end of the Second World War.

The lower ranks of the officer corps suffered less severely. The extent of the manpower losses was lower than most outside observers supposed at the time, though the effect on a military organization in which morale was not high should not be underestimated. The true figures are now available from Russian sources. From 1936 to 1938 a total of 41,218 were purged, but most were dismissed rather than arrested or executed. Of the 34,000 officers sacked in 1937 and 1938 the NKVD arrested 9,500. By May 1940 11,596 officers had been reinstated. As a proportion of the total number of officers these figures are relatively small. Of the 179,000 officers employed in 1938 only 3.7 per cent were still formally discharged by 1940. The net loss in 1937 and 1938, after taking into account new recruits into the officer corps, was approximately 10,000.[56]

The military purge may have had a rationality all its own in the mind of a Yezhov or a Stalin, but it made little sense in terms of the Soviet Union's military development and international security. 'This is worse than when artillery fires on its own troops,' observed General Konstantin Rokossovsky during his two-year imprisonment between 1938 and 1940.[57] The purges profoundly affected the perception of Soviet strength abroad, and contributed to the judgement of most German commanders that the Red Army could be beaten. The destruction of the cadres of young officers around the reformer Tukhachevsky is usually taken as evidence that the Soviet Union took a giant leap backward in military effectiveness and levels of military preparedness. This is a superficial conclusion. Plausible though it seems, the strengths and weaknesses of the Soviet military position in the late 1930s were not simply the result of the purges.

Any argument which suggests that the purges weakened the Red Army (and Navy) rests on a prior assumption that the pre-purge army must have been a more effective instrument. Such an assumption is clearly open to question. For all of Tukhachevsky's enthusiasm for mass tanks and aircraft, there existed a wide discrepancy between theory and practice. Soviet forces had made poor progress in 'command and control', the critical dimension of fast-moving aircraft and tank combat.[58] Communications systems were rudimentary or non-existent. Tanks and aircraft were not equipped with radios and could not easily communicate with each other. Commanders had no way of co-ordinating air and ground action, nor of holding a large group of tanks and armoured vehicles together. These deficiencies rendered the concept of 'deep operations' almost impossible. At most levels of junior command there existed a lack of flexibility and tactical awareness. German soldiers who watched their Soviet counterparts in training and on manoeuvres were unimpressed by what they saw. 'The weak point of the army,' wrote a German army adjutant in 1933, 'is that all commanders, from platoon to regiment commander, are not yet efficient enough. Most of them are capable of dealing with problems only at the level of a non-commissioned officer.' The German military attaché in Moscow the same year detected throughout the army 'a fear of responsibility'.[59] Many of those purged after 1937 were men who had little military education and had achieved office on the grounds of their civil war experience.

By the late 1930s there were thousands of younger officers, some of them trained in the military academies, ready to take their place. By 1941 over 100,000 officers were entering the Soviet armed forces each year. The purges certainly removed some men of talent at the top of the military establishment, but it is questionable whether the aggregate effect was to make the average performance of the officer corps much worse than it had been beforehand, or to make the tank and air war any less capable of realization. The army had severe weaknesses both before and after the purges. What made the situation difficult for the army authorities after 1938 was the vast expansion of the Red Army – 161 new divisions were activated between January 1939 and May 1941 – which required more officers than the training establishments could hope to supply, despite vastly expanded training schemes. In 1941 75 per cent of all officers had been in office for less than a year, not because of the purges but because of the creation of many new military units. By then 80 per cent of those officers purged in 1938 had been reinstated.[60]

Other elements of the Soviet military effort were less affected by the purges. The training schools expanded their intake of new officer trainees. In 1936, 10,500 were drafted from academies and schools, but in 1938 23,000 and in 1939 39,500.[61] The technological threshold still moved forward, if slowly. The system of fortifications begun in the 1920s along the whole western frontier – the Stalin Line – continued to be constructed and extended. Most important of all, the modernization and expansion of the Soviet heavy industrial base accelerated, and with it the large proportion allocated to military production.

Without the economic transformation, the Red Army would have been a feeble force in 1941, relaying on a vast base of peasant manpower. The industrial changes of the 1930s provided the planners, the scientists, engineers and skilled labour necessary to cope with the demands of total mobilization made after the German invasion in 1941. Whatever the weaknesses exposed by the modernization drive, it is inconceivable that the Soviet Union could have withstood the German attack without it.

The most debilitating effect of the purges was the sharp change they signalled in the balance of power between the military and the politicians. After a decade of attempts by the military to win greater independence from political control, the purges brought back close political supervision and intervention. It may well be that Stalin was motivated by concern over the growing independence of the armed forces and recollections of the imaginary Bonapartist fears of the early 1920s when he decided to turn the terror on the military. In May 1937, as the axe fell on Tukhachevsky, Voroshilov reintroduced political deputies into all units above divisional strength. In August the Main Political Directorate of the Army was placed under the care of Lev Mekhlis, the editor of *Pravda*, who was instructed by Stalin to 'bolshevize' the army. He was typical of the new political soldiers. Energetic, brutal and vindictive, a military ignoramus who thought that he understood war, he became the major figure responsible for instilling a correct Communist outlook in the armed forces. He kept the terror alive in the armed forces by insisting that the political officers in every unit should play a substantial military role, as they had done during the civil war.[62]

The result was the triumph of military illiteracy over military science, of political conformity over military initiative. It has been estimated that 73 per cent of the political officers had had no military training, yet they were placed even in small military units, down to the level of platoon and company. This stifling of military independence left commanders demoralized and excessively cautious, since anything judged by the political officers to be an infringement of the Party line carried the risk of the Lubyanka, not just for the commander concerned but for his wife and family. Officers were inclined to stick by the rule book. Any talk of 'deep operations', or massed tank attack, with its echoes of Tukhachevsky, was by association deemed to be counter-revolutionary. In this sense the purges left an indelible mark on the Soviet armed forces, which were once again, as they were in the early 1920s, officially regarded by the Party as an instrument of the people's revolutionary will. Military professionalism was suspect as 'bourgeois expertise'. In February 1939, to mark the twentieth anniversary of the foundation of the Frunze Military Academy, *Pravda* carried the following editorial:

Military thought in the capitalist world has got into a blind alley. The dashing 'theories' about a lightning war, or about small, select armies of technicians, or about the air war which can replace all other military operations; all these theories arise from the bourgeoisie's deathly fear of the proletarian revolution. In its mechanical way, the imperialist bourgeoisie overrates equipment and underrates man.[63]

After twenty years of Soviet rule the mentality of civil war, of a people armed in the righteous struggle against its class enemies, still dominated the outlook of the political élite, most of whom had experienced it at first hand. Workers and peasants were regarded as soldiers in the war against the counter-revolution; soldiers were workers and peasants in uniform, the armed wing of the proletarian movement. The legacy of the civil war helps to explain why Soviet society as a whole, civilian and military, was mobilized to fight against German aggression in 1941, but it also explains why that fight when it came was at first so incompetent and costly.

2

The Hour Before Midnight:
1937–1941

*My people and I, Josef Vissarionovich Stalin, firmly remember
your wise prediction: Hitler will not attack in 1941!*

Beria to Stalin, 21 June 1941

In August 1936 the German dictator, Adolf Hitler, took himself off
to his retreat in the Bavarian Alps at Berchtesgaden. Perched in his
'Eagle's Nest', staring out over his favourite vista of peaks and alpine
meadows, Hitler thought about war. The last time he had written
anything down about his plans for the future was in 1928, when he
dictated a sequel to *Mein Kampf* that was never published in his
lifetime. The book was full of ideas about the necessity of war and
economic conquest. But it had been written when Hitler was still a
struggling street politician, years from power. In August 1936 he had
been ruler of Germany for almost four years. Plans for war took a
back seat while the Nazi Party struggled to consolidate its power and
heal the economic damage of the slump. But by 1936 war was at the
front of Hitler's mind. Hitler rarely set his thoughts down on paper.
But on this occasion he wrote a lengthy memorandum on Germany's
political and economic situation and the inevitability of war.

The memorandum was shown to only a small circle: the Defence
Minister, Werner von Blomberg; the head of the autobahn project,
Fritz Todt; and the Nazi politician and Air Force Commander in
Chief, Hermann Goering. To others around him he gave only hints
that a great war was in the offing, a war that would redraw the map
of Europe as the Thirty Years' War had done three centuries before.[1]
The central argument of Hitler's document was the necessity of war

between Marxist Russia and Western civilization. 'No nation will be able to avoid or abstain from this historic conflict,' wrote Hitler. He compared the age in which he lived with the crisis of the ancient world when it was overwhelmed by the barbarian invasions, and with the long and violent confrontation between Islam and Christianity. The growing military strength of the Soviet Union he regarded as 'menacing'; the prospects for the future were grim unless Germany took up the torch of civilization and rode out to slay the Bolshevik dragon. If Russia won the looming historic struggle it would be, Hitler thought, 'the most gruesome catastrophe which has been visited on mankind since the downfall of the states of antiquity'. The danger had to be confronted: 'All other considerations must recede into the background.' 'I set the following tasks,' Hitler concluded his document. 'I: The German armed forces must be operational within four years. II: The German economy must be fit for war within four years.'[2]

In the autumn of 1936 Goering was appointed head of a Four-Year-Plan organization to create the economic foundation for large-scale war. Two-thirds of industrial investment between 1936 and 1939 was devoted to war-related production. By the spring of 1939 one-quarter of the entire German labour force was working on military contracts. The pace of military expansion, first begun in the late 1920s with Soviet assistance, accelerated. 'The extent of the military development of our resources cannot be too large, nor its pace too swift,' Hitler had written in the memorandum. The German army was to be 'the premier army in the world'.[3] No definite plan for war was formulated, like the Schlieffen Plan that had shaped German strategy before 1914, but the memorandum pointed to an ineluctable contest between Germany and the Soviet Union. It was the seed from which grew the bitter struggle of the years 1941 to 1945.

In Moscow the revival of German military power was viewed with genuine anxiety. Relations between the two states had steadily deteriorated since Hitler came to power in 1933. Soviet leaders were more impressed by the central message of Hitler's *Mein Kampf* than were politicians in the West. At the Congress of Soviets in January 1935 the Soviet Premier, Vyacheslav Molotov, warned delegates that Hitler's stated intention was territorial conquest in the East. When the wealthy American lawyer Joseph E. Davies arrived in Moscow early in 1937 to take up the post of ambassador, he found that all the talk there was of the German threat. Maxim Litvinov, the Soviet Commissar for Foreign Affairs, explained to him that Hitler was consumed by a lust for conquest and for the domination of Europe.[4] It was no accident that Marshal Tukhachevsky and the generals who stood trial beside him were accused of spying for Germany.

The Soviet Union was forced to abandon the isolation of the 1920s. Faced with a hostile Germany in the West and a strongly anti-Communist Japan in the Far East, the Soviet Union began to mend its fences with the Western states, Britain and France. This choice was understandable enough, but it ran entirely counter to the prevailing Soviet view that the West represented the forces of bourgeois imperialism in their most extreme form. Stalin had little time for France, which he regarded as 'the most aggressive and most militarist' of all the Western states. The League of Nations, set up in 1920 as the instrument for international co-operation and collective security, was dubbed by Stalin as the 'organizational centre of imperialist pacifism'.[5] Now, in the wake of rejection by Germany, Soviet leaders found themselves in the unexpected position of suitor, begging favours from a frosty mistress.

As the price of co-operation the Western states insisted that the Soviet Union display its change of heart publicly by joining the League of Nations. On 18 September 1934 Soviet representatives took their seats on the League Council at Geneva. Further gestures of goodwill followed: Stalin ordered Communist parties everywhere to abandon the revolutionary struggle and to collaborate with 'progressive' political forces in a 'popular front' against fascism. The Comintern, the international Communist organization set up by Lenin in 1920, toned down its radical language. All the talk now was of democracy, social co-operation and peace. In May 1935 the Soviet Union replaced the lost friendship of Germany with a pact of mutual assistance signed with France. Non-aggression pacts were signed with Finland, Estonia, Latvia and Poland, all states that were to feel the weight of Soviet aggression in a matter of years.

The public face of good-neighbourliness masked a much more

cautious and pragmatic attitude. Stalin never lost sight of the prospect of Soviet-German friendship, despite the public posture of hating fascism. In 1937, at almost exactly the time that Stalin's executioners were extorting confessions of spying for Germany from terrorized Soviet generals, secret contacts were made with Goering's Four-Year-Plan organization in Berlin to try to revive Soviet-German trade. The negotiations stumbled on Hitler's refusal in March 1937 to countenance parallel political discussions. To cover his tracks, Stalin had the Soviet negotiators arrested, executed or imprisoned.[6] In Berlin the drawbridge was drawn up. The two sides did not talk again until the months leading to war in 1939.

The Soviet Union now entered a new and dangerous phase in its foreign policy. Weakened by the savage purge of the officer corps and the violent effort to transform Soviet society, faced with a rapidly rearming, anti-Soviet Germany, and deeply distrustful of her new imperialist partners, Stalin's revolutionary state was anything but secure. We know little of Stalin's private thoughts from this period. Under Litvinov's influence the Soviet Foreign Commissariat remained rigidly committed to the letter of collective security in the struggle against aggression and fascism. Most foreign observers assumed that this was a front for a more devious and self-interested policy, but the revelations since the 1980s have not yet exposed it, if one ever existed. In the mid-1930s collective security *was* in Russia's self-interest.

Once the Soviet Union had stepped out of isolation into the European theatre, it at once became embroiled in Europe's problems. European Communists and fellow-travellers (of whom there were a great many in the 1930s), quite innocent about the true nature of Stalin's regime, took up the cause of anti-fascism and loudly trumpeted the heroic achievements of Soviet modernization. Very few of them ever saw the Soviet Union; those who did were escorted from model village to model factory, where they met only orchestrated smiles and a terrified loyalty. Among them were to be found the volunteers for the first armed struggle between Communism and fascism, in Spain. When civil war broke out under the Spanish Second Republic in July 1936 the conflict between nationalist and reactionary forces under Franco and the embattled Spanish Popular Front regime of liberals, socialists and Communists quickly became an international issue. The reality of the Spanish Civil War was much more complicated than a crude division between fascism and Communism, but for non-Spaniards the conflict came to symbolize the growing political tensions in Europe. Left-wing sympathizers from all over Europe and America (but not from the Soviet Union) joined the International Brigades which fought alongside the Republican army. Although the Soviet Union formally joined with her new League partners in advocating non-intervention in Spain, Soviet arms and equipment were secretly supplied to the Republican army and air force. But Stalin had other motives for intervening in Spain. Agents of the NKVD, with orders to fight not fascism but 'Trotskyite accomplices' and other anti-Soviet Communists, were sent from the Soviet Union. There were Communists of every kind in Spain, from members of the powerful native anarcho-syndicalist movement to Communist defectors from Stalinist terror. The NKVD hunted down and eliminated any who posed a threat to the Moscow line. Even those who had been sent to do Stalin's work in Spain were summoned back to death or imprisonment.

Throughout the 1930s Stalin conducted a shadow war across Europe, exporting terror to reach the other Communist parties of Europe and the Russian *émigré* communities, right and left, which kept up a ceaseless propaganda war against him. Soviet spies were recruited in every state, even in the heart of the political establishment, driven by greed or idealism or fear. Their methods were the stuff of fiction. In 1937 the head of the Federation of Tsarist Army Veterans in Paris, General Eugene Miller, was kidnapped by the NKVD in an elaborate plot. Two Soviet agents, impersonating senior German officers, collaborated with Miller's assistant, the White general Nikolai Skoblin, who unknown to Miller had been an NKVD agent all along. On 22 September 1937 Miller disappeared in broad daylight on his way to a meeting with Skoblin and the fake German officers. He was taken to the Soviet embassy, drugged, put in a trunk and sent in a Ford truck to the port of Le Havre and on to Leningrad. In Moscow he was subjected to the usual brutalities and shot. Skoblin escaped capture by the French authorities and went to Spain, where his future can only have been bleak, though his exact fate remains unknown.

His wife, Nadezhda Plevitskaya, famous among *émigré* circles for her haunting performances of the folk songs of old Russia, had been for years an NKVD agent. Caught by the French police, she was sentenced to twenty years and died in prison in 1940. According to the Soviet defector Walter Krivitsky, who was murdered by Soviet agents in Washington the same year, Miller's kidnapping was linked directly with the Tukhachevsky case. Skoblin also had contact with the Gestapo. He was used as the conduit for passing disinformation on to Miller about the Red Army command, which was eventually beaten out of him in Moscow and formed part of the conspiracy case. Krivitsky suggested that Stalin and Yezhov were the authors of the Miller plot, but this has still to be proved beyond doubt.[7]

The first real test of the Soviet Union's commitment to collective security came in the summer of 1938. The issue was the fate of Czechoslovakia. At a secret meeting in November 1937 Hitler had told his military and foreign policy leaders of his short-term plans for German expansion. They included the incorporation of Austria into the German Reich and the dismemberment of Czechoslovakia, where three million German speakers lived under Czech rule in the Sudetenland. In March 1938 Austria was occupied by German forces and incorporated into the Reich. In May 1938 Hitler ordered his armed forces to prepare for a brief war to eliminate the Czech state in the autumn. He did not expect a general confrontation, but it proved impossible to avoid, because Czechoslovakia had treaty agreements with both France and the Soviet Union. If Czech territory were attacked by another state, French and Soviet forces were pledged to her defence.

When the promises were made neither power expected them to be called in so soon, if at all. Britain and France put pressure on the Czechs during the summer months to make concessions to the German position, because neither was willing to risk war if the Sudeten question could be solved by negotiation. By September the crisis was as dangerous as that earlier crisis, in July 1914, which had plunged all Europe into war. The British Prime Minister, Neville Chamberlain, flew to see Hitler to persuade him to agree to negotiation. When on his second visit, on September 22, Hitler raised the stakes by demanding the immediate German occupation of the Sudeten area, the crisis reached boiling point. Both Britain and France began frantic preparations for mobilization. Neither wanted war, but neither could accept the invasion of Czechoslovakia. The question that has always hung over the final crisis was the attitude of Stalin. Was the Soviet Union prepared to go to war with Germany in 1938 to defend its Czech ally?

The formal position taken by the Soviet Union was to stand by collective security. As early as March 17, well before it was clear that Hitler wanted war with the Czechs, Molotov publicly stated his country's commitment to collective action to deter aggression against Czechoslovakia, though he did not specifically promise military intervention. Shortly afterwards the Czech President, Edvard Beneš, was privately assured that Moscow would honour its treaty obligation to protect his country as long as France participated as well.[8] As the crisis unfolded over the summer, this remained the Soviet position. Ever since the crisis Western opinion has seen in this simply a gesture, designed to salve the Soviet conscience: words rather than deeds.

Fresh evidence has altered the picture substantially. The memoirs of a senior Soviet staff officer, released finally in 1989, seem to make it clear that Stalin was prepared to offer more than a gesture. On September 20 Beneš was given a firmer indication of Soviet military support. Two days later both the Kiev and the Belorussian military districts facing the long Polish border were put on alert, and troops were redeployed westward. On September 28, the day that Hitler finally backed down and agreed to Mussolini's suggestion of a conference at Munich, all the military districts west of the Urals were ordered to stop releasing men for leave. The following day reservists were called to the colours throughout the western Soviet Union, 330,000 in all. The Czech Government was offered 700 fighter aircraft if room could be found on Czech airfields. The most significant revelation was that Romania, the Red Army's only possible route into Central Europe (given the strong hostility of the Polish Government to any transfer of Soviet forces through its territory, half of which had belonged to the former Tsarist empire), had agreed under pressure to allow 100,000 Soviet soldiers to cross to Czechoslovakia, as long as it was done quickly.[9]

Clearly Stalin had something in mind. When Maxim Litvinov

met Ivan Maisky, the Soviet ambassador to Britain, in Geneva on September 24, he told him privately that Moscow had decided 'in earnest' on war, even if France and Britain did not fight. The critical factor for Litvinov was Czech resistance: 'If they fight, we'll fight alongside them.'[10] The following day Paris was finally informed of Soviet military preparations. On September 28 all three states, Britain, France and the Soviet Union, were poised to fight, though not in concert. Their questionable resolve was never tested. Hitler accepted negotiation; the Czech records now show that Beneš was in the end not prepared to fight, even with Soviet assistance, if Hitler could not be restrained by the other powers.[11]

The new evidence is open to a number of interpretations. The Soviet Union might well have used the crisis to intimidate Poland, a state loathed by the Soviet leadership. On the same day that Soviet forces were put on alert an ultimatum was sent to Warsaw warning the Poles that any move against the Czechs on their part would be regarded as unprovoked aggression. No ultimatum was ever sent to Germany. German intelligence was unimpressed by Soviet military movements and did not interpret the Soviet position as a threat of war.[12] War with Germany would have meant more serious evidence of large-scale mobilization. It is not improbable, given that military preparations were kept secret from the Germans, that they were for domestic consumption – an elaborate military exercise or another war scare like 1927, designed to keep the system on its toes. The most likely answer is that Stalin was keeping his options open. The one option he did not want was to be left fighting Germany alone. Soviet intervention, if it came, was always dependent on the willingness of the 'imperialist states' to fight first.

The Czech crisis forced the Soviet Union to rethink its position in Europe. Stalin's distrust of the Western powers intensified. The Soviet Union had been deliberately kept at arm's length in the Czech negotiations, and, despite its status as one of the major powers, was not invited to the Munich conference. Soviet leaders could not be sure that Britain and France did not intend to divert German ambitions eastward towards them (or Japanese ambitions westward), the very opposite of what they had expected by joining the League. Joseph

Davies reported to President Roosevelt the evident mood of 'hostility to England and indifference to France'.[13] It is tempting to see this as the point where Stalin decided to try the German gambit once again, to win a peace from Hitler rather than fight a war allied with the West. The Soviet Union appeared to be in a strong position. Both sides, Hitler and the West, stood to gain by having Stalin on their side. Stalin stood to gain from whichever side could offer him immunity from war. The Nazi-Soviet Pact, concluded in August 1939, can, on this account, be regarded as the logical conclusion of the Munich crisis.

Here again new evidence has overturned the established picture. The wealth of new documentation on Soviet foreign policy in 1939 paints a picture of uncertainty and vacillation. Far from being the arbiter of Europe, the Soviet Union saw itself as isolated and vulnerable; Soviet leaders did not believe that an agreement with Germany was possible, but they had no confidence that an agreement with Britain and France was worth very much. The fresh crisis in Soviet security was intensified by the toll of experienced diplomats and officials taken by the terror. In the spring of 1939 a further wave of sackings and arrests hit the Soviet Commissariat of Foreign Affairs. On May 3 Maxim Litvinov, the Soviet architect of the policy of collective security, was removed as Foreign Minister. Perhaps because of his links with the West, where he was respected more than most Soviet negotiators, he did not go through the usual horrors but ended up as ambassador in Washington. The rest of his staff was not so lucky. Their punishment for allowing the Soviet Union to drift again into a dangerous isolation was demotion, prison or death. At just the point where the Soviet Union needed all the diplomatic talent she could muster, it was squandered by the regime's lust for scapegoats.[14]

Litvinov's successor was Molotov, the Soviet premier, and one of the few men to keep high office throughout the dictatorship. Like Stalin, whose name means 'steel' in Russian, he adopted a revolutionary pseudonym. From his reputed skill in forcing through an argument he chose the Russian word for hammer. He was an intelligent and shrewd organizer, promoted to premier at the age of forty in 1929. He was entirely Stalin's man, and remained loyal to him even when, after the war, his Jewish wife was arrested and exiled. A second key appointment was made after Munich. On 8 November 1938 the sadistic Yezhov was replaced as head of the NKVD by a young Georgian, Lavrenti Beria. Ambitious, fawning, vicious, depraved, Beria had all the qualifications for the job. Born in 1899, the son of a poor Georgian peasant, he was a student in Baku when the Revolution broke out. He joined the Bolshevik Party in 1917, and became an official of the Azerbaijan Cheka in the early 1920s. He made his reputation slaughtering enemies of Stalin in Transcaucasia, where he rose to be the local Party leader in the mid-1930s; he embellished it relentlessly in Moscow when he became master of the Lubyanka. His sadism was notorious. His bodyguards seized young girls off the streets of the capital for him to molest and rape at leisure. He combined grotesque coarseness and lust for cruelty with a slavish obeisance. He survived the death of Stalin in 1953, if only briefly.[15]

The search for greater security occasioned by the failure of collective action over the Czech crisis was renewed in the spring of 1939. The German occupation of the rest of the Czech state on March 15 provoked from Stalin a public condemnation of the Western states. At the 18th Party Congress he chided Britain and France for 'conniving at aggression, giving free rein to war'. He thought he could detect 'an eagerness, a desire' on their part to push Japan and Germany into a war with the Soviet Union.[16] Since this was regarded as a very real threat, Stalin did not close the door on co-operation with the Western states in restraining Hitler. This was not an attractive option, given the Soviet Union's deep distrust of Western motives, but in the spring of 1939 it was still preferable to isolation. The British and French realized at almost exactly the same time that if they wanted to deter or restrain Hitler in 1939, they would have to move closer to the Soviet Union. On March 1 Neville Chamberlain paid the first official visit by any British Prime Minister to the Soviet embassy in London. Chamberlain did not like Stalin or Communism, but he bowed to the wisdom of Britain's military leaders and the French Government, who argued that Hitler would only listen to superior military force.[17] By the beginning of April Britain had guaranteed Poland and Romania against German aggression, and contacts were pursued with the Soviet

Union to see if a wider coalition of anti-Hitler states could be created to encircle Germany.

The Soviet answer was so straightforward that neither of the two Western states (nor a great many historians since) was willing to take it at face value. On April 17 the Soviet Union offered Britain and France an alliance that would guarantee the integrity of every state from the Baltic to the Mediterranean and bring all three powers into war if any of the states was attacked by Germany. The offer now seems to have been genuine enough. In his speech in March Stalin reminded his listeners – and foreign opinion – that the three of them combined were 'unquestionably stronger than the fascist states'.[18] This was almost certainly true in a material sense, even allowing for the fact that Stalin had an exaggerated respect for the military power of the Western democracies. There remained considerable doubts in Moscow about Western goodwill. Litvinov did not believe that the West was serious about facing up to Hitler, and was sacked in May for his lack of enthusiasm. His replacement, Molotov, was faced with the problem of how to persuade the West that the Soviet Union meant business. Here he ran up against an accumulation of profound mistrust and hostility whose depths constantly frustrated and disconcerted Soviet negotiators.

The first indication of how difficult it was going to be to get the Western states to accept the Soviet offer came with the long delay in the British reply. Not until May 25, six weeks later, did the British agree, not to an alliance, but to the opening of preliminary discussions. Those talks dragged out over the summer. The British and French found endless stumbling blocks. Their guarantee for Poland brought into the equation a state whose leaders were inveterately anti-Soviet; Polish generals made it clear that they would rather fight Germany alone, if they had to, than with Soviet assistance. The British were not prepared to guarantee the Baltic states, where they suspected the Moscow regime had ulterior motives. The NKVD furnished Stalin with regular high-level intelligence, supplied by spies in the heart of the British establishment, about the twists and turns of British policy. Molotov privately fumed about the 'crooks and cheats' he had to deal with, 'resorting to all kinds of trickery and dreadful subterfuge'. As tension between Germany and Poland deepened over the summer months, the talks deadlocked.[19] Finally an exasperated Molotov announced on July 17 that the talks should consider a military pact if they were to have any worth at all. This ambition exposed the difference between the two sides: the Soviet Union wanted an alliance to fight Hitler, the West wanted a diplomatic front to deter him.

The military talks marked the final step in the Soviet effort to establish a common bloc – the diplomatic equivalent of the Popular Front – to encircle Hitler. They ended any illusion that Soviet leaders might have clung to that an alliance with the West on equal terms was possible. Instead of treating the military talks with the seriousness they deserved in view of the imminent German–Polish conflict, the Western states added insult to injury. Their negotiators travelled, not by airliner, but by sea. The British liner *City of Exeter* did not dock at Leningrad until August 10, twenty-five days after Molotov's invitation to talks was issued. The British and French delegations were met by senior Soviet military men and whisked by night train to Moscow. Neither delegation was headed by anyone senior enough for the immense task of forging a military alliance. Soviet leaders drew the obvious conclusion: the West did not regard the Soviet Union as an equal. Even Poland had been more favourably treated.

On August 12 the drama unfolded. The two Western delegations met the Soviet side around a table in a room in the Spiridonovka Palace. The room was crowded with interpreters and stenographers. It was an unusually sultry day. The room filled with the smoke of Soviet cigarettes.[20] The Soviet team was led by Marshal Kliment Voroshilov, Commissar for Defence since 1934, and one of Stalin's closest circle. All the Soviet military chiefs were present, primed to give a full account of the Soviet contribution to the alliance. In only a matter of minutes the whole enterprise was damaged almost beyond repair. Voroshilov announced that he was empowered by Stalin to sign any military agreement then and there. He asked the heads of the French and British delegations for their credentials. General Joseph Doumenc, the French Commander of the 1st Military Region, bent his instructions sufficiently to persuade Voroshilov that he had the same power. But Britain's chief negotiator, Admiral Sir Reginald

Plunkett-Ernle-Erle-Drax, the naval aide to King George VI, did not even have a page of written instructions. He could at best report back to London. He had no power to agree to anything. Voroshilov was visibly surprised. This revelation might have ended the talks at once, but after conferring with his colleagues Voroshilov agreed to continue them. The group reassembled after a cold lunch. The answer to his next question was even more dismaying. He asked whether either Government had made firm arrangements with the other states of Eastern Europe, principally Poland, for the movement of Soviet forces towards Germany. Drax spluttered about principles, but had nothing concrete to offer. Doumenc could make no commitment, for the Poles had refused point-blank to have the Red Army on Polish soil. Voroshilov was now ill-tempered: 'Principles? We don't want principles, we want facts!'[21]

The facts, when they came, killed off the conference. When the British negotiators were asked how many army divisions Britain could field, Voroshilov was told the figure was sixteen. The Soviet team was so astonished they asked for the figure to be retranslated. When pressed for details, the hapless British had to admit that only four were actually ready to fight. When Stalin later asked the British ambassador for the figure, he finally got the truth: two divisions immediately and two later. Stalin simply shook his head in disbelief. The French had more to offer – 110 divisions and 4,000 tanks. Voroshilov then turned to Soviet strengths. In addition to 120 divisions (out of approximately 300), the Soviet Union could field 5,000 heavy guns, 9,000 to 10,000 tanks and 5,000 combat aircraft.[22] The talks were continued by both sides with little enthusiasm. Stalin now realized, if he had not already done so, that the Western imperialist states he had feared so much were considerably weaker than the Soviet Union. The alliance would still have been a formidable bloc and might well have deterred Hitler from war on Poland. But the evident reluctance of the Western states to rise to Stalin's offer and the constant slights and checks directed at Soviet efforts would have tried the patience of the most diffident ally. The failure to secure the alliance ended the search for collective security.

Soviet isolation was ended by a move from the most unlikely quarter of all. While negotiations dragged on with Britain and France, lines began to reopen from Germany. There is still much speculation about Soviet motives, yet the answer is again more straightforward than any conspiracy theory. It was Germany that pursued the agreement with Stalin, not the other way round. German motives were transparent. In April 1939, after swallowing up Czechoslovakia and extorting the city of Memel from Lithuania, Hitler ordered his armed forces to plan a short, annihilating campaign against Poland for the autumn. Although Hitler was confident that Britain and France would not intervene, there were great risks. A revival of the old alliance from the Great War threatened Germany with a conflict on two fronts. In April Hitler began to tone down the propaganda attacks on the Soviet Union. On May 5 the first German feeler was put out. The Soviet chargé d'affaires, Georgei Astakhov, was told that Germany would honour Soviet trade agreements with arms firms in German-occupied Bohemia. On May 20 the German ambassador to Moscow asked Molotov to reconsider opening trade discussions. Molotov curtly rejected the offer: 'The German government is playing some sort of game.'[23] Ten days later the German Foreign Office, led by Joachim von Ribbentrop, ordered the German ambassador to begin political negotiations with the Soviet Union. It was a frustrating experience. For three months no progress was made. Soviet contacts agreed in general terms that it would be well to improve relations – which could hardly have been worse – but would agree to nothing specific. Privately, Molotov and Astakhov dismissed German efforts as 'superficial' and 'non-committal' and doubted that the fascist leopard was capable of changing its spots. By July nothing had changed. Molotov, and Stalin, too, we must assume, were unimpressed by ever more urgent hints from Berlin that Hitler wanted to talk.[24]

Not until the end of July, only a month before war broke out between Germany and Poland, did the German side finally provide some kind of agenda for discussion. On July 26 Germany's trade negotiator, Karl Schnurre, told Astakhov that Germany was prepared to discuss a political settlement in Eastern Europe, which amounted to a division of the spoils. Three days later Molotov told Astakhov to seek clarification. For the first time Soviet ears pricked up. On

August 2 Ribbentrop, with remarkable candour, offered a settlement of the whole area from the Baltic to the Black Sea. Still Moscow did no more than listen. Molotov did not know what to make of the offers. Hitler was not someone to be trusted to keep his word. But the hints from Berlin touched on real Soviet interests. In the Baltic states, Poland and Romania were territories of the former Tsarist empire. The Soviet Union had been forced to abandon them, but had never lost the ambition to replace Tsarist imperialism in the region with Soviet imperialism. Soviet hesitation about Germany's flagrant advances stemmed partly from deep distrust of German intentions, but also from sheer incredulity. This was an offer, wrote Astakhov to Molotov, 'that would have been inconceivable six months ago'. The Soviet side played their cards as close to the chest as ever.[25]

Over the following few days the German negotiators, who were by now desperate for the diplomatic revolution they needed before attacking Poland, laid all their cards on the table in an untidy heap. There was a non-aggression pact; the possibility of a secret protocol on the territorial dismemberment of Eastern Europe; a top-level German mission to Moscow to sign an immediate agreement; generous trade settlements. One by one the Soviet side picked them up. On August 17, when it was already clear that hope for an alliance with Britain and France was dead, Molotov finally agreed to talks. He handed the German ambassador a note agreeing to a non-aggression pact and a secret protocol. This was all and more than Hitler wanted. On August 19 Stalin agreed that Ribbentrop should come to Moscow, but not until August 26 (the day Hitler had set for the attack on Poland). Frantic telephone calls followed. The German ambassador, Friedrich von der Schulenberg, conveyed Hitler's request that Ribbentrop come sooner; two hours later Stalin himself replied to Hitler with another date, August 23. The contrast with the Western approach to negotiation could not have been more marked. The stage was set for a remarkable diplomatic coup.

On the evening of August 22 Ribbentrop boarded Hitler's private Focke-Wulf Condor aircraft with a staff of more than thirty. His aircraft flew to Königsberg in East Prussia, avoiding Polish air space on the way. He stayed the night there in a state of agitated expectation.

At one o'clock in the afternoon of August 23 the plane landed in Moscow. The airport was festooned with swastika flags drawn back-to-front for Soviet anti-Nazi films.[26] At three o'clock Ribbentrop and Schulenberg drove to the Kremlin. To the Germans' astonishment, they were greeted not by Molotov alone but by Stalin himself. Stalin greeted Ribbentrop with the words 'It's been a lovely shoving match, has it not?'[27] The two sides got down to business. The pact was quickly agreed to. The secret protocol took longer. Germany gave away almost everything previously promised, except for part of Latvia, which Hitler wanted to Germanize. It was a bizarre occasion, two sworn ideological enemies locked in secret session, carving up the states of Eastern Europe in an extravagance of *Realpolitik*. Latvia proved a stumbling block. At 6:30, after three hours of historic discussion, the two sides adjourned.

Ribbentrop telegraphed the news to Hitler and asked him to give up Latvia. Two hours later came Hitler's reply: 'Yes, agreed.' At ten o'clock Ribbentrop returned to the Kremlin. He broke the news to Stalin, who seemed to give an involuntary shudder before shaking his hand. While the final drafts were prepared Stalin invited Ribbentrop to celebrate with him. Each side gave elaborate expressions of goodwill to the other. Stalin drank to Hitler's health; Ribbentrop drank to Stalin's. At two o'clock in the morning the documents were ready. Molotov signed for the Soviet Union, Ribbentrop for Germany. Two hours later Hitler was notified at Berchtesgaden. Champagne was ordered, and Hitler, a non-drinker, sipped a little. German delight was impossible to conceal. 'Now Europe is mine!' Hitler is said to have cried out on hearing the news. Ribbentrop returned to a hero's welcome, hailed as the saviour of peace.[28]

In the event it was Stalin alone who got peace. The pact guaranteed that the Soviet Union could keep out of the war. Without a strong Western alliance, Soviet interests could be served in no other way. The third option available in 1939, to make a commitment to neither side, simply perpetuated an uneasy isolation. It has often been argued that Stalin was playing a double game in 1939, pushing for a Western alliance in order to compel Hitler to offer him the maximum not to make it. Such a view gives Stalin, and Soviet foreign policy, too much credit. It is true that Soviet leaders would have preferred a friendly Germany throughout the 1930s rather than one so self-consciously anti-Communist. Ideology made little difference to Stalin. On the far side of the Soviet frontier, *raison d'état* took over. He could as easily make a pact with the imperialist West as he could with fascist Germany. In the Soviet view all the reactionary states of Europe would be ground to dust in the end under the iron wheels of socialism. Yet the German alliance was neither expected nor sought in 1939. Only when the German offer was on the table did it prove irresistible. 'What could England offer Russia?' asked a German official of Astakhov in July 1939. 'At best participation in a European war and the hostility of Germany, but not a single desirable end for Russia. What could we offer, on the other hand? Neutrality and staying out of a European war . . .'[29]

Above all Germany offered something the Soviet Union could only dream about in 1939: the possibility of rebuilding the old Tsarist empire in Europe. The fact that it came with German approval did not diminish the offer. The fact that it would bring a common German-Soviet border, instead of the network of small buffer states, was bearable. Stalin saw only profit. The photographs of the historic meeting with Ribbentrop show Stalin beaming with an unconcealed and childish pleasure. After the pact was safe Stalin told Nikita Khrushchev, the young Ukrainian ex-peasant and a rising star in the Party, 'I know what Hitler's up to. He thinks he has outsmarted me, but actually it is I who have outsmarted him.'[30] Seven days after the pact was signed German armies invaded Poland. Two days later, on September 3, Britain and France, against Hitler's (and Stalin's) expectations, declared war. Stalin had a breathing space; Hitler had a war he did not want.

What followed in Eastern Europe was a consequence of the pact only in an indirect sense. The secret protocol drawn up in August only delimited spheres of interest; it did not arrange partition or control. The Soviet advance in Europe rode on the back of German military successes. Stalin waited until he was sure of his ground before moving. The rapid advance of German troops promised swift Polish defeat. Stalin did not want Germany to drive on to the Soviet border, disregarding the secret protocol entirely. On September 9, after much hesitation, Molotov agreed to German requests to invade Poland from the east. Little had been prepared, and not until September 17, shortly before the Polish surrender, did the Red Army begin rolling across the frontier. For public consumption Molotov announced that the Soviet invasion had come about because of the 'internal bankruptcy of the Polish state' and the dangers this posed to Russia's blood brothers, the Ukrainians and Belorussians living under Polish rule, who had been 'abandoned to their fate'.[31]

This fate proved as terrible as any Stalin had yet imposed on his own people. Almost overnight Soviet liberators became Soviet jailers. Over one million Soviet troops poured into the seven provinces of Poland in the Soviet sphere. By September 24, following brief skirmishes, the whole area was pacified. On September 28 Ribbentrop again flew to Moscow to arrange the partition. The predominantly non-Polish areas were granted to the Soviet Union; the rest went to Germany. The provisional frontier agreed in August was adjusted. In a second secret protocol Hitler now gave up his claim to Lithuania as part of the German sphere. It was this second pact that formally divided the spoils. Stalin now had a free hand to extend the fruits of his revolution to the peoples of Belorussia and the western Ukraine who had escaped Soviet rule following the Polish victory in 1920.

On 29 November 1939 the inhabitants of the new lands became by decree Soviet citizens. This meant nothing less than the extension of the revolution from above by thousands of NKVD troops and Soviet officials. In the first weeks of occupation the Soviet authorities permitted the law of the jungle to prevail. Thousands of the richer landowners and peasants, local officials and policemen, businessmen and politicians were rounded up and shot or imprisoned. The NKVD quickly established a network of informers who gave them lists of known nationalists and anti-Communists. Private wealth was seized by the state; the possessions of those deemed to be enemies of the revolution were stolen by neighbours or corrupt officials. Instructions from Moscow defining 'anti-Soviet' elements included stamp collectors and Esperanto speakers because they had foreign contacts. The NKVD brought in notorious thugs to run the new prisons that sprang up all.

across the region, where they routinely tortured everyone who fell into their hands to force out the names of yet other victims. When the usual instruments of interrogation were lacking, they improvised. Prisoners were beaten with railings broken from fences; their hands were crushed in the doors of their cells; thin books were placed on their heads, which were then beaten with hammers to induce concussion rather than fracture. When they were dragged, crushed in body and spirit, before NKVD kangaroo courts they were subjected to further indignities. One prisoner had his penis wrapped in paper and then ignited.[32]

For ethnic Poles in the new Soviet provinces the descent into hell had one more staircase. In October a long and detailed set of instructions on deportations was drawn up. By February 1940 the authorities were ready. Two million Polish families were moved in four major deportation actions, ending in June 1941. They were sent to the bleakest areas of Siberia or to the harsh landscape of central Asia. They were allowed to take very little, and the male heads of the family were separated from their wives and children when they arrived at the railheads for deportation. They were destined for Russia's concentration camps. Their families were herded into cattle cars, with a tiny grille for ventilation and no water. At each stop along the line the dead were flung out onto the platform. The exact death toll may never be known. Thousands died of malnutrition and disease. Thousands more died at their destination, where they were left without shelter or food at the side of the track. They were forced to live in holes dug in the mud or huts of straw and branches, in temperatures of minus 40 degrees, or worse. Those who survived were used as forced labourers.[33]

Polish prisoners of war followed the deportees, except for the officers, for whom there was a different fate in store. By late September 1939 the Red Army had 230,000 Polish soldiers in captivity. Most suffered deportation and a regime of hard labour. But for the officers, military officials, gendarmes and border guards who fell into Soviet hands separate camps were set up in the former monasteries of Kozelsk, Starabelski and Ostashkov. They held over half of the Polish officer corps. On 3 April 1940 the first contingent of 300 officers was taken to a station near Smolensk and loaded into buses. A diary later found on one of the prisoners ended with the words: 'They took us to a small wood. They took away rings, my watch, belts, knives. What will they do to us?' A few minutes later the soldiers had their hands tied behind them, were led to a large pit dug among the trees near an NKVD rest home and were shot in the back of the head. They were laid in ten to twelve layers in the pits, the feet of one by the head of the next. The murders were over by May 2. The forest of Katyn where the Polish officers lay was restored; young birches and fir trees were planted above the mass graves and the dirt tracks which the buses had made on the grass were covered over. They were the victims of an order from Stalin himself.[34] The death of Poland's military cadres was part of a calculated strategy to rid the occupied areas of any elements capable of raising the flag of national resurgence against the Soviet invader. When the graves were discovered in 1943 by the German army, the Soviet authorities insisted that they were the work of German killing squads.

But in 1940 Germany was still a Soviet ally. The last thing Stalin said to Ribbentrop when they met in August 1939 was that 'on his word of honour' the Soviet Union 'would not betray its partner'.[35] Stalin took the pledge seriously. The pact included a mutual commitment to revive trade between them. Soviet deliveries were made punctually and in full. During the seventeen months of the pact Germany was supplied with 865,000 tons of oil, 648,000 tons of wood, 14,000 tons of manganese ore, 14,000 tons of copper, almost 1.5 million tons of grain and much more besides. In addition Soviet traders bought up materials on world markets to be transhipped to Germany, including 15,400 tons of rubber, which came via Japan. Other military assistance was granted. The German navy was given a base to use near Murmansk for refuelling. Soviet icebreakers were offered to clear a way through Arctic waters for German merchant raiders, hunting down Allied sea traffic. Soviet weather ships sent back meteorological reports for the German air force during the Battle of Britain.[36]

Stalin also saw to it that international Communism toed the new line. References to fascism mysteriously disappeared from *Pravda*. German Communists, sheltered in Moscow from the Gestapo, were handed back, 800 of them, to the sworn enemy of Marxism. The Comintern, many of whose members had been thrown into complete confusion by the conclusion of the Soviet-German Pact, was ordered to end its attacks on fascism and turn its attention instead to the Western warmongers, Britain and France. Molotov publicly declared in a speech in October 1939 that to continue the war was 'not only senseless, but criminal'. Soviet soldiers were supplied with two simple diagrams to explain why Germany was now a friend. The first was a triangle with the word London at the apex and Moscow and Berlin at the other two corners. The heading was 'What did Chamberlain want?' The second was another triangle with Moscow written at the top, and London and Berlin below, under the caption 'What did Comrade Stalin do?'[37]

The sudden change in the European situation brought the Soviet Union a breathing-space. Very soon the conclusion of the pact and the German war with the West were rationalized as a deliberate proletarian strategy. Stalin liked the idea of 'manoeuvring and pitting one side against another', because it fitted with his own analysis, first developed for the Central Committee in 1925 and expressed publicly in 1934, that war was essentially a phenomenon of imperialist rivalry from which a Communist state could only benefit by taking 'action last'. Just as imperialist war brought revolution to Russia in 1917, so the new war would pave the way for popular revolutions in the rest of Europe, aided by Soviet armies. A few months later Molotov told the Lithuanian Foreign Minister that Lenin's vision of world revolution was unfolding before their eyes. The starving masses of warring Europe would rise up, the Soviet Union would move to liberate them and a final apocalyptic battle on the Rhine between the forces of capital and of labour 'will decide the fate of Europe once and for all'.[38]

This was a distant vision, though it must have looked like a possibility, given the Soviet belief that the new war would be a war of attrition like the war of 1914. In the autumn of 1939 Stalin and the Main Military Council looked for ways to strengthen the Soviet military position in the years of reprieve won by the pact. The main lines of strategy, laid down by the chief of staff, Boris Shaposhnikov, in 1938, were unchanged. The Red Army was expected to fight a stubborn defence on the frontier, then, in Voroshilov's terms, carry the war 'on to the enemy land' with 'little loss of blood'. There is little doubt that such a strategic ambition fitted well with the image of a revolutionary state committed to exporting revolution and able to mobilize a whole society of workers and peasants to drive an invader back. However, two alterations to the 1938 plan were to have deadly consequences. It was decided that a new line of fortifications would be built along the German-Soviet border in Poland and the established fortified line abandoned. The 'covering force' that would conduct the stubborn defence was to be positioned behind a defensive line that was barely on the drawing-board. The second change concerned the tank force. In 1939 it was decided, on the basis of Voroshilov's evaluation of the lessons of the Spanish Civil War, to disband the separate tank corps and to split Soviet armour up among local infantry units. This move was intended to strengthen the defensive power of the covering force and enable small-scale incursions to disrupt enemy mobilization. But it meant that just at the time when German soldiers were about to demonstrate the extraordinary hitting power of massed armoured forces, the Soviet tank force faced fragmentation.[39] In both decisions politics played a large part. After the purges, the balance of power between military and civilian now tilted towards the politicians.

Having absorbed half of Poland, and temporarily averted the German threat, Stalin was eager to press on with fulfilment of the terms set out in the secret German-Soviet protocols. The Baltic states were asked to sign treaties of mutual assistance in the two weeks following the Polish defeat. The treaties gave the Soviet Union the right to station troops in Baltic bases. A few weeks later, on October 5, similar demands were made of Finland: a naval and air base at the mouth of the Baltic at Hanko and cession of the Karelian isthmus north of Leningrad to provide a better defence of that vital city. In return Finland was offered a large area of Soviet territory in Karelia. The Finns refused and on November 13 negotiations were broken off. Stalin almost certainly would have preferred a political solution, but when the Finns refused to be intimidated he tore up the Soviet-Finnish non-aggression treaty and prepared for a military campaign to bring Finland entirely into the Soviet orbit. A puppet Communist government-in-waiting was established for Finland, and Stalin drew up plans to incorporate Finland into the Soviet Union as the Karelo-Finnish Soviet Republic. On November 30 Soviet artillery began to shell the Finnish frontier, and Soviet armies rolled forward, expecting a quick victory. Khrushchev later recalled Stalin's remark that 'all we had to do was fire a few artillery rounds and the Finns would capitulate'. Stalin relied in turn on the conceited assurances of Voroshilov: 'All is well, all is in order, all is ready.'[40]

The Finnish campaign was a disaster for the Red Army. It exposed to the world how feeble was the offensive capability of the purged forces and underlined foreign assessments of the damage the terror had done. Despite a numerical advantage, the armies assigned to the Winter War were broken on a solid set of fortifications, the Mannerheim Line. Soviet soldiers fought stubbornly but took exceptional casualties, a total of 126,875 dead in four months. Their frozen corpses lay in grotesque heaps where they fell. The troops were untrained for storming fixed defences; there were shortages of automatic weapons and winter clothing; the food-supply system soon broke down and transport was poorly organized. Frostbite and hunger added to the casualties inflicted by fast-moving Finnish ski troops and snipers. The commanders were too closely controlled from the centre by political officers who knew little about the battlefield. Initiative and flexibility were sacrificed to the rule book. Only after the appointment of Marshal Semyon Timoshenko to command the front, and the transfer of twenty-seven new divisions, strongly supported by tanks, was the Mannerheim Line breached. The Finns sued for an armistice, and the Red Army was too bloodied to go on to conquer the whole country. On 12 March 1940 peace was signed. Finland was forced to give up the territories and bases demanded the year before, but her independence was assured. The Soviet Union was expelled from the League of Nations for the act of unprovoked aggression.

The Winter War was the largest conflict undertaken by the Red Army since the civil war twenty years before, larger even than the border battles with the Japanese at Khalkhin-Gol fought the previous summer, where the Red Army's blushes were saved by the intervention of General Zhukov. Victory over the Japanese relied on Zhukov's exceptional battlefield skills, but also on the more effective deployment of modern weapons in open terrain against an enemy with poor mobility. Zhukov ensured that the logistical tail was well in place before risking battle. None of these things was present against Finland. Here the Red Army fought as an unmodernized army, relying on primitive infantry tactics, with poor intelligence, weak supply lines and, significantly, no Zhukov. Against the Japanese Zhukov acted with characteristic independence, rejecting recommendations from senior officers and instilling in poorly trained troops a better sense of purpose than their comrades displayed in Finland.[41]

The humiliation in the Winter War prompted reassessment at the highest level. In the middle of April 1940 a special session of the Central Committee and the Main Military Council met to consider steps to improve Soviet fighting power. Voroshilov, who had been a dominant voice as Defence Commissar for fifteen years, was subjected to a hostile cross-examination. Stalin dismissed what he called 'the cult of admiration for civil war experience' and finally sacked his civil war comrade, the man Khrushchev regarded as 'the biggest bag of shit in the army'.[42] In his place Stalin appointed Timoshenko, who had brought the Finnish fiasco to a satisfactory close. Timoshenko's career had followed the conventional Soviet path. A former peasant labourer, he rose to become an NCO during the First World War, joined the Red Army in 1918, the Communist Party in 1919. He proved an able organizer and was regarded as politically reliable. In 1940 he was commander of the Kiev military district, the key area for the defence of the Soviet frontier. He was summoned to the Defence Commissariat as a reformer.

He set about his task with the urgency it deserved. Where Voroshilov had persisted in viewing the army as a branch of politics, as a revolutionary force, Timoshenko was determined to take up the torch lit by Tukhachevsky before his fall and to turn the Red Army into a professional force. He enjoyed wide support from other commanders, who wanted to abandon the political supervision of the army by Party commissars which Voroshilov had reintroduced in 1937. The ambition was to rely more on military expertise. General Kirill Meretskov, who had commanded an army against Finland, complained openly at a meeting in May 1940 about the sterility produced by political control:

Our people are afraid to say anything directly, they are afraid to spoil relations and get in uncomfortable situations and are fearful to speak the truth.[43]

It was evidence of the changing mood in the Party that Meretskov not only survived this outspoken challenge to Party interference, but was promoted to chief of staff in August. On the twelfth of that month Timoshenko, with Stalin's approval, reinstituted unitary command, returning the initiative to the military.

This was the most important of the reforms introduced in the summer of 1940, but not the only one. Timoshenko restructured the Defence Commissariat along functional lines; he resurrected the old officer corps. Over 1,000 were promoted to admiral or general, and traditional uniforms were reinstated. The right of junior officers to criticize their superiors was abolished. A tough new code of discipline was introduced, as was a new training regime that cut down on political propaganda, under the slogan 'Teach the troops what they require in war, and only that.' Training was altered to reflect more closely the arduous conditions of combat learned in Finland. At the expense of training for open, mobile warfare, every effort was now made to prepare the troops to attack fixed defences. Progress, however, was slow. At the end of the year Meretskov told the annual conference of the Defence Commissariat that training was still inadequate and blamed the failures on a lack of 'military professionalism'.[44]

The reforms were intended to turn the Red Army and Navy into effective fighting forces, which in 1940 they were not. Timoshenko did not question the wider military strategy adopted in 1939 but concentrated his effort on producing commanders and troops who could carry it out. Like most senior officers, he accepted that modern war would be fought in two stages, a preliminary period following a declaration of war in which the two sides used a screen of forces in forward positions to disrupt the mobilization and deployment of the enemy's main forces, and a second in which the main forces, concentrated behind the first echelon, would mount a crushing offensive. This strategic outlook emphasized the offensive posture of Soviet forces, which the Finnish war had exposed as flawed. It also flew in the face of the evidence of the German campaign in Poland. Soviet commanders did not draw the obvious lesson that modern mechanized armies could deploy at once with remarkable striking power, without any preliminary skirmishing.

If further proof were needed, in May 1940 German armies swept through the Netherlands and Belgium and in six weeks defeated the French army and drove the British from the Continent. The defeat left Stalin's strategy in tatters. The whole object of the pact with Germany was to deflect the threat from Hitler westward for the foreseeable future. Stalin hoped that the war would develop like the war of 1914, and that Germany would emerge from it 'so weakened that years would be required for it to risk unleashing a great war with the Soviet Union'.[45] Instead the war was over in a matter of weeks, leaving the Soviet Union exposed to a German-dominated Europe and without allies. When news of the surrender terms came through to Moscow, Stalin was angry and incredulous. Khrushchev watched him pacing nervously up and down 'cursing like a cab driver'. 'How could they allow Hitler to defeat them, to crush them?'[46]

The obvious military explanation was ignored. The General Staff blamed Polish and French defeat on unusually 'favourable circumstances' for the German army, most prominent of which was the incompetence and operational immaturity of the Polish and French forces.[47] In December 1940 Timoshenko was confident enough to assert during his annual review that the campaigns had revealed nothing new. Senior Soviet commanders clung to the contention that they could expect a two-stage campaign rather than a swift assault and that the defensive skills of the Red Army were sufficient to absorb and contain an initial attack. Four days after the French surrender, Timoshenko ordered work to begin on the fortified zones along the new frontier with Germany that Stalin had authorized the year before. The Stalin Line was abandoned, its guns and equipment placed in storage or sent forward to supply the new defences. A new urgency was evident. Without the eleven fortified zones of defence planned for construction along the length of the border, the Red Army would have nothing to stop a German attack. From the summer of 1940 until the new line was finished the Soviet Union was in a dangerously vulnerable position. Even with the new line, the failure to grasp the nature of German offensive strategy left Soviet forces unnecessarily exposed to a sudden and swift blow.

The sharp change in the strategic situation prompted Soviet leaders to take the remaining spoils assigned to the Soviet sphere under the terms of the secret protocols of the pact with Germany. On June 17, on the pretext that 'acts of provocation' from the Baltic states had to be met with force, half a million Soviet soldiers were sent into the three republics, Estonia, Latvia and Lithuania, which were subjected to the same regime of lawless terror that had been imposed in eastern Poland. Thousands were openly murdered. Thousands more were deported to distant Siberian camps, an estimated 127,000 in total. A list of names of Latvians shot by NKVD forces, discovered when the Germans occupied the area in June 1941, showed only the most feeble attempt to justify their murder: 'she was caught singing Latvian folk songs'; 'his ancestors were bourgeois'; 'he was caught hiding in the woods'; and so on, a dreary litany of trumped-up charges. At the end of June it was the turn of Romania. Under strong diplomatic pressure the Government in Bucharest handed back the former Tsarist territory of Bessarabia, as well as a part of the Bukovina region that had not been included in the pact. The occupation of these areas was begun on June 28 under Zhukov's supervision, and was completed two days later. The Red Army now lay only 120 miles from the Ploesti oil fields, which provided almost all of Germany's wartime supply of crude oil.[48]

The sudden expansion of Soviet territory westward, although conceded in principle in 1939, produced fresh anxieties in Berlin. The Soviet-Finnish war had left Germany in a difficult position, for her sympathies were all with the Finns. After the end of the war German forces were stationed in Finland. The deliveries of machinery and weapons to the Soviet Union agreed upon in the pact were slow and irregular, in sharp contrast with the scrupulous provision by the Soviet side of materials and food. Despite constant Soviet complaints, the

German suppliers dragged their heels whenever they could rather than allow the latest technology to fall into Russian hands. From Hitler's view the most unfortunate consequence of the pact was the rapid forward deployment of the Red Army in Eastern Europe. He was embroiled in a major war, which he had not wanted and which the pact had been supposed to avert. Now, instead of a powerful Germany dominating Eastern and Central Europe following Poland's defeat, Germany was engaged in an unpredictable war against the British Empire, while the Soviet Union was free to extend its influence unchecked. The occupation of Bessarabia was a final blow. A few weeks later Goebbels wrote in his diary: 'Perhaps we shall be forced to take steps against all this, despite everything, and drive this Asiatic spirit back out of Europe and into Asia, where it belongs.'[49]

Hitler had anticipated him. On July 3 instructions were issued to the German armed forces, under the code name 'Fritz', to begin preliminary studies for an operation against the Soviet Union. At first the army believed that Hitler wanted to inflict only a local defeat on Soviet forces so as to push back the frontier between them and force Stalin to recognize 'Germany's dominant position in Europe'. The army told Hitler on July 21 that a limited campaign could be launched in four to six weeks. But Hitler's ideas, which had at first been uncertain, hardened over the course of the month, as a stream of intelligence information came in showing how Soviet diplomats were now pushing on into the Balkans in their efforts to spread Soviet influence. When Hitler's Operations Chief, General Alfred Jodl, called together his senior colleagues on July 29, he had the most startling news. After making sure that every door and window in the conference room aboard a specially converted train was tightly sealed, he announced that Hitler had decided to rid the world 'once and for all' of the Soviet menace by a surprise attack scheduled for May 1941.[50]

Two days later Hitler called a council of war at his summer retreat. Seated in the main hall of the Berghof, his military chiefs learned for the first time of Hitler's motives. The arguments he presented were practical ones. The Soviet Union was Britain's last chance; with the Soviet threat knocked out, Britain would make peace, and America would no longer be a danger. What he had in mind was the annihilation of the enemy – 'to smash the state heavily in one blow'. Two Army Groups would attack through the Baltic states and the Ukraine to converge on Moscow. A third Army Group would attack south towards the oil-rich Caucasus. It was a plan of startling audacity. That same month he had already ordered the build-up of an army 'greater than all enemy armies together'.[51] He would slowly deploy it eastward. Stalin was to be fooled into believing that the troops were for use in the west and were stationed there in order to avoid British air attack.

There can be no doubt that practical strategic issues did push Hitler towards the most radical of military solutions. But a great war in the east had always been part of his thinking. Here was the real stuff of *Lebensraum* – living-space. Hitler's plans assumed fantastic proportions. By August he had decided to seize the whole vast area stretching from Archangel to Astrakhan (the 'A–A Line') and to populate it with fortified garrison cities, keeping the population under the permanent control of the master race, while a rump Asian state beyond the Urals, the Slavlands, would accommodate the rest of the Soviet people. Planning moved forward on this basis. By the spring of 1941 comprehensive programmes for the racial, political and economic exploitation of the new empire had been drawn up. 'Russia,' Hitler is reported as saying, 'will be our India!'[52]

Every effort was made to keep the whole enterprise camouflaged. Hitler maintained relations with his Soviet ally, though they became acutely strained. On 27 September 1940 he signed the Tripartite Pact with Japan and Italy, which divided the world into separate spheres of interest – 'New Orders' in the Mediterranean, eastern Asia and Europe. This realignment was read with unease in Moscow. The same month German troops appeared in Romania for the first time, and in Finland. Hungary and Romania joined the Tripartite Pact. In October Italy, which had joined in the war on the German side in June, invaded Greece and opened up the prospect of fascist expansion into the Balkans. Then on October 13 Stalin received a long, rambling letter from Ribbentrop which ended with a tantalizing invitation to join the Tripartite Pact and revise the world order together.

It is not entirely clear why Hitler authorized Ribbentrop to send the invitation. He may have hoped that the growing threat of the Soviet Union might be neutralized by agreement after all. He may have used it as an opportunity to find out just what Soviet ambitions were. But for Ribbentrop there was reason enough. He hoped that he could create a powerful bloc opposing the Anglo-Saxon powers and pull off another remarkable diplomatic coup. Stalin gave a cautious reply. It was arranged that Molotov go to Berlin in November. The object of the visit, according to General Aleksandr Vasilevsky, who accompanied him, was 'to define Hitler's intentions' and to 'hold off German aggression for as long as possible'. The evidence now suggests that Molotov was pursuing more than this, that Stalin wanted a second pact defining spheres of influence in Eastern Europe.[53]

Molotov arrived by train on November 12. Two days of discussion followed which satisfied neither party. Molotov was so abrupt with Hitler that their meeting on the first afternoon became heated, and Hitler refused to attend the evening dinner to welcome the Soviet party. Hitler and Ribbentrop hinted that the Soviet Union should turn away from Europe towards British India. They talked in generalities, Molotov in details. His instructions were to discuss points that closely concerned Soviet security in Europe, but he found that the Germans were trying to get the Soviet Union embroiled in the war with Britain. There could be no agreement on this basis. In the middle of an embassy banquet on the 13th, Molotov found himself forced to take shelter from a British bombing raid. Taking advantage of the interruption, Ribbentrop presented Molotov with a draft treaty delimiting the Soviet 'New Order' 'in the direction of the Indian Ocean'. With the noise of guns and bombs in the background, Molotov dismissed the suggestion and told Ribbentrop that what the Soviet Union really wanted was hard talking about Bulgaria, Turkey, Sweden, Romania, Hungary, Yugoslavia and Greece. The following day Molotov returned to Moscow. On November 25 he filed with the German ambassador a list of demands that represented the Soviet price for extending the alliance: German withdrawal from Finland, a free hand for the Soviet Union in Iran and the Persian Gulf and Soviet bases in Bulgaria and Turkey. Hitler ordered Ribbentrop not to reply.[54]

Agreement had always been unlikely, as both sides recognized. Goebbels watched Molotov and the Soviet delegation breakfasting with Hitler in the Chancellery. 'Bolshevist subhumans,' he wrote in his diary, 'not a single man of any stature.'[55] On the very day of Molotov's departure, Hitler ordered final preparations 'to settle accounts with Russia'. On December 5 he told his military staff that by the spring German 'leadership, equipment and troops will visibly be at their zenith, the Russians at an unmistakable nadir'.[56] On December 18 he signed War Directive Number 21 ordering the preparation for war on the Soviet Union, 'Operation Barbarossa'. A date was set for the following May, 'the first fine days'. On January 9, at his retreat in Berchtesgaden, he gave a speech on the future of Germany. 'Russia must now be smashed,' one witness recalled him saying. 'The gigantic territory of Russia conceals immeasurable riches . . . Germany will have all means possible for waging war against continents . . . If this operation is carried through, Europe will hold its breath.'[57]

The failure of Molotov's visit did not diminish Stalin's desire to avoid a direct military confrontation with Germany. The Soviet Union was not, as Hitler knew, ready for a major war, and would not be for at least a year. Stalin has often been pictured as a man blinded by appeasement, leading an unprepared country to the brink of ruin in 1941. It is certainly true that right up to the moment of the German attack Stalin did not want war and hoped that it could be avoided by negotiation – a view not very different from Neville Chamberlain's in 1939 – but the absence of preparation is a myth. The Soviet political and military leadership began to prepare the country from the autumn of 1940 for the possibility of a war with Germany. The problem was not the absence of preparation but the fundamental flaws in strategy and deployment that underpinned it.

Consistent with the Red Army philosophy of active defence and massive counter-offensives into enemy territory, Stalin wanted the new zone of defence to be moved right up to the frontier with Germany and its allies. To the astonishment of German forces, Soviet engineers began to build fortifications in full view, right on the frontier itself. The old Stalin Line was almost entirely abandoned; depots and strong points were left to crumble, or were covered over with earth or in some cases handed over to be used as vegetable warehouses by local collective farms. Much of the equipment removed from them was poorly stored or was moved forward to the new frontier, where it sat rusting while the new fortifications were constructed. The new fortified zones, on which the whole strategy of forward defence hinged, were too numerous to complete all at once. By the spring most of them lacked guns of any kind, radio equipment, even electric power or air filters. When Zhukov visited the border districts in April he immediately ordered armoured doors to be installed at the entrances to the fortifications. On the eve of the German invasion the key frontier areas had no minefields, camouflage or effective fields of fire. Of 2,300 strong points set up on Zhukov's orders, fewer than 1,000 had any artillery.[58]

Zhukov was among those who argued that the Stalin Line should not have been abandoned, and was supported by Shaposhnikov. Stalin refused to accept the argument and to authorize defence in depth. For political reasons the newly acquired territories were to be defended at all costs. Only in June 1941, shortly before the German attack, did Stalin grudgingly concede that the old line should in places be manned, at 30 per cent of its garrison strength. The troops found nothing more than a concrete shell. When General Ivan Konev's men occupied the Kiev Fortified Area, abandoned in 1939, they found it 'overgrown with grass and tall weeds', the concrete gun emplacements empty.[59]

In the autumn of 1940, while the engineers wrestled with the impossible task of fortifying the 2,800 miles of frontier, Soviet leaders drew up their contingency plans in the event of an invasion from the west. Like the 1939 plan, the 1940 draft was based on the assumption that there would be a period of time before the main forces clashed. The one concession that the General Staff made as a result of the German victory in Western Europe was no longer to assume that the period would be three weeks, but could be as little as ten to fifteen days. (In the event, by day fifteen German forces were closing in on Leningrad and poised to take Smolensk and Kiev!) The planners started from the assumption that Germany would attack together with its allies Hungary, Romania and Finland. The direction of the main German advance was, at Stalin's insistence, assumed to be south-west, towards the industry, food and oil of the Ukraine and the Caucasus. Stalin seems to have been influenced in this decision by his civil war experience, where control of the major economic resources was regarded as decisive. Other possibilities were explored, but the plan finally agreed upon in October incorporated Stalin's preference.

The forces protecting the Ukrainian frontier were to engage in a vigorous defence, plugging any holes made by the German advance, smashing its forward units with air attacks, and hampering the mobilization of the main forces by bombing attacks and harassing raids in strength. The main Soviet force would deploy far to the rear, then, once assembled, roll forward through the battling frontier forces onto enemy soil. They were to make for the main assembly of German forces, expected to be around Lublin, and there inflict a decisive defeat before wheeling south-west to sever Germany from her Balkan supplies, then north to seize Silesia.[60] Given the state of the Red Army and Air Force, the plan had an air of complete fantasy about it. When it was put to the test in a series of war games in January, the weaknesses of the Soviet position became clear.

The war games followed a week-long command conference that began on December 23. The object was to thrash out the lessons of the year and review the current state of military planning. No serious attempt was made to challenge the central principles upon which Soviet war-planning rested. The war games were staged to confirm what was seen as received wisdom. The first was fought between Zhukov and General Dmitri Pavlov, chief of the Soviet mechanized forces, on New Year's Day, 1941. Zhukov was the German side, Pavlov the Soviet. Although Pavlov was able to bring his main forces to bear on East Prussia, consistent with the strategy of the massive counter-offensive, he was routed by Zhukov. In the second game, played a week later, the players were reversed. This time Zkukov pushed successfully across the frontier into Hungary; Pavlov's weak counter-attack attempted to parry. The outcome said a great deal about Zhukov's battlefield skills, even on a table-top. But there were worrying signs for Soviet strategy. When Stalin assembled the commanders and officials following the second game, a curious drama unfolded.[61]

The chief of staff was asked to report on the outcome of the games. Meretskov spoke hesitantly. Rather than say out loud that the Zhukov Germans had won the first game, Meretskov applauded the early stages, when Pavlov with sixty divisions had overcome the fifty-five German divisions defending the Reich frontier. Stalin angrily took the floor and exposed as nonsense the view that a ratio of little more than one division to one could overcome the fixed German defences. It was all right 'for propaganda purposes', he told the assembly, 'but here we have to talk in terms of real capabilities'. The uncomfortable Meretskov was then asked about the second game but would give no definite answer on the outcome, which was inconclusive. When one of Timoshenko's deputies followed the discussion by insisting on voicing his own belief that infantry divisions should be horse-drawn rather than mechanized, Stalin's patience was stretched to the limit.[62] The General Staff left the conference in a despondent mood. The following day Zhukov was appointed Chief of the General Staff, and Meretskov was put in charge of training.

Zhukov had never been a General Staff officer and expressed his desire to remain in the field. Stalin insisted, and Zhukov took up the key military position at the most critical time for Soviet forces. He approached his task with a ruthless energy, but he was not staff-trained and had to rely more than a chief of staff should on the work of his deputies. The five months that remained before the German invasion were used to press forward the building of the fortifications and the establishment of large numbers of air and tank units in the forward defence zone that were to absorb the preliminary German attack, should it come. In March the Government called for the creation of twenty mechanized corps to be distributed along the frontier, but by June less than half were equipped. The air force was ordered to establish 106 new air regiments, using the new models coming into production, but by May only nineteen were complete. These forces were crammed into a narrow belt behind, or sometimes straddling, the frontier. They absorbed four-fifths of the production of the new T-34 tank, the most advanced in the world, and half of the available modern aircraft, but they lacked the training (and spare parts) needed to operate them effectively. Morale among the forward troops was at its nadir; officers were losing control of their men. Crime and insubordination were widespread.[63]

In May 1941 Zhukov and Timoshenko produced what turned out to be the last version of the deployment plan before the German invasion. It varied little from the plan drawn up the previous October, except that it now postulated two counter-offensives into German-held territory: one towards Cracow, to cut Germany off from her southern allies; one towards Lublin, with the ultimate object of securing German-occupied Poland and East Prussia. A section of this document has been seized upon as evidence that the Soviet Union was planning a pre-emptive strike against Germany in the summer of 1941, a strike undone by the sudden launching of Barbarossa. The document in question, an unsigned memorandum dated May 15, was not an order or directive but an exploratory recommendation for force deployment entirely consistent with the planning of the previous two years.[64] There is no evidence that Stalin saw it, but even if he had there are no grounds for thinking that this was anything other than a continued review of the forward defence posture on which Soviet strategy had relied since the 1930s. Some form of pre-emption through spoiling attacks on the mobilizing forces of the enemy was an integral part of that posture. It did not signify a Soviet intention to launch unprovoked war but was, on the contrary, a desperate gambit to obstruct German mobilization against the Soviet Union.

It is true that in March 1941 Stalin, grudgingly, agreed to Zhukov's request to call half a million reservists to the colours, with a further 300,000 several days later. True, too, that the frantic rearmament called for in 1940 brought new labour laws in June 1940 that lengthened the working week to seven days on, one day off. True, also, that throughout May 1941 Zhukov and Timoshenko argued with Stalin, often heatedly, to transfer more troops as a precaution against certain defeat. Not until June 4 did Stalin relent, authorizing the movement of a further 120,000 men to the frontier fortified zones and the second line of defence, but only over a four-month period.[65] None of this suggests a premeditated assault on Germany. It is also true that Stalin and other military leaders stressed that the Red Army was an offensive force. On May 5 Stalin spoke publicly about the Soviet military: 'The

Red Army is a modern army, and a modern army is an offensive army.' This, too, has been taken as evidence of malign intent. Yet it is entirely consistent with the Soviet view of fighting dating from the 1920s. Defence was regarded neither as an acceptable option for a revolutionary state, nor as militarily desirable. Stalin said nothing that had not been said a hundred times before.

The clearest evidence that Stalin had no plans to attack Hitler first can be found in his almost frantic efforts to appease the German leader right up to June. Despite the efforts of Zhukov to prepare more thoroughly for a possible German attack, Stalin insisted repeatedly that no such danger existed and that nothing should be done to provoke it. Among the wider public, as with the military leaders, there was a growing sense of unease, of impending crisis. In the spring a Soviet film, *If War Should Come Tomorrow*, portrayed a German attack repulsed by heroic Soviet soldiers and the revolutionary over-throw of Hitler. Stalin knew, of course, that a great deal remained to be done. The lamentable performance of the military at the command conference in January could have done little to convince him that the Soviet Union was capable of any effective counter to Hitler (or Japan, with whom a separate non-aggression pact was signed in April 1941). He insisted to all around him that war would not come. Zhukov was widely criticized after the war for not having done more to prepare for the German attack, but it is difficult to see what more he could have done under the circumstances. In 1966 Zhukov spoke in his own defence against the chorus of recrimination: 'Let's say that I, Zhukov, feeling the danger hanging over the country gave the order: "Deploy!" They would report to Stalin. "On what basis?" "On the basis of danger." "Well, Beria, take him to your basement."' Indeed, the hapless Meretskov was taken to the 'basement' that spring and given the worst that the Lubyanka could offer. Not that Zhukov was a coward. He was, Timoshenko recalled, 'the only person who feared no one. He was not afraid of Stalin.'[67] He spoke his mind regularly. The problem was that one man could not change the political machinery. Stalin ordained that war would not come in 1941, and the system was not able to contradict him.

Few military campaigns could have been more clearly signalled.

Despite German efforts at concealment and disinformation, designed to lull Soviet intelligence into thinking that the military preparations were for the war with Britain, there came during the spring of 1941 an almost endless stream of intelligence information about imminent German invasion. There were at least eighty-four such warnings, most probably a great many more. They were passed through the office of the head of military intelligence, General Filip Golikov. His reports classified information as either 'reliable' or 'doubtful'. Most of the information on Barbarossa was placed in the second category. He suggested that much of it was British misinformation, part of a conspiracy to drive a wedge between the two allies. Warnings sent directly from the British Prime Minister, Winston Churchill, which were culled from decryptions of German orders, were regarded as a particularly blatant attempt at provocation. When Hitler's deputy, Rudolf Hess, made his 'peace' flight to Scotland on 10 May 1941, Soviet officials regarded the whole episode as evidence that their mistrust of British motives had been right all along.[68] The most reliable evidence came from a German Communist spy in Tokyo, Richard Sorge, who was indiscreetly fed a diet of detailed information on German moves by German embassy staff. On March 5 Sorge sent microfilm of German documents to Moscow indicating a German attack in mid-June. On May 15 he sent more precise detail, giving the date as June 20. On May 19 he warned that nine German armies with one hundred and fifty divisions were poised on the Soviet frontier. Military intelligence replied simply: 'We doubt the veracity of your information.'[69]

Not even the repeated violation of Soviet air space – an estimated 180 incursions – made any difference. Stalin remained utterly, almost obsessively, convinced that Germany would not invade. On June 14 the Soviet news agency Tass published a stinging rejection of any suggestion of imminent attack. The rumours were spread 'by forces hostile to the Soviet Union and Germany, forces interested in the further expansion and spreading of the war'.[70] When watertight information was supplied from a Czech espionage source, Stalin said, 'Find out who is making this provocation and punish him.' Even when Soviet spies in Berlin, many in positions of responsibility, reported on

June 16 that 'the blow may be expected at any time', Stalin rejected the report on the grounds that no Germans, even Communist sympathizers, were to be trusted. A courageous German soldier crossed the frontier on June 21 to tell the Red Army that Germany would attack the next day. Stalin ordered him shot: more disinformation and provocation.[71]

Why was Stalin so blind? The Soviet Union had the largest intelligence network in the world. Why did Stalin disregard it entirely? He was a man with an almost congenital distrust of others. Why did he apparently trust Hitler, most artful of statesmen? There is no easy answer. Stalin based his calculations partly on rationality. He argued that to invade the Soviet Union with its vast army and overstretched frontier would require a numerical advantage of two to one for the attacker. This Hitler did not have. He was convinced that no leader, however adventurist, would risk a two-front war. When German forces were sent into the Balkans to help Italy they became embroiled in Yugoslavia, Greece and eventually, as late as May 1941, in driving the British from the Aegean. Stalin was no military genius, but he could see no sense in Hitler striking east in June with only a few weeks of combat weather remaining. The Balkan diversion hardened Stalin's conviction, for conviction it was. He projected onto Hitler his own sense of what was possible.

There are other explanations. It seemed plausible that Hitler's military moves in the spring of 1941 were simply a ploy to bring Stalin back to the negotiating table. (Stalin was not alone in drawing that conclusion.) He also felt he had the measure of his fellow dictator. He had the same grudging respect for Hitler that his opposite number reserved for him. He clearly indulged at times in the fantasy that side by side the two leaders, each in his own way a revolutionary, could take the world by storm. On more than one occasion he was heard to complain, 'Together with the Germans we would have been invincible.'[72] Yet in the end Stalin suffered from a failure of imagination. He does not seem to have been able to entertain the idea that Hitler could undertake an assault so breathtaking, so against the grain of military good sense. He must, nevertheless, have had the strongest misgivings. Khrushchev remembered Stalin in the weeks before the

German attack as a man 'in a state of confusion, anxiety, demoralization, even paralysis'.[73] On June 14 Zhukov suggested beginning Soviet mobilization. 'That's war,' replied Stalin, and refused.[74] Perhaps Stalin was simply unable to admit that he had misjudged Hitler. By the weekend of June 21/22 he was of two minds. He put the Moscow air defences on alert, but then complained that he was giving way to 'panic' himself. At half past midnight on June 22, Timoshenko, Zhukov and his deputy, Nikolai Vatutin, went to see Stalin to persuade him to issue an alert. He finally authorized it, but too late for many of the units in the German line of attack. Timoshenko had great difficulty persuading Stalin not to include a sentence asking frontier commanders to treat with the oncoming German officers to settle the dispute. He did insist that no Soviet soldier, sailor or airman was to cross the frontier, the very antithesis of everything that Soviet operational art had taught them.[75]

On the other side of the frontier there moved into place the largest invasion force ever gathered. Over 3 million men, organized in 146 army divisions, with 14 more Romanian divisions to the south and Finnish forces to the north, all supported by more than 2,000 aircraft and 3,350 tanks, gradually moved to battle stations during June. Behind the frontline units special security brigades, Hitler's equivalent of the NKVD, were organized in four *Einsatz-kommandos*. Their orders were to root out all political elements hostile to Germany and exterminate them ruthlessly. On the morning of June 21 the code word 'Dortmund' was released, signalling an attack at half past three the following morning. Soviet border guards could hear the noise of armour moving into position. Stalin retired to bed at three o'clock in the morning, his eyes still closed to the glaring evidence of catastrophe. Thirty minutes later Russia's war had begun.

3

The Goths Ride East:
Barbarossa, 1941

We have only one task, to stand and pitilessly to lead this race-battle. . . . The reputation for horror and terror which preceded us we want never to allow to diminish. The world may call us what it will.

Heinrich Himmler, April 1943

On the night that German forces launched the largest and costliest war in history Stalin had little more than an hour of sleep. By the time he was awakened German aircraft had already attacked the major Soviet air bases behind the frontier and were bombing Minsk, Kiev and Sevastopol. At four o'clock in the morning Zhukov already knew that German forces were attacking all along the Soviet western frontier. He was asked by Marshal Timoshenko to telephone their leader at his villa – the so-called nearer *dacha* at Kuntsevo – outside Moscow. This was an unenviable task. The officer on duty was bleary and unco-operative: 'Comrade Stalin is sleeping.' Zhukov was urgent: 'Wake him up immediately, the Germans are bombing our cities.' A few minutes later Stalin himself answered the telephone. 'Did you understand?' Zhukov asked.[1] Silence followed, broken only by the sound of heavy breathing. Finally Stalin regained himself. Zhukov was ordered to assemble the entire Politburo at the Kremlin. Stalin arrived first, driving through Sunday morning streets filled with drunken, slumbering Muscovites.

Stalin was shocked but he was not, as is often suggested, paralysed by the news. For some time he persisted in his belief that this was a limited act of provocation. When Timoshenko objected that bombing

Soviet cities could not be regarded merely as 'provocation', Stalin replied that 'German generals would bomb even their own cities,' so unscrupulous were they when it came to provoking a conflict. He muttered that Hitler could know nothing about the attacks and that someone should 'urgently contact Berlin'.[2] As his Politburo companions arrived one by one, Stalin addressed them in a slow, faltering voice. He was pale and tired. Molotov was sent off to find out from the German ambassador what German intentions were. Schulenberg was shown into Molotov's office. He stiffly informed Molotov that a state of war now existed between Germany and the Soviet Union. All Molotov could stutter was 'What have we done to deserve this?'; he hurried back to Stalin's office. The news was received by Stalin with unusual calmness. He 'sank in his chair and was locked in deep thought', wrote Zhukov. After a long pause he spoke. 'The enemy,' he assured everyone present, 'will be beaten all along the line.'[3]

Zhukov and Timoshenko promised first to halt the enemy and then, warming to the theme, to destroy them, though neither man could have had any illusions about the difficulties they faced. At 7:15 in the morning Stalin issued the first wartime order, under Timoshenko's signature. The German air force was to be destroyed and air attacks launched up to 100 miles into German territory; the army was ordered to 'annihilate' invading forces, using any means, but not to cross the frontier with Germany. In the evening Soviet forces were ordered to go over to the offensive against the main axes of German attack and to take the battle onto enemy territory.[4] Molotov and Stalin worked on a draft speech announcing the onset of war. Molotov was sent off to read it over Soviet radio at noon. From loudspeakers set up in the main streets of Soviet cities, the people heard the terrible truth. Many were already under attack; refugees were already streaming eastward, the start of a vast exodus of more than 25 million people. Molotov found the words difficult to deliver. He ended on an optimistic, exhortatory note: 'Our cause is just, the enemy will be smashed, victory will be ours.' Stalin thought his performance lack-lustre.

There existed an almost unbridgeable chasm between the confident expectation of victory which Stalin clung to in the first week of the

Map 1 Operation Barbarossa, June–September 1941

war and the state of utter chaos and demoralization at the front line. The attack was the very opposite of what orthodox thinking in the Red Army had expected. Instead of ten days of initial probing attacks, followed by the clash of the two fully mobilized armies, the entire German force swept forward in the first hours much as German leaders had expected, to all appearances a model of purposeful efficiency pitted against Soviet primitivism. 'The Russian "mass,"' wrote a German staff officer, 'is no match for an army with modern equipment and superior leadership.' Most foreign observers agreed. 'I am mentally preparing myself for headlong collapse of the Red Army and air force,' wrote the British politician Hugh Dalton in his diary on the night of the German invasion. British and American military leaders expected German victory in weeks, months at the most.[5]

Soviet forces were capable of a great deal more than their enemies and allies supposed. They were the victims not of Bolshevik primitivism but of surprise. So insistent had Stalin been that Germany would not attack in the summer that even the most rudimentary precautions were lacking. Aircraft were lined up in inviting rows at the main air bases, uncamouflaged. At least 1,200 of them were destroyed at sixty-six bases within hours of the war's beginning, most of them on the ground. Many units in forward positions had no live ammunition to issue. The speed of the German advance overwhelmed the Soviet supply system; 200 out of 340 military supply dumps fell into German hands in the first month.[6] The army itself was in the midst of a complex redeployment. A fraction of the army was stationed in the forward echelon, another fraction was behind it, far to the rear, and reserves, larger than either of the echelons in front of them, were still further back. Stalin continued to insist on keeping most divisions, approximately 100, stretched out opposite the south-west frontier, to protect the resource-rich Ukraine, even after it was evident that the main route of German advance was further north towards Minsk and Moscow. Many units were in the process of moving to new quarters when the attack came. Most were under strength. In the first days army units were posted to the frontier in almost complete ignorance of the enemy's position. No coherent order of battle could be established. Divisions were sent into the line as they arrived. Without air cover, adequate weapons or intelligence, they were annihilated, often in just a few hours. In the first four weeks of Barbarossa, 319 Soviet units were committed to battle; almost all of them were destroyed or badly damaged.[7]

While Soviet units at the front fought in hopeless isolation, their organization and communication systems in tatters, the Kremlin buzzed with urgent activity. After the weeks of vacillation preceding the invasion, Stalin was galvanized into action. Khrushchev later recalled a man who overnight became 'a bag of bones in a grey tunic', but the recollections of those who worked with him in the first week of war paint a picture of an energetic man who, though 'tired and worried', was consumed with anger – at the Germans, at his colleagues, at the disoriented forces at the front, even at himself. He worked around the clock, involving himself in every decision, large and small – the design of a sniper's rifle, the length of bayonets. He was voracious in his appetite for news, but those around him hesitated to tell him the worst. The military discussions had an air of complete unreality, Stalin urging annihilating attacks, his commanders cautiously painting a picture of continuous retreats.[8]

During the first weeks of the war Stalin finally stepped out of the modest shoes of the Party Secretary to concentrate the supreme direction of the war in his own hands. On June 23 he approved the establishment of a Main Headquarters (*Stavka Glavnogo Komandovaniia*). Usually known simply as the Stavka, its name echoed that of the headquarters set up by the Tsar in the previous war. On July 10 he became Supreme Commander of the Armed Forces. On July 19 he replaced Timoshenko as Commissar for Defence. On August 8 the Stavka was finally converted to the Supreme High Command, with Stalin at its head. This was a remarkable political revolution. Stalin had always preferred to operate behind the scenes, while public responsibility was given to others. Stalin's motives for seizing the reins at the hour of crisis are still open to speculation.

In June the Supreme Command was still chaired by Marshal Timoshenko, who had the unfortunate task of trying to interpret the awful news from the front in a form that would bring nothing worse than angry rebukes. Under the circumstances it was perhaps surprising that he survived at all. Stalin was quick to project his own failure onto others. No diploma in psychology was needed to see that Stalin's ferocious anger was fired by his own sense of guilt at so misjudging his fellow dictator.

Stalin's personal battle with reality reached its climax on June 27. News was filtering in that German forces had reached the Belorussian capital of Minsk, some 300 miles into Soviet territory. Following a tense Politburo meeting, Stalin, accompanied by Beria and Molotov, took the unprecedented step of paying a visit to the Defence Commissariat, where Timoshenko and Zhukov were trying to bring some order to the battered Soviet line. Stalin looked at the maps and reports for himself and could see the truth. An angry exchange followed with Zhukov and Timoshenko, who for once dropped the mask of fear always worn in Stalin's presence. Stalin wanted the truth and got it. He looked around at each of them in the room with evident gloom and stalked out. 'Lenin founded our state,' he muttered, 'and we've fucked it up.'[9]

Stalin abruptly stopped ruling. He drove to his *dacha* at Kuntsevo in the forest of Poklonnaia Gora outside Moscow and stayed there, leaving the Government in abeyance. There are a number of possible explanations for Stalin's behaviour. It may well be that, overcome with nervous exhaustion and despair, he could no longer sustain the charade played out in the first week of war, now that the truth was known. He had refused to face the shock of invasion when it came. A delayed reaction was perhaps inevitable, certainly not surprising. Yet Stalin did little that was not calculated. He avoided any kind of identification with the disaster. *Pravda* stopped printing his name. The withdrawal may well have been a ploy to see whether his leadership would survive the crisis. The discovery that Stalin was reading a play about Ivan the Terrible at the time has led one biographer to suggest that he was acting out the game once played by his autocratic predecessor, who pretended to be dying to see how his courtiers reacted. On the cover of the play Stalin doodled the words, 'We'll hold out.'[10] If this was Stalin's intention it was a risky game. He could not be certain that he would survive the disaster. As it turned out the gambit, if that is what it was, worked to Stalin's advantage.

On June 30 the members of the Politburo drew up a plan to create a State Committee for Defence, an emergency cabinet to oversee the whole Soviet war effort. They all agreed that in the country only Stalin had the authority to lead the Committee. At four o'clock in the afternoon they drove out to the *dacha* to plead with Stalin to return to Moscow and take up the reins once more. According to Anastas Mikoyan, they found Stalin sitting in an armchair in his dining room. Another witness of the bizarre encounter recalled that Stalin was thin, haggard and gloomy. 'Why have you come?' he asked nervously. When their mission was explained Stalin looked surprised: 'Can I lead the country to final victory?' Voroshilov is reported to have replied: 'There is none more worthy.'[11] Stalin agreed to take up the heavy task. The leadership crisis was past. Stalin became and remained Russia's supreme war leader.

He returned to the Kremlin on July 1. Two days later he broadcast to the nation for the first time since the onset of the war. It was one of the most important speeches of his life. The delivery was hesitant, interrupted by occasional gulps, as if the speaker were sipping from a glass of water; Stalin had never been a good public speaker. The message was, nevertheless, clear enough. He began by addressing the Soviet people as 'brothers and sisters', 'friends', words generally foreign to Stalin's public political vocabulary. He explained that Germany had launched an unprovoked attack, and that the Soviet Union had 'come to death grips with its most vicious and perfidious enemy'. He invoked the great heroes of the Russian past who had fought off one invader after another. Russia's enemies were 'fiends and cannibals' but they could be beaten. He appealed to popular patriotism rather than revolutionary zeal. (On June 26 *Pravda* described the conflict for the first time as a 'fatherland war'.) He called on ordinary Soviet citizens to undertake a *levée en masse*, like the great popular mobilization that saved the French Revolution in 1792. If retreats were necessary – they could no longer be disguised from the Soviet public – he promised the Germans a wasteland: 'The enemy must not be left a single engine, a single railway car, a single pound of grain or a gallon of fuel.' He finished by reminding his listeners that this was not 'an ordinary war', it was total war, 'a war of the entire Soviet people', a choice between Soviet freedom or German slavery.[12]

To many listeners this must have seemed an unenviable choice, but the response was immediate. Stalin's slow voice gave the Soviet people a reassurance they had lacked in the confused, rumour-filled early days of war. 'It was the end of illusions,' wrote the novelist Konstantin Simonov, 'but nobody doubted his courage and his iron will . . . What was left after Stalin's speech was a tense expectation of change for the better.'[13] The call to establish a popular militia – *opolchenie* – was answered overwhelmingly. In Leningrad 159,000 joined the volunteers; in Moscow 120,000, organized in a dozen divisions. The volunteers came from every quarter – workers, teachers, students, officials. They received rudimentary training and few weapons. When Khrushchev telephoned Moscow from the Ukraine to ask what the *opolchenie* should fight with, he was told to use 'pikes, swords, anything you can make'.[14] When the militia units were thrown into defence of the major cities they were wiped out.

Stalin's speech of July 3 contained not one but two declarations of war. Beside the war on German fascism, Stalin declared war on anyone on the home front who threatened the Soviet struggle. There was no room, he announced, for 'whimperers or cowards, for panic-mongers and deserters . . .' Later in the speech he urged a ruthless fight against 'disorganization of the rear', against 'spies, diversionists and enemy parachutists . . .' Here Stalin was on more familiar territory. The terror was not suspended; it was simply redirected. Draconian regulations were introduced. On June 22 martial law was declared throughout the western Soviet Union. A labour conscription law compelled all men between 18 and 45 and all women between 18 and 40 to work eight hours a day constructing rudimentary defences. In all weathers, hour after hour, the conscripts dug anti-tank traps, trenches and artillery emplacements. On June 26 the working day was extended by a mandatory three hours, and all leave and public holidays were suspended.[15] Every worker had to be a Stakhanovite. On July 16 Timoshenko's reform of the previous year, which kept the Party out of military affairs, was overturned, and dual command was reintroduced. In August the notorious Order Number 270 was issued, condemning all those who surrendered or were captured as 'traitors to the motherland'. The wives of captured officers were subject to arrest and imprisonment. Among the first victims was Stalin's own son, Yakov, captured in early July. Shortly after his capture his wife was arrested and spent two years in a labour camp. Stalin refused a German offer to exchange him for a high-ranking German officer. In 1943 Yakov was shot by a guard for deliberately walking into the forbidden perimeter zone of the prisoner-of-war camp where he was held.[16]

The wartime terror took an almost inevitable toll among those officers who had been unfortunate enough to be in command of the zone that was attacked. Senior commanders were arrested, though not all were executed. But the chief culprit in Stalin's eyes was the commander of the Western Army Group, General Dmitri Pavlov, who made desperate but entirely fruitless efforts to hold the Soviet front line together in the first week of the war. The son of a lumberjack, and an NCO from the First World War, Pavlov was one of those who rose rapidly to high command following the purges. He was arrested at the end of June, accused of treason and shot. The commander of the Western Air District, Major General Kopets, saved the NKVD the trouble by killing himself on the first evening of the invasion. Pavlov's place was taken by Timoshenko, who found himself the target of ceaseless intervention from Stalin and other Party leaders desperate for results. After four weeks Timoshenko was suddenly summoned to Stalin's *dacha*, where he was told that Zhukov was to take his place. Zhukov, who was present, urged Stalin not to change the command at such a critical point, and Stalin obligingly agreed. At almost the same time Zhukov himself clashed dangerously with the politicians. On July 29 he called on Stalin, Malenkov and Mekhlis to outline his plan to abandon the Ukrainian capital of Kiev and withdraw to a defensive line behind the Dnepr River. Stalin told him the idea was 'rubbish', and Zhukov angrily asked to be relieved of his post as chief of staff. He might have suffered Meretskov's fate for confronting Stalin or for his 'defeatism' in suggesting a withdrawal, but Stalin stuck with Zhukov. He was removed as chief of staff but put in charge of the Reserve front, and he remained a member of the Stavka.[17]

The terror was not limited to military scapegoats. On July 20 Stalin authorized Beria to organize special sections in the NKVD to purge unreliable elements from military units and to investigate ruthlessly all soldiers who escaped from German captivity or encirclement. True to Stalin's instructions, the NKVD rounded up suspected rumour-mongers and defeatists, who in a fresh wave of lawlessness were either shot or exiled to the camps.[18] The worst atrocities were perpetrated in the areas vacated by the Red Army. In occupied Poland, the Baltic states and the Ukraine the NKVD indulged in a panic-stricken orgy of killing. Uncertain what to do with their prisoners, they began to murder them randomly in the first days of the German assault. There was no longer any system to restrain them. The NKVD guards killed anyone in their hands, even common criminals or those pending trial. When the prisons were opened up after the Soviet retreat there were scenes of indescribable horror. Bodies had been savagely mutilated; hundreds of prisoners had been tortured to death rather than dispatched with the usual bullet in the back of the head. In one incident in the Ukraine the NKVD dynamited two cells filled with women prisoners. In another prison the floor was strewn with the tongues, ears and eyes of the dead prisoners. The horrors almost defy explanation. What happened in the first few days of the war was very different from the calculated killings in Katyn and elsewhere. The NKVD guards seem to have been convulsed by a spasm of retributive violence induced by fear, desperation and rage. Racism cannot be discounted, for when the advancing Germans put Soviet prisoners of war and Poles together in the same railway cars, they sometimes found, on arrival at prison camp, that the Poles had been murdered on the way.[19]

Where the NKVD had time, prisoners were marched east under escort on what quickly turned into death marches. A column of 2,000 prisoners from the Wilno area was forced to march for six days before reaching a railhead, from which trains were to take them to camps further east. They were given only one meal, on the first day, and water only in sips after that. Hundreds died of exhaustion; others were shot or kicked to death as they fell behind the column. Since the death rate was so high on the marches, it is difficult to understand why the prisoners were not simply killed like all the rest. Few seem to have survived the war. In these western areas of the Soviet Union, so recently incorporated into the state, and in the Ukraine, the victim of Stalin's brutality during the collectivization drive, there were genuine opponents of the regime. When German forces poured into the region they were hailed by much of the population as liberators. For many of them the last experience of Soviet occupation was the sight of straggling columns of prisoners stumbling east and the seizure by retreating troops of anything that could be carried or driven along. Almost half the cattle of Ukrainian collective farms were herded back to Soviet-held territory. Some 50,000 factories, most of them small workshops, were dismantled and shipped east as part of a vast pro-gramme of industrial evacuation and relocation. There were few families that had not been touched by the attention of the NKVD in the western non-Russian areas for at least a decade prior to the German invasion. Nonetheless, it would be wrong to confuse anti-Soviet sentiment with enthusiasm for German rule. Many Ukrainians and Poles reacted with understandable caution to their new rulers. As one observer put it, the Germans had 'not come to Ukraine to do good'.[20]

In the first weeks of 'liberation' a power vacuum opened up in the conquered areas that was rapidly filled with local nationalists or fascists. The Organization of Ukrainian Nationalists (OUN), founded in 1929 and based largely in Poland, sent some 8,000 of its 20,000 activists into the Soviet Ukraine with the German forces. They split up into small units of ten to fifteen and fanned out into the region to spread the gospel of Ukrainian national revival. The OUN distrusted the Germans. Their ambition was nothing less than a Ukrainian homeland, independent of both Russia and Germany. That distrust was not misplaced. By the end of August German occupation authorit-ies ordered the first crackdown on local nationalism. In the Baltic states, Soviet-occupied Poland, Belorussia and Ukraine, all those elements deemed to be hostile to German interests, including national-ists of all kinds, were rounded up by the SS *Einsatzgruppen* and either executed or imprisoned.[21] That summer the first trainloads of emaciated, terrorized workers arrived in Germany, part of an army of more than 7 million workers seized from the areas of German conquest. The local populations were soon made aware that they had simply exchanged despotisms. In October 1941 Field Marshal von Reichenau ordered that no effort should be made to put out fires started by retreating Soviet forces. The destruction of buildings was part of the German 'fight of annihilation' against Bolshevism.[22]

The German plans for the conquered East began to take shape months before the attack in June. They closely reflected the fate of Germany's share of Poland, where the political and intellectual élite had been wiped out in mass killings in the early months of occupation and Polish territory either earmarked for crude Germanization or placed under the rule of Nazi satraps. The Polish population was regarded simply as a resource to exploit for its labour power. Any manifestation of Polish nationality and culture was officially stamped out, though it lingered on in a twilight world of dissent. The war against the Soviet Union was defined by Hitler as a *Vernichtungskrieg*, a war of destruction. The Soviet Union neatly encapsulated, in his view, all the major enemies of German, and European, civilization – Jews, Bolsheviks and Slavdom. This was a war to the death between two different world systems, not simply a struggle for power and territory. Whatever the practical strategic arguments for invasion in 1941, Hitler did not disguise the fact that the conflict was ideologically driven. For here was the unavoidable contest between barbarism and civilization anticipated in his thoughts on war in 1936.

The army and the SS – Heinrich Himmler's élite party paramilitary organization – were given joint responsibility for eliminating the 'Jewish-Bolshevik' menace. In the so-called Commissar Order issued in June 1941 the armed forces were instructed to root out Communists and Jewish intellectuals among Red Army prisoners. The SS *Einsatz-gruppen* had the job of eliminating all Communists, officials and intellectuals. Their fate was death. The German armed forces alone are said to have executed an estimated 600,000 Soviet prisoners during the war. In May 1941 the chief of Hitler's Supreme Headquarters, Field Marshal Wilhelm Keitel, issued guidelines for the troops to be 'ruthless and energetic' in their attacks on Bolsheviks and Jews. Early in the campaign the *Einsatzgruppen* began the mass executions of male Jews aged 17 to 45, as instructed. Soon older men and boys were added to the list. Beginning in August women and children were also rounded up for slaughter, some of them cases denounced or handed over by native anti-Semites in the Baltic states or the Ukraine. The remaining population was to be used as a virtual slave-labour force, ruled by Nazi imperial governors. At a meeting on 16 July 1941, Hitler outlined his own view of the East: 'Occupy it, administer it, exploit it.'[23]

By mid-July Hitler was riding high on a wave of scarcely credible military triumph. Operation Barbarossa had worked like clockwork. The plan, elaborated more than six months before, was to strike a series of heavy blows against Soviet forces on the long western border, followed by encirclement and annihilation. Rapid pursuit was ordered to prevent Soviet forces from falling back in good order and regrouping. German forces were divided in four: a small Norwegian command based in occupied Norway and three larger Army Groups, North, Centre and South. Each Army Group was supported by an air fleet. Army Group Centre got a half share of the German armoured divisions, two Panzer groups out of four. It was to launch a vast encircling movement towards Minsk, with the ultimate axis of attack towards Moscow. The northern Army Group was pointed at Leningrad; the southern armies were to converge on the Ukrainian capital of Kiev. Germany's mobile and armoured divisions spearheaded the attack, though most of the army moved by foot or horse. The aim was to secure through surprise and speed the main axes of attack with the mobile units. The rest of the army would follow through, cleaning up pockets of resistance and strengthening the German front line.

When the German armed forces sprang forward on June 22 they met only slight resistance. Border guards in many cases fought bravely, sometimes literally to the last round and the last man. The great fortress at Brest-Litovsk, right on the frontier, succeeded in holding out until July 12, its defenders fighting to a standstill. German paratroopers trained for special operations infiltrated behind Soviet lines, cutting communications, seizing bridges and adding to the general confusion. Some Soviet commands could establish contact neither with headquarters nor with the units they were supposed to be controlling.

Sheer ignorance about the current military situation was a major factor explaining the disorganized Soviet response. The widespread destruction of Soviet air power made air reconnaissance nearly impossible and meant that forward troops got no respite from the continuous German air bombardment. The Red Army deployed nine mechanized corps in the first two days of the battle, but problems in supplying fuel and ammunition rendered Soviet tank warfare ineffective. Some 90 per cent of the army's tank strength was lost in the first weeks of the war.[24]

By June 26 Army Group North had crossed Lithuania, and was deep into Latvia. After pausing for the infantry to catch up, the armoured formations rushed forward to reach the Luga River, only sixty miles from Leningrad. Army Group Centre under Field Marshal Fedor von Bock drove in two massive pincers towards Minsk. Pavlov's attempt to counter-attack was swept aside, with high casualties. By June 29 German armies had reached Minsk. In their net they caught over 400,000 Soviet soldiers, in this first of the great battles of encirclement. The Panzer corps simply repeated the manoeuvre as they moved on to Smolensk, the last major city before Moscow, which they took on July 16. Timoshenko was sent to command the Western Front and save Smolensk after Stalin assumed the job of Commissar of Defence. Timoshenko improvised a defence using reserve divisions intended as a strategic counter-offensive force. The long, extended flanks of the German attacking force were subjected to a series of fierce assaults. Short of ammunition and supplies, with troops weakened from forced marches through the Russian heat, with few tanks and a great many horses, Timoshenko nevertheless succeeded in slowing the German advance and imposing a fearful level of casualties on an army that had conquered all of continental Europe for the loss of 50,000 men. Eighty miles south-west of Smolensk Zhukov even succeeded in inflicting a local defeat on German forces in the Yelnya salient. On September 6 forces of the Reserve Front retook the battered town in savage fighting but were prevented by the shortage of tanks and vehicles from exploiting their victory.

The actions around Smolensk showed both the strengths and the weaknesses of Soviet forces. Soldiers fought with an extraordinary ferocity and bravery. They inflicted casualties at a high rate and in the early battles often refused to take prisoners. Captured Germans were murdered and mutilated, sometimes ritually – Soviet troops had been told to expect no better from the enemy. It was not Soviet propaganda but the German army chief of staff who observed that 'Everywhere, the Russians fight to the last man. They capitulate only occasionally.'[25] When they ran out of bullets and shells – as was all too often the case in the early stages of the war – they fought with knives or bayonets. Horsemen charged with sabres drawn. Soviet forces soon came to believe that German soldiers disliked fighting away from the support of aircraft and tanks. 'Bayonet charges,' wrote General Rokossovsky, whose forces stood astride the road from Smolensk to Moscow, 'are dreaded by the Germans and they always avoid them. When they counter-attack they shoot without aiming.'[26]

Soviet soldiers were also adept at concealment. Hiding in trees and undergrowth, in grassland or in swamp, infantrymen could maintain a chilling silence while the enemy marched past them entirely oblivious to their presence. German patrols took to placing non-smokers in front because they were more likely to be able to smell the tell-tale scent of the enemy – the coarse tobacco, sweat, even cheap perfume, swabbed on to keep away lice. The ability to blend into the landscape, summer or winter, was exploited by the Red Army to the full in the later years of war.[27]

The savage fighting held up but could not halt the German armies. Soviet forces lacked basic military equipment. The standard rifle dated from Tsarist days and was not generally replaced by automatic weapons until 1944. Radio communications were rudimentary and radios in short supply. Radar was not generally available. Tanks, even the most modern T-34 and KV-1 tanks, were short of supplies and fuel and were attacked repeatedly by German aircraft, which had local air superiority. Though brave, Red Army soldiers were tactically inept, often absurdly so. Officers were trained to undertake only frontal assaults, even across open terrain. A German account of Soviet counter-attacks on a German strong point on the approach to Kiev exemplifies both Soviet persistence and Soviet ineptitude. The attack began with an artillery barrage that fell behind the German emplacement, causing no damage. Then from a thousand yards distant, a hundred yards or so separating each line, wave after wave of infantrymen rose up out of the grass and with bayonets fixed tramped towards the German lines. The first line was mowed down almost to a man by machine-gun fire; the second was hit but was able to reform. Then the men ran towards the German guns, shouting in unison. They moved more slowly when they reached the piles of dead, stepping over or between them. Officers on horseback bullied them on and were shot by German snipers. The attack faltered and broke, then was repeated, using the same methods, four more times, each time without success. German machine-gunners found that their guns became too hot for them to touch. 'The fury of the attacks,' the report continued, 'had exhausted and numbed us completely . . . a sense of depression settled upon us. What we were now engaged in would be a long, bitter and hard-fought war.'[28]

In 1941 the two opposing sides made war in very different ways. Both the Soviet and the German armed forces were committed from strategic tradition to the offensive. But in the summer of 1941 it was German forces who were on the offensive, forcing the Red Army to wage an unaccustomed war of defence, for which there had been almost no systematic preparation. The German armed forces were structured to maximize the offensive posture. The spearhead of the invasion force was provided by nineteen Panzer (armoured) divisions and fifteen divisions of motorized infantry. Each of the latter was a self-contained fighting unit, with its own complement of tanks, motorized infantry in trucks and armoured carriers and on motorbikes, engineers, artillery and anti-aircraft batteries. They were designed to move fast – at some points in the summer of 1941 they covered thirty to forty kilometres in a day – and to strike with irresistible force at an enemy front line. Once that line was fractured armoured forces could pour through and push on past the enemy infantry, which could be mopped up by the slower, horse-drawn infantry divisions trailing in their wake. For Barbarossa there were 119 of them, less heavily armed than the Panzer formations and far less mobile. Most of the army's 600,000 vehicles were with the armoured spearhead; the infantry were followed, like Napoleon's Grande Armée, by horse and cart. For all its modernity, the German army went into its war against the Soviet Union with 700,000 horses.[29]

Above the mobile core of Hitler's army was the German air force, 2,770 modern aircraft, including 1,085 bombers and dive-bombers and 920 fighters. The air forces were divided into four air fleets, each with a complement of bomber, fighter and reconnaissance aircraft. Army Group Centre, pointed towards Moscow, had the bulk of the air force, 1,500 planes. The air fleets were designed to give direct support to the ground forces, seeking out enemy strong points and artillery sites, columns of troops and vehicles and supply dumps and trains. The longer-range bombers were used for attacks on cities in the path of the approaching armies. The swift advance in June and July brought the capital within range. The bombing of Moscow began on July 21. During the war an estimated 500,000 Soviet citizens died from German bomb attacks, more than ten times the number who died in the London Blitz. The 700 reconnaissance aircraft played a vital role in giving the advancing army a clear picture of what lay ahead of them. The whole system was held together by radio communications, which proved to be central to German success. On the ground, tank liaison officers rode with the armoured columns as they moved across the battlefield, directing aircraft overhead to targets on the ground. The whole offensive movement depended on speed and organizational flexibility, and on supplies and reserves keeping pace with the attacking force.

The Soviet dispositions to meet the German attack could not have been worse. The defensive belts were not finished; the reserve army was only just being formed; above all the concentration of forces in the southern zone allowed the weight of the German attack in the north to punch a giant gap in the Soviet front, then swing forces south to eliminate the threat to their flank from Soviet armies that could not be fully deployed. The defensive weaknesses were compounded with the poor state of organization and preparation in Soviet armoured and air formations. Unlike the German Panzer armies, the Soviet tanks and vehicles were organized in unwieldy mechanized corps, with large numbers of tanks spread out along the front to support the infantry armies. Armoured divisions were widely scattered, lacked effective communications, were badly under strength and were equipped mainly with obsolete vehicles. Their function was not clearly defined. Force concentration, the great German strength, was impossible under these conditions. The same was true of Soviet air power. Large though the Soviet air forces were, outnumbering German aircraft by three to one, their planes were mostly obsolete. New aircraft entering service in 1941 came in dribs and drabs, and Soviet pilots had little time to be trained on them. Most aircraft were parcelled out, like the tanks along the front line, in direct support of individual ground armies. A strategic reserve existed behind the front line, directly controlled from the Stavka, but its exact role remained unclear. Soviet air tactics were rudimentary. Few Soviet aircraft had radios, leaving them dependent on close formation flying. Fighters flew three abreast in a fixed line, easy prey for German pilots, who flew in loose vertical formation, using air-to-air communication to help each other. The slow Soviet bombers flew close together at a set height of 8,000 feet and were shot down like migrating geese.[30]

These many differences between the two sides explain the remarkable victories won by German arms between June and September. Soviet forces were sent in piecemeal, to plug gaps in the leaky front line, unable to concentrate for any more ambitious operations. Stalin used his new military powers to push his tired and disorganized troops to the limit, but bit by bit the Soviet line bent and cracked. In the north German armies edged ever closer to Leningrad. When Stalin heard that German forces were shielding themselves behind hostages – delegations of Russians with petitions to the Leningrad command to surrender the city – he ordered his defenders not to be sentimental but to gun down their fellow citizens. 'War is merciless,' he wrote, 'and it will bring defeat in the first instance to him who shows weakness and vacillation . . .'[31] But hardness of heart was not enough; on September 26 the Germans reached the shores of Lake Ladoga behind Leningrad, and the 900-day siege of the city began.

On the other fronts disaster followed on disaster. In the south, where the bulk of Soviet armies had been based in June, progress was slower. But in August Hitler changed his mind about the priority to

Army Group Centre he had given in June and switched the main German effort to clearing the Ukraine and seizing Kiev. The change was strongly resisted by the army leadership, who wanted to capitalize on the victory at Smolensk by pushing on rapidly to Moscow and destroying what remained of the Red Army in the process. Theirs was the view of Clausewitz: concentrate on the destruction of the enemy's forces. They did not share Hitler's view that what counted in war was economics. The seizure of the Ukraine, with its rich grainlands, its mines and metals plants, was part and parcel of the pursuit of 'living-space'. Hitler believed that the loss of these resources would spell disaster for the Soviet war effort and make the new German order invincible.

Hitler prevailed and in the process possibly saved the Soviet capital. The capital of the Ukraine was less fortunate. Though under heavy harassing attack, bogged down by autumn rains, and short of tanks and aircraft, the First Panzer Group from the north and the Second Panzer Group moving from the south met up far to the east of Kiev. In Moscow the German shift from the central front to the southern had been anticipated in August. General Yeremenko, who lost his wife and young child in the initial German onslaught, was given charge of the counter-offensive to save the Ukraine. The attempt failed. Stalin urged Yeremenko to report victories and poured in precious reserves from other parts of the front to bolster the Soviet attack. They were all squandered in the effort to prevent another catastrophic encirclement. Stalin refused to let Kiev be abandoned to the enemy, though only a strategic withdrawal would have saved the Soviet forces, as Zhukov had argued in July. Without a specific order from Stalin, the local commander in Kiev refused all demands from his colleagues that he save the army by retreating – politically prudent no doubt, but militarily disastrous. When even Stalin had to accept the reality that German forces had encircled Kiev and its hinterlands, it was too late. Evacuation of the front was ordered on September 17, but the order never reached the embattled garrison in Kiev, which fought on in the ruins of the ancient city for two more days before surrendering. The rest of the trapped army, except for small groups of stragglers who fought their way out, became prisoners. In all

527,000 men were killed or captured, and the way was open for German armies, though battle-weary and greatly depleted, to occupy the rest of the Ukraine and the Crimean peninsula. Most senior commanders lost their lives in the final battering of the pocket by German aircraft and artillery. The Kiev Front commander, General Mikhail Kirponos, was ambushed with a thousand men as he tried to break out. Wounded in the leg, he fought on until the splinters from an exploding mine abruptly dispatched him.[32]

Kiev fallen; Leningrad encircled; at last Moscow caught Hitler's attention. So swift had been the capture of the southern area that, with one final flourish, the capture of Stalin's capital was within German sights. On September 6 Hitler published Directive Number 35, which inaugurated Operation Typhoon, the destruction of what was believed to be the last significant Soviet forces guarding the capital, in the region of Vyazma and Briansk. The task of holding the last line fell to General Ivan Konev, who took over from Timoshenko on September 13. Konev, a former lumberjack and an NCO from the First World War, was one of the group of outstanding Soviet commanders whose baptism of fire was experienced in the retreats of 1941. He was a tall, rather ascetic-looking figure, with a distinctive bald head and piercing eyes and a reputation for severity. He abstained from drink and disliked drunkenness in others: in front of his troops he adopted a simple, austere life-style. He read widely from Russian literature, which he quoted as he talked, and carried his own library with him at the front. He was regarded as a devoted Communist. He ended his career as Commander-in-Chief of all Warsaw Pact forces in the 1950s.[33]

The force Konev commanded in front of Moscow was scratched together, a mixture of battle-weary remnants of the struggles further west and poorly-trained *opolchenie*, militia units that contained men more than fifty years old, as well as women. There were few modern tanks or aircraft and far too few vehicles. Most of the Soviet divisions were well under strength, with 5,000 to 7,000 men instead of the usual 14,000. They faced forces numbering 800,000 with over 1,000 tanks, organized in three Panzer armies.[34] The plan was a repeat of the formula that had proved so successful since the first encirclements in

June. Soviet forces were to be caught in two powerful pincer movements around Vyazma to the north and Briansk to the south, and the road to Moscow opened up.

Operation Typhoon was launched in the south on September 30. Led by General Heinz Guderian, the architect of the German tank armies, it soon lived up to its name. The storm tore open the southern wing of the Soviet armies, commanded by Yeremenko; the soldier who had failed to save Kiev now faced the nightmare of losing Moscow, too. So swift was the German assault that Guderian's troops entered Orel while the streetcars were still running. A week later Briansk was captured and Yeremenko's three armies were trapped. Little news could be sent to Moscow; Stalin's only instruction was to hold tight to every defence line rather than retreat. On October 6 Yeremenko himself narrowly escaped the German encirclement. He was severely wounded by a shell but lived to fight another, and vital, day at Stalingrad.

Further north the attack began on October 2 under cover of artillery and air attack and a smoke-screen that turned the landscape to deep fog in front of the Soviet defenders. Konev's armies fared no better than Yeremenko's. German forces converged on Vyazma, threatening an even larger encirclement of five Soviet armies. In two days the whole Soviet front was once again in crisis, far faster than Stalin had ever imagined could happen. October 5 was a critical day. Routine air reconnaissance from Moscow found a column of German armour twelve miles long converging on Yukhnov, only eighty miles from the capital. Twice more aircraft went out to confirm the unbelievable news before it was passed on in full to Zhukov's successor as chief of staff, Marshal Boris Shaposhnikov. Finally it was believed, though this did not stop Beria from ordering the NKVD to arrest and interrogate the unfortunate air officer for 'provocation'. Stalin telephoned the Moscow district command at once: 'Mobilize everything you have.' He called an immediate emergency meeting of the State Defence Committee.[35] Stalin, who had been ordering last stands all summer, ordered one more, the most important of his life. In front of Moscow, along the thinly manned 'Mozhaisk Line', the army of the revolution, cornered but defiant, was to face the enemy.

In the first days of October the two dictators were poised on the edge of victory and of defeat. German expectations had been high all summer. As early as July the Army Chief of Staff, Franz Halder, wrote in his war diary that it would not be an exaggeration 'to say that the Russian campaign has been won in two weeks'. In mid-July Hitler ordered a new set of gigantic armaments programmes for the air force and the navy to swing the war back to the West and confrontation with Britain and the United States.[36] The second wave of victories produced at Hitler's headquarters a state of near euphoria. As German forces pressed towards Leningrad and Moscow Hitler's early fantasies about a sprawling German empire in the east began to take on substance and form. On September 29 he ordered that after the capture of Leningrad, which seemed imminent, the city be 'wiped from the face of the earth'. The same month, when he decided on the drive for Moscow, he swore that that city would be razed to the ground, to be replaced by a large artificial lake: 'The name Moscow will disappear forever.'[37] At mealtimes in his headquarters he talked endlessly of his plans for the East, of the Asiatic 'brutes' he had conquered. Finally, on October 2, he returned to Berlin to address his people for the first time since the invasion began in June.

The German public was thirsty for news. On October 4 Hitler vouchsafed to release remarkable news indeed. He arrived at the Berlin Sportpalast, where an audience was assembled to listen to the routine exhortations to give to the Nazi Winter Relief Charity. The first row of seats in the dimly lit hall was reserved for wounded men, and they sat a few yards from Hitler with their crutches stretched out in front of them pointing towards their leader. There were the usual pleas for the German public to dig deep into their pockets. But so buoyant were Hitler's spirits with the news from Russia that he could not resist sharing it with his audience. He had come, he told them, from 'the greatest battle in the history of the world'. The plan had worked. The Soviet enemy was beaten 'and would never rise again'. He detailed the evidence: over 2 million Soviet prisoners, 22,000 artillery pieces seized or smashed, 18,000 tanks destroyed, 14,500 aircraft shot down. Cheers echoed around the hall.[38]

Six days later Hitler put a seal on the victory. His press chief, Otto

Dietrich, was sent to Berlin from Hitler's headquarters to tell not just the German people but the whole world that Germany had won. On October 10, in the richly decorated Theatre Hall of the Propaganda Ministry in Berlin, the foreign press corps gathered. There was an air of suspense, exaggerated by the long, probably deliberate, delay in starting the proceedings. German officials stood at the front, all in uniform, even those whose office was entirely civilian. At last Dietrich emerged, grinning with self-importance. The red velvet curtains behind him were drawn back, revealing a vast map of the Soviet front that dwarfed the huddle of Germans in front of it. Dietrich echoed Hitler, whose words he read. The last remnants of the Red Army were now trapped in two steel vices, tightened day by day by German forces; their destruction, Dietrich continued, was assured. Beyond them was simply undefended space, which German legions were poised to fill. Neutral pressmen in the audience looked glum. The rest, newspapermen from Germany's allies, rose and cheered, their arms outstretched in salute. The next day German newspapers confirmed the tidings: CAMPAIGN IN EAST DECIDED! THE GREAT HOUR HAS STRUCK! In Berlin the faces showed the relief. Bookshops began to display Russian grammars in their windows to serve the officials and colonists of the new German empire.[39] The smooth, sweet taste of victory was on everyone's tongue. Hitler had spoken; the war in the East was won.

In Moscow the mood turned from sombre to panic-stricken. The public there had few illusions about the course of the war, but propaganda kept up the image of tough, improvised revolutionary warfare that was slowing and holding the fascist horde. Few Muscovites knew anything about what was happening at the front save by rumour. Not even Stalin knew clearly what was going on. He saw the defence of Moscow and Leningrad as a unique challenge. They symbolized the new Soviet state. The Soviet Union might survive the fall of its capital and its second city, but the effect on the Soviet public and on world opinion would be devastating. Nonetheless Stalin had to face reality. On October 1 the orders went out to begin evacuating the Government 500 miles to the east, to the city of Kuibyshev. The population of Moscow began evacuating, along with foreign embassies, office staff, archives, art treasures and commissars. Stalin sent his own library and his family. Finally it was decided to send Lenin.

The custodian of Lenin's body was summoned to a meeting of the Politburo. Here he was told by Stalin to take everything he needed to move the embalmed leader to safety. A railway carriage, fitted with refrigeration and shock absorbers, was then prepared. A special train with its ghoulish freight pulled out of Moscow for distant Tyumen. Lenin was housed in a former Tsarist school, guarded by soldiers and scientists. At the mausoleum in Red Square the guard of honour remained in place as if everything were normal. Stalin might have followed. His papers were sent ahead to Kuibyshev. His personal train and a fleet of aircraft were kept on standby.[40] He could not risk capture. He might have made peace, as Lenin had done at Brest-Litovsk in 1918 to save the revolution. It was rumoured in Berlin in early October that Stalin had sought an armistice through Tsar Boris of Bulgaria. It would not have been an irrational choice, any more than was Lenin's.

The evidence on the peace mission is far from clear. The story that emerged in the 1980s suggested that on October 7 Stalin ordered Beria to send out peace feelers to Hitler via the Bulgarian ambassador to Moscow, Ivan Stamenov. The emissary was instructed to say that Stalin would give Hitler the Baltic states, Moldavia and parts of Belorussia and the Ukraine. According to the story the Bulgarian refused, telling either Beria or Molotov that the Soviet Union would, in the end, win. There is no evidence from the German side of any contacts in 1941. More recent revelations suggest a rather different picture. The attempt to make a peace offer may have been part of a political initiative sponsored by Beria to try to confuse the Germans long enough to form a more solid defence line in front of Moscow. This version fits more comfortably with the rest of what is known about Stalin's behaviour in early October – frantic efforts to organize the defence and to recruit American and British assistance and his subsequent decision at the moment of acute crisis to stay in the capital.[41]

Stalin's decision was a historic one. It was taken against a background of mounting chaos in the capital. The sight of trucks removing files and equipment, of smoke curling up from bonfires of documents that could not be carried, of a stream of evacuees, mostly women and children, leaving the crowded railway stations, proved too much for the remaining population. Moscow was under constant aerial bombardment. Not even the threat of an NKVD bullet could stem the wildest rumours. The journalist Ilya Ehrenburg recalled that in Moscow 'the general mood was appalling'. The panic suddenly burst in mid-October, just as Ehrenburg, too, got his marching orders for the east. The scenes he found at the Kazan Station defied description. Trains were swamped by desperate Muscovites, who occupied any space they could. Ehrenburg lost his luggage in the mêlée but was lucky enough to find a place on a long suburban train that took almost a week to reach the safety of the designated capital of rump Russia.[42] For those left behind Beria ordered food to be distributed free to the population to save it from the Germans. But by then people were helping themselves. Looters moved into the empty shops and offices. In the modern apartment buildings in the city centre the managers collaborated with thieves to steal paintings and furnishings left behind. Stalin had almost lost control of his capital not to the German army, now only two or three days away, but to his own frightened people.

The panic was triggered by an unusually frank and grim communiqué broadcast in Moscow on October 16. 'During the night of October 14–15,' ran the report, 'the position on the Western Front became worse.' The Germans, with large quantities of tanks, 'broke through our defences'.[43] The following day the radio announced that Moscow would be defended stubbornly to the death, that no thought had been given to abandoning the capital (which was not, of course, true), but that above all Stalin was still in Moscow. Why he chose to remain we cannot know for certain. But on the 17th, instead of following his Government, he went out to his *dacha*, which had been mined for demolition, to do some work. He found his guards about to blow up the building. He ordered them to clear the mines and started to work in his study. In Moscow the NKVD moved in to shoot looters and restore order, while thousands of not entirely enthusiastic volunteers were formed into labour battalions to dig defences or into ramshackle militia to be moved at once to the front. Every tenth apartment building manager was shot as an example. A state of siege was declared on October 19. The city prepared for the showdown. Stalin informed his guards that he was staying put: 'We will not surrender Moscow.'[44]

4

Between Life and Death: Leningrad and Moscow

'The mortuary itself is full. Not only are there too few trucks to go to the cemetery, but, more important, not enough gasoline to put in the trucks and the main thing is – there is not enough strength left in the living to bury the dead.'

Vera Inber, Leningrad diary, 26 December 1941

One name links together the fate of Leningrad and Moscow in the terrible autumn of 1941: Georgi Konstantinovich Zhukov. Twice he was called upon by Stalin to perform a military miracle and save the cities, once in early September, when he was sent to Leningrad, and again in October, when he was recalled to defend Moscow. He was by any measure a soldier of genius, though certainly not infallible. Stalin came to depend on Zhukov to a degree that he would surely not have tolerated in any lesser man. Left to himself, Russia's Supreme Commander might well have lost the war. Zhukov did not win the war on his own, but no one played a greater part in Soviet victory.

Zhukov was one of thousands whose humble origins were transformed by war and revolution. He was born in 1897 in a small village outside Moscow, the son of a shoemaker. He was a bright pupil, and his father arranged for him to be apprenticed to a Moscow furrier. At nineteen the young artisan was drafted into the imperial cavalry and became an NCO before the Revolution. He stayed with the military, serving in the fledgling Red Army in the civil war. He fought in the defence of Tsaritsyn in 1919, where Stalin was the chairman of the local Military Committee. He remained a regular cavalry officer, but one who was eager to move out of the horse age into the age of tanks. In the 1930s he was sent to Spain as a military observer, but, unlike many others, survived his recall. He also survived the purges. He was a dedicated Communist, devoted to the revolutionary cause and to Stalin, though not even that was a guarantee of survival. As far as can be judged, there was something about him that Stalin liked or respected. In 1939 he was sent on another mission, this time to China, where the Japanese had invaded and occupied much of the north. From there he was posted to the Soviet far east, where he successfully commanded Soviet forces in a full-scale border war with Japan at Khalkhin-Gol.[1]

Zhukov was a good battlefield commander, capable of immersing himself in detail without losing sight of the campaign. He was a soldier's soldier, tough, decisive, outwardly calm and confident, who expected the utmost from his men and gave his all in return. He did not hesitate to sacrifice lives, military or civilian, if that would win battles. He was as tough-minded as his political master; victory was what counted, not the way it was won. He was less popular with his fellow commanders. His was an unusually coarse personality in a profession not noted for its decorum. His language was punctuated by repeated profanities, now expunged from the record. He bullied and threatened other generals with court-martial or execution and did not hesitate to use his access to Stalin to get rid of commanders who had lost his confidence.[2] Since the war many of his colleagues have complained in their memoirs that Zhukov stole their ideas and presented them to Stalin as his own – accusations that should be assessed with caution. Zhukov's brusque manner and intolerant personality earned him much animosity. The important contribution Zhukov made was not strategic insight, much of which emanated from the General Staff rather than from any one individual, but his willingness to stand up to Stalin and to represent the military voice at the highest level so that those strategic ideas could be nourished.

At the age of forty-three he was suddenly catapulted to the top of the military tree. In January 1941 he was appointed Chief of the General Staff over the heads of generals greatly his senior. It was a post that carried its dangers. The man he succeeded, Kirill Meretskov, was arrested a few months later on the usual conspiracy charges and

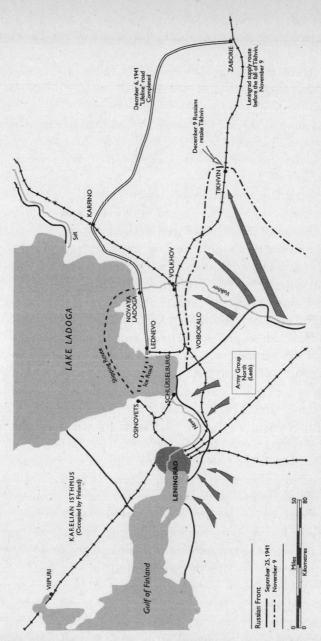

Map 2   The Siege of Leningrad

savagely tortured – 'a veritable meat grinder' was how Beria described it twelve years later – until the usual confession came out.[3] It was also a post not entirely suited to Zhukov's skills. When he argued with Stalin in July over defending the western areas, he avoided Meretskov's fate but was sacked as chief of staff and sent off to the field to command the Reserve Front defending Smolensk. Here he inflicted one of the first and heaviest reverses on the German advance at Yelnya, which may well explain why Stalin called for him again early in September to try to save Leningrad, as it faced complete encirclement and destruction.[4]

During the last two weeks of August one after another of the defensive positions around Leningrad, built with the sweat, and sometimes the blood, of thousands of women and teenagers, were stormed by the German armies approaching the city. The last rail link southward at Mga was cut by August 30. From the north Finnish forces pushed down to the old Soviet-Finnish frontier sixty miles from Leningrad, from which they had been forced back in 1940. To the east of Leningrad Finnish and German forces moved to complete the final encirclement of the city. Hitler had decided in August that Leningrad was not to be stormed but subjected to a close siege. After the experience of German forces in other Soviet cities, where booby traps and mines had killed German soldiers as they advanced through the abandoned streets, Hitler wanted to destroy Leningrad by artillery and aerial bombardment and, eventually, by starvation. Early in September German forces began operations to seal off Leningrad from the outside world. They stood from twelve to twenty-two miles from the city centre. After a further week of fierce fighting, in which the defenders, having few heavy weapons and almost no reserves of trained manpower, fought with anything on hand to slow the German advance, the leading German units were only seven miles from the heart of the city. On September 4 the first artillery shell fell on the central zone; two days later the first bombs fell.

On the very day Stalin sent Zhukov off from Moscow to Leningrad to investigate the crisis, September 8, the German army to the east of Leningrad reached the town of Schlüsselburg and cut off the last land link with the interior. Leningrad was encircled; it was now the task of the German armies to tighten the noose around its neck. Zhukov did not break that noose, but he succeeded in getting a hand between rope and neck. He flew from Moscow in thick clouds to give him cover, but over Leningrad the clouds disappeared. As he flew across the defensive zone German fighters approached but failed to press home an attack.[5] Zhukov rushed straight to the Smolny Institute, where the city's Military Committee was in session. The city command was in crisis. None of the defensive lines had held. Little better could be expected of the new inner lines of defence dug by battalions of Leningraders who had been working since July. The city was commanded by Voroshilov, sent in by Stalin as a troubleshooter in August. He was regarded by everyone as a military incompetent, even by Stalin, but he was sent as an old Communist to instil the political will to fight on. The real work was done by the city's Party leader, Andrei Zhdanov, a popular and independent-minded Communist and an inspiration to the people of Leningrad.[6] Zhukov listened, observed and returned to Moscow. By this time Stalin almost certainly knew from Communist intelligence sources in Berlin, organized in the so-called Red Orchestra, that Hitler was going to lay Leningrad to siege rather than storm it, though nothing could be certain.[7] He sent Zhukov back as commander in Voroshilov's place, with orders to defend Leningrad to the last breath.

Zhukov began his work with a flourish. Arriving back at the headquarters in the Smolny he threw all the maps which the Military Committee had spread on the table onto the floor and turned his gaze towards the single wall map of the city's defences. Voroshilov made as dignified an exit as he could manage, and Zhukov and Zhdanov got down to work.[8] A good deal had already been done. By early August 467,000 Leningraders had been evacuated from the city, including 216,000 children. By the end of the month the figures had reached 636,000, including more than 100,000 refugees from the Baltic states. The plans to evacuate another half a million women and children were frustrated by the German advance, and they remained sealed up with the men. Among those who remained a workers' militia was organized, an echo from the city's revolutionary past. It was in the same city in 1917 that Trotsky had organized factory workers into the nucleus of a revolutionary army to seize power for the Bolsheviks. Now some 36,000 workers, given a rudimentary daily drill and armed with 22,000 rifles and shotguns donated by the population, prepared to defend their city street by street, factory by factory.[9]

Leningrad itself became unrecognizable as primitive fortifications sprang up in every street. Seventeen miles of barricades and anti-tank ditches left long scars across the face of the city. Shops, offices and apartment buildings had wooden sheets and sandbags around the lower floors; windows were covered with plywood or scraps of timber and cardboard. Across each street appeared simple barricades, the symbol of revolution. Made of stones or wood, they were no more than a few feet thick, and dotted with firing slits. Streetcars and buses filled with sand were used as obstacles. Fortified posts for machine-guns or rifles were set up, over 20,000 in all. Air-raid shelters and slit trenches were built to protect the population from artillery fire and bombs, but there were enough for only one-third of those who remained. Around the bizarre furnishings of war Leningraders continued to work and live as best they could.

Zhukov inherited these preparations, and added some of his own. He ordered anti-aircraft guns to be used instead as anti-tank weapons, as the Germans had done with the famous 88-mm anti-aircraft gun. He had the approaches to the city heavily mined and completed a deep defensive zone in the city's suburbs. Guns removed from the ships of the Baltic Fleet were dug in by the coast or set on armoured trains; they kept up a dense and powerful artillery barrage on German positions. Even the guns of the cruiser *Aurora*, which had been declared a national monument for the famous part it played in shelling the Winter Palace in October 1917, were removed and sent to the front line.[10] Zhukov bullied and hounded his commanders and city officials. The NKVD operated everywhere, shooting alleged slackers or deserters and cracking down on looting. The mood by mid-September was sombre and desperate, but nothing like the Moscow panic was permitted to develop. Leningraders did not need to be reminded of the sacrifices they had to make. Surviving testimony showed that many of those scheduled for evacuation did not go; children stayed with their families, wives with their husbands. Alongside the fear of the population there also stood what Zhukov later remembered as the 'courage, endurance and tenacity' of ordinary people. 'September 1941,' he recalled in his memoirs, 'impregnated itself in my memory for life.'[11]

The defence of the city reached its climax in the third week of September, as German forces closed in to isolate the city centre. Forty tons of high explosive were distributed to prepare for the demolition of bridges, factories and military strong points. On September 19 the German artillery began a continuous eighteen-hour barrage of the city, while aircraft bombed food stores, shops and trains. The same day orders came from Moscow to lay and prime the charges. German forces had swept through Zhukov's outer defences, taking the suburban townships one by one. The very last line of defence along the Neva River and the approaches to the city itself were fought for yard by yard. A determined push would almost certainly have brought the German army to the gates of the city, where they would have fought house by house and street by street, much as they did at Stalingrad. But the city was saved by Hitler. On September 20 the pace slackened. Intelligence sources from among the guerrilla groups fighting behind German lines showed that the Germans were digging in. Tanks and armoured vehicles were seen on trains heading away from Leningrad. Forces were evidently moving south for Operation Typhoon and the capture of Moscow. On September 25 the front line stabilized and then halted. The battle for Leningrad became the siege of Leningrad.[12]

No one in the autumn of 1941 could have predicted how long that siege would last. Soviet forces to the south of the city kept up their attacks on the German defences to try to break the circle, but by then Stalin needed everything available to save his own capital. The blockade of the city was complete. The only access was across Lake Ladoga, twenty miles to the east. Part of the southern shore was still in Soviet hands, but the rail line that might have brought the supplies to that shore was in German hands, and shipping to bring supplies across the lake was not yet available. The stark reality was that at the beginning of October the population of over 3.3 million had sufficient food for only twenty days. On November 1 there was enough for seven days. Without more resources famine was unavoidable.

Daily life in Leningrad during the winter of 1941–42 was a story of horrors almost beyond imagining. The city was dark and silent, draped in snow and ice. The only sound came from the German guns, heavy artillery on the hills to the south-west, which kept up a regular bombardment. Every day like clockwork the shells would fall: from eight o'clock until nine in the morning; for an hour before noon; from five until six in the afternoon; and finally a two-hour shelling between eight and ten at night.[13] The shell bursts left great craters in the road, which filled with ice, mud and refuse. Buildings crumbled and cracked; debris lay uncleared in the streets. Transport came to a halt. Electricity was rationed in August to a few hours a day; by November it was limited to the most urgent needs. Private telephones were cut off. The streets were deserted during the night-time curfew; during the day the inhabitants moved nervously about, staying close to shelter. The shelling gave way each day to air attacks. German airmen were ordered deliberately to promote the slow death of the city by bombing food stores, power-plants and water-works. In September the Badaev food warehouses burned to the ground. In the first months of the siege there were over 20,000 casualties from the bombardment. The hospitals could barely cope; medicines and anaesthetics ran out.[14]

Life was reduced to its most primitive. Ration cards were issued to about 2.8 million people in September, leaving as many as half a million with no entitlement. The ration gave workers and soldiers about one pound of coarse, adulterated bread a day and a pound of meat a week. The rest of the population had to subsist on eight ounces of bread a day. In November and December the food supply reached rock bottom. Workers and soldiers got eight ounces of bread a day; everyone else got four ounces. These were levels that could not support life.[15] The whole of Leningrad made frantic efforts to find more food. Ration cards were stolen or traded. Bread was snatched from the hands of the weakest and consumed greedily in front of them. People caught birds, dogs, cats. They ate medicines; they made soup from glue and leather. The famine brought out the best and the worst in people. Mothers sacrificed themselves to save their children. When they died their children died beside them, cold and unnourished, their ration cards stolen by desperate neighbours. Hunger produced a new morality: survive or die.

Leningraders did die, in their thousands. Starvation and cold weakened everyone. Resistance to disease diminished. The weakest died first, old men and infants, then women and children. They succumbed to the same grim cycle. First arms and legs grew weak; then the body became numb and the circulation of the blood slowed; in the last stages of dystrophy the heart ceased to beat. People died at their desks and machines; they died as they walked the streets. Those who were not yet dead took on the expression of a corpse. Eyes stared large and lifeless. The skin was drawn tight over the face, unnaturally taut and glossy, covered with sores. All the fat seemed to have been drained from the people's bodies.[16] Families made pathetic efforts to honour the dead, but there was sometimes no one left with the strength to drag the small wooden sleds to the cemetery. One doctor recorded a visit to a family in January 1942:

My eyes beheld a horrible sight. A dark room covered with frost, puddles of water on the floor. Lying across some chairs was the corpse of a fourteen-year-old boy. In a baby carriage was a second corpse, that of a tiny infant. On the bed lay the owner of the room – dead. At her side, rubbing her chest with a towel, stood her eldest daughter. . . . In one day she lost her mother, a son and a brother who perished from hunger and cold.[17]

With the city death rate rising to 4,000 to 5,000 a day, the official system for registration of deaths and burial of the dead broke down. The dead were left in frozen piles at collecting centres, to be buried in mass graves when the gravediggers regained their strength. The madness of hunger drove some people to cut off the limbs or heads of the unburied dead for food. Cannibalism was condemned by the authorities, who threatened death to those who were caught. Estimates vary on how extensive the practice was, but there is now no doubt that it occurred. Perhaps several thousand may have tried to survive from eating corpses. It is a part of the famine story that can never be told in full.[18]

While people died wretchedly, the city authorities tried to maintain some semblance of organized life. Factories were kept running as long as possible, turning out equipment for the city's defenders. From July to December the factories turned out over 1,100 tanks and combat vehicles, 10,000 mortars, 3 million shells. Unbelievably, Leningrad's starving workforce produced 1,000 guns and mortars for the defence of Moscow, flown out of the city over the German lines.[19] At the famous Kirov Works, close to the front line, the workers bivouacked in the factory, with the shift that was resting putting out fires from German incendiary bombs or training for the factory's defence. Factories became communities, where food, companionship, even warmth could be found away from a bleaker home life. But by December most factories were closed. On December 15 the Kirov Works came to a standstill. There was no fuel, no electricity, no water, no raw materials. A foundry was somehow kept going to repair damaged guns, but production ceased until March.[20] The workers with the highest skills were flown out of the city to continue their work at arms centres far behind the front line.

To keep up morale theatres and orchestras were kept going for as long as they could. The composer Dmitri Shostakovich wrote the early drafts of his 7th symphony, later to be known everywhere as the 'Leningrad', to the sound of shells and bombs. In October he was taken out of the city so that the work could be completed in safety at Kuibyshev, where it was first heard in March 1942. It was not performed in Leningrad itself until August 1942. Musicians had to be recalled from the front lines to rehearse but by the time the symphony was staged many of the players were dead or wounded. Shostakovich dedicated the work 'To the city of Leningrad', and it became an artistic symbol of Soviet defiance in the face of German violence.

At Leningrad's famous Hermitage Museum the curators struggled against bomb damage and cold to salvage Russia's most important art collection. Half of the museum's 2.5 million objects were evacuated in sealed and guarded trains to the Urals city of Sverdlovsk. Josef Orbeli, the Museum's director, stood and wept on the platform as the first trains pulled out. By the time the next objects were ready for evacuation, the rail link had been cut. In September the bombing started. The remaining objects were taken to the basements, where over the winter some 2,000 artists, writers and academics continued to work by candlelight. There was a little light and heat in one room, supplied by the generators of the Tsar's former yacht, the *Pole Star*, tied up on the river outside. Beneath the library an informal mortuary was established, where the frozen bodies remained for weeks until they could be buried.[21]

Almost certainly the bulk of Leningrad's population would have starved to death by the spring had not frantic efforts been made to exploit the one loophole in the blockade – Lake Ladoga. At first small boats and barges made the journey to the tiny port of Osinovets on the west shore of the lake, about twenty miles from Leningrad. Some 45,000 tons of food, ammunition and petrol were brought in this way before November, when the lake began to freeze over.[22] The only remaining option was to make a path across the ice. At some point in November the Leningrad Military Committee decided to build what became known as the 'Ice Road', or the 'Road of Life'. In mid-November groups of Russian fishermen led officials across the ice, gingerly testing its thickness as they went, leaving rough markers on the way to indicate where the road should lie. On November 17 the ice was only 100 millimetres thick, sufficient only for unladen horses. It had to be at least 200 millimetres thick to support a loaded truck. The following day a bitter north wind began to blow, and within days the ice pack had nearly doubled in thickness. On November 20 the first horse-drawn sleds crossed the lake. The exhausted animals stumbled and staggered on the icy path. Those that collapsed were killed and cut up on the spot and sent on to Leningrad to be eaten.[23]

The first trucks edged out onto the ice on November 22. In places the ice was still too thin; trucks plunged into watery crevasses and with their drivers disappeared beneath the ice. But enough got through to load up on the far side of the lake and to return a day later with thirty-three tons of supplies. This was an insignificant amount, but it showed what was possible. It was decided to construct a military road from Osinovets across some eighteen miles of ice to the village of Kabona, then from there through the swamps and forests beyond the German line at Tikhvin to railheads at Podborove and Zabore. The whole length was 237 miles. The army was given two weeks to build it. There was now sufficient food for seven days left in the city. Forced labour, working in sub-zero temperatures, threw the road together in a little over fourteen days. The results were meagre. The ice refused to thicken more and trucks were able to carry only half loads, with a sledge slung behind. The steep gradients and uneven surfaces led to endless breakdowns and accidents. During December an average of 361 tons were brought in each day, one-seventh of what was required to feed the population. Stores fell to one or two days' supply.[24]

In December Zhdanov and Admiral Nikolai Kuznetsov, the Stavka representative in Leningrad, rode out to survey the Ice Road for themselves. They sacked the general in charge, ordered repairs and improvements to the road, designated standard loads and promised handsome bonuses to the drivers. The daily tonnage began to improve. On December 24 the authorities announced an unexpected Christmas present: the daily bread ration was raised for most Leningraders by about two and a half ounces, for workers by about five ounces from December 25.[25] Without radio and newspapers, most Leningraders discovered the increase only when they were at the shop counter. One woman watched a man leave a bakery, 'laughing, crying, clutching his head as he walked along'. The increased ration was a rash move, since the flow of food across the lake was still uncertain. But in early December 1941 a Soviet offensive against the city of Tikhvin, astride the main rail route to Lake Ladoga, pushed back the overextended German line and recaptured the railway. The attack was led by none other than General Kirill Meretskov, reinstated after his bruising encounter with the NKVD. It took time to rebuild the bridges and repair the track, but by January the new railway was in full operation. The truck journey was cut by one third, and thousands of drivers, railway workers and engineers, working in bitter cold and raging blizzards, struggled to organize real relief for Leningrad. Six truck routes were built across the ice; they were permanently posted with sentries, many of them women. As the ice thickened to more than three feet the trickle of supplies became a flood, 1,500 tons a day, then more than 2,000. The bread ration was increased at the end of January, and again in February. Soon a very different cargo began to make the return journey. Refugees were crammed into the trucks going back to the railhead: in January, 11,000; in February, 117,000; in March, 221,000. In four months more than half a million exhausted and emaciated Leningraders made the trek along the Road of Life to safety.[26]

By the spring Leningrad had become a different city. Along with the food came fuel, ammunition, matches – two boxes for every worker and soldier, one for each dependant – and the equipment and materials to restart industrial production. More than 200,000 garden plots were given to Leningraders to grow their own vegetables. Municipal restaurants were opened to provide cheap, warm meals; schoolchildren were given free lunches, bringing thousands of pupils back into the classroom.[27] Over the summer of 1942 the Ladoga route expanded. When the ice melted in April, ships took over. By October more than 150,000 tons of supplies a month were being provided. German efforts to bomb the supply routes had little effect, as the flow was continuous, day and night. Soon food from America, Australia and New Zealand, boxed and stamped 'for Leningrad' or 'for Moscow', began to arrive in the city. German plans to seize the city in August 1942 were frustrated by an energetic Soviet counter-offensive. In January 1943 a Soviet attack prised open a land corridor south of the lake, through which trains could now pass to the besieged city. By the time the journalist Alexander Werth was allowed to visit Leningrad, in the autumn of 1943, he found a population returning to normal, almost oblivious of the regular German shelling and the thunderous symphony of Soviet guns returning the fire. The children were plump and healthy, though many were orphans. Memories of the famine were already fading.[28]

Despite the revival of food supplies in the spring of 1942 it was too late to save the thousands of Leningraders who were too weakened by the weeks of starvation. Death rates remained high into May and June. When the Soviet writer Aleksandr Fadeev visited his stepsister in April he found a handsome woman transformed: 'Before me now was almost an old woman, withered, with puffy eyelids, darkened face and swollen legs. Her dark, smoothly combed hair was heavily streaked with grey . . . Her delicate hands had coarsened and become rough: the knotted hands of a manual worker.'[29] By the spring the deaths and evacuations left a much smaller population, which allowed the individual food ration to be quickly increased. How many died in Leningrad will never be known exactly. The refugees who crowded into the German noose were never counted. The official Soviet figure was 632,253 civilian dead over the whole course of the siege, 16,700 of them from the shelling and bombing. More than one million were evacuated, leaving a total population in the city by March 1943 of 639,000. This leaves well over one million unaccounted for from a population of over three million. Most of that one million perished slowly, painfully, tragically, in the winter of 1941–42.[30]

It was a tragedy that could have been avoided only if the Red Army had withstood the German onslaught and prevented the encirclement of the city. Leningrad might have been declared an open city, as Paris was in 1940, or have surrendered to its besiegers. But Hitler would not hear of surrender; he wanted to wipe the city from the face of the earth. Even if he had been prepared to accept the city's surrender, it is unlikely that the German authorities would have been willing or even able to supply food for its population. Most of the three million Soviet prisoners who fell into German hands in the 1941 campaign were simply left to starve to death behind barbed wire. The same fate almost certainly awaited Leningrad: 'in this war for existence,' declared Hitler in late September 1941, 'we have no interest in keeping even part of this great city's population.'[31] Leningrad was caught, a victim of the surprise and speed of Barbarossa (and of its location). It was a victim, too, of Soviet strategy. It was essential that Leningrad keep fighting. If Leningrad had fallen or surrendered in September, Army Group North might have swung south to tip the scales in the encirclement of Moscow. The desperate defence of Russia's old capital was vital to the desperate defence of the new.

Zhukov was long gone from Leningrad before the famine gripped. On October 5 he received a telegraphed order from Stalin to return to the capital at once to stabilize the front there. Two days later Zhukov was at Stalin's home, where he had retreated with a heavy cold. Stalin was brusque and to the point. He asked Zhukov if Leningrad would hold out and was told it could. He then ordered Zhukov to travel to the front line before Moscow to see the true state of affairs. Zhukov found a chaotic situation. Soviet army groups had lost contact with each other. Defence units were being formed out of stragglers making their way eastward in small groups out of the German encirclements. No one knew for certain where the Germans were. Stalin acted at once on Zhukov's report. On October 8 he sacked the commanders of the encircled Western Front and Reserve Front (which Zhukov had left in September), and on October 10 placed all the Soviet forces before Moscow under Zhukov's command. Only Zhukov's intervention prevented Stalin from treating the sacked Konev as he had treated Pavlov. Konev became Zhukov's deputy. Neither man much liked the other, but they provided a partnership rich in experience and tactical skill.[32]

When Zhukov took charge there were in his command only 90,000 men between the Germans and Moscow, all that was left of the 800,000 men that had started the battle in September. His priority was to strengthen the Mozhaisk defence line, a weakly held system some sixty miles from the centre of Moscow. A second line of defence was built in a semicircle round the city itself, ten miles from the centre. It was built, like the Leningrad fortifications, by hundreds of thousands of women and children, who were drafted to dig ditches and construct tank traps, fire points and rough barricades. Moscow bristled with anti-aircraft guns; barrage balloons hung in the grey air above the city. The atmosphere by late October became, according to one witness, 'austere, military and heroic', a very different atmosphere from the earlier panic.[33] Into the Mozhaisk Line the Stavka ordered six Soviet armies, some of them veterans of earlier battles, all of them under strength in men and weapons. Both sides now struggled in the autumn mud. On October 6 the first snow had fallen, unusually early. It soon melted, turning the whole landscape into its habitual trackless state – the *rasputitsa*, literally the 'time without roads'.

It is commonplace to attribute the German failure to take Moscow to the sudden change in the weather. While it is certainly true that German progress slowed, it had already been slowing because of the fanatical resistance of Soviet forces and the problem of moving supplies over the long distances through occupied territory. The mud slowed the Soviet build-up also, and hampered the rapid deployment of men and machines. During October the front still moved remorselessly towards Moscow. By October 18 German armoured forces had taken the cities of Kalinin to the north of Moscow and Kaluga to the south and were poised for another battle of encirclement. Zhukov's line was outflanked, and he was forced to move further back. He urged Stalin to throw forces against the German armies to disrupt their preparations. There were local triumphs and local disasters. A Mongolian cavalry division attacked across a snowy open field, and was mowed down by machine-gun fire; 2,000 of the horsemen were killed, not a single German. Soviet forces fought better with the weapons of the twentieth century. Where the Red Army could field the new T-34 tank, which could outgun and outfight even the best German armour, German units could be halted. In 1941 there were far too few of them.

While Zhukov and his Western Front waited for a renewed German onslaught to come when the mud became solid with the frost, Stalin decided to proceed with the usual ceremonies to mark the anniversary of the Revolution. The rally on the eve of the anniversary was held traditionally in the Bolshoi Theatre, but its floor had a large bomb crater in it. City officials suggested the ornate hall of the Mayakovsky Square subway station. A stage was erected; chairs were placed on it and it was decorated with flowers. Trains served as changing-rooms and cafés. The audience assembled at seven thirty in the evening. German aircraft had been trying for five hours to breach Moscow's air defences to disrupt it, but without success. On cue, Stalin rose to speak. He spoke of vast German losses, seven times the true figure; he admitted to colossal Soviet losses but understated them by more than half.[34] It was a patriotic speech, not the speech of a revolutionary Communist. The war was a Great Fatherland War, rallying the whole population to the cause of Russia. With the loss of the Ukraine, Belorussia and the Baltic states, it was indeed Russia they were defending, and they would defend it bitterly. 'If they want a war of extermination they shall have it!' Stalin declared, to prolonged and tumultuous applause. 'Our task now will be to destroy every German, to the very last man! Death to the German invaders!'[35]

The following day saw the familiar march in Red Square. Secret preparations went on for days beforehand. The troops for the parade were told that they were training for the front, where they would be sent immediately after the parade was over. They assembled at five o'clock in the morning, in biting cold. By the time the parade began it was snowing heavily, and German bombing was out of the question. In the distance could be heard the rumble of Russian and German guns. Soviet fighter aircraft were ordered to patrol overhead. The review was taken by the colourful cavalry commander, Marshal Budyenny, whose command Zhukov had just usurped. In full uniform, his distinctive handlebar moustaches spattered with snow, Budyenny rode on a white charger from the Kremlin gate. The sand that had been scattered on the roads to prevent the tanks and guns from skidding was blown away by the wind or pushed aside by the soldiers' boots, and the heavy equipment had to be manhandled through the slippery square. Stalin then spoke to the troops, not in person but on a film recorded in the Kremlin.[36] This time he left his listeners in no doubt that their cause was the cause of Russia down the ages: 'May you be inspired in this war by the heroic figures of our great ancestors, Aleksandr Nevsky, Dmitri Donskoi, Minin and Pozharsky, Aleksandr Suvorov, Mikhail Kutuzov!' These figures had fought off the Teutonic Knights, the Tatars, Polish invaders in the seventeenth century and, finally, Napoleon. Stalin was no longer appealing to revolutionary élan but to a deeper sense of nation, and of history.

The parading soldiers marched from Red Square to the front, now only forty miles away. Hitler wanted to finish the encirclement of Moscow, though even he could see that the war in the east would run on into the following year. On October 27 Goebbels was told by Hitler that he was 'waiting only for the roads to dry out or freeze'. Once tanks could roll again 'Soviet resistance will be broken'.[37] In early November the final assault was planned, though the army leadership was unenthusiastic. By the middle of November the ground had finally hardened. To the north of Moscow the 3rd and 4th Panzer Groups attacked towards the city of Klin, which finally fell on November 24, and towards the Moscow-Volga Canal, which was crossed on November 28. The leading units were now only twelve miles from the centre of Moscow. Further south the 2nd Panzer Group attacked towards Tula, whose capture would open the way to the region behind Moscow. That city was defended by General Boldin, a veteran of two previous encirclements. This time his men were dug in more firmly, with a deep defensive zone. Though close to being surrounded yet again, he clung on to Tula and the southern prong of the German attack ground to a halt.[38]

Zhukov had very limited forces to hold the attack. His line now had 240,000 men. There were 500 tanks for the whole front, and many of them were light tanks out of their depth on the modern battlefield. The initial defence of Moscow was conducted not with fresh troops from the Siberian hinterland but with a scratch force made up from the fragments of defeated units, non-combatants from the rear services, Moscow militia and hastily trained men from the townships around the capital. Effort was made to concentrate mobile units in 'shock' armies, rather than parcel them out. Zhukov organized a tighter and more co-ordinated battlefield and did not lose contact with his forces, as had happened in earlier campaigns. Soviet commanders now understood more clearly the nature of German tactics. As before a great deal was demanded of the troops. It was during these critical battles around Moscow that the legend of the 'twenty-eight Panfilov men' was born. A small detachment of Red Army soldiers, armed only with anti-tank rifles, grenades and Molotov cocktails, held at bay attacks by first twenty and then thirty German tanks. They crippled eighteen tanks and repulsed the German attack. At the height of the struggle the Communist political instructor, Klochkov, severely wounded, clutched a pile of hand grenades and threw himself under a tank. Before he did so he told the few men remaining, 'Russia is big, but there is nowhere to retreat.' These stories, like the Stakhanovite tales of the 1930s, had a clear propaganda purpose. Shock workers had now become shock soldiers, exceeding their norms to death. But these accounts should not all be dismissed as fiction, however mendacious the regime they served. There are too many witnesses to the mute valour of thousands of ordinary Soviet soldiers who fought to the death against impossible odds, not least from among their German adversaries, who found the suicidal resistance of the enemy hard to comprehend, and fearful to fight against. Panfilov's story, nonetheless, had a more sinister aspect. In the midst of the battle he received a message from Zhukov ordering him to stand fast or face a firing squad.[39]

At some point in the middle of November – Zhukov believed it was November 19 – Stalin rang to ask him what Moscow's prospects were. 'Are you certain we can hold Moscow? I ask you with this pain in my heart. Speak the truth, like a Communist.' Zhukov obliged by speaking Communist truth: 'We'll hold Moscow without a doubt.' He recalled years later that in fact he had anything but 'total confidence' about the fate of the capital.[40] Stalin promised reinforcements but could offer none of the tanks that Zhukov wanted. By late November the power of the German assault was visibly wilting. Scouting parties approached the outskirts of the capital, but that was the limit. The last offensive demanded too much of the tired German soldiers, short of tanks and ammunition and poorly prepared for the fierce winter conditions. The number of dead and wounded increased spectacularly with stiffening Soviet resistance. Up to the end of July the German army had lost only 46,000 men in the conquest of the whole western area of the Soviet Union. The battles for Kiev, Leningrad and Moscow cost another 118,000 dead. By the end of November more than 25 per cent of the effective strength of German forces were casualties. This was nothing, of course, compared with the losses of their enemy. Between June and December the Red Army lost 2,663,000 killed in action, 3,350,000 taken prisoner. For every German soldier killed, twenty Soviet soldiers died.[41]

At the beginning of December, exhausted though the German units were, the German High Command believed that the Soviet Union had used up all its reserves of manpower, down to the last battalion. 'No more new forces available,' wrote the German army chief of staff in his diary. On December 1 the German army commander, Field Marshal Walther von Brauchitsch, reported that the Red Army had 'no large reserve formations'; it was a spent force.[42] Both were wrong, and by a wide margin. Early in the morning of November 30 Stalin telephoned Zhukov with orders to mount a Soviet counter-offensive to end the threat to Moscow. Zhukov protested that he had neither the men nor the weapons, but Stalin would not be moved. Later that day Zhukov arrived with General Belov at the Kremlin. Walking briskly past bomb craters, the two men entered the underground bunker, which crawled with security men. At the end of a long corridor they entered a brightly lit room. Stalin was waiting to receive them. Belov, who had last seen Stalin in 1933, was staggered by his changed appearance. The public image was of a political giant, tough, brilliant, decisive. In front of him he found a quite different Stalin: 'a short man with a tired, haggard face. In eight years he seemed to have aged twenty. His eyes had lost their old steadiness; his voice lacked assurance.'[43] He looked at Zhukov's plans but merely nodded approval. There were no angry interventions. Stalin was still Supreme Commander, but the balance between the leader and his generals was slowly tilting their way.

The counter-offensive was planned for the first week of December, before German units could dig in for the winter, as they had done around Leningrad. Entirely unknown to the enemy, the Stavka had been holding in reserve no less than twelve armies for just such a strike. Some had been deployed in November to hold the front line before Moscow. While these divisions were expected to fight to the very limit, fifty-eight new divisions were held behind the front, some of them withdrawn from eastern Russia, to strengthen the counter-stroke. When the Soviet spy Richard Sorge confirmed that Japan was preparing to move southward against Britain and the United States, further divisions were transferred from the eastern frontier. These were the tough, fresh-faced 'Siberian boys' that so many Muscovites recalled in the streets of the capital that December. The recruitment and training of whole new armies took the German command entirely by surprise. It was not the tough winter conditions that halted the German army but the remarkable revival of Soviet military manpower after the terrible maulings of the summer and autumn.[44]

Zhukov's plan was a limited one. The two pincers that reached out like a giant metal claw around Moscow were to be pushed back by heavy offensive blows to where they had started in November. Surprise was essential, but the movement of troops and forward armour was spotted by German planes. Fortunately for Zhukov the reports were dismissed by German commanders, who did not believe a Soviet offensive was possible. The force he assembled was no larger than the German force it faced and was much weaker in tanks and aircraft. What Soviet forces did have was winter equipment – the bulky white snowsuits, goggles, heaters, skis and sledges, and the hardy steppe ponies that hauled supplies and carried the cavalry from one encounter to another. The Soviet air force had heated hangars; Soviet vehicles had always been adapted to all-weather driving. These were small but important advantages.

German forces were poorly prepared for the cold. Winter clothing was in short supply, and vehicles in most cases were entirely unsuitable for arctic conditions. Trucks could be started only after small stoves placed beneath the engines had heated them. Aircraft stood on small, open grass airfields with little protection. Mechanics working on the planes froze to the machinery. Shortages of effective lubricants and the extra fuel needed for winter driving reduced the favourable odds in tanks enjoyed by the Panzer armies. Ordinary soldiers found the icy conditions utterly debilitating. Over 133,000 cases of frostbite weakened the German front line. Men lost feet and fingers; their skin was covered with sores. Numbed with cold and fatigue, poorly camouflaged, they were forced to fight a fast-moving enemy that they could not see. The day the Soviet offensive opened, 5 December 1941, the temperature in the morning hours was minus thirteen degrees Fahrenheit.[45]

At three o'clock in the morning of December 5, in deep snow, the Red Army moved forward. The attack began north of Moscow, against the armoured forces on the Moscow-Volga canal and in the small town of Klin. The use of concentrated 'shock groups' broke holes in the German defence. Klin was taken on December 15 after ten days of stubborn fighting. By the end of the month Kalinin was retaken. In the south the encirclement of Tula was broken, and German forces were driven back more than eighty miles to the city of Kaluga, which was taken in a week of ferocious house-by-house struggles, both sides now under orders to yield nothing and to fight to the death. As the German pincers snapped off, Soviet forces became more confident. Much of the fighting had been done in blizzards and freezing winds that took a toll of both sides. For all the hardiness of Red Army soldiers, fighting at the height of winter was easy for neither side. The

Army Group Centre facing the Soviet onslaught was itself threatened with encirclement. German commanders began to petition Hitler for permission to withdraw to better defensive positions. Like Stalin, Hitler would permit no general retreat. He sacked his leading commanders and on December 19 took over the command of the army himself, with the promise that he would 'educate it to be National Socialist'.[46] Hitler and Stalin now faced each other directly, two amateur commanders in charge of the largest forces ever mobilized for war.

On December 13 the population of Moscow was told the news that the German threat to encircle the capital was over. In fact the battle raged well into January. Despite the bitter weather and shortages of reinforcements and vehicles, German troops and commanders fought with tenacity and skill. The situation at the front was far from being clear-cut. German units found themselves surrounded and had to be supplied by air. Soviet units infiltrated behind the German lines and found themselves in turn surrounded. Zhukov wanted to concentrate his remaining reserves for a second stage of the offensive, to push back the strong German formations still in front of Moscow and straighten the Soviet line. Stalin had other ideas. The sight of the enemy in flight was enough to foster fantasies of a larger victory. With both his cities saved, Stalin now wanted to drive the enemy back all along the front, before the spring rains and German reinforcements slowed down Soviet momentum.

It was a hopelessly unrealistic ambition. Stalin's thinking can only be guessed at. It was true that the wider strategic picture had altered in the Soviet Union's favour during December. On December 7 Japan attacked the United States and Britain in the Far East; four days later Hitler declared war on the United States, bringing Stalin a rich and powerful comrade-in-arms. On December 16 the British Foreign Minister, Anthony Eden, visited Moscow, the sounds of battle only fifty miles away. The draft of a British-Soviet military treaty was prepared, while Stalin, more relaxed after the success of Zhukov's offensive, got back to politics. He demanded a treaty agreeing to the restoration of the Soviet frontiers of 1941, in effect handing over Eastern Europe to Soviet domination. While he thought about the offer Eden was

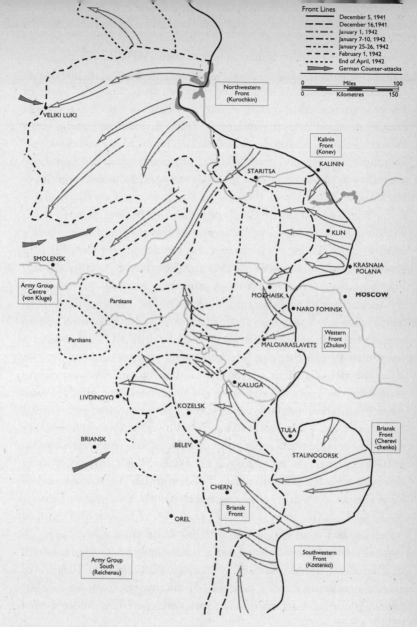

Front Lines
———————— December 5, 1941
— — — — December 16, 1941
—·—·—·— January 1, 1942
—··—··— January 7–10, 1942
—···—··· January 25–26, 1942
– – – – February 1, 1942
············ End of April, 1942
⟹ German Counter-attacks

0   Miles   100
0   Kilometres   150

Northwestern
Front
(Kurochkin)

VELIKI LUKI

Kalinin
Front
(Konev)

KALININ

STARITSA

KLIN

SMOLENSK

KRASNAIA
POLANA

Army Group
Centre
(von Kluge)

Partisans

MOZHAISK

MOSCOW

NARO FOMINSK

Partisans

Western
Front
(Zhukov)

MALOIARASLAVETS

KALUGA

LIVDINOVO

KOZELSK

BRIANSK

Briansk
Front
(Cherevi
-chenko)

TULA

BELEV

STALINOGORSK

CHERN

Briansk
Front

OREL

Army Group
South
(Reichenau)

Southwestern
Front
(Kostenko)

Map 3   The Moscow Counter-offensive, December 1941–April 1942

taken out to see the recently liberated town of Klin. Nothing was agreed upon, but Stalin had thrown his hat in the ring. A pro-Soviet Eastern Europe remained Stalin's position throughout the years of negotiation with Britain and America. In the midst of the critical campaign raging outside the capital, Stalin found time to send Eden off with what Eden later described as an 'embarrassingly sumptuous' banquet staged in Catherine the Great's throne room in the Kremlin.[47]

Stalin was almost certainly eager to try to wrest the military initiative away from Zhukov and the rest of the military leadership. Stalin deliberately crossed out Zhukov's name on a list of those to be awarded honours for saving Moscow. When Zhukov was summoned to Stalin's study in the Kremlin on January 5, he argued against the idea of a general offensive, but everyone else present stayed reverently silent.[48] The offensive stood. In February and March Stalin hounded his commanders to move faster and harder. Offensives were launched to relieve Leningrad, to encircle German Army Group Centre and to liberate the industrial heartlands of the Ukraine. All failed, and at a terrible cost. A further 444,000 Soviet soldiers perished, for the loss of 80,000 more Germans, an indication that the offensive was rich in manpower but poor in weaponry.[49] The Soviet war machine was woefully deficient in the weapons and equipment needed to inflict decisive defeats. The battle for Moscow allowed Stalin to fight another day, but it was not the turning point of the war, as is so often asserted.[50] In December 1941 the Red Army chief of staff, Marshal Shaposhnikov, observed that Russia still needed 'to assimilate the experience of modern war . . . Neither here nor today will the outcome of the war be decided . . . the crisis is yet far off.'[51] Not until 1943 did the Red Army succeed in inflicting a major defeat on the German army in summer campaigning weather, at a time when the invader was still as deep inside Soviet territory as in 1941. Even then the balance of material resources heavily favoured Germany. Moscow was a first, faltering step, a brief success almost squandered by Stalin's own military ineptitude.

The counter-offensive did have one enduring effect. The areas liberated from German occupation showed ordinary Soviet soldiers the nature of the war they were fighting. They found village after village torched or blown up and peasant women and children scrambling in the ruins to find scraps of food in sub-zero temperatures. Zhukov's own village, Strelovka, south of Moscow, was burned down during the German retreat, his mother's house with it. His family was fortunate to have so illustrious a member. Before the Germans arrived he had arranged for his mother and his sister and her children to be moved to the relative safety of Moscow.[52] Some, at least, of the damage had been inflicted by retreating Soviet forces earlier in the year, under instruction from Stalin himself to destroy everything in the path of the oncoming enemy (though the retreat was too disorganized and rapid for this to have been done systematically).

Wherever the Red Army came they found the grisly evidence of atrocities, none more poignant than the fate of the eighteen-year-old Zoya Kosmodemyanska. A member of a local partisan group with instructions to destroy what might be useful to the Germans, she was caught setting fire to some stables. Later rumours suggested that the villagers themselves betrayed her to the Germans. She was paraded through the village with a placard around her neck, then tortured, mutilated and hanged. Her frozen body, with the left breast cut off, was found still dangling when Soviet troops arrived. Her ordeal was recorded first in a poem, then in a play, in which the Zoya of the title is visited on the night of her execution by a vision of Stalin reassuring her that Moscow has been saved. The truth behind the Zoya legend was less uplifting. Her father and her grandfather were both shot during the purges, and the teenage Zoya, as if to redeem them, had become an obsessive young Communist. Her mother shared her desire to clear the father's name and encouraged Zoya to join the Communist youth partisans who were sent out on suicide missions in the region in front of Moscow, into the teeth of the oncoming German forces.[53]

The discovery of atrocities altered the mood of the troops. Ehrenburg, who witnessed the aftermath of the violence outside Moscow, detected at last 'a real hatred for the enemy'. One German infantryman wrote that Soviet soldiers 'bellow like bulls when they attack'.[54] More grimly, he noted that Red Army soldiers were no longer taking prisoners at the front line. A war of extermination was being fought by both sides. Russian culture was a target as well. Museums and galleries were looted. The great Tsarist palaces, preserved for the people by the new republic, were pillaged. The monuments to the great figures of Russian music and literature were defiled. At Tolstoy's estate, Yasnaya Polyana, manuscripts were burned as fuel, and the Germans buried their dead around the great man's grave; Tchaikovsky's house was ransacked and used as a motorbike garage.[55] What had once been merely Party slogans about the 'fascist beasts' now took on real meaning. In 1941 the poet Surkov captured some of that rage in his poem *A Soldier's Oath*: 'The tears of women and children are boiling in my heart/ Hitler the murderer and his hordes shall pay for these tears with their wolfish blood/ for the avenger's hatred knows no mercy.'[56]

1 Josef Stalin (*right*) at Lenin's funeral in January 1924. In his testament Lenin warned the Party that Stalin did not know how to use power 'with sufficient caution'.

2 Victims of the Ukrainian famine in 1933. The death toll is now estimated at over four million. Roadblocks were set up to prevent food from crossing the frontier into the stricken province.

3 Ukrainian nationalist prisoners in one of hundreds of labour camps across the Soviet Union. Latest estimates suggest a camp population of 3.5 million by 1939.

4 The Soviet Foreign Minister, Molotov, reviews a guard of honour on a visit to Berlin in November 1941 during which the Soviet Union sought a further pact with Hitler over the territories of south-east Europe and the Middle East.

5 A sombre crowd of Russians listen to the broadcast of Molotov's speech on
22 June 1941 announcing the German attack earlier that morning across the whole
western frontier of the Soviet Union.

6 Ukrainians greet German soldiers on horseback in the summer of 1941. Many
hated the Stalinist regime and saw the Germans as liberators. Collaboration was
extensive, but unavoidable.

7 Lorries make their way across the treacherous 'Ice Road' to bring much-needed supplies to Leningrad in 1942. 360,000 tons of supplies were brought in over the winter of 1941; without them the whole population might have died.

8 A worker puts out a German incendiary bomb in Leningrad. Those resting from work formed civil defence units in the factories to repair bomb damage and prevent fires.

9 Shostakovich rehearses his 'Leningrad Symphony' in the beleaguered city. By the time it was performed there, in August 1942, many of the players had died or been killed at the front.

10 Soviet ski troops in action in the winter of 1941-2. The Soviet soldiers were better supplied with winter equipment than the Germans, and adapted their tactics to exploit that advantage.

11 A procession passing through a city in the Ukraine, carrying a banner 'Hitler-Liberator'. German troops were widely greeted with the traditional gifts of bread and salt, but repaid them by seizing over ten million tons of grain to feed the German army and the home population.

12 A rare picture of the massacre at Babi Yar, taken from a film shot by a German witness. A total of 33,700 Jews were slaughtered here in two days, and buried in an anti-tank ditch along with Soviet POWs and Soviet officials captured in Kiev.

13 Jewish children starving in a ghetto set up for Soviet Jews in Belorussia. By the end of December 1942 1.1 million Soviet Jews had been murdered, and hundreds of thousands exposed to famine and disease.

14 Collaboration with the German occupiers brought a swift retribution. Partisan gangs shot or hanged suspects. When the Red Army recaptured the occupied regions, thousands of collaborators were given summary justice.

15 A family struggles with a handcart through the ruins of Stalingrad. Many of the civilian population were compelled to stay in the city as German troops approached. An estimated 40,000 were killed in air raids.

16 A woman carrying guns in a trench in the defence of Stalingrad. Thousands of women saw front-line service in the Red Army and air force. Few concessions were made either by their male companions or by the enemy.

17 A Soviet soldier snatches a bowl of soup near the front line in 1943. Army life was tough and discipline harsh, but morale improved after Stalingrad as confidence was restored in Soviet commanders and Soviet soldiers tasted victory.

18 A German soldier captured by a Soviet scouting party before the Battle of Kursk. Soviet forces relied on kidnapped enemy soldiers for much of their information on enemy strengths and dispositions.

19 The fog of war. Tanks in combat at Prokhorovka during the Battle of Kursk. Driving rain and smoke made visibility atrocious: tanks rammed other tanks in a vast armoured duel which left 700 disabled vehicles on the battlefield.

20 The Metropolitan of Moscow gives his blessing to the war effort. In 1942 Stalin revived the Russian Orthodox Church as part of the patriotic rallying of the Soviet people.

21 Lorries drive Lend-Lease goods away from the docks in Murmansk. Soviet authorities disparaged the contribution made by foreign aid, but in private Stalin confessed that the USSR 'would not have been able to cope' without it.

22 A soldier falls in a frontal attack somewhere on the Ukrainian front in 1944. The liberation of the Ukraine was one of the largest and most successful of all Soviet campaigns, but the cost was over one million casualties.

23 German soldiers are paraded through the streets of Moscow in 1944. For the first time large numbers of prisoners were taken in battles of encirclement. Their destination was the work camps in the east.

24 After the Germans were driven through the city, disinfectant trucks were sent to spray the streets as a symbol of the cleansing of the Soviet Union. The enemy were often portrayed as vermin in Soviet cartoons and posters.

25 As the Red Army approached, German forces perpetrated a final wave of atrocities. Jewish workers in a Lublin tailoring shop lie where they have been shot at their benches and machines. Others were slaughtered in the courtyard outside the workshop.

BOT OHA.
проклятая
ГЕРМАНИЯ!

26 *Accursed Germany!* One of many posters on the Red Army's route into German territory. The first towns and villages in the Red Army's path were the victims of a terrible vengeance.

27 An elderly German watches in an East Prussian town as Red Army soldiers march past him. Millions of Germans fled westward in 1945, an exodus which finally totalled more than 13 million.

28 Marshal Georgi Zhukov, the most famous Soviet general of the Second World War, stands in a command post during the battle for Berlin. He was a tough-minded leader prepared to act brutally with his own men for any dereliction of duty.

29 A Soviet cameraman photographs a body that resembled Hitler found in the ruins of the Reich Chancellery in early May 1945. Hitler's remains were later found badly charred in the Chancellery gardens.

30 Millions of homes were destroyed in the western Soviet Union. Many people lived for the first months or years of peace in home-made huts built from sticks and mud, or in caves.

31 Soviet women working on a reconstruction site. Every citizen in the ruined areas was obliged to perform labour service. In Leningrad workers had to put in thirty hours a month, the rest sixty hours.

32 A train full of prisoners for the labour camps in Siberia drives past a vast portrait of Stalin on the hillside. The 'cult of personality' reached new heights after victory in 1945, but the terror was intensified.

5

The Fight from Within: Collaboration, Terror and Resistance

Friends and Brothers! Bolshevism is the enemy of the Russian people. It has brought countless disasters to our country. Enough blood has been spilled! There has been enough starvation, forced labour and suffering in the Bolshevik torture chambers! Arise and join in the struggle for freedom! Long may peace with honour with Germany prevail!

> General Vlasov's appeal to the Russian nation,
> 27 December 1942

In August 1941 the commander of *Einsatzgruppe* B, Artur Nebe, called up experts from the Criminal Technical Institute to help him solve a problem. A short while before, Heinrich Himmler had visited the Belorussian capital of Minsk to witness the execution of a hundred 'saboteurs'. It was the first time he had seen men killed, shot a dozen at a time face down in an open pit. He asked Nebe to test other methods that were less brutalizing to those who carried out the executions. The experts drove to Russia in trucks filled with explosives and gassing equipment. The morning after their arrival they drove out to a wood outside Minsk, where they packed two wooden bunkers with 250 kilograms of explosive and twenty mental patients seized from a Soviet asylum. The first attempt to blow them up failed, and the wounded and frightened victims were packed back into the bunkers with a further 100 kilograms of explosive. This time they were blown to smithereens, and Jewish prisoners were forced to scour the area picking up the human remains. The group then tried a different method at an asylum in Mogilev. Here they herded mental patients into a bricked-up laboratory, into which they inserted a pipe connected to a car exhaust. Fumes from the car took too long to kill the victims, and the car was swapped for a truck, which could generate a larger volume of fumes. The victims died in eight minutes. Gas killing became the preferred option. Altogether an estimated 10,000 died in asylums across German-occupied territory: men, women and children.[1]

These murderous experiments were part of a programme of ethnic cleansing and 'counter-insurgency' in the East that led to the deaths of millions of Jews, Soviet prisoners of war, captured Communists, partisans and ordinary people caught in the crossfire of ideological and racial war – a harvest of dead unparalleled in the history of modern war. Few of those who witnessed German tanks rolling past their villages in the early days of the invasion knew what to expect of the invader. In the Baltic states, Belorussia and the Ukraine there was strong hostility to Stalin and Stalinism, but alienation from Soviet rule did not necessarily mean that German rule would be any more welcome. Even collaboration with the invader, with the usual implication of betrayal and opportunism, should not always be taken at face value.

There is no doubt that some of those who found themselves under German control in the East did work with the invader. Some did so voluntarily, spurred on by a genuine loathing of Soviet Communism. Some did so in the mistaken belief that the Germans had enlightened views on the restoration of private land ownership and capitalist enterprise. (In Kiev a number of Jewish merchants even petitioned the German authorities for permission to restart their businesses.)[2] Some did so because they saw an opportunity to set up independent national states long denied them by Soviet repression. National committees were formed in the Baltic states, in the Ukraine and in the Caucasus area. The largest number of collaborators were to be found helping the German armed forces. The recruitment of Soviet military labour began not long after the invasion. Soviet prisoners or local labourers were used as auxiliary volunteers. They performed mainly menial jobs – building defences, hauling supplies or building airfields and camps. They were employed in secret at first, for Hitler had expressly forbidden the use of Soviet labour. Rather than use their labour power for the war effort, the Germans left millions of prisoners of war in huge open camps to die of malnutrition and disease.[3] But German commanders in Russia soon found they had no choice but to recruit local labour. The vast area of the front and the speed of the advance made it impossible to supply enough German hands to run the whole military apparatus that backed up the front line. By the end of the summer of 1941 Soviet recruits were to be found in the ranks of the fighting force itself, mobilized for the crusade against Bolshevism.

At first the recruits were drawn mainly from the non-Russian nationalities, who were more hostile to the Soviet system. In 1941 the prisoner-of-war camps were combed for prisoners from the Caucasus or Turkestan, who were removed, fitted out with German uniforms, given mainly German officers (only seventy-four of the released prisoners were given officer status) and inferior Soviet weapons. The Islamic units were supplied with an imam each, and Sunni and Shi'ite priests were trained at theological schools in Dresden and Göttingen to meet the high demand for Islamic instruction among the troops. Many of the recruited men were added to existing German divisions, in small numbers as a safeguard against defection.[4] But as the war went on they were formed into larger units. There were two Ukrainian divisions, a division from Turkestan, an SS division raised from Galicia, and more than 150,000 Latvians, Lithuanians and Estonians. Above all there were the Cossacks. These military tribesmen were legendary fighters, with a long and bloody history of service to the Tsars. Many fought against the Bolsheviks in the civil war, and they were never reconciled to a system that denied them a national existence and savagely suppressed the traditions of Cossack life. They made no secret of their desire to build a national homeland – Kazakia – but they were welcomed by German commanders as comrades in arms.[5]

Cossack regiments in the Red Army crossed over to the enemy and volunteered for service. They formed fast-moving cavalry squadrons and were used to hunt down partisans. When in 1942 the Cossack homelands in the south were liberated by German armies, they were greeted by the entire populations of villages and farmsteads singing local anthems and bearing gifts of food and flowers. The men dug up the swords, daggers and rifles that they had buried away years before and rode out in full costume, with the familiar crisscross bullet belts and sabres, to offer their services. One ancient leader, the hetman Kulakov, long believed to be dead, emerged from hiding and headed a magnificent tribal procession into the Cossack capital of Poltava. The horsemen were recruited into the German army that was approaching Stalingrad. They were sent off to hunt down groups of Red Army stragglers, which they did with a ferocious and merciless efficiency. In 1943 even Hitler overcame his prejudice against Asian peoples and agreed to the first full Cossack division. The numbers multiplied. There were by 1944 over 250,000 Cossacks serving on the German side.[6]

In total an estimated one million Soviet soldiers ended up fighting against their country. Many did so out of desperation, as the only alternative to dying in the prisoner-of-war camps or being sent to the Reich as forced labourers, where an estimated 750,000 died of mistreatment and neglect.[7] This was hardly voluntary collaboration in any meaningful sense of the term, though it earned most of them a death warrant or a prison sentence when at the end of the war they found themselves on the losing side. Some of those who defected did so with greater enthusiasm. For the anti-guerrilla campaign the Germans hired gangs of Soviet mercenaries and freebooters to root out the resisters. They asked few questions about what methods were used. A Soviet engineer, Voskoboinikov, virtually ran the area around Orel and Kursk for the Germans. With 20,000 men and twenty-four tanks he terrorized the population, collecting taxes and food by force, murdering anyone who resisted. Soviet paratroopers dropped into the area assassinated him in January 1942.[8]

There were plenty of replacements. Voskoboinikov was succeeded by the most notorious defector of all, Bronislav Kaminsky, another Soviet engineer who established a reign of terror and crime across the region. Backed by 10,000 men and thousands of camp followers, Kaminsky was left to pacify the region as he saw fit. His forces became part of the pretentiously titled Russian National Army of Liberation, though they liberated little save other people's possessions. The reputation of the Kaminsky Brigade vied with that of the SS. Heinrich

Himmler, who controlled the brigade, withdrew it from Russia in 1944 to deal with a Polish revolt in Warsaw. The behaviour of the brigade in slaughtering thousands of Polish civilians in scenes of appalling cruelty proved too much even for the hardened stomachs of the SS. Kaminsky was shot on the orders of his German mentor, and the remnants of his unit were sent off to form the nucleus of another renegade Russian army being formed to fight in the last ditch against Communism. They arrived at the Russian camp in Württemberg under the astonished gaze of their new commander, General Buniachenko, a procession of horse-drawn carts carrying both armed and unarmed men, wearing every kind of uniform, accompanied by their women, who were draped in dresses and jewels they had looted. The officers wore a row of watches on each wrist. Buniachenko was dumbfounded: 'This is what you are giving me – bandits, robbers, thieves?'[9]

The man the Kaminsky outlaws were going to serve was General Andrei Vlasov, who only three years before had distinguished himself in the defence of Moscow and was recognized as one of Stalin's favourites. He was now the head of the Committee for the Liberation of the Peoples of Russia and the nominal leader of those Soviet citizens, more than five million in number, now living under German rule. Vlasov looked the very model of a Prussian general: tall and heavily built, with his hair combed back tightly from a receding hairline and small horn-rimmed spectacles, his appearance was austere and militaristic. He wore no medals or insignia, save a small white, blue and red cockade of the Russian Liberation Army, whose commander he had also now become. He saw himself as the spokesman of a different Russia from Stalin's, but his appeal was always overshadowed by his decision to pursue that Russia at the side of Hitler.

Vlasov was born in 1900, the thirteenth and last son of a peasant. After a seminary education, he was called up into the fledgling Red Army in 1919 and fought in some of the bitterest conflicts of the civil war in the Caucasus, the Crimea and the Ukraine. He became a successful career soldier and, like Zhukov, was lucky enough to survive the purges. He became a Communist Party member in 1930 and won the Order of Lenin (and a gold watch) in 1940. His unit was the last to fight its way out of the Kiev pocket in September 1941; in November Vlasov's 20th Army was defending the northern approaches to the Soviet capital; in January he led the counter-offensive to encircle the whole German force in front of Moscow. In March 1942 Vlasov led the 2nd Shock Army on the Volkhov Front south of Leningrad in its effort to break the German line, but it was encircled and the army annihilated in June. Vlasov was captured on July 12 while hiding in a village hut. He was taken to a special camp for prominent prisoners at Vinnitsa in the Ukraine, where Hitler had his forward headquarters. Here he wrote to the German authorities suggesting the idea of an anti-Stalin Russian Liberation Army, making the most of anti-Bolshevik sentiment among prisoners of war and the populations of the occupied areas.[10]

There are various reasons suggested for Vlasov's sudden conversion. His brother was shot in the civil war for alleged anti-Bolshevik conspiracy; he had given his elderly parents a cow as a present, and they were punished for it as 'rich peasants'; he is reported to have been shocked by the sight of Ukrainians greeting the Germans with flowers, bread and salt, which awoke in him a realization of how unpopular Stalin was.[11] The most likely explanation is the one Vlasov himself gave: he was alienated from a system that traded in lies and deceit, butchered its own people and threw thousands of soldiers into battles for which they were poorly prepared.[12] He soon made his political credentials public. Despite the disapproval of Hitler, leading diplomats and officers conspired to have Vlasov released, in order to establish a Russian liberation movement, whose founding meeting was held in Smolensk in December 1942. The 'Smolensk Declaration' was a direct political challenge not just to Stalin but to the whole Soviet system. Vlasov pledged his movement to abolish collective farms and the state-run economy, and to establish civil rights for all, but within a 'New Europe' modelled on German lines. There was no mention of democracy.[13]

Hitler remained immovably opposed to the Vlasov project. He feared that a Russian liberation movement would undermine Germany's own plans for the East, and he deeply distrusted the motives of any Russian. When in September 1943 the German line broke at a point manned by Eastern volunteer units, Hitler flew into a rage and insisted on drawing the collaborators out of the line and sending them to western and southern Europe. This effectively undermined the whole basis of collaboration. Vlasov and a great many other former Soviet soldiers did not want to fight America and Britain on Germany's behalf. They were interested only in freeing Russia from the Stalinist grip. Nevertheless, thousands of Soviet soldiers were left guarding the West Wall. On D-Day they surrendered to their bemused enemy with shouts of 'Ruskii, Ruskii'. The Liberation Committee was accepted by Hitler only in September 1944, when everyone who could fight was needed to save Germany from Soviet vengeance. Vlasov was given two weak divisions, with not the remotest prospect of liberating anyone in the East. There was one final twist to the story. When Vlasov's Russian divisions finally saw action in March and April 1945 they ended up fighting the Germans again – protecting the people of Prague from an SS force on the rampage against a Czech revolt.[14] Vlasov and his men tried then to reach American lines, hoping that the United States would start a second anti-Soviet war and let them fight alongside. They were caught by the Red Army. Some, including wounded men in hospital in Prague, were shot on the spot.[15] The rest were brought back to the Soviet Union, where a grisly fate awaited them. Refusing to recant, Vlasov and his senior colleagues were tortured with exceptional ferocity. Tried in July 1946 in camera on treason charges, he was sentenced to death on August 1. The following day he was hanged; rumour had it that he was strung up with piano wire, with a hook dug into the back of his skull. Vlasov told one of his interrogators, 'In time, the people will remember us with warmth.'[16]

The reaction to Vlasov after 1945 was mixed. In the Soviet Union the official line was to condemn him as a coward and a traitor who deserved rough Communist justice. Vlasov's supporters saw him as a Russian patriot who tried to steer an impossible course between the two dictators, and his reputation has accordingly been resuscitated since the fall of Soviet Communism. What distinguished Vlasov and the Liberation Army from other Soviet dissidents, however, was their willingness to harness the liberation campaign to the German war effort. Soviet soldiers on the German side shot at ordinary Russians, burned down Russian villages and looted Russian homes. This was more than simple anti-Bolshevism, and it was harder to forgive. Even if Vlasov and his German allies had succeeded in defeating the Red Army and destroying Stalinism, there is little evidence to suggest that Hitler would have allowed an independent, liberal Russian state in place of the vision of harsh empire that drove his conquest on.

In reality the Russian liberation movement, like the national movements in the Baltic states, the Ukraine and Belorussia, was seen by Hitler as a threat. The conquest of the eastern territories was a gigantic colonial war, not a war to emancipate the peoples of Eurasia. Hitler saw the German future in the east in terms of colonial exploitation. A German governing class would rule the region, supported by a network of garrison cities – rather like the fortified towns of the Roman empire – around which would cluster settlements of German farmers and traders. Plans were drawn up for a web of high-speed motorways to link the regional centres with Berlin and a wide-gauge double-decked railway, along which would sweep the new imperial élite through land tilled by modern helots, millions of Slavs labouring for the master race. Any of the new colonial peoples surplus to the requirements of the empire were to be transported to Slavlands beyond the Urals or left to die.[17]

It was a vision of empire straight out of science fiction. For the conquered peoples it became fact. The native nationalist movements were violently suppressed. In the Ukraine the mood of temporary exhilaration felt at the retreat of the Soviet order evaporated when from the end of August 1941 the *Einsatzgruppen*, whose job it was to root out anti-German elements, began systematically to round up Ukrainian nationalists and intellecturals, most of whom were executed.[18] In the Baltic states, hope of winning back their independence was broken by the creation of a Nazi Commissariat *Ostland*, placed under the Nazi commissar Hinrich Lohse, and by Hitler's decision that the Baltic states should eventually be incorporated into the greater German Reich. Lohse was a Nazi 'old fighter' from the early days of the movement who used his new power to indulge in a corrupt caricature of imperial rule – requisitioning palaces and a fleet of cars, and living the life of a pampered sybarite until he fled his

post in 1944.[19] In the Ukraine a second Commissariat was set up in
September, a vast sprawling province that at the height of the war
embraced fifty million people. Its ruler was another old Nazi comrade,
the *Gauleiter* of East Prussia, Erich Koch.

The appointment of Koch was meant as a signal to anyone on
either the German or the Soviet side who was in any doubt about the
nature of the new Nazi empire. At his inauguration speech in Rovno,
a city chosen deliberately because it was not a centre of Ukrainian
culture or historic identity, Koch expressed words which soon became
notorious: 'I am known as a brutal dog . . . Our job is to suck from
the Ukraine all the goods we can get hold of . . . I am expecting from
you the utmost severity towards the native population.'[20] Ukrainians
were regarded as racial inferiors, the lowest kind of humanity. Koch
was by no means alone in regarding the Ukraine as dispensable.
Goering reflected that the solution in the Ukraine was to kill every
man over fifteen years of age. Himmler wanted the intelligentsia
'decimated'. When one of Koch's deputies angrily confronted a German official who was planning to re-establish rudimentary education
in the region, he blurted out the true state of affairs: 'Do you wish to
create a Ukrainian educated class at the time when we want to
annihilate the Ukrainians!' To protests that forty million people could
not be annihilated, the deputy replied: 'It is our business.'[21]

The exact number of Ukrainians who died at the hands of the
German occupiers will probably never be known. Death was meted
out arbitrarily. Peasants who, when questioned by German officials,
admitted to being able to read and write were liable to be shot as
'intellectuals'. Farmers who withheld food stocks or refused to work
the fields for the Germans were hanged as an example to the rest. In
the district of Rivne the German farm administrators introduced
flogging for everything from slack work to the failure of peasants to
remove their caps in the presence of Germans; they imposed curfews;
the carrying of a knife was punishable by death.[22] Thousands of
peasants were hanged or shot for suspected partisan activity. Throughout the Ukraine 250 villages and their populations were deliberately
obliterated to encourage good behaviour in the rest.

Thousands more died of starvation. The seizure of food supplies to feed the vast German army and its hundreds of thousands of horses left the cities of the conquered region desperately short of food. In the Ukraine it was decided to eliminate 'superflous eaters', primarily Jews and the populations of the cities. In Kiev the meagre food ration was cut sharply (200 grammes of bread per week), roadblocks were set up to prevent food from entering the city and the collective-farm markets supplying the cities were suspended. As the supply of food reached famine levels, the peoples of the east were denied effective medical care. In Kharkov around 80,000 died of starvation, in Kiev almost certainly more. During 1942 food seizures were relaxed so that in the spring farmers would be able to sow their fields, but with the following harvest German demands rose higher still. In 1943 people in Kiev were fed only one-third of the minimum they needed for subsistence. The collective farms were not dismantled, as many peasants had hoped, but were run by German officials in place of the local Communists, who had either fled or been killed. In some places grain quotas were fixed at double the level demanded by the Soviet system. Peasants struggled to survive on the food growing on their plots.[23]

The labour programme was as harsh. In the first weeks of the war Ukrainians volunteered for labour in Germany, but their treatment was so poor that labour quotas had to be imposed and labourers recruited by force. The first volunteers were bundled into boxcars without food and sanitation facilities. When they arrived in Germany they were kept behind barbed wire in rough barracks. Their food was less than the necessary level of nutrition; they were segregated from the rest of the population and forced to wear armbands with the word *Ost* (East) sewn onto them. When the flow of volunteers dried up, workers were simply seized at gunpoint. Villages that failed to hand over their quota could be torched and their leaders murdered. Churches and cinemas were raided and the people inside shipped off to Germany. Thousands of young Ukrainians fled to the forests and marshes to join the partisans rather than work in captivity. In 1942 Hitler issued a personal order requiring the deporting of half a million Ukrainian women between the ages of eighteen and thirty-five, to be assigned to German households and Germanized. By the end of the war the

Ukraine had supplied over four-fifths of all the forced labour from the East.[24] The effect of exploitation on this scale was to alienate much of the population in the East as thoroughly from the Germans as from Stalin.

The bloodiest chapter in the history of German conquest was the subject of race. The German imperial concept was in essence a racial one. The East was populated by ethnic groups deemed to be a biological threat to the German people. The ideology of race went beyond mere discrimination. Lesser peoples were deemed to have less right to existence than the master race. In some cases – Russians, Ukrainians – they were to be killed off, allowed to starve or geographically dispersed. For Jews, millions of whom now found themselves trapped under German rule, the German authorities reserved special treatment. The Jew was taken to be the most cunning and dangerous enemy of the German race. Hitler had always equated Bolshevik and Jew in his mind, and the assault on the Soviet Union was waged as war against them both, without discrimination. The war had already sharpened the anti-Semitic policies of the regime. Millions of Polish Jews were forced into ghettoes, where they began to die from disease and malnutrition. Thousands were killed by the SS and security police in the pacification of the German zone of Poland. In the Barbarossa campaign the instructions issued to the troops, the SS and security services before the launch of the attack specified Jews as a target for 'ruthless and energetic measures'.[25]

About five million Jews lived in the Soviet Union in 1941; most in the western regions, which came directly under German rule. Anti-Semitism was no stranger to Soviet Jews. There was a long history of popular anti-Semitism in the Ukraine and the Baltic states, going back far into the Tsarist past. Before the First World War hundreds of thousands of Russian Jews emigrated to Western Europe or America to escape the pogroms. Anti-Semitism was never a formal policy of the new Soviet state – which was officially committed to the socialist ideal of racial equality – but under Stalin, who was described by Khrushchev as 'a dyed-in-the-wool anti-Semite', the Jewish population and its leaders faced an uncertain future.[26]

In the 1920s the Soviet authorities decided to establish a separate

Jewish homeland where Jews from the western regions could settle and till the land. The area chosen was the Crimea, the very area later designated by Hitler for German colonization. During the 1920s thousands of poor Jews from the Ukraine and Belorussia, the old Pale of Settlement, migrated to the Crimean steppe. In the 1930s the plan changed. Stalin did not want a Jewish homeland in the Crimea, half of which was populated by Tatars, who had their own autonomous republic. A new site was found in the Soviet far east, on the banks of the Amur River, in the region of Birobidzhan. This desolate area abutted the new Japanese empire in Manchuria. No Jews had ever lived there. But a new stream of settlers moved across Siberia to set up the Jewish Autonomous Region, with its own Jewish press, Jewish theatre and Jewish authorities. It was not quite a ghetto; Soviet propaganda made great play with the idea that the regime was protecting the culture and identity of the Jewish people. But its remoteness from the traditional centres of Jewish culture and settlement made it an unattractive prospect. Few western Jews moved there. Birobidzhan was a failed experiment in Soviet apartheid.[27]

During the Stalinist terror of the 1930s Jews featured prominently among the list of victims in one show trial after another. Anti-Semitism was never given as the ground for their persecution, and the large number of Jews in the senior ranks of the Party and the state apparatus made it inevitable that they would suffer disproportionately when Stalin turned on his former colleagues. Anti-Semitism was more evident in the savage purge that followed the sacking of Maxim Litvinov from the Foreign Affairs Commissariat in May 1939. Although the Jewish Litvinov was spared, his staff was not. They were arrested and forced to confess that they were all part of a counter-revolutionary circle of spies, headed by Litvinov himself. Almost all of those purged were Jews. The NKVD began to prepare a show trial, the 'trial of ambassadors'. All but one of those singled out for the trial were Jewish.[28] The trial never took place. The unstable international situation made a further purge too dangerous. The Foreign Affairs Commissariat under Molotov was gradually filled with ethnic Russians. The NKVD was purged at the same time, and many Jews prominent in the organization were arrested and murdered. Contact with 'Zionist circles' began to appear in the lists of fabricated crimes drawn up by the Lubyanka torturers.

After war broke out in September 1939 the Soviet regime was drawn into sudden complicity with German anti-Semitism. Thousands of German and Polish Jews flooded across the new Soviet-German border. The Red Army turned many of them back, only to have German guards open fire on the helpless crowds caught in a stateless no-man's-land. German Jews who had sought sanctuary in the Soviet Union during the 1930s were now rounded up and shipped back to Germany, where they were imprisoned or murdered. Other Jewish refugees from German occupation were exiled to Siberia or Kazakhstan or thrown into prison or labour camps (from which they finally emerged in the late summer of 1941, when the German invasion of the Soviet Union made Jews everywhere into allies of the Soviet cause). In the Soviet-occupied area of Poland, where Jews had already been the victims of Polish discrimination, the new authorities launched a further attack on the communities of small-town – *shtetl* – Jews. In just twenty-one months the traditions of Jewish life were demolished. Jewish leaders were arrested and deported; Jewish associations and youth movements were closed down; many synagogues were closed and used as ware-houses or stables. The ideological drive against religion and class distinctions was used to justify the public drive against Jewish religious practice and the richer or more cultured elements of the Jewish community. The Jewish slaughterhouses were closed down, and the public practice of circumcision and bar mitzvah prevented. The Sab-bath was abolished as an official holy day, along with Jewish festivals and holidays. The characteristic Jewish economy of small artisan shops and market stalls was closed down. In the deserted squares of the small towns appeared statues of Stalin.[29]

Suddenly, in August 1941, Stalin ordered a complete turnabout on the Jewish question. Imprisoned Jews were released, including two famous Polish Jewish socialists, Genrikh Erlich and Viktor Alter, who had spent eighteen months in the Lubyanka and had been condemned to death for agitating against the Molotov-Ribbentrop pact – in July 1941, a month after the German invasion![30] On August 24 a rally of Jewish people was held in a Moscow park, and was addressed by prominent Jewish figures from the worlds of film, art and literature. Erlich and Alter proposed the establishment of an international Jewish Anti-Hitler Committee that would unite Jews everywhere in the anti-Nazi cause. This proved too much for Stalin. When government offices were rushed to Kuibyshev in October, as German forces threatened to encircle Moscow, Erlich and Alter were sent there under NKVD guard. They were settled in a smart hotel, whence they were summoned to an urgent meeting in the local NKVD residence. Neither was ever seen in public again. Erlich committed suicide in prison in May 1942 and Alter was executed in February of the following year.[31] The plans for a broad Jewish anti-Hitler movement came to nothing. Instead Stalin sponsored a new organization in April 1942, the Jewish Antifascist Committee. Headed by the actor Solomon Mikhoels, the new Committee was part of the Soviet Information Bureau, the state propaganda agency. Its purpose was to secure funds and support for the Soviet war effort from both inside and outside the country. The hidden hand behind the committee was that of an NKVD official, Sergei Shpigelglaz, whose job was to monitor its activities. Throughout its wartime life it was a branch of the Soviet apparatus, part of the frantic effort to mobilize the energies of all Soviet peoples for the struggle against the invader. Only towards the end of the war, when the committee's leaders began to plan for a Jewish homeland in the Soviet Union, did Stalin turn against it, suspicious that its real purpose was to create a Trojan horse for American capitalism and imperialism inside the Soviet Union itself.[32]

Stalin's fantasies about Zionist conspiracies were nothing compared with the ideological obsessions of his erstwhile German ally. Stalin was an anti-Semite, but he was too much of an opportunist to allow his prejudices to stand in the way of the Soviet war effort. Hitler and the racist circle around him were ideological purists. The war with the Soviet Union opened up undreamed-of opportunities to complete a project of racial engineering unparalleled in human history. Just when Hitler decided in his own mind to initiate the active extermination of the Jewish people is not known with certainty. The most likely hypothesis is that Hitler made the first of a number of decisions that led to genocide in the first flush of victory as German forces rushed forward into Soviet territory, seizing the Ukraine, the Baltic states and Belorussia, triumphant, unstoppable. There were witnesses to the enhanced state of euphoria that overtook Hitler's headquarters in June and July 1941.[33] He was a man on the crest of a wave; his achievements were regarded as extraordinary, world-historic. He had already crossed every moral threshold: he had authorized the liquidation of mentally and physically disabled Germans in the spring of 1939; in September 1939 he approved the liquidation of thousands of Polish civilians; in the months before Barbarossa he had approved the 'criminal orders' to liquidate Communist and Jewish functionaries of the Soviet state. No radical moral leap was necessary to extend these criminal orders to include all Soviet Jews. Adolf Eichmann, the man who organized the transport of Jewish victims in Europe, later recalled that he was told in the middle of July 1941 by Himmler's deputy. Reinhard Heydrich, that Hitler had ordered 'physical extermination'.[34]

By the autumn of 1941 Hitler had almost certainly extended the decision to slaughter the Jews in the East to the Jewish communities of the rest of German-occupied Europe, precipitating full-scale genocide. Preparations for the Holocaust can be found throughout the months of the German advance into Russia: grotesque experiments to determine the most rational form of extermination, rather than simple massacre; the preliminary orders for crematoria and camp equipment; the search for sites suitable for the new death camps. All of this pre-dated the final crisis in front of Moscow. The accumulating evidence of German preparations in 1941 for extermination undermines the argument that the slowdown of the German advance and the sudden reverses before Moscow pushed Hitler over the edge to a policy of Jewish annihilation in revenge for Communist successes. Exultant victory triggered the genocide, not unexpected defeat. The Soviet collapse in 1941 sealed the fate of Europe's Jews.

Whatever the motives and timing of Hitler's decision, the process of killing Jews began almost immediately after German forces crossed the frontier. The *Einsatzgruppen* rounded up any male Jews who worked for the Soviet regime or the Communist Party and shot them outright. They spread the net wide; their situation reports referred to the slaughter of 'Jews', 'intellectual Jews', 'Jewish activists', 'wandering Jews', 'rebellious Jews', but could be applied to 'suspicious elements', 'hostile elements' or 'undesirable elements'.[35] So broad were these categories that within weeks of the invasion the *Einsatzgruppen* were routinely murdering women and children along with adult male Jews. They also got other people to do their dirty work for them. Local anti-Semites were armed by the Germans and encouraged to launch vicious pogroms of their own. The first occurred in the Lithuanian city of Kovno on the night of June 25, when 1,500 Jews were massacred and Jewish property and synagogues destroyed. A few days later another pogrom was staged in the Latvian capital of Riga. Nine further pogroms were instigated, in which thousands of helpless Jews were humiliated, beaten, tortured and murdered.[36] This proved only a temporary solution, however. The local anti-Semitic gangs were soon disarmed and incorporated into the *Einsatzgruppen* or the local German police organization. The systematic slaughter of Soviet Jews then began in earnest.

The mastermind of the killing campaign was an SS general, Erich von dem Bach-Zalewski. In the last two weeks of July 1941 he was given control of some 11,000 SS troops – almost four times the number originally assigned to the *Einsatzgruppen* – so that the pace of the killing could be stepped up. Around 6,000 ordinary police were put under Bach-Zalewski's authority. By the end of 1941 33,000 local auxiliaries had joined them, a total of over 50,000 men whose job was to kill not only Jews, but other race enemies such as gypsies and the mentally and physically disabled.[37] The overwhelming number of victims were Jews. They were rounded up in camps and ghettoes, transported to woods or fields, stripped of possessions and clothes, gunned down and buried in mass graves they themselves had been forced to dig. In rural areas Jewish settlements were simply destroyed, one after another. The villagers were herded into the open and mown down, and the buildings were razed to the ground. Within weeks reports informed Berlin that whole areas of the occupied East were now *judenrein*, free of Jews.

The most notorious crime of all was the massacre of 33,771 Jews in just two days in a ravine at Babi Yar, outside Kiev. Shortly after the German occupation, partisans blew up the Continental Hotel in the heart of the city, the headquarters of the German 6th Army. The authorities decided on 'reprisals'. On 26 September 1941 notices were posted in the city ordering all Jews to report within three days for resettlement. Over 30,000 appeared, most of whom assumed that the Germans meant what they said. They were marched to the outskirts of the city to the ravine, a one-mile-long anti-tank ditch that ran between sand dunes. There they were taken in small groups with their luggage to the edge of the ravine, at the bottom of which a pit some sixty yards long and eight feet deep had been dug. The victims were stripped and their valuables collected. They then stood on planks placed on the edge of the ravine, where they were shot in the back of the neck. Some were made to run the gauntlet and were shot at as they ran. The slaughter took two days, September 29 and 30. According to eyewitnesses thousands of Soviet prisoners and the captured commanders of the city were also murdered at Babi Yar. The pit was then covered with a shallow layer of quicklime and earth was spread over the scar.[38] Six months later small explosions could be heard in the ravine and columns of earth could be seen shooting into the air. Gases from the decomposing bodies had made the burial site physically unstable. Paul Blobel, whose *Einsatzkommando* had carried out the massacre in September, was ordered by Heydrich to exhume Babi Yar and other mass graves to dispose of the bodies more effectively. The dead were unceremoniously cremated to remove any trace of the crime.[39]

The massacre at Babi Yar was not the largest. At Odessa an estimated 75,000 to 80,000 Jews were killed by Germany's Romanian allies and the local *Einsatzgruppe*. In the Ukrainian city of Dnepr-petrovsk only 30,000 of the city's 100,000 Jews remained when the Germans arrived. They were ordered to 'resettle' and were marched eight abreast through the city, clutching their bundles of clothing. In a single operation in October 1941, 11,000 elderly Jews and children were machine-gunned over a two-day period, the noise clearly audible from the edge of the city. The shootings continued until March. In Kharhovsk, with a large and famous Jewish community, 20,000 Jews remained. They were not massacred all at once but were denied food or clothing. Thousands died of starvation and hypothermia. They were forced to inhabit a huge tractor plant. In March 1942 the survivors were taken to a nearby gully and shot in small groups. The tractor plant, piled high with Jews long dead, was burned to the ground in April.[40]

Most Soviet Jews who died at the hands of the German occupiers were murdered in the orgy of killing in the first nine months of the occupation, before the extermination camps had been built and brought into operation. Around four million of the five million Soviet Jews lived in the area. An estimated one and a half million fled before the German invaders. Of the rest the reports of the killing squads suggest that a total of 1,152,000 were killed by the end of December 1942. There were other deaths not inflicted by the SS or the German army. The German authorities found that the local populations were often so hostile to the Jews that they engaged in extermination and property seizures of their own. The *Einsatzgruppen* were inundated with denunciations from the local people of Jews, Communists or political 'undesirables'. In the Crimea, village leaders asked permission of the German authorities to liquidate the Jews themselves. In the massacre at Babi Yar, Ukrainians helped to round up Jews for the march to their deaths. The Germans came to rely on a network of informers who routinely betrayed partisans or Jews in return for bread or the protection of their village.[41] The murder of the Jews brought out the worst in both populations, Soviet and German, but it is unthinkable that atrocity on such a scale would ever have been perpetrated against the Jewish population without the encouragement of the invader. The descent into lawlessness was sparked by one thing: the German treatment of Soviet Jews as vermin, to be flushed out and exterminated. The ultimate responsibility lay with Hitler and the Nazi leadership, who chose in 1941 to make legitimate an unimaginable barbarism.

German rule in the Soviet Union did not go unopposed. For the thousands who collaborated there were thousands who resisted. The guerrilla war waged by partisan forces behind German lines became the symbol of defiance against fascism; the partisans became in Soviet propaganda the shock troops of the Motherland, heroes of the revolutionary struggle against the evil threat of Hitlerism. The historical reality was very different. Partisans were often reluctant fighters for the cause; their military impact was limited; their victims were to be found not only among the German occupiers but among the ordinary Soviet people, who came to fear their own side almost as much as they did the enemy.

Partisan warfare had a long and honourable history in Russia. Peasant bands had attacked Napoleon's great army during its catastrophic campaign in Russia in 1812. Guerrillas fought on the Bolshevik side in the civil war against the forces of the counter-revolution. Partisan warfare was part of the Russian military tradition. But during the 1930s the famous partisan leaders of the civil war were liquidated. Stalin regarded partisan war as a threat, something beyond the reach of the highly centralized and suspicious state apparatus. The existing partisan cadres and the supply dumps of food and weapons which had been set up in the 1930s to nourish and arm them were all closed down. When Germany invaded in 1941 there were no plans for partisan war.[42] The movement grew at first spontaneously and incoherently, a product of circumstances, not of revolutionary spirit.

Stalin soon laid aside his distrust of popular warfare. On 3 July 1941, in his first wartime appeal to the Soviet people, he summoned up the partisan struggle against the invader: 'Conditions must be made unbearable for the enemy and his collaborators; they must be pursued and annihilated wherever they are . . .'[43] The first irregular units were sent copies of an article penned by Lenin in 1906, 'Partisan Warfare', in which terrorism was presented as a legitimate instrument of class struggle. Every partisan had to swear an oath on entering the force promising utmost loyalty to the Soviet cause and swearing to 'work a terrible, merciless, and unrelenting revenge upon the enemy . . . Blood for blood! Death for death!' The partisan committed himself and his family to die rather than surrender; if 'through fear, weakness or personal depravity' the recruit broke his oath, he was asked to approve, in advance, his own death warrant at the hands of his own comrades.[44] More than any other Soviet citizens, partisans found themselves caught between the devil and the deep blue sea.

The first partisans could scarcely be regarded as volunteers. As

German forces swept with breathtaking speed through the villages and towns of the western Soviet Union, large numbers of soldiers and Communist Party officials found themselves left behind German lines. Stragglers from the disorganized, retreating army escaped into woods or marshland. Party members or Jews, fearful of what the Germans would do to them, followed them into the inaccessible terrain. They did not constitute a serious fighting force. They were poorly armed and supplied, usually relying on what could be captured from ambushed Germans. They were in the main desperately short of food; much 'partisan activity' in the early months consisted of little more than the seizure of food from peasants, who had little desire to give it up. This did not endear the partisans to the local population. During the later part of 1941 some 30,000 Party members and young Communists from the Komsomol were infiltrated from the east through the German lines or were parachuted to where partisan groups were thought to operate. The local population in the Ukraine had little love for their former Communist masters either, and many of them were betrayed to the German authorities. Efforts by the newcomers to bring some kind of discipline to the Red Army stragglers and the ragbag of civilian recruits produced fresh tensions. Many partisan units simply sought to survive rather than fight.[45]

Whatever the limitations of the early partisan movement the German authorities reacted savagely to the threat of popular revolutionary warfare. The army regarded civilian resisters and *francs-tireurs* as nothing more than terrorists to whom the laws of war applied not at all. Partisans and their accomplices – a category that was suitably elastic – deserved only immediate death. Savage reprisals were approved at the highest level. On July 23 Hitler directed that his forces 'spread the kind of terror' which would 'make the population lose all interest in insubordination'.[46] Throughout the summer, army and SS commanders vied with each other in approving the most barbarous solutions to the partisan threat. On September 16 Hitler's chief of staff finally announced the notorious hostage order: between fifty and one hundred should be executed for every German death. There was no place for leniency; the stick, not the carrot, was what the Russian understood. Human life in the Soviet state, he continued, counted for nothing. Hence, punishments of 'unusual severity' would be necessary in order to deter terrorism.[47] The stage was set for a war in which neither side would show any mercy, in which terror was met with indescribable terror, in which all conventional morality was banished. Partisans expected the harshest treatment; they were thus under no obligation to treat the enemy any differently.

The German anti-partisan offensive, which came under the general control of the same Bach-Zalewski who operated the liquidation squads, had in 1941 two strikingly contrary effects. On a military level the operations were reasonably successful. More than two-thirds of the occupied area had no partisan activity of any significance, and in the more favourable topography of the north-west, dense forests and inhospitable swamp, thousands of partisans were rounded up and shot or publicly hanged, with placards placed round their necks, as an example to the rest. Thousands more were murdered in reprisal for partisan attacks. In most cases villages held only women, children, the sick and the old when the Germans arrived; the able-bodied had fled or been evacuated when the Red Army retreated. The soldiers, often aided by local militia or helpful Cossacks, murdered a village's entire population in cold blood on the flimsiest pretext: ski tracks in the snow betrayed one hamlet; in another a lone sniper. The 707th Infantry Division in Belorussia in one month shot 10,431 'partisans' in reprisal for the loss of two of their own number.[48] Atrocity on this scale swiftly turned the local population against the Germans, whose campaign of enforced obedience was generally feared and resented more than were the partisans, whose activity had prompted the atrocities in the first place. By 1942 the Germans had done more to promote the partisan war than had any number of uplifting tracts from Moscow.

In the spring of 1942 Stalin at last gave formal structure to the partisan war. On May 30 a Central Staff for Partisan Warfare was established in Moscow under the Belorussian Party Secretary, Panteleymon Ponomarenko, who became chief of staff of all Soviet partisans. The guerrillas, whose life and fortunes were difficult to predict or control, found themselves the victims of a rigid centralization. The partisan groups were organized under regional and frontline staffs; local Red Army officers or Party officials became commanders; each partisan unit had an NKVD cell attached to it to keep the group in line. Something like military discipline was now imposed, although many bands displayed an anarchic refusal to conform. Elements deemed by the Party or the NKVD to be a danger to morale or simply too lazy or fearful to act energetically against the enemy were shot out of hand. Partisan groups were encouraged to see themselves as terrorist Stakhanovites. The Yalta Brigade was given specific work norms to fulfil: 'Each partisan must exterminate at least five fascists or traitors; [and] he must take part in at least three actions a month.' In Moscow 50,000 copies of a partisan guide were published, explaining in detail the behaviour of a Communist freedom fighter, from blowing up railway lines to surviving on bark and moss in subzero temperatures.[49]

The attempt to impose order on a fragmented and shadowy force had mixed results. Recruitment did increase, and because of the behaviour of the German authorities many of the new recruits were motivated by a genuine patriotism or by a deep and fiery hatred forged by what they had witnessed. But many of the newcomers were pushed into the partisan war because they had nowhere else to go. Jews fleeing from their exterminators provided one source. In Poland and Belorussia they fled from the ghettoes and small towns into the thick Belorussian forests. In the woods around the town of Nowogrodek the Bielski brothers assembled a large group of Jewish escapees, armed young men, women, children and older men. They were not partisans in the Soviet sense, since their main aim was to survive the German onslaught on the local Jewish population. Nonetheless, they named the group after Zhukov, already a legendary character. The group lived on what they could beg or confiscate from local peasants, and were constantly on the move to avoid German anti-partisan sweeps, eking out a precarious existence side by side with groups of Russian soldiers or Polish resistance bands hiding in the woods, neither of which were particularly sympathetic to Jews. The different armed bands stole from each other or murdered rival members. Occasionally group members were betrayed by local peasants, who were paid fifty marks by the German authorities for each treachery. Spies or traitors were routinely executed. The young leader of the Zhukov group,

Tuvya Bielski, succeeded in his aim of saving lives. Of the 1,200 in his group, only an estimated fifty died during the war. Bielski himself became a taxi driver in Palestine after 1945 before moving to the United States, where he died in 1987, age eighty-one.[50]

The partisan bands – or *otriad* – drew heavily on young men and women who fled from the threat of forced labour or escaped from captivity. Hundreds of Soviet prisoners of war escaped from the network of camps set up far behind the German front, with conditions so poor that two million prisoners died in the first six months of the war. Knowledge quickly spread of the fate that awaited prisoners. Rather than surrender, surrounded Red Army troops tried to hide in the hope of making later contact with local partisans. By the end of the year there were an estimated 300,000 partisans, but their willingness or ability to fight effectively varied greatly. They remained short of equipment; only one-tenth of the units had regular radio contact with the Soviet side of the front; and partisans depended critically on the shelter of forests, mountains or marshland. In the vast steppe areas of central and southern Ukraine there was almost nowhere to hide. The few partisan brigades sent into the region to drum up support were hunted down and annihilated.[51]

In August 1942 Stalin summoned partisan commanders to Moscow. He lectured them on the duties of the profession: energetic aggression, constant action, a vigilant anti-fascism.[52] It was easy to romanticize the life of the partisan, and Soviet propaganda did just that. Even Hollywood joined in. *The North Star*, screened in 1943, was pure invention, full of heroic stereotypes that would hardly have been out of place in *Pravda*. The real partisans faced a grim existence. They lived in constant dread of discovery; spies and informers could be bought by the German authorities for very little. They fought with poor weapons against an enemy who mobilized Panzer divisions and bomber fleets in the great anti-partisan sweeps, Operation Munich and Operation Cottbus. They had little access to medical supplies, and hundreds of wounded partisans died in caves and forests, lacking even basics like bandages. In parts of Belorussia or around Smolensk or Briansk, the partisans came to control large areas, where they re-established a primitive form of Communist authority, but they

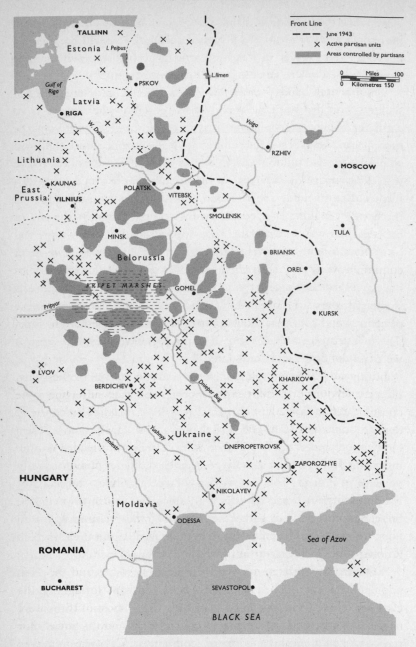

Map 4 Main Partisan Areas in the German-Occupied Soviet Union, Summer 1943

were loath to risk their local power by attacking the enemy. Instead they turned their guns on local traitors, leaders who had been forced to collaborate with the Germans, peasants who had too readily handed over food to the enemy or worked for German favours.

In some areas partisan rule was welcomed, and partisans were fed and sheltered. But until the victory of Stalingrad, when there appeared a greater likelihood of Soviet victory, relations between partisans and their hosts were strained. The diary of a young partisan stationed near Smolensk early in 1942 betrays the roots of that tension: 'Drove to Nekasterek to fetch bread – without success. We shot a traitor. In the evening I went to do the same to his wife. We are sorry that she leaves three children behind. But war is war!!!' Five days earlier, he had shot down three Germans in cold blood in an ambush: 'captured a cigarette lighter, a gold ring, a fountain pen, two pipes, tobacco, a comb.' A week later, 'a rich loot captured'.[53] Partisans sometimes walked a thin line between military hero and gangster. Partisan actions invariably were followed by reprisals. If some were driven to join the partisans by the sight of German atrocities, others resented the risks that the partisan presence imposed on them. Increasingly the partisans began to conscript local men and women into their bands by force. Peasants had little choice. If they resisted they were shot by their own side; if they joined the partisans they were likely to suffer the same fate at the hands of the Germans. They had no military training. Partisan units with large numbers of forced conscripts – and by 1943 they constituted from 40 to 60 per cent of most brigades – took exceptionally high casualties and were conspicuously more inept than units with a cadre of experienced guerrillas.[54] They stare out of hundreds of photographs, gaunt, sullen men, poorly dressed and scarcely armed, fighting for a system that a decade before had forced them into collective farms with the same grim resolution with which it now propelled them into involuntary terrorism.

Nowhere was the tension between Soviet partisans and the local population as marked or as dangerous as it was throughout the Ukraine. There were partisans in the region, but most of them were nationalist guerrillas, fighting both the Germans and the Soviets for the right to an independent Ukraine. The battle lines of the area were pure anarchy. There were nationalists under the hetman Bulba-Boravets who fought on the side of the Germans in 1941, against them in 1942, under the designation Ukrainian Insurgent Army, then in 1943 amalgamated with the Ukrainian Nationalist Organization led by Stepan Bandera, whose estimated 300,000 supporters fought both Germans and Russians. The notorious 'Bandera boys' punished Ukrainians who helped either side.[55] This nationalist militia was, by 1943, strong enough to turn back attempts by the Soviet partisans to penetrate the Ukraine and inflict damage on German communications. Soviet partisans found almost no support among the Ukrainian villagers, whose memories were long enough to recall the famine and the terror. In 1943 the German authorities calculated that 60 per cent of the area of north-western Ukraine was under the control of nationalist partisans. The Ukrainian nationalist force was too large for the Germans to defeat, but they held on to the main lines of communication, after abandoning the forests and mountains. In November 1943 Bandera was confident enough to stage a Conference of the Enslaved Nations of Eastern Europe and Asia, which brought together Tatars, Georgians, Azerbaijanis, Poles, Slovaks, Czechs and Cossacks to draw up a common programme for the struggle against Germany and the Soviet Union. The struggle continued well after the end of the war against the Communist successors to the retreating German army.[56]

By 1943 the partisan movement in the rest of the occupied area had come of age. The growing confidence of the Red Army and the greater availability of military supplies boosted the partisan organization. The units came to resemble the regular army. Tanks, heavy artillery, even aircraft were made available. A total of 22,000 trained military experts were sent into the partisan regions, three-quarters of them demolition experts, 8 per cent of them radio operators. In the spring of 1943 Stalin ordered the Rail Campaign, a co-ordinated attempt to disrupt communications in the German rear. Thousands of explosions forced desperate measures from the German authorities, but the rail network was kept going despite the constant threat of disruption.

The life of Germans caught in the vast expanses of the Russian front was bleak. The roads were no longer safe. Vehicles were forced to move in convoys, with heavy machine-guns mounted on trucks. All main routes were patrolled regularly. Nevertheless the partisans took a steady toll. Lines of vehicles were blocked by simple barricades thrown across the roads at blind corners. Trees were chopped down and laid behind the last truck, while a hail of bullets was pumped into the hapless convoy. Partisans were credited with the destruction of 65,000 vehicles and 12,000 bridges. In one such ambush the SA leader Viktor Lutze was killed. In Minsk the commissar of Belorussia, Wilhelm Kube, a man whose savage reputation made him a prime target, was blown up by a timebomb laid under his bed by a partisan maid. Neither German soldiers, nor the thousands of Soviet citizens who worked for the new masters, were safe. An insidious demoralization was evident among the occupation troops. Repression was tempered in some areas by attempts to buy local peace from the partisans or to negotiate a truce, but for many isolated, frightened, perhaps guilty German soldiers vicious reprisal remained the refrain. Hundreds of ruined villages and a death toll that passed an estimated one million bore terrible testimony to the price paid for Hitler's 'kind of terror'.[57]

In 1944 the partisan war was wound up. As the Red Army swept through the last areas of occupation, partisan units, with their colourful names, 'Death to the Fascist' or 'The People's Avengers', were absorbed into the regular army. One-fifth were rejected as unfit. Others were carefully scrutinized by the NKVD units which followed in the wake of the conquering armies. Membership in the partisans did not bring immunity from the security habits of the regime. All Ukrainian partisans, even Communists, were distrusted as a matter of course. The arrival of the Red Army opened up old wounds and exposed new ones. The tortured history of collaboration, betrayal and resistance left hundreds of thousands dead beside the millions slaughtered by the invader in the name of racial war. The urge for revenge is easy to understand. The journalist Alexander Werth found himself talking in 1944 to a middle-aged Russian partisan who had been appointed mayor of the Ukrainian town of Uman. Short, with pale skin and dark hair brushed back, Mayor Zakharov explained to his guest the rigours of partisan life. He had been able to recruit only a small group, which had hidden in the Vinnitsa forest. Poorly armed, they took consistently high casualties. He had been wounded in July 1941, and captured by the Germans; escaping, he ended up with partisans outside Uman. He was arrested by the Gestapo in 1942, who savagely tortured and beat him and broke his back. He disappeared back into the forest, where the partisans knew him only as 'Uncle Mitya'; here he masterminded attacks on railway lines, while his force was harassed by Cossacks in German pay. 'It was a harsh and grim life,' he told Werth. 'They were merciless and so were we. And we shall be merciless with the traitors now.'[58]

Across a vast no-man's-land from the Baltic states in the north to the shores of the Black Sea in the south was played out a human tragedy that still defies imagination. The population of Balts, Belorussians, Ukrainians and Jews was caught up in a drama not of their making. Why did some choose to collaborate and some to resist? There is no simple answer. Most of those caught in the middle had little choice but were forced to one side or the other by fear, opportunism or accident. Millions had no choice at all, victims of an ideology of discrimination and destruction. Some collaborators actively chose the German side because of their hatred of Communism. A large part of the German-conquered area had been ruled by the Soviet Union for only a matter of months. There was no fund here of Russian patriotism or socialist commitment. No doubt the German invaders could have made more of such anti-Soviet sentiments than they did, but millions of nationalists continued to fight against the Soviet side even when the true nature of German imperialism became clear.

Resistance is no easier to understand. It carried exceptional risks; partisans were the kamikazes of the Soviet war effort. Some who joined did so from fear of what would happen to them when, or if, the Soviet system returned. Others joined from honest conviction. Mayor Zakharov expressed his own choice in simple terms: 'working for the good of his country'.[59] It is easy to be sceptical about the political idealism of those who fought for a system which imposed such heavy burdens on its own people, but it should not be dismissed out of hand. An uncomplicated patriotism is evident in the behaviour and language of many partisans, which we have no reason to disregard.

The German invaders were easy to hate. Stalin encouraged the partisans to see the war in ideological terms; resistance was an expression of commitment to the Soviet cause and the forces of socialist progress. This perception transformed the campaign of resistance into a revolutionary war, a conflict with deep echoes of the civil war, whose confused battle-lines the partisan struggle closely resembled, a war more in tune with the theory of proletarian struggle that permeated military thinking in the Soviet Union in the 1920s and 1930s. The partisan movement was also important to the Soviet leadership because it kept the occupied area in touch with Moscow, and maintained a residual Communist apparatus. Despite the three years of German occupation, the Party and the Soviet state held on to the bare threads of a system that might otherwise have collapsed entirely.

6

The Cauldron Boils:
Stalingrad, 1942–43

*At the bottom of the trenches there lay frozen green Germans
and frozen grey Russians and frozen fragments of human shapes,
and there were helmets, Russian and German, lying among the
brick debris . . . How anyone could have survived was hard to
imagine. But now everything was silent in this fossilized hell, as
though a raving lunatic had suddenly died of heart failure.*

Alexander Werth, in Stalingrad, February 1943

When the spring thaw in 1942 turned the battleground into mud
the two sides paused to draw breath after eight months of almost
continuous, draining conflict. Though Moscow and Leningrad had
both been saved from the annihilating fate intended for them by Hitler,
the Soviet Union found itself in a position of acute weakness. In the
terrible battles of attrition more than 3 million soldiers had been
captured and 3.1 million killed.[1] The tank and air forces which had
been available in June 1941 were severely depleted, and replacements
were slow to arrive. Soviet economic strength was a fraction of what
it had been the previous year. German forces now occupied the Soviet
bread-basket, the rich grainlands of the Ukraine; in 1942 bread and
meat supplies were halved for the 130 million people living in the
unconquered territories. One-third of the rail network was behind
enemy lines. Soviet heavy industrial production – coal, steel and iron
ore – was cut by three-quarters with the loss of the Donbas industrial
region. The materials vital to the production of modern weapons –
aluminium, copper, manganese – fell by two-thirds or more. Millions
of skilled workers were killed or captured. Against an enemy with

Table 1 Soviet and German wartime production 1941–45

A: MILITARY OUTPUT

		1941	1942	1943	1944	1945
Aircraft	USSR	15,735	25,436	34,900	40,300	20,900
	Germany	11,776	15,409	28,807	39,807	7,540
Tanks*	USSR	6,590	24,446	24,089	28,963	15,400
	Germany	5,200	9,300	19,800	27,300	——
Artillery	USSR**	42,300	127,000	130,000	122,400	62,000
	(over 76mm)		49,100	48,400	56,100	28,600
	Germany**	7,000	12,000	27,000	41,000	——

* figure for USSR includes self-propelled guns. German figure includes self-propelled guns for 1943 and 1944.
** artillery pieces of all calibres for USSR (separate figures for pieces over 76 mm). German figure for pieces over 37 mm.

B: HEAVY INDUSTRY
(m. tonnes)

		1941	1942	1943	1944	1945
Coal	USSR	151.4	75.5	93.1	121.5	149.3
	Germany	315.5	317.9	340.4	347.6	——
Steel	USSR	17.9	8.1	8.5	10.9	12.3
	Germany	28.2	28.7	30.6	25.8	——
Aluminium	USSR	——	51.7	62.3	82.7	86.3
	Germany	233.6	264.0	250.0	245.3	——
Oil	USSR	33.0	22.0	18.0	18.2	19.4
	Germany*	5.7	6.6	7.6	5.5	1.3

* synthetic oil production and natural crude oil production and imports.

four times more industrial capacity at its disposal Soviet prospects were bleak indeed.[2]

The most remarkable part of the story of Russia's war lies here, in the revival of Soviet fortunes from a point of near collapse. Few would have gambled on a Soviet victory, faced with the cold statistics of Soviet decline. The Soviet war effort began to resemble the ramshackle structure of the Tsarist war twenty-five years before, which ushered in the Revolution. There was worse to come. In April 1942, confident that German forces on the southern end of the front were weaker than the armies facing Moscow and Leningrad, Stalin ordered an offensive to retake the city of Kharkov, a vital rail junction for the German front. Warned by their intelligence service, German forces drew the Soviet armies into a well-prepared trap. The attack was launched on May 12, with Soviet units poorly prepared and, because of a late thaw, some not even in place. Ten days later German forces encircled them, capturing the equivalent of three Soviet armies. The disaster at Kharkov was a humiliating failure for Stalin's personal leadership. Further south a Soviet attempt to drive German forces out of the Crimea met with a similarly tragic conclusion. The offensive was repulsed at great cost, with three more Soviet armies, the 44th, 47th and 51st, driven into the sea from the Kerch Peninsula, where German forces took savage reprisals against the helpless civilian population. During June the heavily fortified city of Sevastopol, perched on the edge of the Black Sea, was slowly reduced to rubble by systematic German air and artillery bombardment, until it surrendered on July 4. Its conqueror, General Erich von Manstein, was presented with a Field Marshal's baton for his efforts.

The scene was set for a repeat of the disasters of 1941. Hitler was determined to complete during the summer of 1942 the job that had eluded him the year before. His own commanders wanted to complete the seizure of Moscow at the centre of the front, for they believed that the psychological impact of the loss of the Soviet capital, allied to the destruction of the main weight of the Red Army, would bring a quick end to the war. Hitler disagreed. He was dreaming of greater things. Victories in North Africa, which brought Field Marshal Erwin Rommel to within striking distance of the Suez Canal and the vast oil reserves of the Middle East, and Japanese victories in the Far East against American and British Empire forces made him much more ambitious. His aim was to drive Soviet forces from the southern steppes and the Caucasus region, so that Axis forces could link up in the Middle East and also make a final annihilating sweep northward behind the Soviet lines to Moscow and the Urals. Throughout the vast southern region was fresh mineral wealth, above all oil, the key to Germany's final apocalyptic conflict with the resource-rich West. On 5 April 1942 Hitler issued Directive Number 41; its aim was 'to wipe out the entire defence potential remaining to the Soviets'.[3]

The plan, code-named Operation Blue, was to sweep east to Stalingrad and south to the high mountain passes of the Caucasus, then on to Astrakhan and Grozny on the Caspian Sea. The Soviet Union would then be cut off from her own supplies of oil, and her war effort would wither on the vine. The preparation was veiled in absolute secrecy, but the British passed on details of the forthcoming offensive culled from intercepted German signals. Stalin was no more receptive to these warnings than he had been to the warnings about Barbarossa. When on June 19 a light plane crashed behind Soviet lines carrying the precise order of battle for the German operation, Stalin thought it could only be a deliberate and clumsy attempt at disinformation.[4] Habitually suspicious, Stalin preferred to rely on his own intuition, even though it had served him so poorly over the past year. He insisted that the main weight of German attack would be brought to bear on Moscow. This was not an irrational expectation; it was what German generals wanted to do, and many of Stalin's own military leaders concurred with their chief. The irony was that only a year before Stalin had insisted on strengthening the south in the mistaken belief that Hitler wanted oil and grain more than he wanted Moscow; now the south was weaker, and the centre strong.

When the blow finally fell on 28 June 1942 Soviet forces were as ill-prepared to meet it as they had been the previous June. German forces punched forward behind a shield of aircraft and tanks, supported on their flanks by more weakly armed, and less fanatical, allies – Hungarians, Italians and Romanians. By July 9, the northernmost German armies on the southern front reached the River Don opposite

Voronezh. They then swung south to join up with armies moving from the Crimean area. Soviet resistance crumbled. Small groups of stragglers, cut off from their commanders, moved eastward, followed by a train of desperate refugees. Many were simply swallowed up by the vast steppeland, easy prey to the Axis troops who followed in the wake of the fast-moving tank columns. Others struggled to construct makeshift defensive lines, until these, too, melted away. On July 23 Rostov-on-Don, at the mouth of the great river, was abandoned by the panicking soldiers. A few NKVD troops fought to the death before the city fell into German hands. There was no repeat of the frantic defence of Soviet cities witnessed the year before. The demoralization was infectious. By the end of July Hitler was so confident of another victory that he divided his forces in half: von Kleist took the 1st Panzer Army with Army Group A to conquer the Caucasian oil fields; von Weichs's Army Group B moved eastward across the Don with orders to take the city of Stalingrad on the Volga, more than 1,500 miles from Berlin.

The new wave of failures could not be hidden from the Soviet people. In Moscow observers felt a fresh shudder of panic through the population. The news that Rostov had fallen with barely a fight after the terrible sacrifices in Moscow and Leningrad produced feelings of anger and dismay. In the headlong retreat army discipline began to break down. Units abandoned their guns and equipment. Soldiers wounded themselves rather than face the German giant. The authority of the officers and military commissars threatened to disappear. On July 28 Stalin moved to stop the collapse. He issued Order 227, *Ne Shagu Nazad!* – 'Not a Step Back!' The publication of the order came at a time of acute crisis. Stalin told the armed forces that retreat must end: 'Each position, each metre of Soviet territory must be stubbornly defended, to the last drop of blood. We must cling to every inch of Soviet soil and defend it to the end!'[5]

After the war it was forbidden to publish any details about Order Number 227, though it had been distributed to all fighting units. Not until 1988 was its existence first revealed to the Soviet public. The order did not fit with the post-war image of Soviet heroism and self-sacrifice, for it not only called for a fight to the death, but promised

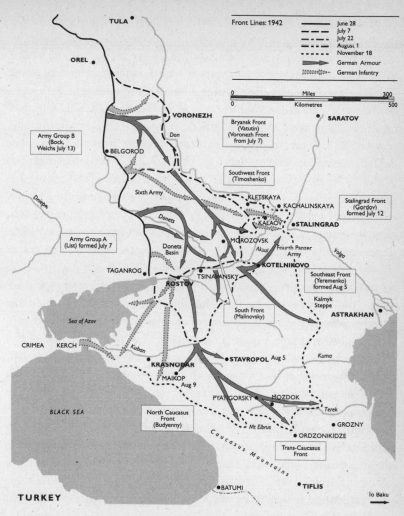

 OREL

Front Lines: 1942
——————	June 28
– – – –	July 7
–·–·–·	July 22
– ·· – ··	August 1
········	November 18
➤	German Armour
▸▸▸▸▸▸	German Infantry

VORONEZH
SARATOV

Bryansk Front
(Vatutin)
(Voronezh Front
from July 7)

Army Group B
(Bock,
Weichs July 13)

BELGOROD

Don

Southwest Front
(Timoshenko)

0 _____ Miles _____ 300
0 _____ Kilometres _____ 500

Sixth Army

Dnieper

KLETSKAYA
KACHALINSKAYA

Stalingrad Front
(Gordov)
formed July 12

KALACV
STALINGRAD

Donets

Army Group A
(List) formed July 7

MOROZOVSK

Donets
Basin

Aksai
Fourth Panzer
Army

Volga

TAGANROG

TSINAMANSKY

KOTELNIKOVO

ROSTOV

Southeast Front
(Yeremenko)
formed Aug 5

South Front
(Malinovsky)

Kalmyk
Steppe

ASTRAKHAN

Sea of Azov

CRIMEA   KERCH

Kuban

KRASNODAR
STAVROPOL Aug 5

Kuma

MAIKOP
Aug 9

PYATIGORSKY   MOZDOK

Terek

BLACK SEA

North Caucasus
Front
(Budyenny)

Mt Elbrus

GROZNY

ORDZONIKIDZE

Caucasus Mountains

Trans-Caucasus
Front

TURKEY

BATUMI   TIFLIS

To Baku ➤

Map 5   Operation Blue: The German Southern Offensive, June–
November 1942

the severest punishments for those who flinched. Anyone caught within the net of the order, the 'panickers' and 'cowards', were liable to summary execution or service in *shtrafbaty*, penal battalions. There were penal units for senior officers who shirked their duty and separate units for junior officers and privates, modelled, according to the order, on German practice during the winter fighting in 1941. Stalin also authorized so-called 'blocking units' (*otryadi zagrazhdeniye*) from the regular Red Army troops, whose task was to prevent panic and desertion and keep soldiers fighting. They were supposed to co-operate with the thousands of NKVD troops who had been performing the same task without a specific order. In practice these new units found themselves carrying our menial tasks or guard duty in the rear when they were needed desperately at the front. On October 29 they were cancelled by a fresh order. The NKVD troops continued to track down anyone accused of slacking or cowardice. Guilt did not need to be clear. The practices of the pre-war terror were reimposed to keep Soviet soldiers fighting.[6] The slightest infringement could be interpreted as sabotage; desertion was punishable by a death sentence, meted out by hundreds of summary courts-martial. Over the course of the war 442,000 were forced to serve in penal battalions; a further 436,000 were sentenced to periods of imprisonment. How many died at the hands of their own side, either shot, or lost in the suicidal missions assigned to penal battalions, may never be known with any certainty. Latest Russian estimates put the figure as high as 158,000 sentenced to be shot during the war.[7] The penal battalions were given the most dangerous work. They were sent ahead through minefields or on air attacks into the teeth of German defences. They could be reinstated only if they were wounded. 'Atoned with his own blood' was added to their reports.

It is easy to argue that from the summer of 1942 the Soviet army fought because it was forced to fight. Yet the impact of Order Number 227 can be exaggerated. It was aimed primarily at officers and political commissars, rather than the rank and file, which had always been subject to very harsh discipline. The order also applied only to un-authorized retreats, not to retreats in general. No doubt legal niceties did not play a great part with the NKVD interrogators, but it was not an order that was applied entirely without discrimination. There was at the time a sense that desperate circumstances called for desperate measures. One soldier later recalled his reaction to 'Not a Step Back!': 'Not the letter, but the spirit and content of the order made possible the moral, psychological and spiritual breakthrough in the hearts and minds of those to whom it was read . . .'[8] Nor should it be forgotten that there was indiscipline and demoralization in the Red Army, which grew in volume as Soviet military incompetence exposed soldiers to unbearable pressures. Stalin was not tilting this time at counter-revolutionary phantoms, but at real soldiers plunged into a nightmare of defeat and uncertainty.

The revelations of terror in the armed forces focus on an evident historical truth, but they also distort our view of the Soviet war effort. Not every soldier stood with a gun to his back; not every instance of self-sacrifice and courageous defiance was a product of coercion or fear. To believe this diminishes the exceptional heroism of thousands of ordinary Soviet men and women, whose voluntary commitment to the Soviet cause can scarcely be in doubt. In the summer and autumn of 1942 Soviet people were animated by more than fear of the NKVD. Stalin called on his people to mobilize the resources of an entire society, to turn the Soviet Union into a single 'war camp'. Soviet propaganda prepared to turn the war into a crusade to save not just the Soviet system, but Mother Russia herself. The war became not simply a defence of Communism, about which many Russians felt uneasy, but a patriotic struggle against a feared and hated enemy.

The mobilization of popular Russian patriotism was forced by circumstances. By 1942 it was evident that the Communist Party alone could not raise the energies of the people for a struggle of this depth and intensity. The war with Germany was not like the war against the kulaks, or the war for greater production in the 1930s, although the almost continuous state of popular mobilization which these campaigns produced in some ways prepared the population to respond to emergency and improvisation. During 1942 the war was presented as a war to save historic Russia, a nationalist war of revenge against a monstrous, almost mythical enemy. The words 'Soviet Union' and 'Communism' appeared less and less frequently in official publications.

The words 'Russia' and 'Motherland' took their place. The 'Internationale', the anthem of the international socialist movement played on state occasions, was replaced with a new national anthem.[9] The habits of military egalitarianism ingrained in the Red Army were swept aside. New medals were struck commemorating the military heroes of Russia's past; the Tsarist Nevsky Order was revived but could be won only by officers. Aleksandr Nevsky, the Muscovite prince who drove back the Teutonic Knights in the thirteenth century, was a singularly apt parallel.[10] In 1938 Stalin had ordered Sergei Eisenstein to produce a film on Nevsky. He interfered with the script to make the message clear about the German threat (and the virtues of authoritarianism). In 1939 the film was withdrawn following the Nazi-Soviet pact, but in 1942 it again became essential viewing.[11]

The mobilization of tradition did not stop with past heroes. During 1942 the Russian Orthodox Church, persecuted ceaselessly by an atheistic regime, was suddenly rehabilitated. For years Russian Christians were forced to live a subterranean existence like the Christians of the ancient world. Churches and monasteries were closed down and their communities disbanded. Before the Revolution there were 50,000 priests and 163 bishops in the Russian Church. By 1941 there were around one hundred priests and only seven bishops.[12] Their lives were closely monitored by the regime. Thousands of practising Christians received communion in secret masses, but the risks they ran were enormous. With the outbreak of war the attitude of the regime began to change. Metropolitan Sergei, head of the Church, appealed to the faithful on the very day of the German invasion to do everything to bring about victory. He published no fewer than twenty-three epistles in the next two years, calling on his flock to fight for the godless state they lived in. Stalin, the ex-seminarian, may never have entirely lost his faith. He told the British ambassador that, in his own way, 'he too believed in God'. The word began to appear in *Pravda* with a capital letter.[13]

Stalin's motives were not primarily spiritual. Religion was allowed to flourish again because it was what ordinary Russians wanted. Even Hitler, who was utterly irreligious, mobilized the Orthodox Church in the conquered areas, where he hoped it would dull the senses of the local population and make German rule more tolerable. When the puppet bishops became too independent-minded they were dispensed with. Metropolitan Sergei Voskrensky of Riga was first recruited by the Germans to preach for a German victory, but ended up being murdered in 1944 by his patrons on the road between Riga and Vilnius.[14] Stalin, like Hitler, appreciated what religion could do. He permitted the reopening of churches and of a number of seminaries. Money was made available to revive church ritual. In 1943 he finally agreed to the appointment of a Patriarch of the Church, the supreme authority, an office left empty since 1926. The Church authorities responded by raising money from the faithful to fund a Soviet armoured column. Priests and bishops exhorted their congregations to observe the faith, God's and Stalin's. The churches soon had larger congregations than they could cope with. Observers in Moscow found crowds standing outside the cathedrals waiting to get in. The end result was a curious blend of traditional Christianity and socialist religiosity. One cold day at a Moscow railway station an elderly Siberian off to the front was observed listening intently to a voice over the loudspeaker, a voice 'low and muffled, yet curiously penetrating'. On hearing the voice he made the sign of the cross, and cried out, 'Stalin!'[15]

The sentiments aroused by popular patriotism in 1942 proved anything but Christian. Russian society was roused to a fever pitch of hatred and vengeance. Hating the Germans and everything German became the central message of the propaganda machine. Soldiers and citizens were encouraged to give way to a blind patriotic rage. The word 'German' or 'fascist' assumed a satanic dimension. 'If you don't want to give away/ all that which you call your country,' wrote the poet Konstantin Simonov, 'then kill a German, kill a German/ every time you see one.'[16] The writer Ilya Ehrenburg, a former anti-Bolshevik who returned from exile in Paris to be rehabilitated by Stalin in 1939, was recruited to fan the flames. In August 1942 he wrote in the army journal *Red Star*:

Now we know. The Germans are not human. Now the word 'German' has become the most terrible swear word. Let us not speak. Let us not be indignant. Let us kill. If you do not kill the German, he will kill you . . . If you have killed one German, kill another. There is nothing jollier than German corpses.[17]

Ehrenburg's own hatred was genuine enough: he had visited areas liberated during the Moscow counter-offensive. The hatred of thousands of other ordinary Russians was not simply manufactured by the state but was born of the sufferings inflicted in a year of defeats. The summer of hate orchestrated in 1942 drew on an incoherent revulsion against the enemy and gave it force and focus, but the patriotism and the grim thirst for revenge had their own source in the Soviet people. The writer Vyacheslav Kondratyev, a veteran of the conflict and a bitter critic of the post-war sanctification of the Soviet war effort, believed that the revival of morale had little to do with Stalin and the Party: 'It was a pure burst of love for our fatherland. That sacrificial incandescence and readiness to give one's life for it are unforgettable. Nothing like it ever happened again.'[18]

In the autumn of 1942 people armed themselves spiritually for the struggle. The summer panic in Moscow appeared to subside. Stalin placed himself at the head of a patriotic rallying unthinkable a few years before. Stalingrad was now to play the role played out by Moscow a year earlier. Its survival became not just a military and economic necessity: the city came to symbolize the new spirit of defiant nationalism conjured up after the disaster at Rostov. The city bore Stalin's name, a gift from grateful fellow-Communists in 1925 in memory of Stalin's alleged role during the civil war in saving the town, then called Tsaritsyn, from counter-revolutionary armies.[19] Within the space of a dozen years the sleepy Volga port was transformed into a sprawling industrial city, populated by giant engineering plants turning out machine tools and tractors – the Red October Factory, the Barricades Works, the tractor plant. A new urban landscape of tall apartment buildings, dull Party offices and workers' housing stretched for forty miles along the riverbank. Along the Volga flowed oil and food from the Caucasus to feed the industrial cities of the north. With the loss of the Ukraine, these southern resources were vital to the Soviet war effort. The rest of Russia could have continued to fight after the loss of Stalingrad and the south, but prospects of victory would have been remote. Both sides knew this. Defender and attacker came to see the struggle for Stalingrad as decisive.

In July the odds were heavily in Germany's favour. Stalin still refused to see the south as the major battleground for 1942 and kept the bulk of Soviet forces farther to the north. The balance on the southern front strongly favoured the attacker: 250,000 troops of Germany and her allies against 187,000, 740 tanks against 360, 1,200 aircraft against 330.[20] Army Group B moved remorselessly forward across the Don River towards Stalingrad. Before them stretched an endless steppe. 'It was,' recalled a German survivor, 'easily the most desolate and mournful region of the East that came before my eyes. A barren, naked, lifeless steppe, without a bush, without a tree, for miles without a village.'[21] Across the bleak terrain drove the German 6th Army, commanded by General Friedrich Paulus. Resistance melted in front of him. Desperate Soviet counter-attacks in the last two weeks of July did little to slow up the German advance and proved costly in men and tanks. Soviet commandeers began to lose control over the battle as communications broke down. Late in July Stalin sacked Marshal Timoshenko, who was struggling to create a coherent defensive line in front of Stalingrad, and appointed General Gordov as commander of the Stalingrad Front. On July 23 6th Army encountered Gordov's two armies, the 62nd and the 64th, along the Chir River, eighty miles from Stalingrad. These two Soviet armies bore the brunt of the savage battle for the next four months.

Against heavily armed mobile forces Gordov's troops could do little. Bleak though it was, the dry steppe country suited German commanders. The Red Army was pushed back towards Stalingrad day by day. By August 19 Paulus was ready to mount his first assault on the city, supported now by the 4th Panzer Army, which had been detached from Army Group A in the Caucasus. The attack almost produced disaster. On August 23 German forces reached the Volga north of Stalingrad and created a salient five miles wide along the riverbank. The same day German units reached the outskirts of the city. The German air force launched a 600-bomber attack on the city, creating a blazing inferno across the centre and killing, according to

Soviet estimates, 40,000 of the inhabitants, who had been ordered to stay in the city rather than clog the military supply lines.[22] At Hitler's headquarters in the Ukraine, where his southern strategy had aroused bitter criticisms from senior generals, there was, according to one eyewitness, an 'exultant mood'. Paulus confidently expected to seize the city and cut the Volga route in a matter of days.[23]

Once again Stalin stared calamity in the face. This time, Zhukov recalled, Stalin did not lay the blame on his subordinates. The strong implication was that, at last, he blamed himself for all the shortcomings of the first year of war. On August 27 Zhukov was summoned to Moscow from his command of the Western Front defending the capital. Late that evening he arrived at the Kremlin, where Stalin was discussing the crisis with the State Defence Committee. Stalin's study was a dimly lit room, dominated by a large map table. At one end of the room stood a large globe. On the walls hung pictures, not of the leaders of world revolution, but of Russian military heroes. Stalin never beat about the bush. He told Zhukov that he must travel to Stalingrad himself and try to rescue the situation. He then announced that Zhukov was to be made Deputy Supreme Commander to Stalin. Zhukov's reply is not recorded. He accepted the new post, drank tea with Stalin and left to ascertain the facts.[24]

Zhukov responded with his usual energy. On August 29 he flew south to the banks of the Volga. At the headquarters of the Stalingrad Front he met Stalin's new chief of staff, Aleksandr Vasilevsky, who had replaced the despondent Shaposhnikov in July. The two men set about stabilizing the front, but they were faced with critical shortages of men and munitions. Three reserve units released by Stalin from the rear were to be used to try to break the 6th Army's grip on the Volga north of Stalingrad. The attack, launched on September 5, achieved little in the face of furious German air attacks. Stalin continued to hound his new deputy to find some way of plugging the gap. On September 12 Zhukov flew back to Moscow to report in person. Accompanied by Vasilevsky, he told Stalin that with existing forces the front could not be held. Reserves were needed. While Stalin stared grimly at the maps spread out before him, Zhukov and Vasilevsky muttered to each other about the need to find 'another solution'. Stalin abruptly looked up. 'What "other solution"?' he asked. He sent both men away with orders to return the following day with a clear picture of what needed to be done to save Stalingrad.[25]

When Stalin met them on September 13 he was livid with rage at his British ally for arguing over military aid. 'Tens, hundreds of thousands of Soviet people are giving their lives in the struggle against fascism, and Churchill is haggling over twenty Hurricanes.'[26] It was over a year since Britain and the United States had pledged to send the Soviet Union the military and economic aid necessary to keep the Soviet front from collapsing. Though there was popular hostility in both Western states to co-operation with Communism, the alternative of a German victory in the East was regarded as even less palatable, since it would leave Britain at the mercy of a military giant and the United States with little realistic prospect of fighting a major war 3,000 miles distant from its shores. Yet for all the importance attached to Soviet resistance, neither Western power contributed enough during 1942 to ensure Soviet survival. Churchill candidly told the Soviet ambassador, Ivan Maisky, that all Britain could offer was 'a drop in the ocean'. The American Lend-Lease aid programme, begun in March 1941 for the British Empire and extended to cover the Soviet Union in August that year, provided $5.8 billion of goods for Britain by the end of 1942 but only $1.4 billion for the Soviet Union.[27] Throughout the year Stalin had pressed Britain and the United States to provide direct assistance by opening a 'second front' in Europe to divert German forces away from the Eastern campaign. The war with Japan and the immature state of American rearmament made it difficult for the West to do more. The British army was hard pressed to keep a small Italian-German force from conquering Egypt, and the Royal Navy was fighting the Battle of the Atlantic, on which the future of any Western war effort depended. The only direct pressure Britain applied came from a long-range bombing offensive against Germany's western industrial cities, which because of its modest scale had achieved only meagre results by the end of 1942.

In July 1942 Churchill suggested to Stalin that a face-to-face meeting between them might help to smooth the path of inter-allied coalition. A meeting was arranged for early August. Stalin had scant respect for the British, whom he regarded as opportunists and cowards. 'We must be guarded in relations with the English,' he had told Maisky a year earlier. 'They want, it seems to me, our weakening.' He was blunt and ungracious when he met Churchill in an awkward confrontation on August 12. Churchill seemed ill at ease, fidgety; Stalin gazed impassively at his guest, insultingly restrained. He outlined the grim news from the south and assured his guest that he was 'determined to hold Stalingrad'.[28] Churchill then had the unhappy responsibility of telling Stalin that no 'second front' could be opened in 1942. Stalin was visibly angered. He was patronizing and insulting about British resolve and competence, to an extent that reduced his guest to a scarcely suppressed fury. After the first meetings Churchill was all for returning home rather than face further humiliation at the hands of a man he cursed as a 'brigand'. But he stayed on, and a greater cordiality was established. Churchill revealed details of planned Allied landings in North Africa – Operation Torch – and for the bombing of Germany, which pleased Stalin, though nothing could assuage Stalin's evident disappointment that his allies could not relieve the pressure on Stalingrad by attacking in force in the west. That night, in the Catherine Hall of the Kremlin Palace, Stalin entertained his guest at another lavish state banquet. As they sat drinking coffee after the meal, Churchill asked Stalin if he could forgive his consistent hostility to the Soviet system. Stalin could not bring himself to say yes. His eyes narrowed, and he stared silently at Churchill before replying: 'It's for God to forgive – not me. In the end, history will judge us.'[29]

Stalin was left to fight for Stalingrad on his own. He accepted Churchill's arguments against risking a premature invasion of continental Europe with manifest resentment. Vasilevsky and Zhukov's 'other solution' held the field. They brought a map to the Kremlin, which they laid on the table. Zhukov did the talking. He proposed a counter-offensive across the long exposed flanks of the German thrust towards Stalingrad that would encircle Paulus and break the German front. The counter-attack would take forty-five days to prepare thoroughly, drawing on strategic reserves which Stavka had garnered for the expected German assault on Moscow that had failed to materialize. The Soviet operation had to penetrate far to the German rear to be sure of opening up an impregnable corridor between Paulus and the rest of the German front. Stalin was critical, but not dismissive. Zhukov and Vasilevsky were sent away again to produce clear plans.

There has always existed a dispute over who first thought of the counter-offensive plan. The commander of the Voronezh Front, General Vatutin, whose forces stood opposite the long northern German flank, may have been the initial author. Vasilevsky played a central role as chief of staff in drawing up the detailed plans. The operational conception owed something to Zhukov's clear battlefield mind. There was no single inspiration behind the plan; it was a collective effort. This in itself was a revolutionary development. Stalin left the rescue of Stalingrad to the experts. The offensive plan still needed his final approval, but by mid-October both its technical feasibility and its prospects for success were clear, and Stalin did nothing to obstruct it.[30]

The advantages of the operation were many. Along the flanks of the German advance had been posted weaker Romanian, Italian and Hungarian divisions. They were less well armed than the German units and had less stomach for a do-or-die contest with an angry Red Army. They were stretched taut along the edges of a salient in which there were now few reserves. German forces themselves were running out of steam. With only one usable railway line, the supply system struggled to cope. Shortages of fuel and spare parts made it difficult to keep German tanks and vehicles going. Aircraft were forced to operate from rough grass airstrips, and their attrition rate was high. In the Caucasus the rapid advance of Army Group A was halted on a line in front of the oil city of Grozny. German soldiers reached the snow-clad passes of the Caucasus mountains but could advance no further. The balance of forces still favoured the attacker at Stalingrad – Paulus fielded twenty-five divisions against the ten under-strength divisions of the 62nd Army in the city itself. But in the second half of 1942, against every reasonable expectation, the rump Soviet economy, a triumph of improvised and urgent revival, began to produce larger quantities of tanks, aircraft and artillery than the Germans, who had four times as much steel.

The Soviet military revival in 1942 and 1943 was inextricably linked to the recovery of the battered industrial economy. The Soviet war effort was saved only by a most remarkable exodus of machines, equipment and manpower from the areas under German attack in 1941. Two days after the German attack a Committee of Evacuation was set up, with a staff of eighty-five planners and officials under the leadership of a Party favourite of Stalin's, Lazar Kaganovich. Unable to cope with the scale of the emergency, he was replaced in July by the trade union leader, N. M. Shvernik. Evacuation was carried out under exceptional difficulties. Subjected to air attack, with German forces often at no more than a few hours' distance, thousands of engineers and workers swarmed like ants over their factories, dismantling machinery and hauling equipment and vital materials to the nearest railhead. Here it was loaded, often manhandled, onto flatcars or into boxcars, for the long journey east. Whenever possible, each train carried a whole plant and its workforce. The workers were packed into cars equipped with rows of bunks and a stove. At their destination in the Urals, Kazakhstan or Siberia, they poured out of the cars and began the arduous work of reassembling their workplace.[31]

They worked with few tools in almost impossible conditions, in snow or permafrost, short of food and shelter. Where possible the refugee factories were coupled to an existing plant. In many cases they were set up on undeveloped sites where amenities were non-existent; two-thirds were restarted in the open countryside. At one tank factory the 8,000 female workers lived in holes carved out of the earth, industrial bunkers that unintentionally mirrored the harsh trench conditions at the fighting front.[32] During the second half of 1941, the latest Russian estimates suggest, at least 2,593 enterprises were moved eastward; the final tally was almost certainly higher. As many as twenty-five million workers and their families went with them, a human exodus without parallel that was to prove vital to the revival of the industrial economy and Soviet agriculture.[33] Priority was given to men of military age, skilled workers and engineers and Communist Party workers, but millions of women and children were moved as well, many in long, gruelling marches on foot, to escape an invader whose reputation for brutality preceded him. With the influx, the work-force in the Urals industrial region increased by 36 per cent; in western Siberia and the Volga basin the increase was almost one-quarter.[34]

Inevitably, mistakes were made in the chaotic conditions. Machines were left rusting by railway tracks. Trains loaded with equipment spent weeks trying to find a route to the east. Some factories, moved only a short distance, were threatened by the next German advance and had to be moved again. Yet an extraordinary amount was achieved despite the lack of a central plan, the shortage of railway equipment and the threat of enemy attack. By the end of 1942 only 55 out of the 1,523 major factories moved to the east were still idle. The rest were either in full operation, or on the way to achieving it. By concentrating everything on the single task of producing weapons at the expense of almost all civilian production, the shrunken Soviet economy in the second half of 1942 produced over 13,000 tanks and 15,000 aircraft, as against 4,800 and 9,700 for the same six months of 1941. In these six months Soviet industry turned out as much as, or in some cases more than, the German economy produced during the whole year.

The Soviet plan of attack, which was given the code name Operation Uranus, hinged on one critical factor: the defenders of Stalingrad had to hold out for the forty-five days Zhukov needed to organize the campaign. This seemed at the time an improbable ambition. In early September Stalin expected the city to fall in a day or so. German forces penetrated south of Stalingrad and reached the Volga once more, splitting the Soviet defence, and leaving the hapless 62nd Army encircled in the city, with its back to the river, relentlessly battered by aircraft and artillery. The German army began to move forward through the deep ravines that led to the outskirts of Stalingrad, sealing off and capturing successive sections of the city. By September 3 some German units were only two miles from the river. The Soviet defenders were confined to the workers' estates and factories to the north, the area around the Central Railway Station and river quays in the central zone and the small hill that dominated the centre of Stalingrad, Mamayev Kurgan. Around them the city collapsed. Bombing and shellfire reduced buildings to stark, twisted skeletons. Wooden houses were reduced to ashes, their metal stovepipes still standing amidst the debris. In the dark, recalled Konstantin Simonov, who immortalized the conflict in his novel *Days and Nights*, the city looked like a flat, undulating plain: 'It seemed as though the houses had sunk into the ground and that grave mounds of bricks had been heaped over them.'[35]

So unendurable was the battleground that the commander of the 62nd Army, General Aleksandr Lopatin, began to evacuate troops across to the eastern shore of the Volga. His commanders viewed this as an abdication of responsibility, and Lopatin was sacked. His replacement proved to be an inspired choice. General Vasily Ivanovich Chuikov was appointed commander of the 62nd Army on September 12. In July Chuikov had been brought back from assignment in China, where he had been a military adviser to Chiang Kai-Shek. He played a major part in stiffening the resistance on the steppe in front of Stalingrad. He was able to gather together scattered, leaderless soldiers and weld them into a more effective fighting force, learning all the time from German military habits, searching for their weaknesses. He was a tough, burly man, his ready smile revealing rows of gold-capped teeth. He endured what his men endured and faced death without flinching.[36]

He was thrown into the cauldron of Stalingrad at a decisive juncture. The day he arrived, September 13, Paulus had massed his army for the final push to the river. The sight that met Chuikov's eyes astonished him: 'The streets of the city are dead. There is not a single green twig left on the trees; everything has perished in the flames.'[37] He made his way to the rough dugout on the slopes of Mamayev Kurgan where the army headquarters was based. Almost at once he was engulfed by the battle. German forces stormed the hill and forced him to withdraw to the banks of the Tsaritsa river where it joined the Volga. Here in a hot, unventilated underground bunker he improvised a command centre for an army with whose outer units he could scarcely communicate. His lifeline was the Volga. A fleet of small ferryboats brought food, ammunition and occasional reinforcements, returning heavily laden with the wounded.

On the far bank of the Volga lay the main part of the Soviet front line. During September Stalin reorganized the line. The Stalingrad Front was renamed the Don Front, since its forces had been cut off north-east of the city by the German thrust to the Volga on August 23. Stalingrad itself and the area immediately to the east of the city was renamed the Stalingrad Front and was placed under a tough Ukrainian, General Andrei Yeremenko. A peasant by origin, like so many of the successful Second World War commanders, he became a cavalry NCO during the First World War and stayed in the service after the Revolution. He survived the purges as a divisional commander before going on to command the Soviet Red Banner Army in the east in 1940. He returned to take command of a front in the collapse in 1941 and was fortunate to survive serious injury. He was ambitious and temperamental; Zhukov became a particular target of his military jealousy. He was famously courageous and fought with a vengeful determination. At Stalingrad he was wounded seven times, four times seriously. He continued to exercise command from his hospital bed and eventually recovered to survive the war.[38]

In Yeremenko and Chuikov, Paulus found unyielding adversaries. The September battles pushed the Red Army to the very edge of human endurance and to the very edge of the Volga. In three days of fierce fighting, which began on September 13, German forces struggled forward through the rubble and ruins to the Central Railway Station and the slopes of Mamayev Kurgan. The station changed hands fifteen times. Small detachments of Soviet soldiers attacked at night to reverse the gains made by the Germans by day. The summit of Mamayev Kurgan was seized first by one side, then the other. The hill became a moonscape of craters and grey ash. Greatly outnumbered, Chuikov's tired troops, each group the remnants of what had once been whole divisions, retreated house by house, block by block. On the far side of the Volga there was little left to send. In desperation Stalin ordered the 13th Guards Division, led by Aleksandr Rodimtsev, a Hero of the Soviet Union, to race to the rescue. They disembarked at a bleak railhead set up on the bare steppe miles behind the front. They undertook a gruelling forced march and arrived by ferry tired, in some cases weaponless. Yet like the proverbial cavalry, they arrived just in time. With just fifteen tanks and a handful of men Chuikov held off the furious efforts of the 6th Army to reach the central jetties. Rodimtsev's Guards were brought across a boatload at a time and were thrown into the mouth of the battle with almost no preparation. They took casualties of almost 100 per cent, but they did what was needed. The 62nd Army kept its slender grip on the western bank of the Volga, and the city was saved.[39]

The battlefield that Rodimtsev's men were flung onto resembled no ordinary field of combat. The city looked as if it had been the epicentre of a giant earthquake. Over the whole area there settled a layer of thick, dark ash from the burned-out buildings, which gusted into clouds of grey dust with the thud of each new shell or each blast of wind from the steppe. There hung in the air the acrid fumes of scorched wood and brick and the occasional stench of burning flesh. Each fresh barrage or bombing contorted the ruins afresh. Soviet and German soldiers hid or lived in the cellars; they fought among the piles of masonry that gave them rough shelter from the constant fire of heavy machine-guns and tommy-guns. The front lines had no clear edges. The two sides were no more than a grenade's throw apart. Soviet soldiers who found themselves trapped behind German lines carried on fighting. Almost everyone was wounded, but light wounds no longer earned a reprieve from combat. The severely wounded were taken out when possible, but hundreds died where they lay, prey to the swarms of rats that flowed like a warm river over the living and the dead.[40]

The strategy pursued by Chuikov and Paulus was greatly simplified by the battle. The Soviet commander had to stay in Stalingrad, come what may; the German aim was to push the defenders back into the Volga. The conflict hinged not on strategy but on tactics. Chuikov became overnight a master of the urban battlefield. He instructed his men to keep their front line as close to the German one as they could, to prevent the enemy, for fear of hitting his own side, from deploying his superior air and fire power. By late September this was a fact of life, for only a matter of a few hundred yards separated the forward German units from the riverbank itself. From beyond the river on the eastern bank came a ceaseless barrage of artillery and rocket fire from Soviet positions, which had a much broader target to aim at. The German army found urban conflict dauntingly different from the fast air and tank operations across the steppe. In Stalingrad they had to fight against an enemy frustratingly elusive and deadly. Chuikov ordered his men to take every advantage of the terrain and of their own fighting skills. When they could Soviet forces fought at night. They infiltrated German units until on a given order they let out a barrage of fearsome yells and machine-gun fire against their nervous enemy. At night a blanket of fear descended on German troops. The tough Siberians and Tatars on the Soviet side used knives and bayonets to slaughter isolated German units inept at hand-to-hand fighting among the shadows. By day snipers sat in wait for anything on the German side that moved. From Berlin came crack shots to neutralize the sniper threat, but they too fell victim to the Red Army's hidden war. 'Bitter fighting,' wrote one German NCO. 'The enemy is firing from all sides, from every hole. You must not let yourself be seen.'[41]

By day the initiative lay with the attacker. The 6th Army was able to deploy more tanks and heavy weapons than its enemy, and the Soviet front line was ground down yard by yard. In late September much of the central area of the city had fallen. The giant Univermag department store in Heroes of the Soviet Union Square was defended to the death by Soviet soldiers holed up in the shop basement. Paulus then made it his headquarters. To the south a giant grain elevator became the scene of a fifty-eight-day siege, the Soviet garrison holding out floor by floor as German tanks and guns reduced it to a twisted shell. On September 25 Paulus turned his attention to the northern factory district, where most of the remnants of 62nd Army was besieged. Here the same tactics of armoured thrust and Soviet counter-thrust were employed for every factory building and every warehouse. Three under-strength German infantry divisions and two Panzer divisions attacked along a narrow, three-mile front until they had driven the defenders out of all but one factory complex. The surviving Soviet forces huddled in the Barricades Factory on the very banks of the river. Chuikov's other troops clung to small pockets of territory along the edge of the Volga. They were so reduced in number that they were organized in small detachments or 'storm groups', capable of launching nothing more than local forays.

How the Red Army survived in Stalingrad defies military explanation. Chuikov inspired his men. Despite a bomb attack on his headquarters in September and a flood of burning oil through his bunker in October, Chuikov stayed where he was, at the front line among his own. His determination infected others. A different commander might have asked less of his men, and he was savagely intolerant of those who failed to rise to the terrible challenge of Stalingrad. During the battle it has been claimed that 13,500 men were executed for cowardice, though they may not all have been regular soldiers, and almost certainly not all were cowards. Chuikov displayed a grim fatalism that was reflected in the morale of those he led.[42] Soviet soldiers, like soldiers everywhere, fought better when they knew what they were fighting for and were confident of their leaders. After that, what Simonov called the 'dour determination' of the ordinary Russian took over. Simonov's hero, Saburov, contemplates the distant, burning city as he arrives at the front: 'He felt that his own fate would be decided on the other side, together with that of the city. If the Germans took the city he would die. If he prevented them from taking it he might live.'[43] Alexander Werth also detected a changed mood among the veterans he talked to at the time of Stalingrad. Men arrived, shocked and fearful, on the riverbank, under continuous German shelling. Some were men in their fifties who had fought in the First World War, some boys of eighteen. Yeremenko was forced to send cooks and mechanics from the rear, with almost no battle experience. A quarter of them might be dead before they reached the front line, a few hundred yards beyond the bank. But the rest developed a tough survival instinct. Viktor Nekrasov, the novelist, who fought as a lieutenant through the Stalingrad battle, recalled that the ill-assorted reinforcements soon became 'wonderfully hardened soldiers. Real *frontoviks*.'[44]

During the struggle Chuikov was not alone. To the south, separated from him by German troops, stood the remnants of the 64th Army, which kept up an active defence against the German flank. From beyond the river came artillery fire and the deadly assault of the multiple rocket-launcher, the Katyusha. Set in the back of a truck, each launcher could send a salvo of four tons of explosives over an area of ten acres. German forces feared them more than artillery. There was no familiar rush of sound, and once released the rockets distributed their fatal loads quite randomly. Chuikov had them on the west bank. Trucks were driven perilously close to the river's edge to get the maximum trajectory. By October the ground barrage was joined by a growing weight of Soviet air power. As Luftwaffe activity was reduced by the loss of crews in combat or from accident, the Soviet 8th Air Force, drawing on extensive new production, could field 1,500 planes instead of the 300 the defenders had started with. Soviet pilots were given intensive training in night flying, which they had lacked. A more effective system of radio communication produced radical improvement in Soviet air fighting.[45]

All of this was watched from Moscow, as Zhukov and Vasilevsky put the finishing touches to Operation Uranus. Zhukov was determined that everything should be in place before launching the attack. Previous Soviet counter-offensives had foundered because they had been started prematurely, at the bidding of an impatient leader. The temptation to relieve Chuikov by pushing Soviet reserves into the city was resisted at the cost of a terrible harvest of death within the cauldron. During October and November reserves of men, equipment and horses were brought up to strengthen the fronts to the north and south of the long German salient. The moves were made with the maximum of security. Using the advantages of the weather and the lessons of camouflage and deception painfully learned in the first year of war, the Red Army built up a force of over one million men, 14,000 heavy guns, 979 tanks and 1,350 aircraft. The deployment went undetected by German intelligence, which expected that Soviet forces, bled white in the city battle, had few reserves left for more than local spoiling actions.[46] During early November the General Staff debated the precise details of the operation. Their conclusions were passed on to the front and divisional commanders so that everyone would be clear about what was expected of him. This in itself represented a great advance on the frantic operational planning before Leningrad and Moscow and helped to secure the success of Uranus.

On November 13 Zhukov and Vasilevsky visited Stalin to lay before him the final plans for the operation. He was in unaccustomed good humour and agreed to everything. The launch date he left to Zhukov's discretion. After one final inspection, November 19 was fixed as the

date for the blow on the northern flank, November 20 for the attack
from the south-east. Though Chuikov did not know it, he had to
endure unaided for only a few days more. They were critical days.
On November 9, after clearing most of the factory district and pressed
on by his frustrated Führer, Paulus made one last attempt to take the
city. When the German Army chief of staff, General Zeitzler, asked
Hitler to consider abandoning the city and shortening the German
line, Hitler shouted, 'I won't leave the Volga!'[47] Paulus was ordered
to assemble seven divisions for the task. In the early hours of the
morning they crashed forward and succeeded in splitting the 62nd
Army once again. German troops punched a corridor 500 yards wide
through to the Volga. They were subjected to heavy fire from the
opposite bank, while Chuikov sent storm detachments to try to force
the Germans from the new salient. The attacks failed, and the small
bridgeheads in the north of the city were surrounded by German
troops. Supplying Chuikov's troops was made difficult by the ice floes
that began to choke the river. They were saved only by the exhaustion
of the enemy. By November 12 the German offensive ground to a
halt, and both sides dug in. Slowly the Red Army began to win back
here and there a section of factory or a blockhouse. After two months
of the most gruelling combat since Verdun the two sides had fought
to a standstill. Neither possessed the means to defeat the other; neither
could retreat.

On November 18 Chuikov received a call from front headquarters
to expect a special order. He and his men knew nothing of Operation
Uranus. It was kept from them to ensure that they would continue to
fight with suicidal energy. At midnight the special order arrived, telling
Chuikov that the Germans he was fighting were about to be cut off
by a massive counter-offensive launched from neighbouring fronts. If
it heightened the morale of the beleaguered defenders of Stalingrad,
it gave them little immediate respite. Ice prevented the shipment of
further supplies until the river froze solid on December 16, and the
first small sled was pulled across. Nor did encirclement stop Paulus
from fighting. For another six weeks Chuikov and Paulus fought a
punch-drunk duel around Mamayev Kurgan and the Barricades Factory, while the noose tightened around 6th Army.

The counter-offensive was successful beyond all expectations. On November 19 Vatutin's South-western Front and Rokossovsky's Don Front swept forward against the 3rd Romanian Army and elements of the German reserve forces. The Romanian front collapsed in hours. Fast-moving Soviet armoured columns, moving over the now frozen steppe, caused the kind of panic German Panzer divisions had provoked the year before. By November 21 Romanian forces had surrendered, and 27,000 of them became prisoners. From the south a powerful armoured thrust hit the 4th Romanian Army, which disintegrated with the same dramatic speed. Resistance stiffened as German units began to be encountered, but so unprepared were Axis forces for an attack of this speed and weight that within four days the two Soviet pincers met up on the Don some sixty miles west of Stalingrad. The bridges over the river were vital to the success of the operation, and as Soviet forces approached they detached small mobile units to race ahead and seize them. At the town of Kalach Colonel Filippov, with a small detachment of tanks, drove into the centre at night with lights blazing. German guards thought it must be their own forces; before they had time to realize their mistake Filippov had seized the bridge and key areas of the town.[48] He held off German counter-attacks until the rest of his division arrived. The encirclement was sealed when advance guards from south and north met at the village of Sovetsky, some miles south of Kalach.

The German southern front was in disarray. Men, horses and guns lay in grotesque, frozen heaps where they fell. The Red Army cleared the steppe around them, until a corridor over a hundred miles wide separated the German front from Paulus, the 6th Army and remnants of the 4th Panzer Army, a total of more than 330,000 men. The first reaction was to try to break out. Paulus later complained that he 'could easily have done so'.[49] But Hitler, who flew back to his headquarters on November 20 to deal with the emergency, told him to stand fast at all costs. Hermann Goering, who accompanied Hitler, promised to supply Paulus from the air with 500 tons a day. Field Marshal von Manstein was given responsibility for cutting a corridor through to Stalingrad to re-establish overland contact with the encircled army. The Soviet staff had anticipated this. They filled the circle around

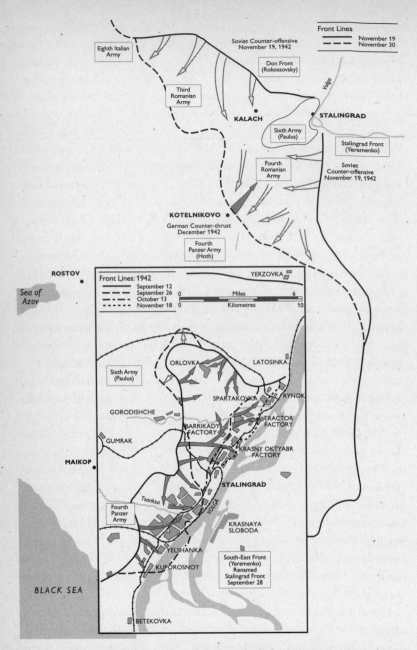

Front Lines
— November 19
---- November 30

Eighth Italian Army

Soviet Counter-offensive
November 19, 1942

Don Front
(Rokossovsky)

Third
Romanian
Army

Volga

KALACH

STALINGRAD

Sixth Army
(Paulus)

Stalingrad Front
(Yeremenko)

Fourth
Romanian
Army

Soviet
Counter-offensive
November 19, 1942

KOTELNIKOVO

German Counter-thrust
December 1942

Fourth
Panzer Army
(Hoth)

ROSTOV

YERZOVKA

Front Lines: 1942
— September 12
---- September 26
—·—·— October 13
········ November 18

Miles
0   6
Kilometres
0   10

Sea of
Azov

Sixth Army
(Paulus)

ORLOVKA

LATOSINKA

SPARTAKOVKA

RYNOK

GORODISHCHE

BARRIKADY
FACTORY

TRACTOR
FACTORY

GUMRAK

KRASNY OKTYABR
FACTORY

MAIKOP

STALINGRAD

Tsanksa

VOLGA

Fourth
Panzer
Army

KRASNAYA
SLOBODA

YELSHANKA

KUPOROSNOY

South-East Front
(Yeremenko)
Renamed
Stalingrad Front
September 28

BLACK SEA

BETEKOVKA

Map 6   Operation Uranus, November–December 1943

Paulus with sixty divisions and 1,000 tanks. A strong defensive perimeter was established facing east and west. When Manstein's Don Army Group finally assailed the circle on December 12, in driving rain and sleet, his prospects were poor. German forces hit hard against fierce resistance. At one point they advanced forty miles towards Stalingrad. In a state of confusion and in atrocious weather a Soviet counter-thrust was organized with reserve armoured divisions. On December 24 Manstein's relief column was itself threatened with encirclement. It was hastily withdrawn, and Paulus was left to his fate.

The Soviet plan had been well prepared. There was scant possibility of Paulus fighting his way out of Stalingrad. Short of vehicles, ammunition and fuel, constantly subjected to air attack, the 6th Army was still capable of fighting but not of moving very far. Manstein's counter-stroke caught the Red Army off guard, but the skilful redeployment of reserves and the considerable numerical superiority favoured the Soviet side. For the first time Stalin's military machine had been able to prepare and execute a large-scale operation involving millions of men and hold it together under the fog of war. Stalin became eager for more. This time his staff had thought ahead. Two new operations were on the table. The first, Operation Saturn, was a more ambitious plan to cave in the German southern front and recapture Rostov, cutting off German forces in the Caucasus. The second was the operation to annihilate the encircled German armies at Stalingrad, Operation Koltso, or Ring. The first had mixed success. Substantial German forces managed to escape capture in the Caucasus by fighting their way through a narrow corridor along the Black Sea coast. The German front was rolled back across the Donbas industrial region towards the Dnepr River. Once Zhukov had provided the trigger, Stalin returned to his old habits of command, pushing his armies on beyond what they could realistically achieve. By March Manstein had not only stabilized the German front in the south but could undertake limited counter-offensives against exhausted Soviet troops. Once again Stalin had overplayed his hand.

Further to the east there was a battle still to be won. The German 6th Army, with remnants of Italian and Romanian forces and part of the 4th Panzer Army, was bottled up in the Stalingrad pocket, but it was not yet beaten. Though prospects of rescue were remote, German forces continued to fight, if for no other reason than Hitler's insistence that they should not surrender. The pocket was a large one. German forces occupied an area of steppe in front of the city, around which they threw a defensive cordon, a circle of guns and tanks to keep the enemy at bay. There were still three operational airfields, to which a trickle of supplies was brought in by the slow transport aircraft of the Luftwaffe. German air power over Stalingrad evaporated. A new generation of high-performance Soviet fighters enacted a grim toll. Losses amounted to 488 transports and over 1,000 crewmen. Wounded soldiers were flown out of the pocket, but hundreds of them died in air crashes. The supply operation was a failure. Instead of the promised 500 tons a day, the average was less than 100, and it fell even lower during the poor weather of December and January.[50] Paulus was left to fight with what he had.

General Friedrich Paulus was not the stuff of military legend. A bourgeois officer in an army still dominated by Germany's military gentry, he made his reputation as an able organizer and staff officer. He took control of the 6th Army only because of the sudden death of its flamboyant and tough commander, Walther von Reichenau, in January 1942. He was Reichenau's opposite: a quiet, subdued, unassertive individual who never lost his temper or became overexcited, loved Beethoven and hated the boorish side of military life. He was fastidious, even fussy, about his personal appearance. A fellow officer recalled a man 'well-groomed and with slender hands, always beautifully turned out with a gleaming white collar and immaculately polished field boots'. Stalingrad was the last place on earth for the tidy and the timid. Paulus could not bring himself to disobey Hitler, and his leadership was a poor example to his men. He was remembered as 'tired and listless', prone to bouts of debilitating illness, devoured by an unspoken bitterness at the role fate had assigned him.[51]

It was now the turn of German soldiers to suffer. They were subjected to an endless bombardment from guns, rockets and aircraft. They were short of ammunition and spares. They fought in temperatures which by January were as low as minus thirty degrees. To keep warm they wrapped torn shreds of material around their feet and legs, and covered their shoulders with anything that came to hand. Military standards gave way to a crude instinct for survival. One veteran recalled that in the icy atmosphere the German soldiers were overcome by feelings 'of the bitterest disillusionment, hidden terror and mounting despair'.[52] Food rations were cut to a minimum: two ounces of bread and half an ounce of sugar a day. Occasionally there was horsemeat. The lucky ones caught cats or rats. Rumours of cannibalism persist.

It was not until late December that Zhukov and Stalin turned back to the Stalingrad cauldron. They believed that only 80,000 poorly supplied soldiers and non-combatants were sealed up in the ring and that they would probably surrender once the option was given to them. In case they did not, a force of forty-seven divisions was drawn up around the perimeter, reinforced with 300 aircraft and 179 tanks.[53] It took time to divert the necessary supplies, and to Stalin's irritation the attack could not begin until January 10. Two days earlier Paulus was given the option of capitulation. Two Soviet officers, accompanied by a bugler and carrying a red flag, approached German lines. Firing started, and they beat a hasty retreat. They came back, and this time were conducted blindfolded to meet senior officers. The surrender terms were dismissed out of hand.[54] The following day the heaviest artillery barrage of the war heralded the final struggle for Stalingrad.

German troops fought a final desperate contest, against the Soviet enemy, against the cold, against hunger and fear. They were condemned men. They were forced to fight and die rather than surrender, but there was little to fight for except to postpone death. Under the terrible bombardment the snow-clad cauldron turned from white to black and grey. In three days Soviet forces cleared the grasslands in front of the city, then resistance stiffened. It became clear from the interrogation of German prisoners that not 80,000 but more than 250,000 troops were now ensnared. Instead of a few days, Operation Ring took three weeks. By January 17 the pocket was reduced to half its original size. Paulus was again invited to give up. Without instructions from Hitler he again refused. His men were pressed back into the city itself, where they fought with methods they had learned from Chuikov's troops.

On January 22 the Soviet forces regrouped for the final push into the city, while Chuikov's 62nd Army, still fighting an increasingly pointless battle of its own, pressed from the river towards the German positions. Some German troops began to surrender of their own accord, since surrendering could be no worse than death. But others killed their wounded as they retreated rather than let them fall into enemy hands. At Gumrak, the last airfield in German hands, the final flights to safety provoked a frantic and unseemly scramble for a seat. Officers tried to bribe their way onto the planes. The Red Army isolated and reduced one section of the city at a time.[55] By January 26 the vanguard had established contact with the 62nd Army by the Barricades Factory. The men of both forces embraced, in tears. The last Soviet push took them to Heroes of the Revolution Square. Paulus had so far eluded efforts to capture him, but interrogators knew from the conversations of captured officers that he was still somewhere in the centre of the city. On January 31 it was learned that he was in the Univermag building on one side of the conquered square.

The building was shelled and flame-throwers were brought up. A German staff officer emerged from the entrance and signalled to a young Soviet officer, Lieutenant Fyodor Yelchenko. With two other soldiers, Yelchenko followed the German inside. In the basement he found hundreds of German soldiers, dirty, reeking, fearful. Here Yelchenko agreed to the terms of German surrender, not with Paulus, but with his staff. Finally he made his way into a room at the back of the headquarters and found Paulus lying on a bed, unshaven and sour. Yelchenko later remembered saying, 'Well, that finishes it.' Paulus gave him 'a miserable look' and nodded assent. A little while later a car was brought up, and Paulus was rushed away to the headquarters of Rokossovsky's Don Front.[56]

To the north a fanatical resistance was kept up until February 2, but after that the city was still. News of the surrender shocked Hitler. On January 30 he had promoted Paulus to Field Marshal to stiffen his spine. The same day Goering issued a communiqué to the battling forces: 'Stalingrad will remain the greatest heroic struggle of our history . . . fighting to the very last.'[57] On February 1 Hitler raged in his headquarters against Paulus's betrayal: 'In peacetime in Germany, about 18,000 or 20,000 people a year chose to commit suicide, even without being in such a position. Here is a man who sees 50,000 or 60,000 of his soldiers die defending themselves bravely to the end. How can he surrender himself to the Bolshevists!'[58] The mood of despondency was evident throughout the Reich. The following day German radio repeatedly played Siegfried's Funeral March from Wagner's *Götterdämmerung*.

On the Soviet side Stalingrad was greeted as a turning point in the war. 'Up till then one believed in victory as an act of faith,' wrote Ilya Ehrenburg, 'but now there was no shadow of doubt: victory was assured.' The mood in Russia was not 'noisily exultant', observed a war correspondent, but displayed a feeling of 'deep national pride'.[59] A high price was paid for the victory. The Red Army had lost another half million men in the struggle.[60] The people of Stalingrad, who began to filter slowly back into the city to search for belongings or shelter, lost almost everything. Yet for the first time German losses were also catastrophic: 147,000 dead and 91,000 taken prisoner. German forces lost their reputation for invincibility. There was, according to General Malinovsky, who led the defeat of Manstein's relief column in December, 'far more drive and punch in our troops than there used to be'.[61] The moral contrast between the two sides was as significant as the material victory.

In the days after the battle the strangest thing about the city was its silence. Fresh snow covered the ruins. The frozen carnage was grimly visible here and there. German stragglers were rounded up from the cellars and Soviet soldiers searched for snipers and booby traps. Most of the remaining Germans were too weak or ill to move. The prisoners who could walk were marched to the rear, to be fed and clothed. A few days after the end of the battle a primitive war memorial was raised on one of the cliffs overlooking the city, its foundations dug out by German prisoners. In Moscow Zhukov and five other generals were awarded the Order of Suvorov, 1st Class. Stalin made himself Marshal of the Soviet Union, his first military rank. From then on he wore his new uniform in public in place of the familiar plain tunic.

7

The Citadel:
Kursk, 1943

To a distant land is our comrade now departing,
His native winds a sad farewell are piping,
His beloved town, his home, his lover's tender gaze,
Vanish with his native fields in a deep blue haze.

Popular wartime song

The German defeat at Stalingrad soon passed into legend. The Soviet soldiers who found themselves packed into airless boxcars deep inside Russia, in an atmosphere laden with the familiar smells of Russian life – black bread and cabbage, leather and coarse tobacco – had poured into the Stalingrad front with evident trepidation. But after the victory it became a status symbol to have fought at Stalingrad (and survived). The stories of heroic resistance were embellished; memories of the initial panic were officially suppressed. It has remained in the modern memory unique among the battles of the Second World War. It was a victory necessary for the self-belief of ordinary Russians; it was a victory necessary for the Allies at a critical juncture in the war. Stalingrad symbolized the change in Soviet fortunes.

Yet the battle was not decisive. The Stalingrad victory was won in harsh winter conditions, against an overstretched and demoralized enemy, many of whose troops were drawn from Germany's weaker allies. This is not to diminish the extent of the victory, for it showed not only the raw fighting power of the Soviet soldier when effectively employed, but the ability of the Red Army to organize large and complex operations against the world's most effective armed forces. (It is difficult to imagine British or American forces in 1942 winning the battle around Stalingrad.) Soviet strengths – as well as German weaknesses – explain the outcome at Stalingrad. But the Red Army faced a still formidable enemy. The counter-offensives in March 1943 around Kharkov were a timely reminder that though the German army had lost a battle it had not yet lost the war. German forces were still deep in Soviet territory. They remained unbeaten in summer campaigning weather, when the German brand of well-organized, concentrated, mobile warfare was most deadly.

The eventual victory of Soviet arms in 1943 and 1944 has usually been portrayed as a result of the Soviet Union's overwhelming resources, of what one German general later described as 'the gigantic Russian superiority of men and material'.[1] More commonly German defeat has been interpreted as a result of German errors – Hitler's poor strategic grasp, sloppy intelligence, logistical overstretch and so on. Neither interpretation does justice to the historical reality. In the decisive battles from Stalingrad to the autumn of 1943 the numerical imbalance was much less marked than it was to become in the final stages of German defeat. German forces were not overwhelmed by sheer numbers, like some wagon train ambushed by Indians, nor did the Red Army win simply because its enemy declined. The operational experience and technological assets at the disposal of German forces in 1943 rendered their fighting power more remarkable than it had been in 1940. Soviet victory came as the result of a profound transformation of the way the Red Army made war.[2]

The transformation began at the top. At the height of the war, with Germany perilously close to seizing the whole of southern Russia, Stalin at last confronted his own inadequacy as Supreme Commander. Zhukov's appointment as his deputy signalled the dictator's gradual abdication from the role of military supremo that he had played since June 1941. The appointment marked one of the critical turning points of the Soviet war effort, not because of the qualities of leadership that Zhukov had already displayed, but because it symbolized yet another revolution in the relationship between the politicians and the army. The reassertion of political influence following the purges, renewed again in the disastrous summer of 1941, was reversed in 1942. Lev Mekhlis, the incompetent and vindictive head of the Main Political

Administration of the Armed Forces, was removed from office in June and confined to propaganda activities. On October 9 political commissars were abolished in all smaller military units, and even at the level of fronts and armies the right of the political representative to interfere in purely military decisions was much reduced. In October their counter-signature on operational orders was no longer required, and in December they became assistants to the commander. During 1943 122,000 former political officials were drafted to the front as junior officers, where they learned the lessons of military command the hard way. The officer corps was encouraged to take initiatives and to assume responsibility. For many this was an unaccustomed opportunity, and they responded to it slowly. Self-reliance and flexibility in command did not spring up overnight. As if to demonstrate that the Supreme Commander was in earnest about the change, the term 'officer', rather than the familiar 'comrade', was used more widely. Officers once again were permitted to wear the trappings of the old imperial army, the gold braid and shoulder boards that revolutionary crowds had torn off in 1917. Divisions that distinguished themselves in combat were given the Tsarist designation of 'Guards'.[3] The planning and running of the war effort, from operations to communications and supply, was increasingly handled by the General Staff rather than the larger Military Council, on which the politicians also sat. Stalin still insisted on being informed about the decisions made by the staff. In the mornings he telephoned the chief of operations for a detailed survey of the front, whose intricacies he knew perfectly; in the evening around eleven o'clock the chief of staff, or his deputy, would come to the Kremlin to make a detailed report, which could last well into the night. The difference lay in Stalin's attitude. He seldom interrupted the reports. He allowed the staff to suggest operations; he came to insist that front commanders should be consulted for their views first. The soldiers slowly overcame their natural caution and began to argue openly with Stalin. It was discovered that Stalin could tolerate dissent, if forcibly and sensibly expressed. He liked to be told the truth, however unpalatable. He took advice and bowed to others' judgement.[4]

The experts Stalin surrounded himself with were men of exceptional character, promoted in the heat of battle on merit. Their capability allowed Stalin to shift the responsibility downward; their success ensured their survival. The appointment of General Aleksandr Vasilevsky as chief of staff in July 1942 set the pattern. A veteran of the First World War and the civil war, Vasilevsky was one of that younger generation of officers which survived the purges. He was a model staff officer. He was picked out by Stalin as a man able to give quick, accurate accounts of the tide of battle, and he spent much of the early part of the war touring from front to front, often under fire, reporting to Moscow the true state of affairs. He had the gift of a natural commander: he could grasp the battlefront as a whole and its likely course of development, but he was alive also to the many hundreds of details that can turn a battle. He developed clear views of his own on each major operation, but he was willing to listen patiently and deliberately to others, and arrive at judgements that he stuck to resolutely and consistently. His ideas were communicated to Stalin with a tactful firmness in hundreds of evening meetings. From all accounts he was liked by the men who worked with him on the staff's gruelling eighteen-hour shifts.[5]

Vasilevsky came to rely on one subordinate above all others: the chief of operations, General Aleksei Antonov. Between June and December 1942 Stalin appointed no fewer than seven different men to the post, one after the other. On December 11 the forty-six-year-old Antonov stepped into the role which was more directly exposed to Stalin's inquisitive leadership than any other. Antonov rose to the challenge. Instead of rushing off to report to Stalin when he arrived in Moscow, he spent the first week familiarizing himself thoroughly with the General Staff and the state of the front. Only when he was fully primed did he go to see his commander. The two men developed the most effective working relationship of the war. Antonov displayed a calm intelligence married to a massive energy and exceptional industry. According to his deputy, General Sergei Shtemenko, Antonov never lost his temper or allowed circumstances to get the better of him. He was firm, caustic, slow to praise and a tough taskmaster, but the rigorous regimen that he imposed on his staff won their respect. Above all he was adept at manipulating Stalin. He did not sugar-coat his reports. He was prepared to stand up to Stalin with what his deputy regarded as a 'brave outspokenness'. So skilled was he at providing the evening situation reports concisely and accurately that even Zhukov bowed to his capability and allowed Antonov to present them in his place. The trust that Stalin came to place in Antonov was reflected in his survivability. He retained his office until February 1945, when he was made chief of staff in Vasilevsky's place.[6]

None of the new military stars survived long after the war's end. They became victims of Stalin's paranoiac jealousy. During the war, however, they created a central team of military managers and thinkers which radically altered Soviet fighting power. Their model was again the German one, as it had been in the 1920s. In the summer of 1941 Soviet air and tank forces, though numerically large, proved incapable of inflicting more than local damage on the concentrated tank and air forces of the enemy. Tanks were divided up to support infantry regiments in small numbers and as a result lost the advantages of striking power and mobility that they should have offered. In the spring of 1942, under the stress of war, Red Army leaders began a thorough overhaul of the organization and technical quality of both army and air force. The new army was built around the concept of the tank corps, a fast-moving unit armed with 168 tanks, anti-tank battalions, Katyusha rockets and anti-aircraft artillery. Two tank corps and an infantry division made up a tank army, the equivalent of a German Panzer division, a self-contained and highly mobile fighting instrument complete with vehicles, riflemen, defensive armament and military services. The infantry went into battle clinging dangerously to rails on the tank's sides, giving it considerable mobility. In September 1942 the army established the equivalent of the German motorized divisions. They called them mechanized corps, having more infantry and fewer tanks than the tank armies. They were more mobile and heavily armed than the regular divisions. From December 1942 they were joined by self-propelled heavy artillery, which gave the Soviet offensive added momentum. To increase the hitting power of the new divisions, infantry went into an attack side by side with tanks and guns. They took heavy losses, but they were able to overwhelm German positions before the enemy had time to regroup.

Between 1942 and the end of the war the Red Army activated forty-three tank corps and twenty-two mechanized corps. In 1943 and 1944 these armoured formations were greatly strengthened by the addition of larger quantities of tanks and guns. A tank corps now had 228 tanks, but fewer men, and was capable of concentrating 70 to 80 tanks and 250 guns on each kilometre of front. In late 1941 the density had been more like three tanks per kilometre. For the rest of the army, largely horse-drawn, the later war years saw a further change in the balance between weapons and manpower, between capital-intensive and labour-intensive warfare, as the former became more plentiful and the latter much scarcer. The firepower of a typical infantry division quadrupled over the war years: under 250 pounds per artillery salvo in 1941, over 900 pounds by 1944. As junior commanders became more familiar with the tactics of modern armoured warfare, and with significant improvements in logistical supply and radio-based communications, the Red Army began to approach German battlefield performance. In 1941, six or seven Soviet tanks were lost for every German one; by the autumn of 1944 the ratio was down to one to one.[7]

The Soviet air force also learned lessons from the enemy. In 1941 it was stretched out across the front, supporting each small army unit. Aircraft were not concentrated, nor were the principles of modern air combat well understood. Reform was begun in the spring of 1942 by a young Communist air officer, Aleksandr Novikov, who had won his spurs defending Leningrad in the autumn of 1941 and reaped his reward when Stalin appointed him commander-in-chief of the whole Soviet air force in April 1942. Novikov was another fortunate choice. He was a fanatical enthusiast for air power. He grasped that the deficiencies of Soviet aviation were organizational as much as technical. He insisted on concentrating air forces, like the air fleets of the enemy, so that they would be capable of carrying out wide-ranging and devastating air strikes rather than being frittered away in small front-line engagements. The new air armies were composed of fighters, bombers and ground-attack aircraft. They were to be closely controlled from the centre, where a large strategic reserve was built up to be used at critical junctures in the battle. Each air army was assigned to a front commander, but the air force retained considerable flexibility in the conduct of the air offensive. The aim was to smash enemy air power first, then support the army on the ground by closely co-ordinated attacks against enemy strongholds, using the redoubtable Ilyushin Il-2 fighter bomber, generally regarded as one of the finest battlefront aircraft of the war.[8]

Novikov's emphasis on organization and striking power gave Soviet forces the air/tank punch they had lacked. But he also recognized that air power was only as effective as its large tail of supplies and services. He reorganized communications, introducing air-to-air and air-to-ground radio contact. Radar was gradually installed. The creaky maintenance system was overhauled so that damaged aircraft could be swiftly returned to combat. A vast programme of airfield construction was undertaken, including a good proportion of dummy fields to deceive the enemy. After the mauling in June 1941, Novikov insisted that airfield camouflage be given priority. Aircraft were concealed in woods and farm buildings. Their rugged design and construction allowed them to take off from rough grass fields close to the front line. Concealed supplies of fuel, brought forward laboriously from the rear, were stored at the front-line airfields. They provided enough petrol for each aircraft to mount twenty operations right in the heart of the battle. During 1943 the Soviet air force was at last brought to the point where it could contend for air supremacy on more equal terms.[9]

The organizational reforms came at just the time that Soviet military equipment was being significantly improved. The main Soviet battle tank, the robust T-34, which first appeared in small numbers in the battles of 1941, had better armour and a heavier gun (76 mm) than German tanks, but suffered from small, debilitating defects. They lacked radios, which left them to fight on their own, in ignorance of the battle around them. The turret was cramped, with room for only two crewmen, so that the tank commander had to load the gun and operate the machine-gun in addition to his command duties. Visibility was poor, through an unsatisfactory periscope. Because the tank hatch opened forward it was difficult to look out. By the battles of 1943 the T-34 had become a much more effective fighting vehicle. The redesigned cabin held a crew of three; a new cupola gave all-around vision; radios were installed to keep tanks in communication with their commanders. In 1943 Soviet factories turned out some 24,000 tanks, of which 15,812 were T-34s. In 1943 Germany produced 17,000 tanks.[10]

During 1943 the T-34 was joined by a new generation of mobile artillery. The SU-76 self-propelled gun was poorly armoured and gave scant protection to its crew when it first saw service in 1942. An upgraded model, the SU-76M, which rectified earlier deficiencies, appeared from May 1943. A heavier model, the SU-122, went into mass production in January 1943, and a giant anti-tank gun, the SU-152, was rushed into production in just twenty-five days in February 1943. The SU-152 was nicknamed the 'Animal Hunter' because of its ability to destroy the new generation of German heavy tanks, the 'Panther' and the 'Tiger'. In the pipeline were the huge IS-1 and IS-2 'Josef Stalin' tanks, which became in 1944 the most effective armoured vehicles of the war. With its thick, crudely machined hull, daubed in muddy green, and reinforced in places with concrete, and a gun so large that it looked as though the tank would topple forward, the IS-2 displayed an awesome, primitive power.[11]

The most serious gap in the Soviet armoury at the start of the war was in radio communication and intelligence. In the early months of war there were desperate shortages of radio equipment, which made effective command and control of large numbers of aircraft and tanks impossible and made it difficult to hold together a regular infantry division. And when radio was used German interceptors caught the messages and dispatched air or tank strikes against the unfortunate command post that had relayed them. Soviet commanders soon grew uncomfortable with using radio once they realized it could betray their whereabouts. The system was disrupted in the fast-moving defensive battles of 1941 and 1942, as one communications post after another was overrun by the enemy. The effort to provide effective communication in 1942 was central to the final successes of Soviet mass operations in 1943 and 1944.

It could not have been achieved without supplies from the United States and the British Commonwealth. Under the Lend-Lease agreements drawn up with America and Britain in 1941, the Soviet Union was supplied with 35,000 radio stations, 380,000 field telephones and 956,000 miles of telephone cable.[12] The air force was able by 1943 to establish a network of radio control stations about one and a half miles behind the front, from which aircraft could be quickly directed to targets on the battlefield. Tank armies used the new radios to hold the tank units together, increasing their fighting effectiveness by the simplest of innovations. Finally, the Red Army began to organize its own radio interception service in 1942. By 1943 five specialized radio battalions had been raised; their function was to listen in on German radio, jam their frequencies and spread disinformation over the air waves. In the battles of summer 1943 the battalions claimed to have reduced the transmission of German operational radiograms by two-thirds. In the last years of the war Soviet signals-intelligence underwent an exceptional and necessary improvement. The systems for evaluating intelligence from radio interception, spies and air reconnaissance were overhauled by the spring of 1943, and a much clearer picture of German dispositions and intentions could be constructed.[13] Moreover, radio came to play a major part in the evolution of sophisticated tactics of deception and disinformation, which on numerous occasions left the enemy quite unable even to guess the size, the whereabouts or the intentions of Soviet forces.[14]

Soviet reaction to Allied aid during the war was mixed. While sending out extravagant shopping lists to the Western powers, the Soviet authorities complained constantly about delays in supply and the quality of some of the weaponry they were sent. Offers by British and American engineers and officers to follow up the deliveries with advice on how to use and repair the equipment were met with a stony refusal.[15] It was true that aid deliveries were slow to materialize in the fifteen months after the promise was made in August of 1941, due partly to the difficulties in establishing effective supply lines, partly to the demands of America's own rearmament. But neither Roosevelt nor Churchill were in any doubt that aid for the Soviet Union was vital to the anti-Axis coalition; they bore Soviet complaints without a serious rupture. When the first aid programme was finally settled in October 1941, Maxim Litvinov, by then the ambassador to Washington, leaped to his feet and shouted out, 'Now we shall win the war!'[16] Yet after 1945 Lend-Lease was treated in the official Soviet histories of the war as a minor factor in the revival of Soviet fortunes. The story of Lend-Lease became a victim of the Cold War. Even in the late 1980s it was still a subject of which the regime would not permit open discussion. The significance of Western supplies for the Soviet war effort was admitted by Khrushchev in the taped interviews used for his memoirs, but the following passage was published only in the 1990s: 'Several times I heard Stalin acknowledge [Lend-Lease] within the small circle of people around him. He said that . . . if we had had to deal with Germany one-to-one we would not have been able to cope because we lost so much of our industry.' Marshal Zhukov, in a bugged conversation in 1963 whose contents were released only thirty years later, endorsed the view that without aid the Soviet Union 'could not have continued the war'. All this was a far cry from the official history of the Great Patriotic War, which concluded that Lend-Lease was 'in no way meaningful' and had 'no decisive influence' on the outcome of the war.[17]

Table 2 American Lend-Lease supplies to the USSR 1941–45

A: BY MAIN PRODUCT TYPE 1941–45

	1941	1942	1943	1944	1945
(Per cent of total supplies)					
Aircraft	——	22.4	17.4	16.3	12.7
Guns and Ammo.	——	15.8	12.8	5.6	2.6
Tanks	——	13.1	2.6	4.9	4.0
Other Vehicles	——	11.0	14.1	14.7	19.3
Shipping	——	0.8	3.2	2.5	2.1
Total Military	20	63.2	49.9	43.8	40.7
Industrial goods	80	23.1	29.6	39.3	39.5
Agricultural goods	——	13.7	20.5	16.9	19.8

B: SELECTED STATISTICS ON THE SUPPLY OF EQUIPMENT 1941−45

Aircraft	14,203
Fighters	9,438
Bombers	3,771
Tanks	6,196
Trucks	363,080
Jeeps	43,728
Motorcycles	32,200
Explosives (tons)	325,784
Radio Stations	35,089
Field Telephones	380,135
Radio Receivers	5,899
Telephone Wire (miles)	956,688
Canned Meat (tons)	782,973
Boots (pairs)	14,793,000
Belts	2,577,000
Copper (tons)	339,599
Aluminium (tons)	261,311

Source: H. D. Hall, *North American Supply* (London, 1955), p. 430; M. Harrison, *Soviet Planning in War and Peace 1938−1942* (Cambridge, 1985), pp. 258−9; H. van Tuyll, *Feeding the Bear: American Aid to the Soviet Union 1941−1945* (New York, 1989), pp. 156−61.

It was true that the quantity of armaments sent was not great when compared with the remarkable revival of Soviet mass production. The raw statistics show that Western aid supplied only 4 per cent of Soviet munitions over the whole war period, but the aid that mattered did not come in the form of weapons. In addition to radio equipment the United States supplied more than half a million vehicles: 77,900 jeeps, 151,000 light trucks and over 200,000 Studebaker army trucks. One-third of all Soviet vehicles came from abroad and were generally of higher quality and durability, though most came in 1943 and 1944. At the time of Stalingrad only 5 per cent of the Soviet military vehicle park came from imported stocks. Imports, however, gave the Red Army supply system a vital mobility that was by 1944 better than the enemy's. The Studebaker became a favourite with the Soviet forces. The letters 'USA' stencilled on the side were translated as '*Ubit sukina syna Adolfa*' – 'to kill that son-of-a-bitch Adolf!'[18] The list of other supplies, equally vital to the Soviet supply effort, is impressive – 57.8 per cent of aviation fuel requirements, 53 per cent of all explosives, almost half the wartime supply of copper, aluminium and rubber tyres. Arguably the most decisive contribution was supplies for the strained Soviet rail network, much of which was in the occupied areas in 1941. From America came not only 56.6 per cent of all the rails used during the war but 1,900 locomotives to supplement the meagre Soviet output of just 92, and 11,075 railway cars to add to the 1,087 produced domestically. Almost half the supplies, by weight, came in the form of food, enough to provide an estimated half-pound of concentrated nourishment for every Soviet soldier, every day of the war. The shiny tins of Spam, stiff, pink compressed meat, were universally known as 'second fronts'.[19]

The provision of Lend-Lease supplies was slow in the early stages of the war, but from late 1942 it became a steady flow through the Soviet eastern provinces via Vladivostok, by the overland route from the Persian Gulf and the more dangerous and inhospitable convoy journeys from British ports to Murmansk or Archangel. Foreign aid on such a scale permitted the Soviet Union to concentrate its own production on the supply of battlefront equipment rather than on machinery, materials or consumer goods. Without Western aid, the narrower post-invasion economy could not have produced the remarkable output of tanks, guns and aircraft, which exceeded anything the wealthier German economy achieved throughout the war. Without the railway equipment, vehicles and fuel the Soviet war effort would almost certainly have foundered on poor mobility and an anaemic transport system. Without the technical and scientific aid – during the war 15,000 Soviet officials and engineers visited American factories and military installations – technological progress in the Soviet Union would have come much more slowly. This is not to denigrate the extraordinary performance of the Soviet economy during the war, which was made possible only by the use of crude mass-production techniques, by skilful improvisation in planning and through the greater independence and initiative allowed plant managers and engineers. As a result of the improvements in production, the Red Army faced the German enemy in 1943 on more equal terms than at any time since 1941. The modernization of Soviet fighting power was an essential element in the equation. The gap in organization and technology between the two sides was narrowed to the point where the Red Army was prepared to confront German forces during the summer campaigning season in the sort of pitched battle of manoeuvre and firepower at which German commanders had hitherto excelled.

With the coming of thaw and rain in March 1943 both sides sat back to consider the strategic options for the coming year. Hitler was far gloomier about German prospects than he had been a year before, and, like Stalin, he gave his commanders a greater latitude in defining and planning operations. Field Marshal von Manstein formulated a plan which was given the code name Citadel. The operation was aimed at the large Soviet salient around the city of Kursk that formed a bulge into the German front 120 miles wide and 60 miles long. Here was concentrated the main weight of the Red Army. Manstein planned to envelop the bulge with two heavily armed pincers that would cut the neck of the salient from north and south. The aim was to destroy a large part of the Red Army at a critical juncture of the front, allowing German forces either to recapture the southern area, or to swing north-east behind Moscow. Manstein was eager to attack in April or May, before Soviet forces had had time to regroup and dig in, but Hitler was anxious to avoid another risky campaign, and insisted on waiting until June, when more tanks would be available. He eventually postponed the launch of the offensive until early July to be more certain of prevailing.

Soviet commanders faced a critical challenge. Twice before, in 1941 and in 1942, they had miscalculated where the weight and direction of German attack would come. This time the guess had to be right. The General Staff put themselves in Hitler's shoes. They could see from the available secret intelligence that German forces were not yet ready for a full-scale campaign. From the concentration of German forces around Orel to the north of the Kursk salient, and Kharkov to the south, it seemed evident that the main thrust would come there. From their two-year experience of German battle planning they correctly assumed that the attack would be made by two strong armoured thrusts to cut the salient in the rear and encircle Soviet armies strung out across the bulge. Zhukov assumed that Moscow was the ultimate target. No one dissented from the evaluation. For the first time the Soviet high command guessed right.[20]

The more difficult decision was how to respond. Stalin followed his instinct and called for a pre-emptive offensive before the German line had solidified. Zhukov used his head and argued for defence in depth, absorbing the German right and left hooks, wearing down the enemy strength before delivering a knockout punch from large reserve forces hurled forward from the rear – the strategy that some senior soldiers had advocated in 1941. The outcome of the disagreement demonstrated a very different Stalin. On 8 April 1943 he was with the General Staff when the report arrived from Zhukov rejecting Stalin's plans for 'a pre-emptive offensive' and confirming the intelligence that the Kursk salient was the German target. Stalin expressed no view, nor, as Shtemenko recalled, did he resort to the usual complaints about misinformation and deception he had thrown at intelligence assessments of the enemy's intentions in 1941 and 1942. Instead he called a conference for April 12, where he listened carefully to the analysis of German intentions, took account of the reports from front-line commanders, all but one of whom supported the Zhukov option, and finally approved the Zhukov plan. He became agitated only when it was suggested that the probable German aim was to encircle Moscow. Zhukov was instructed to create an unbreachable defence along the central front around Kursk.[21]

Stalin's uncharacteristic willingness to bow to the experts almost certainly saved the Red Army from yet another disastrous summer campaign. The Zhukov plan prevailed (if indeed it was his plan). As with the Stalingrad counter-offensive, there remains doubt about who originated the concept that served as the foundation for the Kursk battle. The important point is that Zhukov, whatever he owed to the local front commanders, was able to persuade Stalin, in defiance of Stalin's own preferences, that this was the right course. The plan represented a return to the traditions of Soviet, indeed Russian, military thinking expressed in the concept of 'deep battle'. The defensive field was prepared with a depth and thoroughness hitherto denied to Soviet forces. It was designed to maximize Soviet firepower and to allow the defensive forces to manoeuvre effectively to counter German thrusts. The buildup of reserves in the rear to inflict the counter-punch provided the General Staff with difficult challenges of co-ordination and timing. The whole operation rested upon the precise management of a battle-field larger than any Soviet commander had mastered before.[22]

Preparations began at once. The main burden of the defence fell on the Central and Voronezh Fronts, which held the north and south of the salient. The Central Front was commanded by General Konstantin Rokossovsky, the man who had reduced the Stalingrad pocket and who was among the most distinguished wartime commanders on either side. Like Zhukov, with whom he had an awkward rivalry, he was the product of a Russian working-class background. The son of a train driver, he was orphaned at fourteen and started work as a building labourer. He saw service in 1914, was promoted to a cavalry sergeant and joined the Red Army in 1918 at the start of a career as a cavalry officer that took him to command of a corps by 1936. This was prominence enough to bring him into the purge net. He was imprisoned for three years, an experience which left him scarred with a deep loathing for the political officials who hovered around the edges of the armed forces, searching for prey. He was a powerful and outspoken man, one of those who dared to cross Stalin when he thought it necessary, and Zhukov, too. The commander of the Voronezh Front, Nikolai Vatutin, was closer to Zhukov, and had served as his deputy in 1941. He worked as a General Staff officer until he was sent to command the key front for the counter-offensive at Stalingrad. He played a central part in planning that campaign and was, at Zhukov's urging, moved to command the front at Kursk because of his proven strategic capability, one of many senior commanders who won their spurs in the Russian tradition, on the basis of success in the field.

Into the bulge around Kursk, Vatutin and Rokossovsky crammed seven armies. To the north and south of the salient the Briansk and South-western Fronts were reinforced to provide the springboard for the counter-offensive. More than 150 miles from the front line the reserve forces were concentrated in the Steppe Front – a tank army, two infantry armies and the 5th Air Army under the command of General Konev, whom Zhukov had saved from Stalin's vengeance in 1941. The defensive zone consisted of six lines inside the salient, with a further two defence belts in front of the reserve armies. The population of the salient were ordered to stay where they were. They were needed to help the troops dig more than 3,000 miles of trenches, which were laid out in a criss-cross pattern to allow defenders to move easily from one firing position to another. The salient bristled with anti-tank traps made from stakes cut from the local forests. Artillery and anti-tank guns were set so that German armour would be met by a veritable 'curtain of fire'. Over 400,000 mines were laid.[23] Streams were dammed up, so that floodwaters could be released, trapping enemy tanks. A gigantic obstacle course stretched out for miles across the rich farmlands and orchards. Dotted here and there were a hundred and fifty airfields; fifty dummy air bases were built to draw the attention of the enemy. When all was complete, 1,336,000 men, 3,444 tanks, 2,900 aircraft and 19,000 guns were moved into place. 'It was,' recalled Vasilevsky, 'a huge, truly titanic task.'[24] Across the front line they were faced by 900,000 German soldiers organized in fifty divisions, with 2,700 tanks, 2,000 aircraft and over 10,000 guns.[25] They were about to fight the largest set-piece battle in history.

Both sides sensed that the fight when it came would be a decisive one. The Red Army had 40 per cent of its manpower and 75 per cent of its armoured forces compressed into the battle zone. The loss of these forces would have spelled disaster. On Hitler's part the success of Citadel was critical, which is why he postponed its starting date until he was more confident of German strength. The German leader was now forced to balance the war in the east with the demands of the wider war effort. By the summer of 1943 Germany faced heavy bombing raids from British and American bomber forces, which tied down growing numbers of men, aircraft and guns that would otherwise have been available for the eastern front. In the Mediterranean the gamble in North Africa had failed, and Axis forces were finally defeated in Tunisia in May, with the surrender of 150,000 German and Italian troops. While Citadel was in preparation, German leaders were aware that the Western Allies might well use North Africa as a springboard for the opening of a southern front in Italy or the Balkans. The initiative still lay with German forces in the east, but it would be dissipated entirely by a summer defeat.

Soviet forces needed to know one thing above all: when would the German attack begin? There began to appear in May strong hints of an imminent German offensive. The Soviet defensive fronts were not yet complete, but a high state of alert was ordered. Hitler, however, postponed the attack, planned for May 3, to June 12. The Soviet high command became increasingly edgy. They launched air strikes against German positions and airfields to disrupt their preparations. A fresh scare arose from each new piece of intelligence: an attack was predicted between May 10 and May 12, then between May 19 and 26. Stalin became nervous and irritable as each scare subsided, to be replaced by another.[26] His urge for action was hard to restrain. The intelligence that began to come in from beyond Soviet borders painted the same pattern of contradictions that Stalin had been faced with in 1941.

One source was a Communist spy ring in Switzerland, which indicated an offensive around June 12, which was correct, but then began to pass on German disinformation that suggested that Citadel had been postponed. Soviet intelligence had access to British Ultra decrypts of German messages from two sources. One was the Communist spy John Cairncross (the 'fifth man' in the Cambridge spy ring that included Burgess, Philby, Blunt and Maclean), who had succeeded in getting a job at the British cipher and code centre at Bletchley Park. On his days off he drove to London in a car supplied by his NKVD recruiter, Anatoli Gorsky, to hand over details of Luftwaffe airfields on the eastern front. This information provided the basis for the pre-emptive strikes against German bases that destroyed 500 German aircraft in three waves of attack. Cairncross could not stand the constant strain and abandoned his task before the battle started. The British Government also passed on details of Citadel, including the code name, on April 30, but later used intercepted comments from the Japanese ambassador to Berlin, Hiroshi Oshima, to suggest to Moscow that Citadel had been abandoned.[27]

The longer they waited the more disconcerting the German delay became. For the men in the Kursk salient the lull meant weeks of oscillating between a nerve-racking state of alert and spells of dull military routine. The wait of over two months strained the morale of troops who knew that the hurricane was coming and that many of them would be swept away by it. In the last week of June the army's own intelligence services detected a sudden change. From intercepted messages and captured German soldiers, snatched by Soviet patrols, it was clear that the enemy was preparing for battle stations. A state of high alert was declared. The attack was expected between July 3 and July 6. On July 2 the Soviet forces went on full alert.

Then suddenly on July 4 activity on the enemy front ceased. An unbearable silence descended. A prisoner captured on the southern front of the salient confessed that the German offensive was timed for dawn on July 5.[28] General Vatutin's Voronezh Front, which held the line opposite Belgorod and Kharkov, was ordered to begin an artillery barrage to disrupt the German front. In the north, where Rokossovsky's Central Front held the line, Zhukov was at the army headquarters to co-ordinate the battle. Around two o'clock in the morning of July 5 news came that a captured German infantry engineer had yielded the precise time. At three o'clock the German force was to attack. Without waiting for Stalin, Zhukov ordered air and artillery strikes. No one could rest. Stalin's own anxiety was evident to Zhukov when he telephoned to Moscow. At half past two in the morning there could be heard 'a terrible rumbling'. The noise of guns, rockets and bombs all merged together, to Zhukov's ears, into a 'symphony from hell'.[29]

The German commanders were caught completely by surprise. For some time they thought that they were the victims of a Soviet offensive of which they had had no inkling. When it became evident that they had been the object of nothing more than a spoiling attack, the order went out to proceed. At half past four on the morning of July 5 Citadel was unleashed. Field Marshal Walther Model's 9th Panzer Army, supported by heavy Tiger tanks and the new Ferdinand self-propelled gun, moved forward in force on a narrow front to pierce a hole in Zhukov's fortress wall. They were met by a web of defensive fire unlike anything the German army had yet encountered. Tanks and men were pinned down while they waited for aircraft to batter a way through. They edged forward a few yards at a time. The hundreds of obstacles were reinforced by mobile anti-tank commandos who launched suicidal attacks on enemy tanks with petrol bombs and crude jamming devices to immobilize them before anti-tank guns could be brought to bear on the more vulnerable rear and sides of the machines. Soldiers hid in ditches and hurled grenades under passing vehicles. The heavy armour of German guns and tanks forced Soviet units to engage them at close range. After the first day the attack had reaped four miles of ground.

On July 6 Model brought up more tanks. A force of 3,000 guns and 1,000 tanks attacked on a front only six miles wide. The movement of armoured reserves from deeper in the salient held the attack and inflicted high losses. The following day proved to be decisive. On July 7, having moved on more than seven miles, the German tanks were turned on the village of Ponyri. The battle was continuous. The thunder of guns and bombs and the heavy smoke soon made it difficult either to hear or to see. German armour was pushed against the main defence line and ground to a halt. The following day a second village, Olkhovatka, was singled out for the German breakthrough. The concentration of tanks in the narrow approaches to the village made them easy prey to the waiting Soviet dive-bombers and the concentration of accurate crossfire from anti-tank guns and heavy artillery. On July 9 German forces in the north reached their limit. Zhukov told Stalin that the time had come. The counter-offensive in the north was timed for July 12. When it began, the German attack crumbled. Rokossovsky's divisions, reinforced by a flood of supplies and men brought in on new rail lines built for the campaign, forced the attackers back over the pits and trenches they had breached a week before, past the grim detritus of a lost battle.[30]

On the southern front of the salient the situation was less encouraging. Although Soviet intelligence on German intentions had been more complete than a year before, the distribution of German forces had

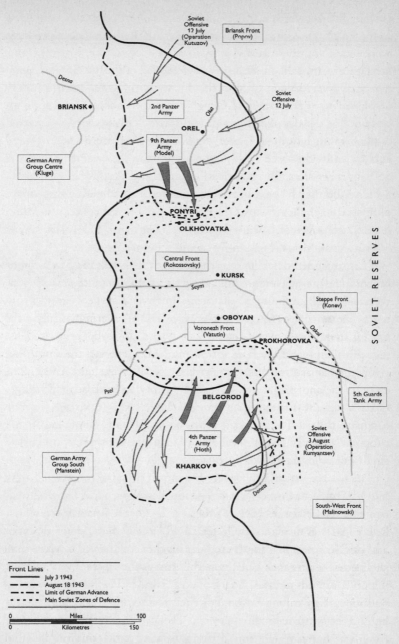

Soviet
Offensive
17 July
(Operation
Kutuzov)

Briansk Front
(Popov)

Desna

BRIANSK ●

Soviet
Offensive
12 July

2nd Panzer
Army

Oka

OREL ●

9th Panzer
Army
(Model)

German Army
Group Centre
(Kluge)

PONYRI ●

OLKHOVATKA

Central Front
(Rokossovsky)

KURSK ●

Seym

OBOYAN ●

Steppe Front
(Konev)

Voronezh Front
(Vatutin)

Oskol

PROKHOROVKA ●

5th Guards
Tank Army

Psel

BELGOROD ●

4th Panzer
Army
(Hoth)

Soviet
Offensive
3 August
(Operation
Rumyantsev)

German Army
Group South
(Manstein)

KHARKOV ●

Donets

South-West Front
(Malinowski)

S O V I E T   R E S E R V E S

Front Lines

——— July 3 1943
– – – August 18 1943
—·—· Limit of German Advance
▪▪▪▪ Main Soviet Zones of Defence

0   Miles   100
0   Kilometres   150

Map 7   Battle of Kursk, 1943

been badly miscalculated. The main weight of the attack was expected in the north, and Soviet defences were stronger there. German forces were in fact more powerful in the south. General Hermann Hoth's 4th Panzer Army fell on the less well-defended of the two Soviet fronts. The Red Army fought to hold the enemy with all the frantic energy displayed to the north, but General Vatutin lacked the weight of armour and density of artillery fire with which Rokossovsky ensnared Model. Hoth had nine Panzer divisions, the cream of the German forces, led by the three most powerful units in the German army, the SS Panzer divisions 'Death's Head', 'Reich' and 'Adolf Hitler Guards'. So hard did they hit that in two days of ferocious fighting they drove almost twenty miles towards the key Oboyan–Kursk road. At German headquarters Manstein waited with mounting confidence for the Soviet front to crumble as it had done so often before.[31]

This time the Soviet enemy stood firm. On July 7 the SS divisions reached the main defensive line, after a gruelling assault against what were only the preliminary obstacles. In their way now stood a full force, the 1st Tank Army. The pace slowed to a crawl. On July 9 the Panzer divisions grouped themselves into a powerful armoured fist and punched one more hole in the line. They crossed the small Psel river, the last natural barrier between the Germans and Kursk. The advance units of the Death's Head division dug in to a small bridge-head. It was the furthest point they reached, the last gasp of a German offensive that had begun two years before. Unable to make further progress, Hoth swung the weight of his attack north-east, towards a small rail junction at Prokhorovka.[32]

The five days from July 9 were the most critical of the whole Kursk battle. The SS armoured corps regrouped and prepared for what was expected to be the decisive manoeuvre against a Soviet force whose heavy losses of men and machines could be seen in the charred bodies and buckled guns that smothered the blackened landscape. More than 500 heavy tanks, many of them the powerful Tigers and Panthers, which could outgun the T-34, rolled forward. The Soviet command had reacted by calling in some of the precious reserve, held back far behind the battle in readiness for the decisive counter-stroke. On July 6 Stalin in person telephoned the commander of 5th Guards Tank

Army, General Pavel Rotmistrov, to order the advance towards Prok-horovka, a gruelling three-day forced march of more than 230 miles. It was Rotmistrov's birthday; a dinner had been arranged. When his guests arrived they found nothing but a table covered with maps. Rotmistrov delivered the details for the march. His health was drunk in champagne captured from a German unit, and at half past one in the morning of July 7, the 5th Guards Tank Army began to move.[33]

The trek was arduous. The army had to march by day and night, despite the threat from German Ju-87 dive-bombers, armed with tank-busting cannon, which had already taken a heavy toll of Soviet armour. The Soviet air force flew overhead to keep German aircraft at bay. Rotmistrov travelled with his men in trucks converted into headquarters, controlling the whole body by radio, as it moved for-ward in a vast phalanx, twenty miles wide. The commander of the reserve front, General Konev, followed in an airplane at a discreet distance to watch the reinforcements in action. It was the first time that a whole tank army had moved under its own power rather than by rail. Conditions soon deteriorated. The heat was already unbearable by eight o'clock in the morning. The endless stream of vehicles threw up a thick, grey dust that covered men, vehicles and horses with a grimy film. The soldiers were soon soaked with sweat and oppressed by a choking thirst. It proved to be a remarkable test of the ruggedness and durability of Soviet vehicles. Surprisingly few were lost despite the rough terrain and the dust. When the army halted on July 9, sixty miles from the front, it was still an intact fighting force. That day Rotmistrov was ordered to bring his force to battle stations and to advance the remaining distance at once. On July 10 the exhausted troops reached the front.[34]

Rotmistrov was ordered to prepare for a large tank battle, but he could have had little idea of what was in store. Against the superior Tiger tanks and Ferdinand self-propelled guns of the enemy he was directed to use his T-34s in the mechanized equivalent of hand-to-hand combat. Up close the T-34s' greater manoeuvrability allowed them to attack German armour at the sides and rear, where at close range real damage could be inflicted. Two days were spent digging in the artillery and priming the tank force. German pressure mounted to the west and east of Prokhorovka, and desperate efforts were made to hold the flanks and prevent a German breakthrough before the reserve army was ready. Zhukov ordered ten regiments of artillery to set up tank-busting units around the township. Stalin ordered Vasilevsky, the Red Army chief of staff, to take over command of the battle himself. On the morning of July 12 two massive tank forces faced each other, 850 Soviet against more than 600 German, the largest tank engagement of the war.

Rotmistrov drove to a dugout in an orchard above the battlefield. Stretched below him was a vast grainfield, tinged yellow with the rising sun. Beyond lay dark woodlands where he knew the German tank force lay concealed. Scouting parties had heard the roar of hundreds of engines during the night, as the SS divisions swung into position. Now the whole scene was strangely quiet, except for the chatter of the communications lines. At exactly 6:30 the first German aircraft appeared. Half an hour later the German bomber force, massed like some swarm of alien insects, their drone growing louder and more filled with menace as they drew overhead, disgorged its bombs on the woods and the villages surrounding Prokhorovka. Before their work was finished Soviet fighters attacked them in large numbers. Aircraft of both sides began to fall out of the sky; the explosion of stricken aircraft replaced the thud of bombs. The bombers turned back to their base.[35]

Waves of Soviet bombers and fighters took their place, smothering the woods ahead with bomb and rocket fire. Soviet artillery opened up, shells and bombs dropping in a continuous rain on the sheltered SS troops. Then at 8:30 Rotmistrov ordered the codeword to attack – 'steel, steel', which in Russian is *stalin*. The word flashed through the force. The T-34 tanks moved from their hiding places across the fields. At exactly the same time, as if 'steel' had been their signal, too, German tanks and guns began to roll out of the fringe of woodland. In an area of little more than three square miles, over one thousand tanks were crashing towards each other. Neither side had intended a head-on clash, but now it was unavoidable. Tanks seldom fought other tanks in pitched battle. Now, like two prehistoric herds, they lumbered towards each other, one savage predator against another.

The ensuing battle was scarcely visible from the hill above, where Rotmistrov stood. Smoke and dust soon obscured the fight. During the day, heavy lashing rain and fierce thunderstorms added nature's portion to the drama. The tanks were soon so enmeshed that both sides had to cease artillery fire and air support. The T-34s, though outgunned, drove in as close as they could to the Tigers and Panthers to inflict real damage. When they ran out of ammunition they rammed enemy tanks. As their machines became immobilized, enemy tanks closed in. Tanks with broken treads or wheels continued firing until their ammunition ran out. When the tanks ran out of shells, Soviet soldiers darted about the battlefield, hurling petrol bombs or grenades. There was little order to the struggle. Both sides suffered debilitating losses. By the end of the day over 700 tanks lay battered and broken, caught in death in grotesque shapes, their hulls pierced, their guns askew, turrets blown off by the force of exploding ammunition or a lucky strike. Beside them lay thousands of burned and burning corpses. After eight hours both sides stopped. Everywhere there were fires burning, in the farms, in the villages, in the meadows and orchards, turned black by the endless blast. When Rotmistrov was at last able to leave his dugout that evening, the rain had cleared. The air itself seemed scorched. After the deafening thunder of battle, he heard the subdued noise of recovery and preparation. Small parties scouted the battlefield for their wounded. The German troops blew up tanks that could not be towed away for repair. A stream of ammunition, fuel and supplies was brought up by truck. Engineers laid new minefields. Rotmistrov fell asleep just before dawn and was awakened several hours later by the morning chorus of falling bombs.[36]

The battle was not over on the first day, but its outcome was more certain. German losses were too great to allow a decisive breakthrough. Soviet forces held the German attack, but made little progress themselves. Flanking movements by heavy German forces to right and left were repulsed. When the attacks began again the following morning, there was no mêlée of tank against tank. German forces probed Soviet defences to find a way through, but Vasilevsky and Vatutin moved their units around quickly enough to blunt German assaults. Two days of further fighting showed that the coveted breakthrough was beyond German strength. On July 15 the battle finally ended with both sides more or less where they started. The SS divisions were devastated. The Death's Head division, which bore the brunt of the fight at Prokhorovka, was withdrawn from the front. The Panzer army lost more than half its men and half its vehicles. Some divisions were down to as little as seventeen serviceable tanks. Soviet losses were also high. On the day after the tank confrontation Rotmistrov had only half his force left, though reinforcements continued to arrive from other parts of the front.[37]

The great tank battle left senior Russian commanders deeply affected. Marshal Zhukov arrived on July 13 to see the damage for himself. He was driven through the stark battlescape with Rotmistrov and Nikita Khrushchev, the Party representative on the Military Council of the front. He stopped the car several times to gaze at the tanks, metal locked to metal. Rotmistrov observed in his guest an uncharacteristic despondency. The man who moved whole armies on the map table was 'awed by the scene' of actual combat.[38] When Vasilevsky, on July 12, watched the tank battle unfold in front of him, it left, he later recalled, 'an indelible impression'. The tank clashes 'had no equal in the war'. For weeks after the battle a whole region, thirty miles long and thirty wide, remained, as one war correspondent described it, 'a hideous desert'; several miles away the air still reeked from the stench of hundreds of unburied bodies, bloated in the summer heat.[39] Here, at Kursk, it was possible to understand the haunting expression coined by Ilya Ehrenburg to describe that summer – 'deep war'.[40]

The battle of Kursk ended any realistic prospect of German victory in the east. A few days before the Prokhorovka clash an Anglo-American force invaded Italy, forcing Hitler to begin shifting valuable army units from the eastern front. On July 13 Citadel was officially cancelled, and Hoth's Panzer army was ordered to mount a fighting retreat back to the lines it had held before July 5.[41] The second stage of Zhukov and Vasilevsky's plan was now activated. There seems to have been almost no suspicion on the German side that the Soviet armed forces had any formal objectives beyond stopping the German attack, nor did German commanders believe that after the exceptional cost imposed on Soviet defenders there existed any serious counter-offensive capability. Yet the real significance of the Kursk battle lay not in the steadfast defence of the salient but in the offensive to follow.

Operation Kutuzov began on the northern edge of the salient on July 12. Soviet forces in their turn had to attack a heavily defended front, with line after line of minefields, trenches, barbed wire and pillboxes. The object was to destroy the German concentrations around Orel and Briansk and unhinge the whole German central front. The attack met strong resistance, but was remarkably successful. Shock forces were concentrated on a narrow front to force open a thin gap in the German line. Strongly supported by aircraft, a combined infantry and tank assault was followed up by a whole tank army, which poured through the gap and fanned out to destroy the German defensive position, an attack that owed a great deal to the vision of Tukhachevsky a decade before. By August 5 Soviet forces recaptured Orel; on August 18 the city of Briansk was again in Soviet hands. The southern counter-offensive, code-named Operation Rumyantsev, was brought under Zhukov's direct control. On August 3 the attack was launched using the reserve Steppe Front to bolster the tired forces that had held back the German attack in July. The objective was the city of Kharkov, where Soviet forces had twice been routed by skilful German counter-strokes. The city of Belgorod fell to the Red Army on August 5. But on the approaches to Kharkov the regrouped German Panzer divisions launched a counter-attack against exposed Soviet tank armies, threatening to repeat their earlier successes. This time Soviet forces were much more effectively deployed, the assault was parried and on August 28 Kharkov fell.

The mood throughout Russia was one of growing elation. Victory prompted Stalin to make what was to be his only visit to a Soviet front. On August 1 he left his *dacha* at Kuntsevo by special train. The locomotive, carriages and platform were camouflaged with branches. He arrived at the Western Front, now many miles to the west of Moscow, where he spent an uneventful night. The next day he went on to the Kalinin Front to the north, where he stayed in a peasant hut (a visit still commemorated by a plaque). He visited neither officers nor men and returned to Moscow the next day.[42] His motives can only be surmised. Perhaps he hoped to impress his own entourage, though so modest a demonstration could scarcely suffice; perhaps he felt real unease that he had sent so many of his countrymen into battle zones of which he had no experience. Having accused so many others of cowardice, he had strong motives for wanting to avoid an accusing finger himself. Whatever his intention, he soon made capital out of the visit. A few days afterwards he wrote to Roosevelt to explain his delay in replying to a message: 'I have to make personal visits to the various sectors of the front more and more often . . .'[43] Two days after his return he ordered a victory salute in Moscow to mark the liberation of Orel and Belgorod. At midnight on August 5 twelve salvos from one hundred and twenty guns thundered over the city, the first of more than three hundred salutes by 1945. 'Eternal glory,' ran Stalin's communiqué, 'to the heroes who fell in the struggle for the freedom of our country.'[44]

The victories of 1943 were won at a high cost in heroes, though the cost was very much less than it had been a year before. Stalingrad cost the lives of 470,000 soldiers and airmen. The battle of Kursk was won at a cost of only 70,000 dead. The German line was broken for the loss of another 183,000. But these are still extraordinary figures. In two months of fighting the Red Army lost almost as many men as the United States or the British Empire did in the entire war.[45] The level of sacrifice imposed on the Soviet people might have debilitated any other society. The terrible haemorrhage of Soviet manpower had been sustained for more than two years, in which time more than 4.7 million were killed, and millions maimed or scarred. So severe was this toll that by the autumn offensives of 1943 Soviet divisions were down to as little as 2,000 men, though bolstered by a large increase in guns and tanks. During the war the labour–capital balance in Soviet military units shifted from high labour input to high capital input. It is a myth that the Soviet Union won the war because it had the endless spaces in the east from which to suck its manpower. In the east there was more space than people. The Soviet Union survived only by mobilizing two-thirds of its women to run the factories and farms, and by modernizing its armed forces so that it did not have to rely any longer on raw numbers of men, but could rely, like the American army, on mass-produced weapons.[46]

Unanswered questions remain, however. The central explanation for the endurance of the Soviet war effort and its final victory lies in the fact that hundreds of thousands of Soviet citizens laid down their lives in the suicidal battles for Leningrad, Kiev, Moscow, Stalingrad and a dozen other cities. There exist so many stories of defence to the death that they cannot all be a product of Stalinist propaganda. Why were casualty rates so high? Why did Red Army soldiers and airmen so often fight with a stubborn disregard for the physical dangers they faced?

There are easy answers: the high death rate and fanatical resistance were a product first of an oppressive political system and second of the Soviet way of war. There is some truth in both of these contentions. The army was kept in constant touch with the Party through the political officers attached to each unit, and the large number of Communist Party members and activists in the armed forces who were under special instructions to show a uniquely socialist brand of courage. The regime regarded them as the moral cement which held the army together; their task was to maintain confidence in victory, and to instil 'contempt for death'.[47] During the war three million Party members lost their lives in combat. In addition there was the NKVD, whose three-quarter of a million troops brought the terror right up to the front line. They played a part in 1941 and 1942 in keeping the battle going.[48] The ability of the political system to compel sacrifice through propaganda and force certainly played a part, but a poem by Yuri Belash, a veteran of the conflict, suggests that the link between the regime and the troops was more tenuous than might have been expected from the endless uplifting talks: 'To be honest about it/ in the trenches the last thing we thought about/ was Stalin./ God was on our minds more./ Stalin played no part at all/ in our soldiers' war.'[49]

There is more to recommend the second argument. The Soviet way of war did produce excessive casualties. Even before the war there existed a harsh disciplinary code. Soviet officers took the view that the army had a task to perform; saving lives was not a priority as long as the objective was achieved. 'In our country,' complained another veteran, 'results of some kind are always more important than anything else, more than people. Russia has plenty of people, she has enough of them to waste.'[50] Officers applied this to their own station. During the war 973,000 officers were killed or captured, a casualty rate of more than 35 per cent.[51] They spurred on the men, and, in the Russian military tradition, led by example. Yet the carnage can hardly have been their first choice. The high casualty rates were dictated more by the nature of the conflict and the demands of a political system that placed incompetent Party men in positions of military responsibility.

Faced with a brutal and efficient enemy, fighting a desperate, improvised defence, with poor supplies of weapons, widespread disorganization of command and a remarkable degree of tactical ineptitude – symbolized by the methodical tramping of rows of riflemen with bayonets fixed towards German machine-guns – losses were certain to be high. These early losses created a vicious circle. By 1942 only 8 per cent of the cadres of the army remained.[52] The new recruits, both officers and men, were inexperienced and suffered further high losses as a result. Surviving officers were promoted rapidly to fill vacant senior posts, leaving insufficiently trained juniors to replace them. They were quickly hardened by battle, but inexperience took its toll. When by 1943 the supply of weapons improved and the quality of leadership and organization forged in war created growing confidence among the troops, losses dropped significantly. By the time of Kursk, the Soviet high command had created conditions of combat in which casualties could be kept at supportable levels. The Soviet theory of the 'field of fire', where a proper balance among artillery, tanks and infantry could reduce troop losses and multiply the effectiveness of gunfire, was well known in the 1930s. Only by 1943 were the weapons available to try to achieve it. At Kursk the casualty rate was half that at Moscow; by the battles of 1944 the rate was only one-quarter.[53] Without such improvements in battlefield performance the Soviet war effort would have collapsed in 1943. The reconstruction of an almost entirely new army on the ruins of the collapse in 1941, one capable of holding its own against the attacker, ranks as the most remarkable achievement of the war.

One awkward fact makes it difficult to accept that the Soviet system as such squandered its manpower in war: the Tsarist armies between

1914 and 1917 averaged 7,000 casualties a day, compared with 7,950 a day between 1941 and 1945.[54] The figures are not entirely reliable, but they give a sense of proportion. During the First World War the sacrifice of human lives, in a contest that proved unwinnable, was little less than the sacrifice of the Second. This strongly suggests that the explanation lies not in the Soviet system, but in the traditions of Russian life, military life in particular. In the Tsarist army the readiness of the soldier for self-sacrifice was regarded as a true test of the moral preparation of the force. Dereliction of duty or desertion were treated as harshly as they were after 1941, with summary executions and 'penal battalions'. It was General Dragomirov, a prominent pre-1914 military thinker, who argued that proper military training inculcated an ability to suppress the natural instinct for self-preservation in favour of the group.[55] The distinction between the 'we' and the 'I' was symptomatic of a deeper social outlook in Russian life, where collectivism was preferred to individualism. These cultural traditions were borrowed and enlarged by Soviet Communism. Years later, in 1942, a military commissar complained about the egoism of many around him: 'All that one can hear is: "I", and yet again "I". They have long forgotten about "us".'[56] This tradition alone does not explain the death rates in Russia's war, but it does suggest a shared social and cultural environment in which the individual was perceived to matter a great deal less than the whole, whether village, community or motherland.

These are, of course, abstractions. They can scarcely do justice to the suffering of the millions of ordinary Soviet citizens, more than half of them former peasants, who had to live for years in the constant shadow of violent death. 'Mine was a noisy age,' wrote Ehrenburg. 'Men were swiftly extinguished . . .'[57] Soviet soldiers coped with this reality in a number of ways. Many were already used to a way of life that was harsh and unrelenting. The physical hardships and brutality of everyday life, in the villages and in the factories, were very different from life in the West, although such differences are seldom acknowledged with sufficient force. In the course of little more than a generation much of the population had endured the upheavals of Tsarist modernization, war, revolution and a savage civil war. The 'revolution from above' accustomed many Soviet citizens to the death or forced migration of millions of their own kind. The state of war was an acute one, but it was endured by a tough and fatalistic people as they had endured earlier sufferings.

Death was inescapable, ever present, but, as Ehrenburg found on his many visits to the front, the soldiers deliberately distanced themselves from it: 'The men lived in such close proximity to death itself that they had stopped noticing it; a way of life had been established.'[58] No one talked about death. There was a pervasive sentimentality, captured in the poetry and literature of the war and its popular songs. Ehrenburg's soldiers preferred to think about the past or hope for the future. They each believed with a superstitious conviction that they would survive while others perished. The future kept a great many soldiers fighting. For some it was a future in which the German enemy was smashed and the motherland regained; but for most soldiers the future must have beckoned in more mundane ways. 'I do not complain of my lot/,' ran one poem, 'but long to see, if only for one day/ a day that is an ordinary day/ when the darkness of the thick shade of trees means nothing more than summer, silence, sleep.'[59]

The fatalism of the ordinary soldier was at the root of that willingness for self-sacrifice which many of them exhibited throughout the war. It is easy to romanticize Russian stoicism. The artist Aleksandr Dzhikiya, writing in 1990, argued that during the war 'in spite of all the deprivations, burdens and victimization' there existed 'some kind of spiritual light'.[60] Soldiers may indeed have felt at certain moments an intense spirituality, a mobilization of the soul, a longing for a beautiful death. These sentiments seem less out of place in the context of Russian culture than they would be in much of the rest of Europe, and they should not be overlooked. Yet the day-to-day reality of a soldier's existence was less elevated. They were fearful, tired, bullied by their officers, often short of food and endlessly homesick, but despite the climate of deprivation most displayed a stubborn resilience and a simple, unselfconscious patriotism in the daily struggle for existence. They continued to fight and to die in their millions, not for Stalin, not for Communism, but for numberless smaller ambitions.

After Kursk the war made greater sense to the Soviet public. Its object was to drive the Germans from what remained to them of the Soviet Union, from the Ukraine, from Belorussia, from the Crimea. In August 1943 Stalin again pressed for a general offensive from Leningrad to the Black Sea, before the enemy recovered from the losses of the previous two months. In the centre, where German forces had had eighteen months to prepare a defence in depth, the Red Army made slow progress. After a complex and costly operation they captured Smolensk in late September. Stalin's chief objective was the Dnepr River, which ran from Kiev in the north down to the Black Sea. This became Hitler's objective too. German intelligence, which had misjudged the size and depth of Soviet forces at Kursk, now produced a gloomy picture of a Soviet colossus bearing down on a weakened German front. 'All hell is loose on the eastern front,' wrote Hitler's chief of staff to his wife.[61] Hitler at last approved a general retreat. German forces, while pursuing an active defence to slow down the Soviet steamroller, were ordered to move to the western bank of the Dnepr and to stand fast there at all costs.

Soviet forces were not as fearsome as the German picture suggested. The numbers of men and tanks were much reduced after Kursk. Rotmistrov's 5th Guards Tank Army was reduced from five hundred tanks to fifty. As he advanced towards the Dnepr he divided the fifty into three separate units, then set up a phantom radio communications net to persuade German eavesdroppers that he had a whole tank army at his back. In the south, German forces faced large infantry armies with a weak sprinkling of Soviet armour. Red Army divisional strength was approximately half the number it had been in 1942. Soviet weaknesses prevented a more decisive attack, and although much of the Donbas industrial region was recovered, German forces eluded capture and re-formed a powerful Panzer group to defend the lower reaches of the river from Zaporozhe to the Black Sea.

Nevertheless the movement was almost all one way. The Red Army had a string of victories behind it; German forces knew that, with operations in Italy and the threat of a cross-Channel invasion, they could not provide the strength now to hold everything in the East. By the third week of September the Red Army had reached the Dnepr north and south of Kiev. Stalin announced that he would award the

August 23
September 16
September 30
December 23
Fronts As From October 20

Miles 100
Kilometres 200

MOSCOW

Kalinin Front
1 Baltic Front
(Yeremenko)

VITEBSK

Belorussia
SMOLENSK

Western Front
(Sokolovsky)

KALUGA

MOGILEV

KIROV

Army Group
Centre
(Kluge, Busch later)

Briansk Front
(Popov)

BRIANSK

OREL

GOMEL

Pripet

SEVSK

Central Front
Belorussian Front
(Rokossovsky)

KURSK

VORONEZH

Desna

OBOYAN

Voronezh Front
1 Ukrainian Front
(Vatutin)

KIEV
ZHITOMIR

Nov 6

BELGOROD

Steppe Front
2 Ukrainian Front
(Konev)

Psel

KHARKOV

POLTAVA

Army Group
South
(Manstein)

Ukraine

South-West Front
3 Ukrainian Front
(Malinovsky)

Vorskla

Donets

VOROSHILOVGRAD

Yuzhny Bug

DNEPROPETROVSK

STALINO

South Front
4 Ukrainian Front
(Tolbukhin)

KRIVOY ROG

NIKOPOL

ZAPOROZHYE

Army Group A
(Kleist)

Dniepr

ROSTOV

Dniestr ODESSA

KHERSON

Sea of Azov

Danube

ROMANIA

CRIMEA

KERCH

North Caucasus
Front (Petrov)

KRASNODOR

SEVASTOPOL

BLACK SEA

Map 8   From Kursk to Kiev, August–December 1943

coveted title of Hero of the Soviet Union to the first soldiers to cross to the other side of the river. Over the following week no fewer than forty small bridgeheads were established on the far bank. Soldiers improvised as best they could. Hundreds took small boats under constant enemy fire in their eagerness to breach Hitler's rampart. A few swam across. The German army surrounded the bridgeheads, but could not dislodge them.[62]

One bridgehead they neglected. North of Kiev, near the village of Liutezh, one infantry division had negotiated the swamps and marshes of the upper Dnepr, where it waited in what the Germans regarded as impassable terrain. On the east side of the Dnepr lay Vatutin's Voronezh Front, which had begun the campaign defending Kursk, now many miles to the rear. It was renamed the 1st Ukrainian Front as an indication of its new destination. Vatutin was ordered to send armour and men into the swampy enclave as a stepping-off point for an attack on Kiev. Soviet methods of deception and concealment were now so sophisticated that the enemy guessed nothing of what was happening. The first tank corps to arrive crossed the marshland by sealing up every orifice of their T-34 tanks and rushing at full speed through the mud. In October a second group, 3rd Guards Tank Army, was moved in complete secrecy into the bridgehead. Poor weather conditions prevented German air reconnaissance, and extensive deception measures further south persuaded Field Marshal von Manstein, in command of the Kiev defence force, that the enemy would attack from its larger and drier bridgeheads below the city. Instead, on November 3, the German defenders were taken by complete surprise as two whole armies poured out of the swamps to the north of the city.[63] Two days later the armies entered Kiev itself. At four o'clock in the morning of November 6 the Ukrainian capital was captured, just in time for the annual celebration of the Russian Revolution.

In Moscow the liberation of Kiev was welcomed with an extravagant display of fireworks. Stalin talked of the 'year of the great turning-point' in his commemoration speech. On November 7, while Soviet forces fought pitched battles against Manstein's Panzer divisions to enlarge their grip on Kiev, the Soviet Foreign Minister, Vyacheslav Molotov, threw a sumptuous party. It was later reported to be the most opulent of the war. Soviet officials were dressed in a newly designed pearl-grey uniform, hung with gold braid. The atmosphere was lush, the drink plentiful, so much so that the British ambassador fell face-first onto the table, cutting himself. Other diplomats were carried out unconscious. Shostakovich appeared in full evening dress. Endless toasts were drunk to the successes of Allied armies, and to international goodwill. The mood was reported to be exuberant, even bohemian.[64]

After five months of continuous campaigning, almost two-thirds of the area once occupied by Axis forces was cleared. Stalin was now in a position to think about the future, after German defeat. He accepted an invitation from Roosevelt to meet outside the Soviet Union, in the Iranian capital of Teheran, to discuss the future of Allied strategy and the politics of the post-war world. On November 24 he boarded a special train for the south, accompanied by Molotov and Voroshilov and officers from the General Staff. The train travelled through the broken city of Stalingrad. At intervals Stalin summoned the staff officers to give him the latest information from the fighting fronts. The train arrived in the oil city of Baku, where two aircraft were waiting to take the party on to Teheran. Stalin was invited to fly with the more senior pilot, a general. He refused on the grounds that 'generals don't do much flying', and flew instead with a colonel at the controls, escorted by twenty-seven Soviet fighters.[65]

The Teheran Conference marked a clear change in the relationship among the three Allied powers. Churchill found himself isolated between the two new superpowers. After Stalingrad and Kursk, Stalin was now arguing from a position of strength, and he wanted his allies to honour their commitment to absorb some of the German army's fighting capacity and relieve the drain on Soviet manpower. Roosevelt came to the conference curious to meet his Soviet partner and eager to lay the foundation for a more permanent relationship. On the first day Stalin informed the President of a possible German plot to assassinate him and invited him to stay in the Soviet embassy, where the conference was to be held. Roosevelt agreed, unaware perhaps of Stalin's persistent paranoia about assassination but pleased to be able to establish closer physical contact with the Soviet delegation. Stalin and his party were housed in the embassy grounds, in the ambassador's residence. The rest of the Soviet delegation was housed in a former harem close by.[66] Stalin and Roosevelt began the conference on November 28 with an informal, private conversation that excluded Churchill. The two men, according to the interpreter's recollection, established a quick rapport. After the usual small talk, Roosevelt made it clear to Stalin that his aim was to start up a front that would 'divert some thirty to forty German divisions away from the Soviet-German front'. Stalin gave a laconic reply – 'It would be very good if that could be done'[67] – before moving on to a wide range of lesser issues.

The question of a western front was the central issue. Roosevelt arrived in Teheran determined to force the British to commit themselves to a cross-Channel invasion in 1944. This early conversation laid the groundwork. When the three leaders met later that afternoon the second front was raised by Stalin in his opening remarks, delivered in a voice so soft that the whole conference room descended into a deathly hush in order to hear him. Stalin asked his coalition partners for a firm commitment to invade northern France as soon as possible. The invasion plan, Operation Overlord, had been in preparation for some months, but Churchill was personally less attracted to the plan than Roosevelt and his advisers. Stalin's insistence on a commitment to Overlord made Churchill's position difficult. Stalin unfurled two cigarettes as he was talking and placed the tobacco in his pipe, lit it, screwed up his eyes and stared at the President and Churchill. Roosevelt was observed to wink at Stalin. When Churchill finally spoke, he knew that he was outnumbered. He described the possibility of other fronts in the Mediterranean. Stalin interrogated him as he might a senior commander. The discussion became awkward and tense, and was postponed.

Churchill continued to argue that Overlord could not be mounted the following spring, when Stalin wanted it, but on the second day, following a direct question from an exasperated Stalin, Churchill was forced to concede in front of the assembly that he, too, favoured a cross-Channel invasion in the spring. The following day the President began the conference session by baldly stating the Western Allies' intention of invading in force in May 1944. Stalin showed little outward sign at hearing the news. His interpreter noticed a slight paleness and a voice softer than ever: 'I am satisfied with this decision.' In return Stalin pledged the Soviet Union to invade Japan after the defeat of Germany. Some inconclusive discussion was begun on the post-war settlement in Europe and the fate of Germany and its leaders. The main decision made, the mood of the conference lightened. That night the British embassy hosted Churchill's sixty-ninth birthday celebration. Stalin toasted his allies after the feast: 'My fighting friend, Roosevelt,' 'My fighting friend, Churchill.' Churchill was more circumspect after the bruising engagements with Stalin around the conference table. He toasted 'Roosevelt, the President, my friend!' but 'Stalin the mighty,' a shift of emphasis that needed no interpretation. Roosevelt, who had acted the peace-maker for much of the conference, hailed, not his partners, but his ideal of world co-operation: 'To our unity – war and peace!' The conference broke up with mutual expressions of goodwill.[68]

Stalin flew back to Baku, where he changed into a simple soldier's greatcoat and cap without insignia. The train taking him back to Moscow stopped briefly at Stalingrad, where Stalin alighted to look at the destroyed city before going on to Moscow. The Soviet side placed little trust in the promise extracted at Teheran. The second front was needed to ease the strain on the Red Army. But Stalin came away from Teheran with the knowledge that his own armed forces had inflicted defeats on a force three times greater than the armies manning the Atlantic wall. On his return from Teheran he told Zhukov, 'Roosevelt has given his word that extensive action will be mounted in France in 1944. I believe that he will keep his word. But even if he does not, our own forces are sufficient to complete the rout of Nazi Germany.'[69] This was a bold statement. Kursk did not win the war, but after the Soviet Union had lived for two years in the shadow of defeat, it opened the door to the possibility of victory.

8

False Dawn:
1943–44

It is five o'clock in the morning of a grey, rainy, autumn day; the foremen are driving out the hungry men, drenched and angry, clothed in rags and torn boots, many of them hardly able to move their feet from exhaustion; and there on the platform near the gates a band is playing a lively march tune.

a Gulag prisoner

If the term 'total war' has any real meaning it surely describes the Soviet Union at the height of its war with Germany. No other state diverted so much of its population to work for the war effort; no other state demanded such heavy and prolonged sacrifices from its people. Life on the home front was a struggle that mirrored the bitter conflict at the warring front. The victories after 1943 were purchased at a heavy price. Stalin's promise to turn the Soviet Union into a single war camp was no mere rhetoric. War dominated every element of daily life.

From the very start of the war normal civilian life ceased. Peasants grew food for the war; factory workers produced weapons for the war; scientists and engineers invented new ways of waging war; bureaucrats and policemen organized and oppressed the rest. In the shadow of impending defeat in 1941 and 1942 the lives and interests of individuals counted for very little. The country's scientists, drawn from no fewer than seventy-six research institutes, were uprooted and transplanted into the Ural city of Sverdlovsk and organized under a State Science Plan, published in May 1942. Committees of scientists were given responsibility for different parts of the war effort – some for tanks, some for aviation, some for agriculture and so on. Geologists were sent into the remote areas of Siberia to find new sources of minerals and oil to compensate for the losses in the Ukraine.[1] Even some experts were recruited who had fallen foul of the regime in the 1930s and ended up in labour camps. The aircraft designer Aleksàndr Tupolev and his team, imprisoned because Stalin turned against the large multi-engined aircraft they designed, worked, in 1941, on drawing-boards inside the camp compounds.[2]

Daily life was at its grimmest on the land. The villages gave up their male workers to the armed forces. By 1944 nearly three-quarters of the men who had worked the collective farms had gone. Those who remained were the sick or the elderly, or farmers who had been disabled at the front. The great bulk of the work to produce the food supplies vital to the cities and the fighting front was done by Russian women. They made up half the rural workforce in 1941; by 1944 the figure was nearly four-fifths.[3] Their routine was relentless and miserable. Unlike the rest of the population, peasants did not qualify for ration cards. At the collective farms they were given a few chunks of bread or an occasional potato. They were expected to subsist on what they could grow themselves on their small garden plots. The lucky ones might sell their surpluses on the open market – after the Government had taken its quota. Some peasants grew temporarily rich by exploiting the black market. But for most peasant women, and the boys and old men who helped them, the war years were uniformly bleak. They lacked the tools and horses to plough and sow. They hacked away at the ground with sticks and rods; teams of women hauling ploughs became a familiar sight. When they finished their daily shift, some were forced to join local logging gangs, hauling the wood often long distances, summer and winter, to provide vital fuel for the cities. Many peasants went hungry and cold for want of the food and firewood they produced for others. They lost millions of their menfolk at the front. They found themselves the unwilling hosts of thousands of refugees from the west, many of whom starved to death in the early years of the war, abandoned by the regime and victimized by villagers who saw no reason to feed unwanted guests.

Life in the city was harsh, but in one important respect it was easier to bear. Work earned food. Everyone who was fully employed was entitled to a ration card. Those who would not or could not work either lived from the charity of their families or starved to death. In the bleakest months of the war, in 1942, the weakest perished. There was in this a cruel rationality. Those who worked and fought were rewarded. The rest were dispensable. Work was difficult to escape. On 13 February 1942, the Supreme Soviet decreed the mobilization of every able-bodied citizen for the war effort. Not every factory was placed under martial law, but NKVD troops were always on hand. New conditions of work were set. A sixty-six-hour week became the norm, with one rest-day a month. Vacations were suspended. Compulsory overtime was introduced.[4] More than half the factory workforce were women; many were young boys, waiting until they were old enough to trade in their overalls for a uniform. The hours they worked, in factories where safety standards were at best rudimentary and work norms fiercely imposed, were uniformly debilitating. Health declined over the war years, as the city populations, short of medical personnel and medicines, became prey to typhus, dysentery, tuberculosis and scurvy.

It was food that kept the system going. The quantities were low, the food was often adulterated and its supply unpredictable, but the regime made strenuous efforts to avoid the mistakes which had led to revolution in 1917. A comprehensive system of ration standards was introduced in July 1941. They were not uniform. Children and elderly dependants got very little, around 700 calories a day; those who worked literally at the coalface got over 4,000. Most ordinary workers got between 1,300 and 1,900, well below what was needed to sustain the interminable routine of work with efficiency, but enough to keep it going.[5]

Very soon the population found ways to supplement the monotonous diet of grey bread, potatoes and perhaps a quarter pound of meat and fat a week. The Government gave permission to set up urban gardens. By 1942 there were over five million of them, by 1944 over sixteen million, sown in parks and public gardens or in long ribbons beside the roads to the cities.[6] How workers found the time to play part-time peasant is hard to understand. Even more extraordinary was the yield: by 1944 they supplied one-quarter of the country's potato crop. 'Digging for victory' became an everyday part of urban life. So too did pilfering. Food shortages created a crime wave across Russia. The gardens were difficult to guard; food stores were regularly looted. In 1943 600,000 'social controllers' were appointed to stand guard over food supplies or to report thieves to the authorities. Food theft carried the death penalty.[7]

Another source of food was the black market. The authorities turned a blind eye to the food trade. Anything left after the fixed state quotas – around 90 per cent of production on the collective farms – was left to the peasants to sell at any price they could get. They gathered at the city food markets, selling food openly at more than twenty times what it had cost in 1941. An American visitor at the Moscow central market in 1944 found that a kilo of bread cost almost the equivalent of a week's wages. The whole covered area was a gigantic bazaar, crowded with Muscovites eager to barter. Women sold honey or flowers at vastly inflated prices; one old lady offered a calf's head 'with the hair on and glassy eyes open', infested with flies; other women, defying Communist morality, offered the farmers sex in exchange for food, 'big, strapping girls . . . all fixed up with lipstick, red shoes, red ribbons in their hats, their eyelashes smeared with stove blacking'.[8]

Few ordinary Russians could afford the prices unless they had something precious to trade with. For many workers the factory, for all its forbidding, exhausting routine, became a source of nourishment and warmth. Canteens provided a warm meal at least once a day. Nurseries were built so that mothers could work. Factories set up their own farms and stored food to reward the workers. Bonuses for work above the norms were paid in food, since money meant little in the market-place. For the new wave of wartime Stakhanovites – and there were many – consistent high performance earned a place at the special tables in the canteens reserved for exceptional workers, who got exceptional diets. Workers who volunteered to give blood regularly for the medical services at the front got a month's salary, a three-course meal, 500 grams of butter or sugar and an extra ration card. In Moscow alone up to 300,000 people gave blood. Thousands who did not qualify for food cards gave blood to keep alive – blood for food, food for blood.[9]

The Soviet home front kept going, despite the massive losses on the battlefield, the shattered families, the stream of refugees and migrants, the constant struggle for food and necessities, the tough regimen of labour. It was an extraordinary collective achievement for a system that was widely regarded in the West as primitive and fragile, dominated by the heavy hand of state planning. In the chaotic circumstances of the early months of war the regime resorted to emergency measures and hectic improvisation, which worked more effectively than the desperate military measures, in part because civilian officials, unlike military ones, did not have to account to a military commissar for every move. Slowly a more settled and centralized planning system was installed. It was based on that of the peacetime economy, which proved readily adaptable to the peculiar circumstances of wartime organization.[10] The Five-Year Plans had familiarized officials and producers with national planning and the allocation of resources. It is unlikely that any other system would have succeeded in extracting either the food or the weapons, given the conditions that existed after the invasion. Planning did not work perfectly. In Kuibyshev at times workers were given chocolate instead of bread until they grew sick of it; the coveted meat ration sometimes turned out to be pickles or jam, or whatever the city authorities had to spare.[11] But on balance the ability of a shrunken economy, with severe shortages of food, materials and labour, to out-produce its seemingly more prosperous and productive enemy can be explained only by the corresponding ability of the Soviet state to keep a grip on its scarce resources and their allocation.

The more sinister face of state power was never very far away. The Gulag prisons beckoned for any act of dissent or negligence, for the theft of a ration card or food or the 'sabotage' of production targets. The network of camps was drawn into the war effort along with the rest of Soviet society. They provided, as they had done in the 1930s, a ready supply of captive workers for state projects.[12] Until the opening of Soviet archives in the 1980s the nature and extent of the system were open to speculation, though the recollections of its victims long ago revealed the cruel price of Soviet slavery. Now a great deal more is known about the details of the system itself. The Gulag (the name is an acronym of Main Directorate of Corrective Labour Camps) controlled only a fraction of the slave labour force. High wartime death rates from malnutrition and disease and the release of some of the inmates reduced the number of Gulag prisoners in its fifty-three camps from 1.2 million in 1942 to 660,000 in 1945.[13] For prisoners on short sentences there was a separate 'labour colony' organization that by 1945 held 850,000 prisoners, in conditions often worse than those of the Gulag. The NKVD prison population added another quarter of a million. The largest group consisted of deportees who were resettled in Siberia or Kazakhstan, a total of 1.4 million. The total of these and all other categories of forced labour was 4.3 million in 1942, falling slightly to 3.9 million in 1945; they were held in a total of 131 camps and colonies, and 1,142 smaller branch camps, in which conditions were often poorer from lack of effective supervision.[14]

These figures on the size of the camp labour force are substantially below the older estimates, which ranged from 10 million to 20 million, but the evidence is overwhelmingly in favour of the more modest sums. As they stand the statistics are bleak enough. They do not cover all of those who passed into and out of the camp system at some time between 1941 and 1945. During the war years 2.4 million were sent to the Gulag and 1.9 million were freed. These figures make clear that a substantially larger number of people experienced prison life at some time during the war than the figures on the size of the prison population at any one time suggest. Nor do the figures on those inside the camps indicate the numbers who died in transit, who were killed deliberately, or who perished from the cold, hunger or disease. The official figures show 621,000 deaths in the Gulag.[15]

This is the tip of an iceberg whose exact size may never be known. The labour colonies had a higher death rate than the Gulag camps for most of the war. In 1942 the death rate reached 27 per cent, against a figure of only 2.4 per cent in the first half of 1941.[16] Most died from malnutrition and disease. The millions deported to Siberia suffered particular hardships. They were packed in railroad cars with little or nothing to eat and drink; the bodies of those who died were unceremoniously dumped beside the railway track. When they arrived they were left in open fields, behind wire, with no more than tents to shelter them. Death came from neglect rather than from murder. Violent death was, by the war period, more unusual. In the camps death was meted out for insurrection or camp crime. The toughest criminals were sent to the camps along with political prisoners; they formed a kind of mafia in the prison, intimidating, murdering and robbing other inmates. Genuine dissidents always ran a risk. In 1942 the NKVD was ordered to murder all prisoners suspected of Trotskyite sympathies, though how many were actually killed remains unknown.

The camp and colony population came from all parts of the Soviet Union and all walks of life. The majority were ethnic Russians, almost two-thirds in 1944.[17] Many were genuine criminals and sociopaths. Some were genuine dissidents in the eyes of the regime, like the artillery officer and future novelist Aleksandr Solzhenitsyn, or the engineer Dmitri Panin, both of whom have left vivid accounts of life inside the camps. But most were innocent of any crime, political or otherwise. They were peasants unable to fill grain quotas, workers who failed to keep time, thousands who were guilty of nothing more dangerous than conversations with foreigners. Women who fraternized with Westerners at the transit ports for Lend-Lease goods or with the foreign legations in Moscow found themselves classified as spies and swelled the growing number of women in the camps and labour colonies. For the regime the nature of the deviancy did not matter a great deal. The camps came to be seen as a convenient source of emergency labour. When one harassed Gulag official was asked for more workers he replied, 'What are we to do? The fact is we haven't as yet fulfilled our plans for imprisonments. Demand is greater than supply.'[18]

The descriptions of camp life all reveal an unbroken cycle of deprivation and wretchedness. Though thousands died from the effects of cold, poor diet and disease, they were not extermination camps like Auschwitz. The NKVD had separate 'execution camps' where prisoners were kept whose fate was the standard bullet in the back of the neck. The object of the labour camps was to use the raw labour power of the unfortunate inmates to carve out quarries, dig canals and roads or work in mines in areas so remote and frozen that no one else would work there. For many this meant a slow death. In 1943 a new category of heavy labour (*katorga*) was introduced for the worst offences. Heavy labour meant twelve-hour shifts with no rest days and small quantities of potatoes and soup. According to one estimate these conditions were bad enough to kill off 28,000 prisoners sent to the Vorkuta mines in their first year of operation.[19]

Camp life was primitive and brutal. Prisoners lived in wooden barracks, which were often poorly heated. They slept in bunks on crude bedding stuffed with straw or wood shavings, set in tiers of two or three. They were summoned at five o'clock in the morning for roll call. They then set off in work details dressed in crude boots and jerkins. In winter, when the temperature seldom rose above minus thirty degrees, they were inadequately clothed. Food was poor and served at irregular intervals. Twelve-hour shifts were worked without a meal. Prisoners stole or bartered for extra food. A curious residual trade flourished in the camps among prisoners and between prisoners and guards. In the evening there was a second roll call; the counting continued until all those who had become sick, died, escaped or simply fallen asleep beyond waking were satisfactorily accounted for. When the dead were carried out of the camp gate in makeshift coffins, the guards in Panin's camp drove a bayonet through the head of each corpse to ensure that no one feigning death should escape. The routine of prison life was repeated day in, day out. In most of the prisoners it produced a dull resignation. At the end of a day in his camp, Solzhenitsyn's anti-hero Ivan Denisovich did not know 'whether he wanted freedom or not . . . Freedom meant one thing to him – home. But they wouldn't let him go home.'[20]

During the war the camp population became an emergency source of labour, shifted from one project to another and from one ministry to another, as the need dictated. There was no alternative to work. A refusal to work brought public beatings and no rations. A third refusal was met by a death sentence, carried out in the sight of the other camp inmates. Only a serious illness – not merely the debilitation brought on by the tough routine – brought exemption, but a serious illness was likely to be fatal. As a result opponents of the regime found themselves compelled to work for the victory of a system they wished to see destroyed. This placed them in fresh danger, for the camps reproduced on a smaller scale the system of arbitrary terror which had put them there in the first place. Camp informers and *agents provocateurs* were paid in food and favours to denounce their fellow-prisoners for slacking or sabotage.

One of these 'double victims', the engineer Dmitri Panin, found himself in a situation reminiscent of a Kafka novel. An indiscreet critic of the regime, Panin was denounced by an acquaintance in 1939, and arrested and incarcerated in the Vyatka labour camp. As an educated technician he found himself in charge of the camp machine shop, where he was responsible for inspecting the camp's engineering output. Despite his hatred of the regime, he was scrupulous in checking the quality of the goods his workshop produced, since any mistake might have landed him or some other worker in the punishment cells. When the first order came in for casings for anti-personnel mines he supervised the change-over to war production and had the first machine running in twenty-four hours.[21] Every day the camp commandant visited Panin to ask whether the production quota had been met, demanding detailed explanations when it was not. Panin realized that he would be held responsible for any mistake. He continued to introduce improvements and speed up production, but finally he fell foul of a camp director named Yevko, a former member of the secret police, whose attempt to introduce an unsuitable machine into the workshop was vetoed by Panin. A few months later Panin was arrested with twenty-seven other prisoners as an 'insurrectionist', having been betrayed to the unsympathetic Yevko by several camp informers with grudges against him. He was arrested by armed men and held with almost nothing to eat in a punishment cell. Production at the workshop declined. Panin defended himself as a valuable expert: 'I am only a prisoner, but I nevertheless set up our war-production line and got it moving.' It made no difference. He was accused and convicted of a range of implausible crimes and given ten years' *katorga*. (Convicted with him was a former lighthouse-keeper who had been imprisoned in the first place on the unlikely charge that he was spreading anti-Soviet propaganda from his isolated look-out.) He nearly starved in the punishment block and survived a murder attempt by a deranged serial killer with whom he was forced to share a cell, before being transported to the notorious Vorkuta mines after the war's end.[22]

The camps made a formidable contribution to the war effort, thanks in part to men like Panin. The Gulag camps produced approximately 15 per cent of all Soviet ammunition, including 9.2 million anti-personnel mines and 25.5 million large-calibre shells; they produced uniforms, leather goods, 1.7 million gas masks and large quantities of food. Over 2 million prisoners were used on railways and roads, in mines and lumber plants. They were a new breed of serf – mere objects, unfree and expendable, passed from one hand to another for their labour alone, as many of their grandfathers had been.[23]

During 1944, as each German-occupied territory fell to the Soviet advance, Stalin began to exact a terrible revenge upon the millions of Soviet people who were accused of collaboration with the fascist enemy – reviving the spirit and practices of the civil war. The axe fell not only on those individuals who had worked for the German authorities or fought in military units organized by the German army, many of whom were executed out of hand, but on whole nations. Stalin had never been a friend to the many non-Russian peoples. Ever since the early 1920s, when as Commissar for the Nationalities he used brute force to unite them under Russian Communist rule, Stalin had entertained a deep distrust of nationalism. Never one to embrace half-measures, Stalin used the war as an opportunity to settle scores with any nationality whose loyalty he doubted.

The first victims were the Volga Germans. They were Russians of German descent who had settled on the reaches of the Volga river several centuries before. They were no longer 'Germans' in any real sense, but to Moscow their German roots were enough to condemn them. In August 1941 Soviet parachutists dressed in German uniforms were dropped among the villages of the Volga German Autonomous Region. They asked to be hidden until the German invaders arrived. Where villagers complied the NKVD wiped out the inhabitants: the test of loyalty had been failed. On 28 August 1941 the area was formally abolished and the population of more than 600,000 was deported to western Siberia and northern Kazakhstan, on the grounds that they constituted an army of 'wreckers and spies', although only nine cases had been brought by the security authorities against Volga Germans since the beginning of the war.[24] In all, over 948,000 Soviet citizens of German descent from all over the Soviet Union were sent east, loaded into the familiar cattle cars for a long, airless, foodless trek, and discarded in open country, where they were compelled to fight hunger and the elements with nothing more than the small bundles of possessions they had been allowed to bring.[25] They were only casually supervised by the NKVD. Thousands died from the familiar killers, hunger, cold and disease. One letter from a woman exiled to the Kirghiz steppe betrays the full horror of the deportations:

. . . [T]here is nothing but grey emptiness. We live in a hut. The sun burns terribly; when it rains the hut leaks, all our things are wet. We sleep on the ground. We work all day till we fall. We have been forced to work on the dungheaps, mixing dung by hand with fertilizer eight hours a day, even during the worst heat. The only reward once every ten days is a kilo of black, sour flour.[26]

The exiles lived under a regime that was less rigid and brutal than the camps, but one that was paradoxically more fatal.

In 1943 and 1944 the Volga Germans were joined by a stream of other nationalities from the areas bordering the Black Sea and the Caucasus: the Crimean Tatars, Chechens, Ingushi, Karachai, Balkars, Kalmyks and Meskhetians. Some had indeed collaborated with the invaders and done so willingly. The rest were found guilty by association. Beria encouraged Stalin to act and was instructed to proceed with their collective punishment. The operation in Chechnya was carried out with military precision. In February 1944 NKVD troops entered the tiny republic as if on a military exercise. On the evening of February 22, the annual Red Army Day, the population was assembled in the village squares to celebrate. The crowds were suddenly surrounded by NKVD troops and the deportation orders read out to them. Scuffles broke out as unarmed Chechens fought to escape. Some were shot down. The rest were ordered to pack at once, no more than a hundred pounds of baggage per family. Heavy snowfalls and frost hampered the operation, but within twenty-four hours most of the Chechen population was loaded into trucks and trains, destined for Siberia. In one township those left behind were gunned down, buried in pits and covered with sand. It says much for the invincibility of the national spirit that the Chechens retained their identity in exile and rebuilt their national homeland when they were finally allowed to return home after 1956.[27]

In all over one and a half million men, women and children were uprooted from their homes. It has been estimated that as many as 530,000 died from the bleak conditions of the journey and the inhospitable new homelands, though the figures recently made available from the NKVD archives give a death total of 231,000, more than one-quarter of those deported between 1943 and 1949.[28] Their possessions were looted by NKVD troops. Attempts to escape from exile were punished with twenty-five years in the camps. The local NKVD commanders of the exiled communities became petty monarchs over their new kingdoms; their subjects were restricted in everything they did: their choice of jobs, their education, their movements. They even had to petition the commander for permission to marry. The Crimean Tatars were singled out for the harshest treatment, as some of them were still fighting alongside the German army when the Crimea was liberated. Estimates of the number of victims vary. Of the 400,000 claimed by Tatar leaders to have been deported, almost half were said to have died within eighteen months.[29] Beria reported that 191,000 were deported, of whom 52,000, or 27 per cent, had died by 1949. When the round-up in the Crimea was over, Beria wrote to Stalin asking for medals for NKVD troops 'who have distinguished themselves' in the war against the 'traitors to the fatherland'; 413 were awarded.[30]

The other war, against the real enemy, was still to be won. During the winter months the liberation of Kiev was followed by almost continuous campaigning to clear the southern front of German troops. In January Konev organized the seizure of the last element of the Dnepr line, which Hitler wanted to hold at all costs. The German salient was subjected to a sophisticated Soviet assault, which demonstrated how, even in harsh winter conditions, the newly learned art of mobile warfare could be deployed to deadly effect. By a brief deception, Konev succeeded in blinding the German defenders to his intentions. A limited attack on the south part of the salient masked the movement north, in complete secrecy, of the larger part of his forces. On January 24 his forces struck suddenly and ferociously. The German front was pushed back three miles, and the 5th Guards Tank Army moved through the Soviet infantry to exploit the breach and open the way to the German rear. Two days later another tank army on the north-west part of the salient cut through to join the 5th Guards and encircle the German forces in what became known as the Korsun-Cherkassy Pocket. Leaving a thin outer cover to preserve the encirclement, Konev's troops, in bitter weather, cut into the pocket, reducing it step by step. Four Panzer divisions were mobilized to rescue the trapped Germans; they succeeded against an inexperienced tank army in breaking into the outer ring, but the concentration of air power (orchestrated at Stalin's insistence by the commander-in-chief of the Soviet air force himself) and the supply of fresh reserves blocked the relief column.

In mid-February, in fierce blizzards, the surviving troops in the pocket were flushed out by an incendiary attack that burned down the township sheltering them. The German commander, General Stemmermann, ordered his men to break out, marching in two columns across the bare, snowy landscape. Unaware of what lay in wait, they set out to try to reach the relief force. As they moved forward into open terrain without a sign of the enemy, they relaxed. Some shouted out, others fired their automatic weapons. Suddenly, as from nowhere, Konev released his forces in a terrifying finale. The German columns were caught in the open with no heavy weapons. Soviet artillery blasted them and tanks crushed them beneath their tracks while a Cossack cavalry unit hunted down the German soldiers, slaughtering them with their sabres as their ancestors had done in generations of service to the Russian crown. 'It was a kind of carnage,' recalled one eyewitness, 'that nothing could stop till it was over.' Survivors tried to scramble clear, but of the 30,000 who had set off across the snow, 20,000 were dead, including Stemmermann, who had refused an earlier Soviet offer for him to surrender, and 8,000 were taken prisoner.

Stalin was reported to be delighted with the massacre; Konev was promoted to marshal, but the hero of the initial encirclement, Nikolai Vatutin, blamed by Stalin for the time it took to reduce the pocket, received no acknowledgement. He died a few weeks later from wounds received in an ambush by Ukrainian separatists on February 28.[31]

By May 1944 most of the Ukraine and the Crimea had been liberated in a series of heavy, concentrated blows by the six major tank armies, led by Zhukov and Konev. The Red Army now stood on the Romanian frontier in the south and threatened to break through the Carpathian mountains towards Hungary. Further north, Leningrad was at last freed from its ordeal, despite a clumsily executed operation in which Soviet commanders, after years of trench warfare, failed entirely to grasp the new tactics of armoured penetration and exploitation that had served so well at Kursk and beyond. On February 26 Leningrad was formally declared liberated. The main obstacle still facing Soviet forces in 1944 was the large concentration of Axis forces in Belorussia. The German Army Group Centre withstood the winter offensives and inflicted heavy casualties. It was here that the Soviet leadership decided to unleash the largest operation yet undertaken by the revamped Red Army.

The military campaigns on the eastern front in the last year of the war were larger than any of the earlier operations. This was thanks largely to a very great increase in the size of the Red Army and air force. By the end of 1943 the large German losses, the growing threat from bombing (which forced the Germans to divert two-thirds of their fighter force, one-third of their artillery and 20 per cent of all ammunition to the defence of the Reich), and the likelihood of an invasion of Western Europe combined to produce a steady decline in the forces available to stop the Soviet army.[32] The 3.1 million Axis soldiers in the east faced almost 6.4 million of the enemy; the 3,000 German aircraft were vastly outnumbered by the 13,400 they opposed; their 2,300 tanks could not match the 5,800 Soviet machines. During 1944 the gap continued to widen. At the Stavka Stalin's commanders knew that they enjoyed a decisive advantage. The object was to make that advantage tell against an enemy skilled in active defence, with battlefield weapons of the highest quality, and whose troops and commanders were now fired by the same fatalistic defiance the Red Army had shown in defence of its own country. Soviet commanders wanted to finish the war as swiftly as possible and to do so with less prodigal use of men and equipment. Stalin, for his part, was motivated by more than the desire to bring his enemy down. Poised to begin the march into Eastern Europe, he was aware that the Soviet Union would soon be in a position to reconstitute the German 'New Order' in the Soviet image.

In March 1944 the Soviet General Staff and the State Defence Committee began a thorough assessment of the whole front to establish where the next blow should be struck. Even Stalin had come to accept that 'general offensives' did not work, even with a clear numerical advantage. The General Staff view was that offensives should be mounted one after another against attainable objectives. This allowed forces to be concentrated and kept the Germans guessing about the main locus of attack. By May the decision was made to mount an assault on Field Marshal Ernst von Busch's Army Group Centre, which was the only significant force still on Soviet territory.[33] It was stretched out around Minsk in a giant salient whose shape earned it the nickname Belorussian Balcony. The German army expected the main assault in the south, from the Ukraine, where most of the Soviet armoured forces were concentrated. The success of the attack on Belorussia depended, as so often on the eastern front, on persuading the enemy that the main attack was to come somewhere else.

The Soviet summer offensive in this sense closely resembled the vast amphibious Operation Overlord, which American and British Empire forces were preparing in the west. The invasion of northern France, scheduled for May or early June, was critically dependent on success in shielding from German eyes the exact location of the main invasion force and the intended landing site. It says little for the German intelligence network that both operations, east and west, managed to achieve complete surprise. On the Soviet side the plan of concealment was given the topmost priority. Only five people knew of the operation as a whole – Zhukov, Vasilevsky, Antonov, Shtemenko and one of the deputy operations chiefs. Any correspondence between them by letter, telephone or telegraph was forbidden. Reports from the front were handled by no more than two or three people, who reported in person. No one else was told anything more than he needed to know for his particular part of the plan. No definite date was set until shortly before the last stages of preparation.[34]

The deception extended right along the Soviet front line. In May commanders were ordered to go ostentatiously over to the defensive to give the impression that the Red Army was digging in and consolidating, after almost nine months of continuous activity. Major radio stations were closed down all along the front, and a cloak of complete radio silence was imposed. An entire dummy force was set up further to the south, like the phantom force set up in southern England opposite the Pas de Calais, to give the impression that the southern flank was the one under threat. The fake force was given added credibility by the stationing of anti-aircraft artillery to 'protect' the dummy tank and gun parks, and by flying regular fighter patrols overhead. In the north, on the Baltic front, a second dummy force was constructed. German intelligence swallowed the deception. Air reconnaissance was difficult, given Soviet air superiority – except in those areas which the Soviet commanders *wanted* the Germans to see. The network of native spies and informers, on which German intelligence had relied in the past, dried up as the Red Army moved closer. In the late spring, just weeks before the Soviet attack, the German head of military intelligence in the east told Army Group Centre to expect 'a calm summer'.[34]

This intelligence ranks as one of the worst blunders of the war. The German commanders expected their enemy to take the easy route, to the south, and retained their persistent belief that Soviet forces were not capable of mounting large and complex operations against experienced German troops in entrenched positions. The success of the Soviet deception plan rested not only on the competence with which it was mounted, but on the willingness of the enemy to be duped. By the time the attack on Army Group Centre began, Soviet intelligence knew that the deception had worked. German forces were stronger in the south and in the far north; the centre had a tough outer shell, but inside it was hollow.

The Soviet plan for the summer was to have five separate offensives unfolding in sequence. The first offensive was to be in the north, a limited assault on the Soviet-Finnish border to break the Finns' resistance and to lure German reinforcements to the Baltic states. The second and third offensives were to be launched by the Western Front (which was divided and renamed the 2nd and 3rd Belorussian Fronts) against the main German concentrations around Minsk. This was the core of the main operation; it was designed to allow a further exploitation towards the Baltic coast and East Prussia if the German front collapsed. The fourth offensive was then to be undertaken by Konev's 1st Ukrainian Front towards the Polish cities of Lvov and Lublin to try to cut off the retreating forces of Army Group Centre. The final offensive, to be commenced only when the central objectives had been gained, was in the far south, against Romania and the Ploesti oil fields.[36]

The planning was designed to avoid unnecessary risks; each stage of the offensive was intended to create conditions to make possible its successor. The key was the assault on Minsk. The two fronts primed to attack the main German concentrations were unobtrusively reinforced with men and stores. So secret was the coming campaign that the units were not told where they were going or why. Trains heading for the front were cordoned off when they stopped *en route* and the men allowed off only in small groups under constant watch. Train engineers were not told where they were heading, only the number of the train they were to drive.[37] As the plan unfolded it became clear that the two main fronts were too weak for the task they had been set. With no single tank army, they lacked the mobile striking power needed for a rapid breakthrough. In the last days of May they were given Rotmistrov's 5th Guards Tank Army, which had played a dramatic part at Kursk. On May 20, Stalin hosted a final top-level meeting in the Kremlin, in which the whole enterprise was placed under critical scrutiny. The start date was set between June 15 and 20. The operation lacked a name. Stalin was asked for his view, and he selected the name 'Bagration', a hero of the war against Napoleon in 1812 and a fellow Georgian.[38]

German forces were faced in May 1944 with the prospect of countering two offensives, one in the west, one in the east. For neither of them did they have any clear view of the size of the forces they would be fighting, where they would come or when. In the Soviet Union the constant disappointments about the second front had produced a widespread cynicism about Western intentions. The tone was set by Stalin himself, who on the very eve of Overlord still doubted Western resolve: 'What if they meet up with some Germans! Maybe there won't be a landing then, but just promises as usual.'[39] Second-front jokes were widespread in Moscow. 'What is an Old Believer?' asks one Russian. 'A person who still believes the second front will open,' replies another.[40] The second front did open. On the morning of June 6 the Western Allies invaded the beaches of Normandy; by the evening they had secured a narrow bridgehead on the coast. That night Moscow's restaurants were crowded with celebrants. On June 7, *Pravda* carried news of the operation across four columns, with a picture of General Eisenhower, the Supreme Commander in the West. But after that the news died away. Newspapers carried small, matter-of-fact reports on 'Military activity in Western Europe'. The tone of the press was, according to a British journalist posted in Moscow, carping and condescending.'[41] The general view was that the Normandy campaign was being waged with insufficient vigour; Western success was widely attributed to the fact that most German divisions were still deployed on the Eastern Front.

This point at least was true. In the east Germany and her allies had some two hundred and twenty-eight divisions, compared with fifty-eight divisions in the west, only fifteen of which were in the area of the Normandy battle in its initial stages. More manpower and anti-aircraft artillery were deployed against bombing in the Reich than were available in France. The German army was well aware of the greater threat. There was no major movement of manpower westward to cope with the invasion of France. The Allied bridgehead in Normandy was contained, though not eliminated, with the troops already there. The first attack in the east followed a few days later. The initial assault was a feint, part of the plan of deception to confirm German suspicions that the main attacks would come in the north and south, not against Army Group Centre. On June 10 the campaign began against the Finns. Soviet forces had learned from the mistakes of the Winter War. This time they prepared the ground with sufficient thoroughness that they were able to achieve their limited goal with a third of the casualties suffered in 1939. Further south Zhukov and Vasilevsky, assigned to co-ordinate the main attacks, supervised the final preparations. Troops were trained and retrained. It was found that the exercises lacked conviction when they were played out with dummy bullets. Zhukov ordered them to use live ammunition. Almost a million tons of supplies and 300,000 tons of oil were ordered from the rear.[42] Delays in the movement of tank reinforcements pushed the date for Bagration back to June 22, the third anniversary of the launch of Barbarossa.

In the event the start of the new campaign was less coherent than might have been expected from the months of secret preparation. The 'mighty avalanche', as Shtemenko called it, began with the usual trickle of stones and ice.[43] Nevertheless, the destruction of Army Group Centre showed how effectively the lessons of the first two years of warfare had been learned. It was perhaps the best example of Soviet operational art at work during the war. The campaign bore a strong resemblance to the 'deep operations' of massed aircraft and armour first outlined by Tukhachevsky in the early 1930s. First of all, on the night of June 19 partisan units began a systematic assault on the German communications web, knocking out a thousand transport targets and crippling the German system of supply and redeployment. This was followed by air attacks of furious intensity. On the eve of the anniversary, June 21, Soviet bombers launched co-ordinated air strikes against the German rear areas. The German 6th Air Fleet could muster, according to one German account, only forty operational fighters.

Some of the bombing strikes were carried out by women pilots flying at night in biplanes with open cockpits. Despite some resistance from male aviators, by 1944 women were introduced in larger numbers to actual combat. The 46th Guards Women's Night Light-Bomber Regiment was run entirely by women, from armourers to pilots and mechanics. Twenty-three of its members became Heroes of the Soviet Union. Other women served in the army; by 1945 there were 246,000 women in uniform at the front. Few concessions were made. The 1st

Belorussian Front boasted a chief gynaecologist, but sanitary and medical amenities for women at the front were rudimentary or non-existent.[44] Male comrades and officers expected women to bear the same hardships that they did, while the women themselves often volunteered for more hazardous work to prove themselves to the men.

On the very anniversary of Barbarossa Soviet reconnaissance battalions moved into the German front in force, seizing German patrols and hunting out German artillery positions in order to gain the intelligence necessary to target the main Soviet thrusts effectively. The full-scale attack finally took place on June 23, starting at the north of the German salient and rolling slowly southward over the next two days. Despite the evidence that there would be some kind of attack, the German defenders were unprepared for the scale and ferocity of what struck them. The usual artillery barrage, which might have alerted them to what was coming, was reduced in favour of a general attack, with infantry, tanks and artillery rolling forward together under cover of darkness. The first wave was made up of special plough tanks, which carved a way through the minefields. They were followed by infantry supported by self-propelled artillery and more tanks. The way ahead was lit with flares and searchlights were used to dazzle German defenders. The German defence crumbled away, leaving room for the following mechanized forces to exploit the gap and push on to the next objective.[45] This time Soviet commanders were under orders to leave pockets of German resistance where they were and to press forward before the line consolidated, precisely the tactics used with such alarming success by the German army between 1939 and 1941.

The terrain was in the defenders' favour. The ground was alternately marshy and hilly, with wide river systems unsuited to rapid troop movement. Nevertheless Soviet forces made lighter work of the problems posed by topography than did the Allied forces enmeshed at the same time in the Normandy *bocage*. When Rokossovsky's 1st Belorussian Front launched its part of the rolling offensive on June 24, his tanks and guns appeared out of the swamps at the northern edge of the Pripet Marshes, to the alarm of the German defenders. Undetected by the enemy, Soviet engineers had prepared the ground with wooden causeways. Down the makeshift roads poured Soviet armour, making gains of twenty-five miles in a day.[46] Whole German army units were threatened with encirclement; they fought back, in a state of mounting disorganization, battered by a remorseless air bombardment and uncertain where the enemy would appear next. This was sweet revenge for the Red Army; three years before it had been their turn.

In a little over a week Bagration had proved to be an astonishing success. A few makeshift units around Minsk were all that remained of the German front. On July 3 the Belorussian capital was seized, but Soviet forces were already past the city, pressing on at all costs to prevent the German front from digging in to form a stronger line of defence. From Hitler's headquarters came frantic calls to stand fast no matter what, or to hold defensive positions long since overrun. On June 29 Field Marshal Model was given command of Army Group Centre to try to stop the avalanche, but he could see no sensible alternative to withdrawal (though he could not say so openly to Hitler). Within two weeks a hole 250 miles wide and almost 100 miles deep had been gouged out of the German front. For the first time, large numbers of prisoners were taken, more than 300,000 around Minsk, and an additional 100,000 over the next few weeks. Stalin must have gained a special satisfaction from the fact that while the Red Army had swept everything before it in two weeks, the Western Allies remained mired in a narrow bridgehead.

So swift was Soviet success that it proved necessary to stop to think about where to move next. On July 8 Stalin called his staff together. Zhukov and Antonov arrived to find Stalin 'in good humour'; during the conference 'his gaiety increased'.[47] This was an altogether unfamiliar Supreme Commander. Although it was two o'clock in the afternoon, Stalin asked them to share his breakfast. The three men discussed Soviet strategy. Stalin insisted that the Red Army could finish the job by itself but welcomed the second front as a way to end the war sooner. Then he asked Zhukov if his forces could liberate eastern Poland and reach the Vistula River in the current offensive. Zhukov said he could do it with ease. Poised at the southern end of the Soviet offensive were a further 1 million men, 2,000 tanks and

3,350 aircraft. Stalin ordered him to unleash them towards Warsaw and the gateway to Berlin.[48]

On July 13 the fourth of the five offensives was begun with a drive on the Polish city of Lvov. In this case poor initial reconnaissance of German strong points, together with atrocious rainy weather, made for slow progress. On July 18 a second assault was launched against Lublin. This had much greater success, and within a week German forces were again in disorder. Lublin was seized on July 23, Brest-Litovsk, where in March 1918 the notorious capitulation to the Germans had been signed by Trotsky, fell on July 26. The drive on Lvov, spearheaded by General Rybalko's 6th Guards Tank Corps, was renewed on July 16. A narrow corridor was carved through the German line, and Rybalko took the risk of pushing through the 3rd Guards Tank Army in single file and under continuous fire in order to move rapidly behind German lines and encircle the force in front of Lodz. While other tank forces held the corridor open, a daring sweep completed the encirclement of eight German divisions around Brody. By July 22 the pocket was conquered, and Soviet tank forces moved to surround Lvov itself. On July 27 the city fell as German forces retreated to the Vistula; the whole front line in southern Poland had been destroyed by Soviet mobile operations in ten days.

This was a week of disasters for the German high command. On July 25 the Western Allies at last broke out of the Normandy beach-head, and American forces, like the Soviet, began to sweep aside weakened German armies. That same day the first units of the Red Army reached the banks of the Vistula, the giant waterway across Poland, which cuts Warsaw literally in two. Within days small bridgeheads were established across the Vistula at Magnuszew and Pulawy. Both bridgeheads were subjected to fierce German counterattack. The commander at Magnuszew was General Chuikov, the hero of the Stalingrad siege. Not one to be pushed backward, he held fast to his tiny bridgehead, reduced at one point to a dozen men and guns. Stalin now ordered Soviet forces to converge on Warsaw and cut off what was left of Army Group Centre. But the Soviet attack, which had covered hundreds of miles in four weeks, began to slacken. Heavy wear and tear on tanks and men left the Soviet vanguard

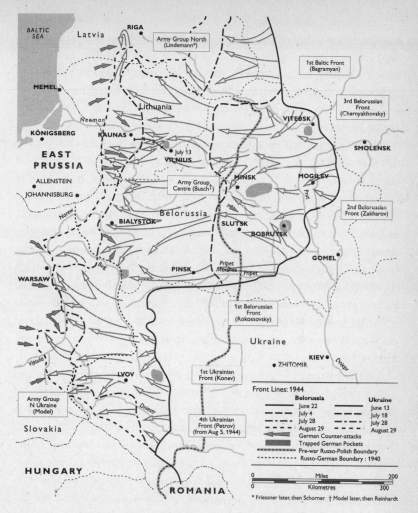

Map 9 Operation Bagration, June–August 1944

vulnerable to counter-attack. In late July the German army mounted a desperate spoiling action: heavily reinforced Panzer units, including the Hermann Goering Division and the SS Viking Division, held the Soviet advance and so severely damaged the leading tank corps that 2nd Tank Army, far from reaching Warsaw, was forced to withdraw and refit. The limits of Bagration were finally reached east of the Polish capital.

The Polish capital was no stranger to war. In September 1939 the German air force flattened large parts of it in an effort to force Polish capitulation. In April 1943 the surviving population of the Warsaw Ghetto rose in revolt, only to be destroyed by 2,000 troops of the Waffen-SS in a savage act of reprisal which reduced the area to rubble and left over 20,000 men, women and children dead. The 49,000 who survived were sent to the camps, some for a quick death from gassing, some for a slow death in the labour colonies. In August 1944, with the Red Army in full pursuit of an apparently beaten enemy, fighting broke out in Warsaw again. The Polish resistance, organized as the Polish Home Army (*Armia Krajowa*), launched a rising in the capital on August 1 in an attempt to liberate it before the Soviet armies arrived.

The revolt was led by General Tadeusz Bor-Komorowski and 20,000 poorly armed patriots. At five o'clock in the afternoon of August 1 the signal went out to the fighters of the Home Army. Germans found themselves all at once under a hail of fire from doorways, windows and balconies. Home-made bombs and mines exploded around the city. Parts of the German garrison were overwhelmed and large parts of central Warsaw were seized, but the rebels failed to capture the railway stations or any of the bridges over the Vistula. Lacking artillery, tanks or even adequate quantities of hand weapons and ammunition, they were worn down in two months of fighting against German troops under orders to raze the city and exterminate its people. Some 225,000 civilians died, in the largest single atrocity of the war. The German troops went on a rampage. They were led by the same Bach-Zalewski who had commanded the *Einsatzgruppen* in 1941 and run the brutal anti-partisan war behind the front. Hospitals were burned down with staff and patients imprisoned inside; gas was used to flush out Poles fleeing through the sewers; women and children were murdered in their thousands. On October 2, to save his city further suffering, Bor-Komorowski surrendered. His men went into captivity and Warsaw's remaining population was deported to German camps. Stone by stone, street by street, the ancient city was utterly demolished.[49]

It has long been conventional in the West to hold Stalin and the Red Army responsible, indirectly, for the horrors that befell Warsaw. Churchill in his memoirs berated his former ally for lack of 'considerations of honour, humanity, decent commonplace good faith', characteristics with which Stalin was indeed poorly supplied.[50] It is said that the Polish Home Army expected help from the Soviet Union. Instead the Red Army sat on the Vistula and watched the destruction of the city in front of them. Churchill was only one of many who assumed that Stalin did this in order to let the German army liquidate Polish nationalists instead of having to do so himself. In this sense the agony of Warsaw could be regarded either as the final flourish of the Nazi-Soviet Pact or as the first battleground of the Cold War.

The truth is far more complicated than this. The Warsaw rising was instigated not to help out the Soviet advance but to forestall it. Polish nationalists did not want Warsaw liberated by the Red Army but wanted to do so themselves, as a symbol of the liberation struggle and the future independence of Poland. This ambition was all the more urgent because only days before, on July 21, a Communist-backed Polish Committee for National Liberation was set up with Stalin's blessing. At Lublin on July 22 the Committee was declared to be the new Provisional Government; four days later a pact of friendship was signed, with the Soviet Union recognizing the new Government.[51] All of this was at least technically within the terms agreed at Teheran, where Churchill and Roosevelt had half-heartedly acquiesced to Stalin's request to keep the frontiers of 1941 and his share of Poland as divided in the German-Soviet pact. What Polish nationalists and the Western Allies could not tolerate was the almost certain fact that any new Polish state born of German defeat would be dominated by the Soviet Union. The Polish Government-in-exile in London, led by Stanislaw Mikolajczyk, urged the Home Army to launch a pre-emptive nationalist insurrection and remained unalterably opposed to any idea that the Soviet Union should keep the territory seized in 1939.[52]

The real issue was not political – there was nothing new about the hostility between Soviet leaders and Polish nationalists – but military. Could the Red Army have captured Warsaw in August 1944 and saved its population from further German barbarities? The answer now seems unambiguously negative. Soviet forces did not sit and play while Warsaw burned. The city was beyond their grasp. In the first days of August the most advanced Soviet units were engaged in bitter fighting on the approaches to the city; the small bridgeheads over the Vistula were subject to a fierce German onslaught. To the north both sides desperately contested the crossing of the Bug and Narew rivers, which might have opened up another avenue to the Polish capital. This was hardly inactivity, though it could little benefit the Poles. Stalin was completely, and no doubt correctly, dismissive of the military potential of the Polish army. 'What kind of army is it?' he asked Mikolajczyk, who was visiting Moscow in early August, 'without artillery, tanks, air force? In modern war this is nothing. . . .'[53] Soviet commanders knew that this was not like Kiev or Minsk; their forces were tired and short of arms, and the Germans had made the defence of the Warsaw district a priority. Late in August 1944 General Rokossovsky, whose troops were tied down on the Warsaw front, told a British war correspondent that 'the rising would have made sense only if we were on the point of entering Warsaw. That point had not been reached at any stage . . . We were pushed back. . . .'[54] When Zhukov was sent to the Warsaw front in early September to report to Stalin on the confused situation there, he concluded on military grounds that the Vistula could not yet be crossed in force. German war memoirs, which are less suspect as a source, confirm that the Red Army was prevented from helping Warsaw by the sudden stiffening of the German defence.[55]

Some effort was made to help the insurgents. Churchill and Roosevelt were shocked by Stalin's attitude to the rising; they began to drop arms and supplies from heavy bombers, but the quantities were tiny. On August 4 two aircraft managed to reach Warsaw; on August 8 only four. The accuracy of high-altitude parachute drops was negligible, and it is likely that most of the material fell into German hands. This was Stalin's reason for not dropping supplies.[56] There was little military realism behind the Western plan. It is out of the question that Allied air drops could have sustained Polish resistance in Warsaw for long; they were gestures prompted by humanity certainly, but by politics as well. When Stalin finally relented in September and began to drop supplies into the surviving pockets of resistance in Warsaw, he was almost certainly motivated by politics alone. No doubt he did welcome the destruction of anti-Soviet Polish nationalism, which was certain by this stage. But even his Polish Communist allies wanted some kind of gesture towards the fate of their future capital, and by early September the military situation had altered. The Polish 1st Army under General Berling joined the front line opposite Warsaw on August 20. On September 10 the attack was renewed; this time the Praga, the eastern suburb of Warsaw on the Soviet side of the Vistula, was captured. Air shipments by low-level parachute drops began. The Polish 1st Army then launched its own attack across the Vistula into Warsaw itself, but after heavy losses was forced on September 23 to retreat back across the river. Even at this late stage the Polish Home Army distrusted their pro-Communist compatriots so profoundly that they refused to co-ordinate their operations with the new attacking force.[57] A week later they surrendered, victims not so much of cynical Stalinist calculation but of their own nationalist fervour: love of their country and hatred of the two great powers at either shoulder which had conspired to crush it.

Bagration did not lead to the liberation of Warsaw, for it had not been part of the original plan. In all other respects the operation was a resounding success. Belorussia was liberated, as was eastern Poland. In August the last of the five offensives was unleashed in the southern sector of the front, at the point where German and Romanian forces had been poised to absorb the Soviet punch in June. Now Axis forces were much weakened by the effort to reinforce the fighting further north, as Zhukov's plan had intended. Soviet forces were larger than the armies they attacked, but the two months of fighting to the north had drained their reserves also. Some of the men were poorly trained, recruited hastily from the very areas the Soviet army had liberated only a few months before. Here too, the remodelled Red Army relied on tanks, guns and aircraft rather than on raw manpower.

The blow struck in the south once again exceeded expectations. Between August 20 and August 29 Army Group South collapsed entirely. Over 400,000 prisoners were captured, including most of the German 6th Army, which had been reconstituted after Stalingrad, only to fall to another annihilating encirclement on the banks of the Siret river, in northern Romania. On August 23 the pro-German Romanian Government fell, and Romania switched sides. Some Romanian army units were back in action only weeks later, fighting at the side of the Red Army. By September 2 the Ploesti oil fields, Germany's last major source of crude oil, were in Soviet hands, and Bucharest had fallen. The Red Army swept on through Bulgaria and into Yugoslavia; by early October it was poised on the boundaries of Hungary for a drive on Budapest. The Hungarian capital was laid under siege by December, and after bruising armoured battles, which sucked much of the German army's remaining tank services into the Hungarian bloodbath, Budapest fell on February 14.

The Soviet drive into the Balkans had a firm foundation in Soviet military planning in the summer of 1944, but its real impact was political. Stalin found himself in a little over a year transformed from a leader who had control of only two-thirds of his own country to the master of large parts of Eastern Europe. Soviet leaders were determined to use German defeat to create a political structure in Eastern Europe that would give them the security they had failed to get from the pre-war system. In effect that meant Soviet domination in place of German. What that amounted to in practice was already in evidence from the treatment of eastern Poland and western Belorussia between 1939 and 1941. Stalin told the Yugoslav Communist, Milovan Djilas, that the nature of the conflict required that this be so: 'This war is not as in the past; whoever occupies a territory also imposes on it his own social system. Everyone imposes his own system as far as his army can reach. It cannot be otherwise.'[58] Soviet leaders expected their Western Allies to do the same.

There was certainly one sense in which Stalin's analysis was correct.

Britain and the United States did not want the countries liberated in Europe to become Communist. They wished them to remain as far as possible within the Western camp and the world market. For much of the war Roosevelt genuinely believed that there existed some prospect of an American-Soviet axis in the post-war world, by which they would co-operate to preserve the peace. Churchill had a more cynical view. He knew that the Soviet Union could hardly be expelled militarily from Eastern Europe, having defeated what had been only a few years before the most effective armed force in the world. He was much more prepared for horse-trading. Stalin had no real liking for Churchill – he told Djilas in the summer of 1944 that he had not forgotten who the English and Churchill were: 'They find nothing sweeter than to trick their allies . . . Churchill is the kind who, if you don't watch him, will slip a kopeck out of your pocket.'[59] When Churchill arranged to visit Moscow in October 1944 to discuss the future of Europe, Stalin found him more realistic than Roosevelt.

The meeting between the two men that convened in the evening of October 9 at the Kremlin found two of Europe's great powers doing what they had done for centuries: disposing of the future of the lesser powers with scant regard for any principle but their own interests. Churchill in his memoirs dramatically recounted how he scribbled down on a piece of paper a list of Eastern European countries, against which he set a percentage for Soviet influence, a percentage for British. For Stalin there was 90 per cent in Romania, 50 per cent in Hungary and Yugoslavia, 75 per cent in Bulgaria. Greece he wanted for himself: 'In Greece it was different. Britain must be the leading Mediterranean power . . .'[60] He handed the sheet to Stalin, who with a casual gesture drew a large blue tick and handed it back in silence. The reality was a little different. The negotiations were more protracted. They involved Poland, where Churchill merely suggested that its fate be left to the nationalist and Communist Poles to sort out between them.[61] The tick on the piece of paper, if such there was, did not indicate approval or agreement, but was a habit of Stalin's to show that he had read something. But in essence Churchill's version of the story was true. The whole discussion made a mockery of his later credentials as a Cold Warrior, just as it compromised his relations with Roosevelt.

It amounted to a virtual acceptance of more than Stalin could have hoped for in Eastern Europe.

Churchill later had cause deeply to regret the character of his intervention in Moscow. No formal agreement was signed or asked for. The 'piece of paper' had no more political weight than that more famous 'piece of paper' Hitler gave to Chamberlain late at night in Munich in September 1938. Soviet leaders did not need British permission to establish Soviet domination in the areas of Soviet liberation. British acquiescence, on the other hand, simplified the Soviet position. Britain and the United States had, to Stalin's intense irritation, refused to allow the Soviet Union a part in the occupation of liberated Italy. Churchill's unforced candour would make it all the more difficult to challenge the Soviet monopoly in the east and the establishment of regimes modelled on the Stalinist dictatorship.

The widening gap between East and West remained a subterranean fissure as long as the war against Germany and Japan persisted. It was agreed among the three Allied leaders that they should meet at yet another summit conference. Stalin suggested the Crimean resort of Yalta. Roosevelt, now in the final throes of the illness that dispatched him in April 1945, agreed, against the strong advice of his doctors and colleagues. Stalin had been offered a site in Scotland, then Malta or Athens (even at that stage of the war a risky choice), but on the advice of his own doctors rejected them all. Roosevelt now had to travel 4,883 miles by sea and a further 1,375 miles in the new presidential aircraft, oddly named 'The Sacred Cow'. According to Churchill ten years of research could not have found 'a worse place in the world'.[62] The President was to be lodged in the Livadia Palace, built for the Tsars. His cavalcade from the airport took five hours to reach Yalta. The party was driven through the wreckage of war, along a route lined by Soviet soldiers, both men and women, who clicked their heels to attention as the cars swept by. At the palace Roosevelt was attended by a staff brought down from three Moscow hotels. The furnishings were pre-Revolutionary, dark, heavy and wooden. The local countryside had been scoured for everything from coat hangers to ashtrays.[63]

The conference was conducted throughout with a level of cordiality and collaboration that belied the growing mistrust between the two sides. Stalin had the advantage over his allies of secret intelligence from NKVD agents, including the highly placed State Department official Alger Hiss, and information revealed through the many microphones concealed about the Livadia Palace.[64] The agreements that were reached on the future conduct of the war almost certainly reflected the influence of this secret intelligence. Stalin agreed to enter the war with Japan as long as the Soviet Union was guaranteed the return of former Russian territories in Sakhalin and the Kurile Islands which he knew the Americans were willing to concede. This was granted with few misgivings; the Americans were convinced that Japan would take another year or two to defeat, and Soviet help would shorten the time. There were more misgivings over Germany. It was agreed that Germany be demilitarized and de-Nazified, and that spheres of influence for the three major Allies and for France be established. The Soviet Union asked for, and won grudging approval of, a bill of $20 billion in reparations from Germany. Stalin insisted on including the word 'dismemberment' to describe Allied policy on Germany. This was resisted at first but finally conceded. The future of Poland was hotly debated, but again a rough agreement emerged, giving the Soviet Union slices of Polish territory in the east in return for the transfer of German territory in Silesia and East Prussia to Poland. The only concession wrung from Stalin was his agreement to allow Polish nationalists into a broader provisional government. (Soviet spies had revealed how important this issue was to the West.) It was a tactical move, to be set aside when the time was ripe.[65]

Roosevelt had one ambition above all. He wanted to give real shape to the United Nations. Like Wilson in 1918, Roosevelt believed that a new idealism in world affairs might end what he called 'the system of unilateral action, the exclusive alliances, the spheres of influence, the balances of power . . .' Stalin did not reject this vision out of hand – he had no need to – but he refused to accept the principle of self-determination of peoples. Harry Hopkins, Roosevelt's confidant, who arrived at Yalta in even worse health than his master, believed that Yalta signalled 'the dawn of the new day'. No one on the American side doubted, he continued, 'that we would live with them and get along with them peacefully for as far into the future as any of us could imagine'.[66]

It is sometimes suggested that the West was fooled by Stalin at Yalta. Certainly Roosevelt and Hopkins projected a misplaced idealism which three years of alliance with Stalin ought to have dissipated sooner. Yet even the more cynical Churchill was moved after Yalta to tell the House of Commons that he came away from the conference with the impression that Stalin wished to live 'in honourable friendship and equality with the Western democracies. I feel also that their word is their bond.'[67] The Soviet side of the story of Yalta remains locked in the archives, but it can be assumed with confidence that idealism played a more junior role, as it always had.

Stalin did not fool the West; they fooled themselves. Nothing in Stalin's record suggested that he would forgo political opportunism and national self-interest for long. In 1944 he picked up where Soviet expansion in Eastern Europe had begun in 1939. His priority was Soviet security, which is why Poland mattered so much to him: 'Throughout history,' he reminded his allies at Yalta, 'Poland has been a corridor through which the enemy passed to attack Russia.'[68] In almost all the discussions at Yalta the West failed to extract a watertight agreement on their terms, though they agreed to what Stalin wanted. Re-reading the discussions, it is difficult to place on them the optimistic gloss that Stalin's visitors later gave them. Stalin had not survived in the jungle of Soviet politics for more than twenty years for nothing. He was an opportunist, accustomed to move cautiously, as circumstances allowed. There is unlikely to have been any master plan to take over Europe. He knew that at that point he could not risk an open breach, for the Soviet Union was hoping for an extension of economic aid from the United States to help with industrial reconstruction; but he made few concessions on the things that mattered. In one of the many toasts at one of the many dinners at Yalta, Stalin sounded a warning: 'The difficult task will come after the war, when diverse interests will tend to divide the Allies.'[69] Here was the voice of realism.

9

Fall of the Swastika:
1945

Victory

Not in paradise, but on this vast tract of earth,
where at every step there is sorrow, sorrow, sorrow,
I awaited her, as one waits only when one loves,
I knew her as one knows only oneself,
I knew her in blood, in mud, in grief.
The hour struck.
The war ended.
I made my way home.
She came towards me, and we did not recognize each other.

Ilya Ehrenburg, 9 May 1945

Stalin was determined that Berlin, Hitler's capital, should be his prize. 'I think it's going to be quite a fight,' he told Zhukov.[1] The capture of Berlin was heavy with symbolism. Stalin wanted the Red Army to seize it as a reward for its almost four years of ceaseless conflict, carrying the main weight of the war against Hitler. He also wanted to command the last campaign himself, and in November 1944 he restored the Stavka to direct control of the front. Vasilevsky, the chief of staff, was pushed aside and in February resigned his post. Zhukov was chosen to command the front which would close in on Berlin, but the accolade was tarnished by Stalin's evident intention of seizing back the reins of command. Berlin was to be Stalin's triumph as well as Zhukov's.

The capture of the German capital was not a foregone conclusion. Stalin did not trust his Western partners not to drive on to Berlin simply to forestall him. He did not trust the Germans not to abandon the fight in the west in order to concentrate everything on the war against Communism, and he strongly suspected Churchill, who Stalin believed 'wouldn't flinch at anything', of seeking a separate German surrender in order to achieve just this.[2] Stalin was right that German forces would fight stubbornly to defend German soil and the German capital. He was right that Nazi leaders would try to divide the Allies. German propaganda leaflets were dropped over the advancing Western troops, calling on them to join with the German army to hold back the tide of 'Asiatic' barbarism. But he was wrong about his Allies. The voices that were raised in favour of a rush to Berlin were stifled, and the agreements made at Yalta, which placed Berlin in the Soviet sphere, were honoured. Nonetheless, British and American forces got closer to Berlin than had seemed possible when they stood on the boundaries of western Germany in December 1944. The collapse of German resistance in the west made the race for Berlin a possibility. Stalin eventually accelerated the timetable for the Berlin operation to ensure its conquest. Unlike the other major operations since the end of 1943, the strike at Berlin was hurried and improvised.

When Stalin assumed control of the front line in November, almost 500 miles separated the Soviet armies, stretched out along the Vistula, and the German capital. The character of the war now changed. Soviet forces were fighting for the first time away from Soviet soil. Russian armies had last traversed the heartland of Europe as victors in 1813, when they fought side by side with Germans to overthrow Napoleon. In the First World War the vast imperial army lumbered westward to defeat at Tannenberg and Lodz. In 1920 the young Red Army was stopped humiliatingly in its tracks by the Polish legions of Marshal Pilsudski in the approaches to Warsaw. Perhaps recollection of defeats explains Stalin's growing caution. He did not want a repeat. He could not afford to have the final triumph turn sour, even if German successes were as short-lived as the Battle of the Bulge, Hitler's final failed offensive in the west in December 1944. So it was that each new drive westward was halted in order to secure the flanks and straighten the Soviet line. In January 1945, after months of careful preparation, a second great operation, less daunting than Bagration but vast in scale, was launched between the Vistula and the Oder rivers to bring the Red Army to within forty miles of the German capital.

The unglamorously-named Vistula-Oder Operation began on January 12. Along the whole eastern front over 6 million Soviet soldiers were faced by 2 million German troops and 190,000 of their allies, a dwindling remnant of the army of two years before. Some of the German troops were of high quality and heavily armed with the most modern defensive weapons, but many were scratch regiments of under-age conscripts or older volunteers, short of fuel and ammunition and desperately short of tanks and vehicles. They stood behind prepared defences that proved more of a threat on paper than in battle. Soviet forces were also very short of trained manpower, the numerous divisions all well under strength, but they now had an exponential lead in weapons, vehicles and aircraft. They also enjoyed the element of surprise, for once again German commanders were almost entirely in the dark about the intentions of the enemy. To confuse the Germans still further the assaults were again staggered. As one front advanced, German reserves were hastily deployed to repel the attack, only to find that a second front had exploded far to the north or south. Konev's 1st Ukrainian Front began the campaign on January 12 and in two weeks was deep in Silesia. Zhukov's 1st Belorussian Front attacked on January 14, and in a little over two weeks swept German forces from central Poland. On January 29 Zhukov stood on the banks of the Oder river with Berlin in his sights.

At times Soviet armies travelled fifty miles a day, driving before them an increasingly disorganized and demoralized German army and streams of frightened German refugees, who sought any avenue out of the clutches of an enemy whose thirst for vengeance was terrible and undiminished. When on January 13 the armies of the 2nd and 3rd Belorussian Fronts in the north began the operation to clear East Prussia, Soviet forces at last found themselves deep in German territory. German resistance was frantic, even suicidal. By February 2 a large German garrison was bottled up with thousands of civilians in Königsberg and along its coastline, subject to constant air and artillery attack. The rest of East Prussia lay open to Soviet revenge. There can be no disguising the treatment meted out to the German

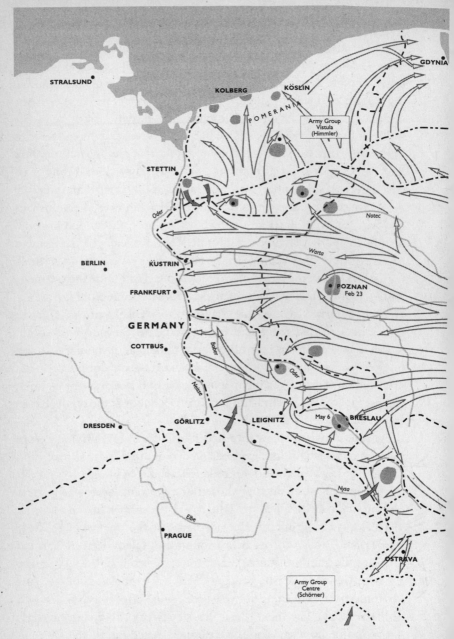

Map 10 The Vistula-Oder Operation, January–May 1945

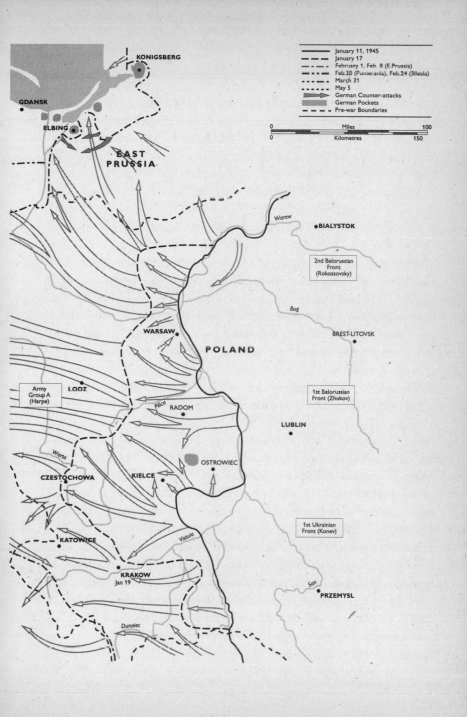

KÖNIGSBERG

GDANSK

ELBING

EAST
PRUSSIA

	January 11, 1945
	January 17
	February 1, Feb. 8 (E.Prussia)
	Feb.20 (Pomerania), Feb.24 (Silesia)
	March 31
	May 5
	German Counter-attacks
	German Pockets
	Pre-war Boundaries

0   Miles   100
0   Kilometres   150

Warew

●BIALYSTOK

2nd Belorussian
Front
(Rokossovsky)

Bug

BREST-LITOVSK

WARSAW

POLAND

Army
Group A
(Harpe)

LODZ

Pilica

RADOM

1st Belorussian
Front (Zhukov)

LUBLIN

Warta

OSTROWIEC

CZESTOCHOWA

KIELCE

1st Ukrainian
Front (Konev)

KATOWICE

Vistula

KRAKOW
Jan 19

San

●PRZEMYSL

Dunaiec

population. The trail of savagery had unmistakable echoes of an earlier age. In the first villages they occupied in October 1944 the soldiers slaughtered the population, raping and torturing the women, old and young. Refugees were shelled and bombed and crushed beneath the tracks of advancing tanks. In Silesia and on the banks of the Oder the orgy of violence threatened the discipline of the troops at what was a critical point of the campaign, and commanders took harsh steps to rein in the wave of atrocities and the widespread looting.[3]

Vengeance was easy to understand. As troops arrived at the frontier they read notices posted along the way reminding them of their hatred for things German. For years Soviet soldiers had been taught that the enemy were beasts fit only for destruction. 'The Fascists,' wrote Ilya Ehrenburg, author of the poems of hate penned in the summer of 1942, 'brought with them savagery, atrocities, the cult of violence, death.' Outside Minsk, in 1944, Ehrenburg came across a pile of the charred bodies of Russian women and girls. Red Army soldiers found them, too, and took instant revenge upon the Germans in their path. 'Nowhere,' wrote Ehrenburg, 'was the fighting so ferociously cruel.' In East Prussia he found the same deep loathing. He accosted a demented Belorussian soldier who was repeatedly stabbing a shop-window dummy with his bayonet in futile vengeance for the death of his wife.[4] The advance across the shattered, depopulated landscape of Belorussia and eastern Poland led Soviet forces to their first encounter with an extermination camp at Maidenek in July 1944. They found around 1,000 sick, emaciated prisoners.[5] The Jewish inmates had been taken westward on one of the hundreds of death marches. Most of those who remained were Soviet prisoners of war. General Chuikov ordered his men to file through the camp. 'How much hate raged in the heart of our soldiers,' he later wrote.[6] Soviet soldiers were horrified less by the camp than by the warehouses stuffed with clothes, hand-bags, shoes and children's toys, all taken from the doomed prisoners. Lists were found containing detailed requests from the Reich for warm children's clothing for evacuees from the bombed German cities.[7]

Maidenek was given wide publicity among the troops. By the time the Red Army reached Belzec, Sobibor and Treblinka, those camps had been obliterated by the German authorities, the land ploughed under and farmed once again. That left Auschwitz, most notorious of all the camps. In January 1945, as the Red Army approached the camp, the population of slave workers, surrounded by SS guards, was made to march off into the snow. Those who remained, most too ill to march, were abandoned by their German captors as the roar of Soviet artillery drew nearer. On the afternoon of January 27 a Soviet patrol reached the camp. Prisoners, waving improvised red flags made from clothing or bedding, swarmed around the soldiers. There were only 2,819 prisoners left, hundreds of them on the point of death. All around the Red Army discovered the grisly evidence of mass murder. The soldiers found (and counted) 348,820 men's suits and 836,255 women's coats and dresses.[8] Some of the liberated prisoners were Soviet citizens. To their horror they were interrogated, in the same Auschwitz buildings they had just been freed from, by agents of Smersh, a military counter-intelligence agency set up in 1943 to root out spies and counter-revolutionaries in the army and among prisoners freed during the Soviet advance. The name was thought up by Stalin himself, an abbreviation of the Russian words 'Death to spies!' Auschwitz shocked the Soviet soldiers who liberated it; the news of German atrocities made it ever more likely that the Red Army would seek a merciless revenge. The authorities, however, remained silent on this occasion. The details of the liberation of Auschwitz were revealed only on 7 May 1945, at the end of the war in Europe. In the Soviet report no mention was made of the Jews. The victims were '4,000,000 citizens of various European countries'.[9]

Stalin was not ignorant of the behaviour of Red Army soldiers, but it worried him little. When he was told of the treatment meted out to German refugees he was reported to have replied: 'We lecture our soldiers too much; let them have some initiative.' When the Yugoslav Communist, Milovan Djilas, complained to Stalin's face that the Red Army was raping Yugoslav women he received a lecture on the Russian attitude to war:

You have, of course, read Dostoevsky? Do you see what a complicated thing is man's soul, man's psyche? Well then, imagine a man who has fought from Stalingrad to Belgrade — over thousands of kilometres of his own devastated land, across the dead bodies of his comrades and dearest ones? How can such a man react normally? And what is so awful in his having fun with a woman, after such horrors? You have imagined the Red Army to be ideal. And it is not ideal, nor can it be . . . The important thing is that it fights Germans . . .'[10]

Stalin adopted the language of oriental despotism: the multiple rape and murder of captured women became nothing more than 'fun with a woman'; looting was transformed into taking 'some trifle'. Stalin did not order the Red Army to commit atrocities against the German population, but he did nothing to prevent it. Ordinary soldiers treated atrocity as routine, a cruel perquisite of war. Aleksandr Solzhenitsyn, an artillery officer in East Prussia in 1945 shortly before his arrest, later recalled without comment the attitude of his comrades: 'All of us knew very well that if the girls were German they could be raped and then shot. This was almost a combat distinction. Had they been Polish girls or our own displaced Russian girls, they could have been chased naked round the garden and slapped on the behind . . .'[11] Only when this violence and disorder, generously fuelled by the many German wine cellars liberated from fascism, threatened military discipline did the tide of barbarism ebb.

Red Army atrocities also owed something to the ferocity of the fighting for the last few hundred miles to Berlin. The Soviet casualty rate had dipped down sharply during 1944, but in the months of conflict on German soil the rate began to rise again. The offensive into East Prussia cost 584,000 casualties; in the battles from October 1944 to April 1945 a total of more than 319,000 Soviet soldiers were killed.[12] Officers were under pressure to finish the war quickly and ordered tired and overstretched units to suicidal advances. German soldiers were under a general mandate from the Führer to stand and die. For Soviet soldiers and their families heavy losses so close to final victory were undoubtedly harder to bear. The conquest of Berlin called for the sacrifice of thousands more Red Army soldiers only days away from victory.

At the beginning of February 1945 Stalin faced a dilemma. The capture of Berlin seemed within the Soviet grasp. Yet there remained islands of powerful German resistance at Königsberg, at Breslau in Silesia, at Poznan and the great Oder fortress at Küstrin on the approaches to Berlin. Zhukov's front reached the Oder on February 2, and the fiery Chuikov, who commanded the 8th Guards Army, the first to arrive and cross the river over treacherously thin ice, wanted to drive on to Berlin without stopping; he argued that the remaining German strongholds could be mopped up later. Whether the forces defending the capital could have coped at that stage with a sustained Soviet thrust is open to question. It was an attractive proposition for Zhukov, who was as eager as anyone to be the conqueror of Hitler's capital, but there were other factors to consider. The Soviet front line was by early February in a vulnerable position. To the north of Zhukov's armies lay a group of German forces in Pomerania. They consisted at first of a scratch SS force made up of office personnel drummed into combat and the dregs of other broken units. During January and February the force was strengthened with a view to mounting a spoiling action against Zhukov's exposed northern flank. Stalin was more than usually anxious about the rallying of forces in Pomerania. The babble of German radio signals caused by the large number of tiny remnants of military units was interpreted by Soviet intelligence as evidence of a much greater strength than actually existed. Further south in Silesia Konev's front had lost contact with Zhukov's, and German forces were rallying here, too. Beyond Konev, the struggles for Hungary and the approaches to Vienna were as fierce as anything in Prussia.

Stalin bowed to military reality and abandoned an immediate thrust towards Berlin. On February 8 Konev began an offensive in Silesia to encircle Breslau and join up with Zhukov at the Oder. On February 10 Rokossovsky's armies in East Prussia were ordered to clear the Pomeranian threat. Two weeks later they were joined by Zhukov's forces, which to the Germans' surprise turned northward to clear the flank threat instead of advancing on Berlin. Fighting for the fortress of Poznan was not over until the central fort, the citadel, was stormed by Chuikov's men on February 20. At ten o'clock in the evening of February 22 the German garrison surrendered. Of 40,000 men, some 12,000 were fit for fighting. They marched out of the fortress into captivity, some of them shouting the words '*Hitler kaput*' wherever they went in the hope, perhaps, of better treatment by their captors.[13] The struggle for the great island fortress of Küstrin also fell to Chuikov. Stalin had been told that Küstrin had fallen in early February. In fact it had not even been encircled. On March 22 the area was finally cut off by Soviet forces, which were then subject to a fierce counter-attack by a hastily gathered German force from Frankfurt an der Oder. These ramshackle divisions of ill-trained and over-age Germans were pushed out by Hitler in a last effort to stem the Soviet tide. On March 27 they attacked almost unprotected across open ground. Eight thousand were killed, sitting ducks for Soviet artillery. On March 29 the Küstrin fortresses were subjected to a gruelling bombardment. Then swarms of Soviet infantry in boats crossed the river to the island. Altogether, a thousand men of the garrison fought their way out to the west. By the afternoon of the 29th the island was in Soviet hands. When Chuikov telephoned Zhukov to report at long last the fall of Küstrin, he was asked: 'Did you give it to them hot?' 'As hot as we could,' replied Chuikov.[14]

The cleaning-up of the Soviet front took much longer than Soviet leaders might have wanted, but it was an indication that Chuikov's idea of a rush for Berlin in early February might well have produced a messy ending rather than a clean punch. It was not until the end of the first week of March that Zhukov was summoned to Stalin to begin the planning for the Berlin operation. He found the Supreme Commander in a sombre mood, and uncharacteristically reflective. In his memoirs Zhukov recalled Stalin's words to him: 'What a terrible war. How many lives of our people it has carried away. There are probably very few families of us left who haven't lost someone near to them . . .'[15] It was one of the few occasions on which Stalin let down his guard. Zhukov recalled that he seemed close to exhaustion, 'utterly overworked'. When they ate together, Stalin did not fall upon his food, as was his habit, but sat silently for a long time without eating. Eventually he sent Zhukov away with orders to begin at last the detailed planning for the Berlin operation. Zhukov sat with Antonov until deep into the night, putting the finishing touches to a plan which had been worked out in general the November before.

On March 8 it was presented to Stalin, who approved it. Over the next three weeks the logistical services brought up the last trainloads of ammunition, fuel and food. The troops were redeployed to the Berlin axis as soon as the mopping-up operations were over. On April 1 Stalin summoned Zhukov and General Konev, commander of the 1st Ukrainian Front, to a conference in Moscow, where the detailed operational plans were presented and approved and the date for the operation fixed for April 16. Both Soviet fronts had only two weeks to complete the preparations for what Stalin hoped would be a showpiece campaign in front of his allies, who by then were no more than eighty miles from Berlin themselves.

The operational plan was straightforward. Zhukov was to attack from the bridgeheads on the Oder with a frontal assault on the city over the Seelöw Heights; further to the north was a wide flanking operation, designed to bring Soviet forces around Berlin to attack it from the west. Konev's task was to drive his front towards Leipzig and Dresden, with his northern flank, next door to Zhukov, deployed north-westward towards the southern outskirts of Berlin to complete its encirclement. There was a good deal of rivalry between the two commanders for the privilege of delivering Berlin to Stalin. Their recollections of the meeting of April 1 were very different. Zhukov recalled that Stalin, looking at the two operational plans, told Konev that he should move into Berlin itself from the south if Zhukov got bogged down. Konev remembered no such instruction, though he did remember that when Stalin drew the demarcation line between his front and Zhukov's, he suddenly paused, erased the section to the south of the German capital and deliberately left the line unfinished. Konev took this as an invitation to join in the attack on Berlin if circumstances permitted, which he later did, to Zhukov's intense irritation. Another version of the story had Stalin announce to both commanders, 'Whoever breaks in first, let him take Berlin,' but neither Zhukov nor Konev recalled his saying it.[16]

Whatever the truth, the two men lost no time. Konev admitted that he had 'a passionate desire' to seize Berlin. The two commanders arrived at Moscow's Central Airfield on the morning of April 3, and flew off only two minutes apart through a thick spring fog, which failed to lift throughout the journey.[17] There then followed a little under two weeks of frantic preparation to meet the deadline of April 16. In all, twenty-nine Soviet armies had to reposition themselves, some moving more than two hundred miles over rail networks swamped with the demands for shells, bombs, fuel and fodder. The task of seizing Berlin was different from the campaigns that brought the Red Army across the Ukraine and Poland. Berlin was the largest city in Germany, 320 square miles of urban and suburban territory. Before the war it housed four million people; by 1945 the number was only half that, as the population fled from Allied bombing. Its geography made fighting potentially as difficult as Stalingrad. The area was criss-crossed with rivers and canals and surrounded by fortified strong points. Pressed into the defence of the capital were approximately one million men, of whom about three-quarters were regular front-line forces. They were supported by 1,519 tanks, 9,303 artillery pieces and small numbers of aircraft. Many of the defenders were young conscripts of fifteen or sixteen, or old men of the *Volkssturm*, a volunteer militia set up to defend the Reich. They crouched behind a network of rough fortifications – barricades of vehicles and furniture – or hid in the network of bunkers and pillboxes built as the Soviet threat came nearer. In their midst, in the bunker of the Reich Chancellery, was their Führer, Adolf Hitler, who wanted his people to share the final death agonies rather than surrender.

Facing the German defenders was a solid wall of weaponry. Zhukov's front alone had almost 14,600 guns, with 7,147,000 shells in store, supported by seventy-seven divisions (reduced to about 4,000 men each), 3,155 tanks and self-propelled guns, and 1,531 rocket launchers. Over 2 million combat troops and 7,500 combat aircraft were assigned to the Berlin operation.[18] Zhukov planned to push his units forward in a night attack, dazzling the defenders with a force of 143 searchlights. In front of him lay the Seelöw Heights, rising to 200 feet above the Oder banks, with German guns that could fire across his whole field of advance. Zhukov was sufficiently worried by this threat to change the original plan to use his tank armies for a flanking attack; instead he concentrated his tank force for a direct assault on the Heights, behind Chuikov's 8th Guards. Stalin approved the change without demur.[19] On paper Konev had a more difficult task than Zhukov. His men were exhausted from the long struggle for Silesia. They had been fighting heavily since mid-January. Their point of departure was the east bank of the Neisse river. They had to cross to the higher and heavily-defended west bank across a wide stretch of water. Konev relied on a careful reconnaissance of enemy firing points so that they could be neutralized by very precise artillery fire when the attack began.

During the two weeks of preparation Stalin was faced by pressures from all sides. Rumour and counter-rumour circulated about the intentions of the Western Allies, only partly stilled by a direct message from General Eisenhower, the Supreme Commander of Allied Forces in the west, that his main axis was to the German south and north, leaving Berlin for the Red Army.[20] The Polish issue became deadlocked over interpretation of the Yalta agreements on the composition of the Polish Government. On April 5 the Soviet Union revoked its non-aggression pact with Japan. On April 12 Roosevelt died. The response of the Soviet leadership seems to have been genuine grief and shock, not least at the loss of a man whom Stalin trusted a great deal more than he trusted Churchill. The Vice-President, Harry S Truman, a newcomer arriving at a very sensitive stage of the war's finale, was suspected of having anti-Soviet feelings. Expressions of sympathy and goodwill were extended by a 'deeply distressed' Stalin to the American ambassador on the following day, but it was difficult to disguise the sense that Roosevelt's death symbolized the passage from fruitful collaboration to damaging distrust.[21]

Berlin beckoned ever more powerfully. To his allies Stalin pretended that Berlin no longer held any strategic importance. He had no intention of revealing his immediate plans as disarmingly as had Eisenhower. By April 14 millions of men and thousands of guns and tanks were packed into a wide semicircle around the German capital. German troops manned the outer layer of eight defence fields between the Oder and the government quarter around the Tiergarten in central Berlin. The tension had a particular quality, like the tension Soviet troops had felt over three years before outside Moscow. Zhukov's forces were more exposed than usual, for there was little greenery, and the flooded, sandy soil made it impossible to dig deep trenches or foxholes. German searchlights and flares, hunting for Soviet positions, lit up the ground at night. By the final night Chuikov was in a state of high nervous tension, unable to sleep. 'When you are awaiting great events,' he later wrote, 'time drags very slowly.'[22]

Just before dawn Zhukov arrived at Chuikov's headquarters. At five o'clock precisely he gave the order to fire. The roar of thousands of guns was soon followed by the roar of bombs and bombers. Even without the searchlights, the view in front of Zhukov became like daylight. After half an hour, with no response from the German forward positions, Zhukov ordered a halt to the barrage and the first units moved forward. The result was chaotic. Zhukov's golden touch had deserted him. The 143 searchlights were duly switched on, but because of the dense smoke and dust the lights revealed little and their reflections dazzled advancing Soviet infantrymen. So concentrated was the bombardment that the ground was impassably churned up. The vehicles and guns were soon stuck on the narrow routes out of the bridgehead, piling up one behind the other. Worse still, the German forward defensive line had been abandoned, following information from a Soviet soldier captured near Küstrin on April 15. The German commander, General Gotthard Henrici, pulled his men back to the second defensive line, so that many of the bombs and shells fell on empty trenches and shelters. For Chuikov and the unfortunate Zhukov the battle soon became utterly obscured by a pall of thick dust that drifted over the command post when the wind suddenly altered direction.[23]

If they had been able to see the battle it would hardly have cheered them. The attack faltered at the edge of a canal after just a mile. Armoured vehicles could not negotiate the steep sides of the Heights. By midday part of the front had not moved at all, and much of it was stuck at the foot of the Heights under constant bombardment. Zhukov then made one of his few errors, and a most conspicuous one. Ignoring the hard experience in using tank armies, which had taught that they should not be deployed until they could penetrate freely and break into the enemy rear, Zhukov ordered his two tank armies to move forward to speed up the conquest of the Heights. The problem was compounded, as Chuikov warned his commander it would be. The tanks blocked the roads already crowded with vehicles and men; when they reached the sandy, marshy ground they were forced to move at a snail's pace. As men and armour crowded into an area too small to support them all, the enemy was able to exact a heavy toll of both. Zhukov, so used to reporting rapid movement and instant success, had to telephone Stalin to tell him that the breakthrough he so coveted had failed. He was treated brusquely. Stalin told him that Konev had been more successful that day and that he would be ordered after all to move his tank armies northward to try to take Berlin from the south. Zhukov heard nothing more from Stalin for three days.[24]

Zhukov needed swift success, but progress on the second day was sluggish, with more high losses. The rear areas were combed for replacements. Liberated prisoners of war were drafted, along with Russian labourers who in many cases had little or no military training. Soviet soldiers, like German, were taken from younger age groups as the Soviet Union scraped the bottom of the manpower barrel. Rising casualty rates reflected the poor quality of soldiers available. By the end of the second day the Seelöw Heights were stormed, but most of the defenders withdrew to the third line of defence, which had not been properly reconnoitred before the battle. On the third day Chuikov was obliged to breach this line, under heavy fire and an occasional counter-attack, with the two tank armies still bunched uncomfortably behind him. By April 20 the forward units at last reached the eastern suburbs of Berlin and, using small assault groups, began to push the defenders back block by block. The same day long-range artillery came within firing distance of the centre of Berlin. Zhukov's front began to recover its momentum. The northern flank now opened up the weak German defences in front of the city and swept around the capital to reach the Elbe river beyond it. Though the German forces in Berlin defended with fatalistic courage a city beyond saving, those spread out to the west of the capital, squeezed between enemy armies, were swiftly reduced to a feeble fighting force. In the capital itself Chuikov's men began to push towards its centre.

Zhukov pressed his commanders to drive on. Once again he ordered his tank army to follow the infantry, this time into the city streets,

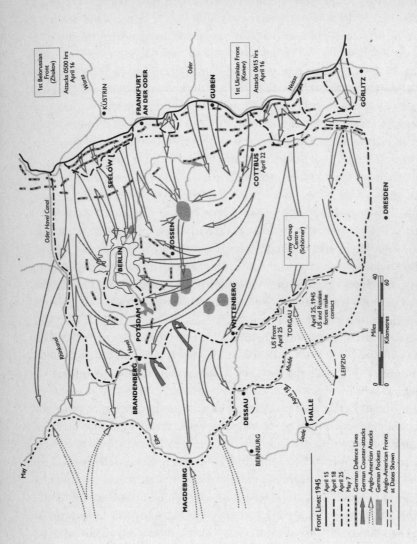

Map 11 The Assault on Berlin

1st Belorussian
Front (Zhukov)
Attacks 0500 hrs
April 16

1st Ukrainian Front
(Konev)
Attacks 0615 hrs
April 16

Army Group
Centre (Schörner)

KÜSTRIN

FRANKFURT
AN DER ODER

GUBEN

GÖRLITZ

Oder

Warte

Neisse

SEELÖW

COTTBUS
April 22

DRESDEN

Oder Hovel Canal

JOSSEN

WITTENBERG

US Front
April 25

TORGAU

April 25, 1945
US and Russian
forces make
contact

BERLIN

POTSDAM

Havel

BRANDENBERG

Rhinkanal

Elbe

DESSAU

BERNBURG

MAGDEBURG

HALLE

Saale

April 19

Mulde

LEIPZIG

May 7

Front Lines: 1945
April 15
April 18
April 25
May 7
German Defence Lines
German Counter-attacks
Anglo-American Attacks
German Pockets
Anglo-American Fronts
at Dates Shown

0   40
Miles

0   60
Kilometres

where mobile warfare was almost impossible and where the German anti-tank *Panzerfaust* gun exacted a heavy toll of Soviet armour. To cope with the threat, it was found that thin sheets of tin or iron set at an angle, or piles of sandbags, could be attached to the tanks to deflect the full impact of the new weapon. These devices gave a simple, crude but effective protection. Tanks were difficult to manoeuvre across the canals and rivers. They relied on the engineers, who, under heavy fire, threw pontoon bridges across each water obstacle. By April 24 Chuikov's forces had crossed the Spree and the Dahme rivers and were closing in on the central zones of the city. At six o'clock the following morning units approached the Schönefeld Airfield, only to find that there were Soviet forces already in occupation. They were units of General Rybalko's 3rd Tank Army, attached to Konev's 1st Ukrainian Front. When Chuikov reported the discovery to Zhukov there was consternation. Zhukov had asked his generals to keep a close eye on Konev's progress, but he seems to have had no idea that they had moved so far, so fast. When Zhukov himself confronted Rybalko only 300 yards from the Reichstag building he shouted, 'Why have you appeared here?'[25] The two fronts were now fighting side by side in southern Berlin; the race for Berlin took on a fresh meaning.

Konev's forces had begun their attack on April 16 with none of the problems Zhukov faced. Artificial fog was laid during a prolonged and thunderous artillery attack. Under its shelter a swarm of small boats crossed the Neisse, some of them towing the assault bridges for the infantry. In just fifteen minutes the broad river barricade was crossed and small bridgeheads were established. In two hours pontoon bridges capable of carrying thirty-ton loads were in place. In four hours bridges for sixty-ton loads had been constructed. In all, 133 crossings were set up within hours of the attack. Konev's forces pushed the German defenders back more than eight miles on the first day. In three days they swept west and north-west. On April 17 tanks drove across the Spree through water three feet deep. By April 18 they were almost thirty miles beyond it, approaching Berlin.[26]

Unlike Zhukov, Konev found that he could fight the battle on the approach to Berlin like the battles in the Ukraine and Poland: a rapid penetration of defensive lines, then the swift deployment of the following armour. Stalin could see the contrast. He rebuked Zhukov for ordering his tanks to support the infantry attack, and he rewarded Konev by ordering him to rush for the capital. Over the next two days 3rd and 4th Guards Tank Armies pushed on without halting, a remarkable sixty miles. On April 21 they were in Berlin. Rybalko's 3rd Guards Tank Army seized the German army's main headquarters at Zossen, leaving stranded German commanders to improvise as best they could. Konev pointed his two tank armies north towards the heart of the city and the Reichstag building, which housed the German Parliament. It was at this point that Zhukov's forces at last caught up. Over the next three days the two forces fought for control of the southern areas of the city. On April 25, uncertain exactly where Zhukov's forces were, Konev ordered a final heavy assault across the centre to the Tiergarten and the Reichstag. As his forces began firing it soon became clear that in front of them were not German troops but Soviet. Chuikov had spent the previous day driving west to cut across the line of Konev's advance. Both armies arrived at the Land-wehr Canal, which shielded the Tiergarten, but Chuikov was in position first and it was here that Zhukov and Rybalko clashed. Konev telephoned Rybalko and ordered him to stop and turn west to clear the rest of the city. There were strong protests, but in the end Rybalko complied. In his memoirs Konev displayed no rancour, but it is easy to sense that his disappointment was as deep as Rybalko's.[27] The plum was to fall to Zhukov.

On the morning of April 29 Chuikov's 8th Guards Army prepared to storm the Tiergarten from the south. From the north another of Zhukov's armies, General Kuznetsov's 3rd Shock Army, crossed the river Spree, moving in the same direction. 8th Guards had just 400 yards to cross, but they were filled with tall government and party buildings and crammed with the last remnants of the army and militia defending the Führer. In their midst was the Reich Chancellery, in whose cavernous basement Hitler sat contemplating the utter, irretrievable collapse of his fantastic dreams of empire. To the north stood the broad classical façade of the Reichstag building. It was this edifice, rather than Hitler's battered Chancellery, that was chosen by the Soviet side as the symbolic heart of the Nazi empire, though its credentials were more democratic than those of most of its surroundings. The troops were told that whoever raised the standard of victory above the Reichstag building would be decorated a Hero of the Soviet Union.

The night before the final assault Chuikov again could not sleep. He chain-smoked from the tension. During the night of April 29 isolated assault groups crossed to the far side of the canal and secured a bridge. Their orders were to capture a major building which could be used as a stepping-off point for the final storming of the centre. They made slow progress against suicidal resistance. But the Reichstag was not to be their prize either. From the north General Pereveretkin's 150th Rifle Division reached the building first. At one o'clock on April 30 artillery opened up. Under covering fire a small group of Soviet infantrymen crawled forward holding one of nine red banners handed out to the closest troops. They burst through the central entrance to the Reichstag and in grim hand-to-hand fighting secured the first floor. Thousands of German soldiers occupied the upper floors and the basement. At about two-thirty the banner was waved from a second-floor window. It took another eight hours for the Soviet assault force to clear enough of the upper levels to reach the roof. Fighting with hand grenades and machine-guns, 300 soldiers succeeded in holding at bay a much larger German force until two Soviet sergeants, Yegerov and Kantariya, finally succeeded, at ten minutes to eleven, in hoisting the banner from the Reichstag. The scene, later photographed from an airplane, became one of the most famous images of the war.[28]

That same day Hitler took his own life. All around him the centre of Berlin was covered by a pall of dust and smoke, dark grey and stifling. On every side fires blazed out of control. The air was torn by an endless roar of artillery and rocket fire, and the shriller notes of machine-guns. The Reich Chancellery, built as a vast monument to the new German empire in the 1930s, was a ruined shell, its marble floors and pillars splintered and shattered. In the bunker, which Hitler had occupied since late March, surrounded by security men and secretaries and a handful of the party faithful, the mood swung from deep depression to desperate optimism with each report from the front line. Since communications were poor, Hitler conjured up in his mind whole armies of Siegfrieds battling through to free the capital from the Soviet dragon. In his more sombre moments the truth was unbearably real. On April 20, as he said farewell to one of his secretaries, who was to take the last flight out of the city, he announced: 'It is all over.'[29]

He had no intention of surrendering his capital and entering captivity. In the last weeks he turned against his own people for their failure to sustain his glorious ambition. In lengthy monologues, faithfully recorded by his secretary, Martin Bormann, he explored the long path he had taken from the heady days of Munich and Poland to the field of Armageddon in Berlin. He blamed the Jews as usual, but this time he also blamed the German people for not being worthy of the trust he had put in them. He hailed the Slavic peoples, whose resilience and fighting power had brought them to the gates of Berlin, as the new master race. Germany would have to wait.[30] Goebbels echoed his master's voice when he told those of his staff who were still in the bunker that the war was lost and that the German people 'deserved the fate that will now descend upon them'.[31] On April 29, with all hope gone, Hitler ordered his commanders never to surrender the city. He refused to flee. Instead he played out the final act according to the script. 'I must now obey the dictates of Fate. Even if I could save myself, I would not do so.'[32]

Late in the evening of the 28th he called a typist into the conference room in the bunker. The map table, usually covered with materials, was empty. He stood in front of it and dictated to her his last political testament. After a further diatribe against the Jews for bringing the peoples of Europe so low, he announced that he would choose death in Berlin. From his sacrifice, and that of millions of other Germans, would come the seed of National Socialism's rebirth. He announced a new German government to succeed him, to be led by Admiral Karl Doenitz, head of the German navy.[33] He then declared in a second, personal, testament that he would marry his long-time mistress, Eva Braun, before dying. The ceremony was performed just before midnight. Hitler had a final meal at lunchtime the following day with his cook and two secretaries, though there must certainly have been little point in eating. Then he solemnly shook hands with the population of the bunker, and retired with his new wife to his private rooms. At half past three, while Soviet soldiers battled for the upper floors of the Reichstag, and Soviet tanks ground down the roads around the Chancellery, Eva Braun took poison and Hitler shot himself in the head.[34]

That evening the German garrison sent out an emissary under a white flag to open negotiations. At half past three in the morning of May 1, the chief festival day of the socialist calendar, General Hans Krebs, the last German army chief of staff appointed by Hitler, arrived at Chuikov's headquarters. He reported Hitler's suicide and then tried to insist that he would negotiate only with the Soviet leadership. He refused to order a military surrender. Chuikov telephoned Zhukov, who said that anything other than unconditional surrender was out of the question. Zhukov then telephoned Stalin, to be told that he was asleep. He got the orderly to wake him up and gave him the still uncorroborated report of Hitler's death. 'Now he's done it, the bastard,' replied Stalin. 'Too bad he could not have been taken alive.'[35] He issued orders for nothing less than full surrender, then went back to sleep. Krebs held out stubbornly for an armistice, to be negotiated with the new German government detailed in Hitler's final testament. He hinted at 'a peace advantageous to you and to us', though what advantage the beaten German army expected was not spelled out. When Chuikov pressed him for a full surrender he replied, 'We will fight on to the last.'[36] They fell to small talk. By five o'clock in the morning the two men were exhausted. They sat together in unlikely companionship, conqueror and vanquished, sipping cognac and eating sandwiches.

The issue could not be resolved that morning. After almost twelve hours Krebs left, and the Soviet order went out to finish the conquest of Berlin. A heavy artillery and rocket barrage smothered the government quarter and the zoological gardens, and Soviet forces moved methodically from block to block clearing out the last defenders. At four o'clock Krebs sent back a reply, countersigned by Goebbels, rejecting surrender. The war began again. At six-thirty in the evening every Soviet gun and rocket launcher erupted in a vast display of firepower, and the German garrison was reduced to small pockets of resistance.

During the night Chuikov was roused twice from much-needed sleep. At one-thirty arrived news that the garrison commander, to prevent further slaughter, wanted to surrender. At six in the morning of May 2 the German defenders laid down their arms. Shortly beforehand a delegation of civilians, headed by Goebbels's deputy, Hans Fritzsche, made their way to see Chuikov, to say that Goebbels had killed himself, Krebs had disappeared (as it turned out, also to commit suicide) and that they were willing to surrender. Within the hour Zhukov confirmed that Soviet hostilities would cease. By midday the struggle was over. The final shots were fired by German soldiers who could not be reached by radio or telephone. When Chuikov went out into the street he was struck by the silence, which rang in his ears after the tumult of battle. In his memoirs he recalled the heady thoughts spurred by the sudden coming of peace to Berlin: 'the flame of world war was quenched there, whence it arose.'[37]

The war was, however, not yet over. While the fight for Berlin was reaching its height, Allied forces from east and west converged on the Elbe river. On April 25, at Torgau, the two sides first made contact. Over the next week the whole line of the Elbe was occupied. Further to the south 600,000 German troops entered Czechoslovakia, where they continued a fruitless resistance. They were pursued by Konev's 1st Ukrainian Front, which had to swing south again, after its efforts in Berlin, to complete one more task. The fighting in the south was not finally over until May 11, two days after the day officially declared in Moscow to be the end of the European war.[38]

The war ended as untidily as had the conflict in Berlin. Chuikov and Zhukov both felt that the war was over with the fall of Hitler's capital. Zhukov toured the Reichstag and the Chancellery as the conqueror of Berlin. He was eager to find the body of Hitler, but on his visit to the bunker only the bodies of Goebbels, his wife and their six children were identified. He began to have doubts about the truth of Hitler's suicide. On May 3 *Pravda* carried on its front page an article which declared that Hitler was not in Berlin: 'If he fled, we shall unearth him, wherever he tries to hide.' An opinion poll published soon afterwards showed that most Muscovites shared this scepticism and thought Hitler was in hiding.[39] At his headquarters Stalin ordered a top-level security officer to Berlin to hunt for Hitler. A popular fear began to develop, which Stalin may well have shared, that a living Hitler might ignite the dying embers of resistance if he should reappear.

The Chancellery was a burning shell in early May, difficult to search effectively. On May 2 a detachment of Soviet troops had found a body which seemed to resemble Hitler's, but the worn clothes indicated a man of lesser station. According to a Soviet report not released until 1968, Ivan Klimenko, a colonel in Smersh, discovered two bodies on May 4, one male, one female, in a small crater at the back of the Chancellery. Both were burned beyond recognition. They were wrapped in sheets and reburied, since it was thought that Hitler would not simply have been dumped in the garden. But the following day Klimenko returned, disinterred the remains and took them for autopsies. The dental work was examined by one of Hitler's dentists and the identity of both Hitler and Eva Braun was confirmed. The report concluded that Hitler had died of cyanide poisoning; there was no heroic suicide by handgun, the report continued, despite all the evidence collected by the British at the end of the war that Hitler did indeed shoot himself (and despite the portion of skull with a bullet-hole through it, alleged to be Hitler's, that was kept sealed away in Moscow for almost fifty years).[40] Though Stalin must have known of the report shortly after it was produced, he continued to pretend that he had no knowledge of Hitler's whereabouts. Not even Zhukov was told. No details were officially released until fifteen years after Stalin's own death.

The reasons for Stalin's silence can only be guessed at, though the official explanation, that Stalin wanted to 'hold it in reserve' in case the evidence were needed to unmask an impostor, is not entirely unbelievable.[41] Hitler's jawbone and the portion of skull were kept in a box in Moscow, where they were finally made public, along with his cap, Iron Cross and personal effects, only after the Soviet Union had collapsed, in 1991. The rest of his burned body took a different trail. Under the code name Operation Myth, Smersh undertook an intensive investigation in 1945 and 1946 into the fate of Hitler. They were satisfied that the body they found was that of the Führer. His remains, and those of Eva Braun and the Goebbels family, packed in empty ammunition boxes, travelled in the baggage of the Smersh unit until February 1946, when they were buried beside the garage of a house in Klausenerstrasse, Magdeburg, on a Soviet military base. In April 1970, under orders from the head of the KGB, Yuri Andropov, the bodies were disinterred and the mummified remains were burned again, pulverized, and scattered in a nearby river. The Soviet authorities wanted to avoid any chance that Hitler's burial site could become a place of pilgrimage for neo-Nazis.[42]

While the hunt went on for Hitler, alive or dead, in the first week of May 1945, the question of a general German surrender became paramount. The conquest of Berlin did not mean the end of a German government. Admiral Doenitz, Hitler's anointed successor, and other ministers had fled to Flensburg in north Germany. Negotiations with the Western Allies brought about the decision to surrender to Eisenhower, not to the Soviet authorities. On the morning of May 7 General Jodl, Hitler's chief of operations, was authorized by Doenitz to sign an act of unconditional surrender. The ceremony was a modest one. At twenty to three in the morning, in a small schoolhouse in Reims, which Eisenhower had made his headquarters, in the presence of the American General Walter Bedell Smith, a gaggle of Allied service chiefs and seventeen selected newsmen, Jodl signed the surrender with a gold-plated pen. Smith, Eisenhower's chief of staff, then signed with a different pen of solid gold, followed by a Soviet representative, General Susloparov, and the French General Sevez. The unfortunate Susloparov was caught unprepared. He had been posted to Eisenhower's headquarters in April as an observer and had no specific instructions from Moscow. If he did not sign he risked a German surrender with no apparent Soviet participation; if he signed he risked Stalin's fury for acting without permission. In the end he signed with a caveat that would allow Moscow to repeat the ceremony. Shortly after the signing a directive arrived for him from the Stavka telling him to sign nothing.[43]

The ceremony in Reims was galling for Stalin, who saw himself as the senior ally, and, with justice, regarded the Soviet war effort as the real source of victory over Germany. To compound the insult he received a letter from the head of the American military mission in

Moscow asking him to co-ordinate the Soviet declaration of the German surrender with the Americans and the British on the 8 May. He called his military staff and senior ministers together to the Kremlin. He was in an angry mood, pacing the carpet back and forth. He accused his Western allies of stitching up a 'shady deal' with the beaten enemy. He would not recognize the surrender in Reims: 'The surrender must be arranged as a most important historical fact, and accepted not on the territory of the conquerors but at the place where the fascist aggression sprang from: in Berlin.'[44] He pressed his allies to accept a second ceremony in the German capital which would demonstrate to the world the important part the Soviet people and their leader had played in the downfall of Hitler. He telephoned Zhukov with instructions to act on his behalf and to find a building still standing in which to stage the surrender.

Zhukov found a two-storey building at Karlshorst in eastern Berlin that had once housed the canteen of the German military engineering school. There, at a little before midnight on May 8, the Allied representatives gathered. New surrender documents had been drawn up in Moscow and hurriedly brought there by Vyshinsky, the chief prosecutor at the Moscow trials in the 1930s, who had become deputy minister for foreign affairs. Hours were spent trying to reconcile Soviet and Western versions. The text was typed and re-typed on a small portable machine by candlelight, following an electric power failure. At last, exactly at the stroke of midnight, Zhukov led the representatives of the other Allied powers, Air Chief Marshal Arthur Tedder, General Carl Spaatz and General de Lattre de Tassigny, into the hall. They sat at a long green table, and the German military leaders were ushered in, led by Field Marshal Wilhelm Keitel, Hitler's headquarters chief of staff. Keitel struggled to maintain his dignity. His face was blotchy and red, his hand shook. As he walked to the table to sign the surrender his monocle dropped from his eye and dangled by its cord. He had, Zhukov later recalled, 'a beaten look', though other witnesses thought the Germans 'arrogant and dignified'. At exactly forty-three minutes past midnight the ceremony was complete. Zhukov made what Stalin regarded as a dull speech for such an historic day, then hosted a night-long banquet, which ended with the Soviet generals, including Zhukov, dancing in the tradition of their country.[45]

Victory was announced in Moscow in the early hours of the morning of May 9. The day was declared Victory Day and a public holiday. The streets were filled with schoolchildren and students chanting 'The war's over.' Crowds gathered outside the American embassy shouting 'Hurrah for Roosevelt!'[46] In the evening two million to three million people gathered in Red Square and the streets around it. A thousand-gun salute was fired, and hundreds of airplanes flew low over the city, releasing red, gold and violet flares. There was wild, unrestrained jubilation, tinged, some observers noted, with a seriousness that bordered on the religious. The working men and women from the industrial suburbs wore their Sunday best. Police and guards allowed the revellers a free rein. Ilya Ehrenburg remembered 'an extraordinary day, both in its joy, and in its sadness; nothing happened, and yet everything was full of significance'.[47] He was recognized and tossed in the air by a crowd of well-wishers. He realized how much he had come to hate war. On May 9 he found people mourning their dead as though they had died that day. 'To the thunder of guns,' the poet later wrote, 'for the first time we bade farewell to all who died in the war, the way the living say farewell to the dead.'[48]

Victory brought Stalin to the pinnacle of his dictator's career. For a great many ordinary Soviet citizens the propaganda image of the supreme military leader was all they knew. Petr Grigorenko had, as a young man at the beginning of the war, begun to have second thoughts about Stalin's leadership. The war expelled that uncertainty. 'I connected the turnabout in the course of the war with Stalin,' he wrote; 'though I had begun the war with doubts about the "wisdom" of Stalin's leadership, I ended it believing that we had been lucky, that without Stalin's genius, victory would have taken much longer to achieve and would have entailed far greater losses, had it come at all.'[49] Stalin was appointed to the new rank of Generalissimus, though he complained that the new uniform made him look like a hotel waiter. The celebrations of victory went on intermittently for more than a month. Stalin played the part of warlord, basking in the reflected glory of his armies.

The high point was reached on 24 June 1945 with a Victory Parade through Red Square. Stalin allowed his generals to take the honours. On June 19 he summoned Zhukov to his *dacha* and asked him if he could still ride a horse. Zhukov said he could and was told to take the salute in the victory march-past. When he argued that Stalin as Supreme Commander should take on the responsibility he received from the sixty-five-year-old dictator the reply: 'I am too old to review parades.'[50] The ceremony took place in a downpour. The fly-past had to be cancelled. A bedraggled Zhukov sat astride his horse while the regiments marched past, led by a Hero of the Soviet Union, Marshal Rokossovsky. Zhukov confessed in his memoirs to an unaccustomed nervousness. Line after line of drenched soldiers arrived in front of the Lenin Mausoleum, where they hurled down the regimental banners of the defeated German army. In the evening Stalin hosted a banquet for 2,500 marshals and generals, where he took the unusual step of praising the ordinary Soviet people, 'the little screws and bolts' of the military machine that had made victory possible.[51] The victory banquet was conducted in the familiar way, awash with toasts to socialist progress and Stalin's genius. But the one group that Stalin left out, surely with deliberate intent, was the assembly of marshals and generals around him, which quite literally glittered with gold braid and battle honours. It was the first indication that Stalin was not prepared to allow the military heroes to overshadow their new Generalissimus. The working relationship established between Stalin and the generals in the middle years of the war, when he needed their expertise and their collaboration, was drawing to a close.

There remained a great deal of unfinished business. The future of Germany, discussed at Yalta, was not decided by the documents of surrender. The settlement in Eastern Europe was not resolved. The war with Japan was not yet over. The three wartime allies agreed to meet for a conference in which they could explore the many political issues left over from the defeat of the Axis powers. The date agreed upon was July 15. Stalin persuaded his allies to add to the symbolism of surrender by meeting in Berlin. The site chosen was Potsdam, home of Prussian militarism. Zhukov was once again asked to find a suitable venue. He chose the Cecilienhof, a former palace of the Prussian royal family. Other villas were requisitioned for the thousands of officials who followed in train behind their heads of state. Zhukov organized the refurbishment of thirty-six rooms and an assembly hall in the palace. By request Truman's headquarters were painted blue; Churchill asked for pink; the Soviet delegation chose a stark white. No circular conference table large enough and in one piece could be found in Berlin, so the Lux furniture factory in Moscow was asked to build one in time for the conference.[52]

Stalin was invited to travel to Potsdam in a Dakota airliner, but after his one and only flight, to Teheran, he refused to take to the air again. Beria arranged a trip by rail, with armoured carriages and an armed guard. The security arrangements exceeded anything yet seen. Stalin was more obsessed than ever with his personal safety, for he now travelled to the heart of what had been, only weeks before, enemy territory. Seventeen thousand NKVD troops and 1,515 regular soldiers lined the route, between six and fifteen men for every kilometre of track. The route was patrolled by eight armoured trains with NKVD troops. In Berlin the complex of sixty-two villas where the Soviet delegation stayed was defended in depth by three concentric circles of NKVD men, seven regiments strong. Beria set up two airfields for Soviet use, also bakeries and working farms, all staffed from Moscow. When Stalin arrived on July 16, resplendent in a white high-collared tunic with burnished epaulettes, the uniform of the Generalissimus, he was met at the station by Zhukov.[53]

The Big Three – Stalin, Churchill and Truman, Roosevelt's successor – met at the centre of a European order transformed from the old world of 1939. In the 1930s European, and much of world, politics was dominated by the European great powers, Britain, France, Germany and Italy. In 1945 the dominant powers were the Soviet Union and the United States. Britain maintained its claim vigorously, but the change in the balance of power was evident from Churchill's own gloomy petulance. In American and Soviet domination lay the seeds of either a new peacetime collaboration or a new confrontation. Despite growing tension in the alliance, some form of co-operation was not entirely out of the question. The parties around the conference table were, in Dmitri Volkogonov's words, 'both friends and enemies'.[54] The difference this time was that neither side needed the other, now that Germany was defeated. The Soviet Union knew by Potsdam that the generous supply of American goods begun in 1941 was drying up and would not be renewed. Reconstruction had to be planned without American aid. Likewise, the war with Japan did not now need Soviet assistance. Truman refused Churchill's offer of troops and was privately unhappy about Stalin's promise of armed assistance, which had been extracted at Yalta in rather different circumstances. The self-interest of the three parties at Potsdam did not require continued friendship. A peacetime union depended in the end on goodwill.

This was a commodity with a poor future. Despite the gestures of warmth and celebration at Potsdam, the two sides were separated, as they had been for most of the time since 1917, by a canyon of mistrust and aversion. For Westerners, as for Stalin, this was a return to a familiar battlefield. Stalin saw imperialistic capitalism as the real enemy, from which he had been diverted by the contest with Hitler. At the end of the war the Soviet security agencies began to describe the United States as 'Main Adversary' in their reports. 'I think we can tear off the veil of amity,' Stalin wrote to Molotov in the autumn of 1945, 'some semblance of which the Americans are so eager to preserve.'[55]

This view certainly overstated the Western position. Churchill anticipated his famous speech on the division of Europe, which he delivered at Fulton, Missouri, in March 1946, when he wrote to Truman in May 1945, four days after the end of the war in Europe:

An iron curtain is drawn down upon their front. We do not know what is going on behind. There seems little doubt that the whole of the regions east of the line Lübeck–Trieste–Corfu will soon be completely in their hands . . . It would be open to the Russians in a very short time to advance if they chose to the waters of the North Sea and the Atlantic.[56]

Churchill remained a constant critic of Soviet intentions throughout Potsdam. Truman kept to the form of Roosevelt's goodneighbourliness, but not to the substance. He privately viewed the Soviet delegation as 'pig-headed'. He was surrounded by men who could see no grounds for collaboration. Secretary of War Henry Stimson argued that there were no grounds for 'permanently safe international relations' between 'two such fundamentally different national systems'. George Kennan, who had long experience of trying to work with the Soviet Union, viewed Potsdam 'with unmitigated scepticism and despair'. Zhukov observed the 'strained atmosphere' of the conference.[57]

The immediate reasons for this distrust were exposed by the issues themselves. Stalin would not budge on the question of Poland. His control of the Baltic states could not effectively be challenged. He ignored the 'percentages deal' made with Churchill in 1944, as he had every right to do. Both sides agreed to a joint policy of de-Nazification, democratization and demilitarization in conquered Germany, but no one was under any illusion that democracy to Stalin meant something very different from Western practice. Over reparations there were protracted and bitter arguments. Truman and Churchill refused to abide by the figure of $20 billion of reparations for the Soviet Union talked of at Yalta. Since most of German industry had fallen into Western hands, there was something to bargain with. The Soviet side was compelled to accept a scaling-down of reparations from the other occupied zones, which Stalin took only because the West did not press the Polish question to the limit. A peace settlement with Germany was touched upon, but nothing firm could be decided as long as the two sides were unwilling to trust the other not to bring Communism westward or capitalism to the east. Germany was partitioned in all but name at Potsdam. Though Stalin announced at the conclusion of the conference that it could be regarded as a success, the final statements betrayed the reality of a divided Europe.

This was still some way from Cold War, further still from anything hotter. Neither side was in a position to risk a violent confrontation. The West was aware of Soviet land power, made stronger by the day as American troops were pulled out of Europe. There was no question of American forces storming to the liberation of Warsaw or Budapest. There was no serious prospect of Red soldiers standing, as Churchill feared, on the Channel coast. The Soviet Union was aware of Anglo-American power in the air and at sea. Stalin was not inclined to take risks with what he had already won. He haggled, but he had a price he would accept. The United States also had the atomic bomb. The first successful test of the new weapon was carried out while the Potsdam Conference was in session. Truman was eager to tell Stalin about it so as to strengthen his own hand in negotiation. At the end of the session on July 24, the day that Churchill learned that he had been defeated in the election in Britain ('One party is better,' Stalin had smugly told him at Yalta), Truman walked up to Stalin and declared the momentous news that America now had a bomb of awful destructive power.[58] Witnesses recalled that Stalin showed no reaction. He replied that he hoped Truman would know how to use it. The President was taken aback by Stalin's apparent indifference. But in subsequent meetings Truman's colleagues noticed a new forcefulness, a new confidence in their President's behaviour towards Stalin. The interpretation of those who watched the exchange, including the despondent Churchill, was that Stalin did not understand what Truman was talking about. He knew all too well. That night he telephoned Beria to speed up the Soviet nuclear programme, which had been placed under NKVD control. 'They are trying to bid up,' Molotov remarked. Stalin laughed: 'Let them.'[59]

The bomb was intended for use against the Japanese, whose war in the Pacific and in China was drawing to a close under the relentless heavy bombing of Japanese cities. Stalin's promise to Truman, made at their first meeting, that he would help to finish off Japan was kept a week after the Potsdam Conference closed on August 2. The Soviet attack on Japanese armies in northern China brought the prospect of solid strategic gains at little military cost. Stalin wanted specific territorial gains, but he wanted much more than this. Participation in the defeat of Japan placed the Soviet Union in a strong position in the re-establishment of the Chinese state. It promised to make the Soviet Union into one of two major Pacific powers, along with the United States. There was revenge, too, for the humiliating defeat of the Russian empire in the war of 1904.

Soviet and Japanese forces had first clashed in 1938, and again in 1939 along the Manchurian border. The victor in 1939 was a younger Zhukov, but it had needed all his operational skill to achieve it. The war then opened up an unbridgeable gap between the two sides in military power. Preparations for the offensive into Manchuria began in June. They were well under way by the time the Big Three met at Potsdam. Some ninety divisions crossed Russia to fight Japan. By August there were 1.5 million Soviet troops against a little over one million Japanese, many of them from the very bottom of the barrel of recruitment. Against 5,500 heavy tanks the Japanese could muster only 1,155 light models. Against the 26,000 guns of the Red Army the Japanese could muster only 5,000.[60] It was nonetheless a difficult operation. Soviet troops were tired from months of warfare. They faced an enemy whose defensive line was buttressed by formidable geographical obstacles – narrow gorges through high mountain barriers. To the north and north-west permanent concrete fortifications provided an artificial supplement to Manchuria's natural protection.

Yet Soviet victory was emphatic. Following the detonation of the first atomic bomb at Hiroshima on August 6, Stalin ordered an immediate attack, in case Japan surrendered. On August 9 the attack began. Japanese soldiers expected the Red Army of the 1930s, but they met a massively armed army, led by skilful officers who used their forces with a sophistication learned from the harsh battlefields of Europe. In just ten days their resistance was over. The war on mainland Asia went on for five days after the Japanese surrender on August 14, following a second atomic bomb. Some Japanese soldiers fought as Soviet soldiers had done on occasion, dying to the last man, but most surrendered: more than 600,000 prisoners were taken. Soviet forces covered vast distances to occupy Manchuria. By August 23 they had occupied the Kurile Islands, southern Sakhalin and the Pacific coast around Mukden. Without telling his allies, Stalin had also planned for a landing on the northern Japanese island of Hokkaido, in order to make the Soviet Union party to the post-war settlement in Japan, but at the last moment he cancelled the operation, from fear of alienating the United States and spoiling what had already been gained, which was a good deal.[61] Mongolia remained a virtual Soviet satellite. Manchuria and North Korea came under Soviet influence. Port Arthur became a Soviet naval base. On September 3 a second national holiday was declared throughout the Soviet Union. Peace came at last; Stalin took his first vacation since 1941.

At the end of the war the Soviet Union had recovered much of the territory the former Tsarist state had lost in the earlier wars of the century. Stalin was well aware of the achievement. Molotov recalled a visit to Stalin's *dacha* when the Generalissimus was presented with a new map of Soviet territory. Stalin pinned it to the wall and stood gazing at it. 'Let's see what we've got, then.' He listed the new territory seized at Finland's expense in the north; the Baltic states, 'Russian territory from ancient times'; western Belorussia, taken back from the Poles; and Moldova, unshackled from Romania. In the east he ran his pipe across China and Mongolia, then on to the Kurile Islands and Sakhalin, with evident satisfaction. Only in the south, around the Black Sea, did he find room for further improvement, at the expense of Turkey. This, too, was an historic axis of Russian advance, which long pre-dated 1917.[62]

Stalin's empire was won with reservoirs of Soviet blood. The cost of the war dwarfed the sacrifices of any other fighting power. By the time the last salvo had been delivered in Manchuria, Soviet forces alone had casualties of over 29 million: 6.2 million killed, over 15 million wounded, 4.4 million captured or missing, 3–4 million incapacitated by illness or frostbite. Of the 34.5 million men and women mobilized an incredible 84 per cent were killed, wounded or captured. Total military deaths from all causes, according to the official figures recently published, are given as 8.6 million. Other recent estimates produced by Russian historians suggest an even higher figure, in one case 23 million, in another 26.4 million. These higher totals have been arrived at on the basis that the official figures did not contain all of those who were mobilized, particularly in the frantic effort to create a popular militia in the first year or so of war, and that many of those killed were not listed as dead because of the difficulty of accounting for them during the period of retreat. Both of these factors should be taken into account, but it seems implausible that they should yield more than double the official total. For the present the figure of 8.6 million must be regarded as the most reliable. To these figures must be added the estimates of civilian deaths. No precise figure can be agreed upon, because for the thousands of murdered men and women, or the hundreds of thousands who starved to death, there can be no

Table 3 Soviet losses in World War Two

A: MILITARY LOSSES

Total mobilized armed forces	29,574,900
Total mobilized manpower (including other agencies)	34,476,700
Total losses (dead/POW/missing)	11,444,100
Total killed in action, died of wounds etc	6,885,100
Total missing/POW	4,559,000
Total dead 1941–45	8,668,400
Total medical casualties	18,344,148
of which: wounds/psychiatric disablement	15,205,692
sickness	3,047,675
frostbite	90,880

B: ESTIMATES OF CIVILIAN LOSSES*

Sokolov	Total civilian dead	16,900,000
Korol	Total civilian dead	24,000,000
Kozlov	Total demographic loss**	c40,000,000
Kurganov	Total demographic loss**	c35,500,000

* all figures exclude the figure of 8.6 million military dead
** includes civilian deaths from all causes + loss of potential demographic growth due to casualty

Source: J. Erickson, 'Soviet War Losses: Calculations and Controversies', in J. Erickson, D. Dilks (eds.), *Barbarossa: the Axis and the Allies* (Edinburgh, 1994) pp. 256–8, 262–6; B. V. Sokolov, 'The Cost of War: Human Losses of the USSR and Germany 1939–1945', *Journal of Slavic Military Studies* 9 (1996), pp. 156–71; V. E. Korol, 'The Price of Victory: Myths and Realities', *Journal of Slavic Military Studies* 9 (1996), pp. 417–24.

neat statistical record. Many were victims of Soviet brutalities and would have died anyway, war or no war. The best estimate available suggests a further 17 million dead from all causes. Taken together with the military deaths, total Soviet war dead may have been as high as 25 million, one quarter higher than the official figure of 20 million announced by Khrushchev in 1956, but consistent with the numbers publicly declared by Mikhail Gorbachev in 1991.[63] Precision in the record is hardly necessary. There is no dispute that the Soviet population suffered out of all proportion to the sufferings of Soviet allies, and suffered in many cases not a quick end from bomb or bullet but an agonizing end from starvation, or torture, or enslavement, or from countless atrocities whose mere recital still, after the accumulation of almost sixty years of further miseries world-wide, humbles and defeats the imagination.

10

The Cult of Personality: Stalin and the Legacy of War

'Turned into a deity, Stalin became so powerful that in time he ceased to pay attention to the changing needs and desires of those who exalted him . . . He knew that he was one of the cruelest, most despotic personalities in human history. But this did not worry him one bit, for he was convinced that he was executing the judgement of history.'

Milovan Djilas

For Stalin the victory of 1945 was a paradox. His identification with total victory over an enemy that Soviet propaganda had for years made out to be the very force of darkness invoked a personality cult that turned Stalin, for millions of his people, into something approaching a deity. A different leader might have revelled in it all, but not Stalin. His paranoiac fear of enemies, real and imagined, at home or abroad, reached a ferocious climax. His intense, irrational jealousies placed everyone around him in danger. No one was permitted to cast even a portion of his shadow over the divine countenance. Stalin's own fears oozed out over the whole system, smothering it with a blanket of terror and uncertainty. Victory did not bring in its wake the promise of a better, freer future – that was reserved for the defeated Germans and Japanese – but instead plunged the Soviet people into a second Dark Age.

The dictator was sixty-five years old when the war ended. The strain of the previous four years showed in his thinning hair and sallow face. He had put on weight, which gave his slight figure a more avuncular, even, at times, genial appearance. Over time Stalin had developed two very different personalities. He was not schizophrenic, as far as can be judged. Yet the Stalin who greeted Roosevelt or Churchill, smiling, courteous, self-effacing, was a different creature from the man who routinely ordered the deaths of thousands, sparing neither his family nor close friends and colleagues. The divided personality reflected a more profound division in Russia's own past, the divide between Westernizers and Russophiles, between the modern and the ancient, between openness and despotism. These divisions produced a tension in Russian history that was evident throughout the two centuries that preceded Stalin. In the figure of the Soviet dictator the two elements of Russia's past jostled with each other in uncomfortable proximity.

The modern Stalin was instantly recognizable. Averell Harriman, who saw a great deal of Stalin during the war as Roosevelt's emissary and then ambassador, was deeply impressed by him: 'his high intelligence, that fantastic grasp of detail, his shrewdness . . . better informed than Roosevelt, more realistic than Churchill . . . the most effective of the war leaders'.[1] At Potsdam President Truman was soon under the spell. He liked the way that Stalin 'looked [him] in the eye when he spoke'.[2] At Teheran the British Chief of the Imperial General Staff, General Sir Alan Brooke, thought that Stalin's grasp of strategy was the fruit of 'a military brain of the highest calibre'. At Teheran Stalin did not, in Brooke's view, put a foot wrong.[3] Stalin was no pampered potentate. He worked exceptional hours on affairs of state, major and minor. He achieved some understanding of modern technology; he knew that modern warfare, to which he was completely converted, needed weapons, supplies and transport, and he placed these areas of the war effort on the same level as the military campaigning. Stalin's contribution to the modernization of the Soviet war effort and to its ultimate triumph cannot be ignored. He worked for a more modern state before 1941, and its achievement made possible Soviet victory.

The pursuit of the modern age continued after 1945. Stalin's priority was to repair the material damage inflicted by the war. It was an extraordinary catalogue of loss – 70,000 villages, 1,700 towns, 32,000 factories, 40,000 miles of railroad track. Over one-third of Soviet wealth was destroyed; 25 million people were homeless.[4] The whole modernization project of the 1930s had to be begun again almost from scratch throughout the war-scarred areas of the western Soviet Union. Stalin saw the project as another kind of war. The population, used to almost twenty years of mobilization, in peace and in war, was rallied for one more effort. In Leningrad the entire able-bodied population was made responsible for reconstruction work, ten hours a month for juveniles, thirty hours for workers, sixty hours for the rest. The regimented workforce absorbed the cost in low wages, few goods, inflation and shoddy housing. In three years industrial production was restored to pre-war levels. By 1950, if the statistics are to be believed, the economy was double the size it had been in 1945. The output of cement to rebuild Soviet cities rose 1,000 per cent.[5]

Stalin's other face was kept from the public gaze. Harriman was not fooled by the mask of 'courtesy and consideration', the face to the West. He knew that Stalin was a 'murderous tyrant', capable, if he chose, of 'ghastly cruelty'.[6] The other Stalin would have been equally recognizable to his people. Not for nothing was Stalin steeped in Russia's past, or an Asian past more ancient still. His reading betrayed him – books on Genghis Khan, on Ivan the Terrible, on Peter the Great. This was not a very Marxist bookshelf, but as Stalin told the biographer Emil Ludwig, 'Marxism has never denied the role of heroes.' Stalin saw his despotism as something necessary for Russia: 'Somebody else could have been in my place,' he told Ludwig, 'for somebody had to occupy it.'[7] Stalin seems to have believed that the very nature of Russian life and Russian traditions made such a relationship between ruler and ruled inescapable: 'The people need a Tsar.'[8]

The despotic Stalin, coarse and malevolent, ruled over a terrified and sycophantic court. He baited and humiliated those around him. He sensed their fear and played upon it, half-humorous, half-threatening. They inhabited a world in which everything was reduced to what Djilas later called 'a horrible, unceasing struggle', avoiding the traps set for them, competing for favours, fawning upon the wisdom and generosity of their master.[9] The art of tyranny was practised effortlessly in the post-war years. Stalin's dinner-time talk was transformed by his zealous staff into commandments; witnesses watched as Stalin's

guests blanched or blushed, trembled or perspired, with every dictatorial snarl or rebuke.

Stalin had one conspicuous vulnerability, which grew more marked
in the post-war years. He had an exaggerated fear of dying. There lay
in this a sinister paradox. His own morbid fears competed with a
studied indifference to the mortality of others. It is not unlikely that
they were connected, his own sense of doom exaggerated by the
cheapness of Soviet lives under his dictatorship. The source may lie
somewhere in his seminary education: a nagging fear of damnation, a
seed of anxiety planted in a fertile, superstitious soil. His preoccupation
with age and dying was present too often in his private conversations
to be merely accidental. At the end of one dinner he raised a toast to
the memory of Lenin. The toast was boozily endorsed, but Stalin
remained lost in thought, 'earnest, grave, sombre'. When the guests
rose to dance, Stalin tried a few steps before complaining, 'Age has
crept up on me, and I am already an old man!' Did he mark down
the names of those obsequious courtiers who reportedly flattered
him with 'nonsense' or 'you look fine' or 'you're holding up'?[10] The
excessive security measures, the desperate terror of assassination, the
grim Hobbesian view of the world in which no mortal, however
powerful, could escape from a ceaseless striving against death – all
of these betray a personality consumed by an intense morbidity. Did
he, along some unconscious path, seek to appease the gods with the
offering of other deaths than his? As he grew older he became more
bitter, more bloodily vindictive. In victory there was none of the
proverbial magnanimity. While the Soviet Union rebuilt its economy
and established the foundation of its new superpower status, Stalin
indulged a capricious lust for post-war retribution.

Some of that thirst for vengeance was rational enough. He agreed
at Potsdam that the leading Nazis should be put on trial to answer
for their crimes. There was an ironic twist to this decision. The British
Government, half-heartedly supported by the American, had favoured
a short, sharp end before a firing squad. The object was to avoid a
long and complicated legal process, with the prospect of political
disagreements and German popular protests. According to Churchill,
it was Stalin who insisted on a trial. Stalin argued that a death sentence

needed a trial; otherwise the senior Nazi prisoners could only be given lifelong confinement.[11] When Truman, too, insisted on due process of international law, the idea of summary execution evaporated. There remained a great deal to argue over. Western politicians found it difficult to sit in judgement on German leaders over 'crimes against peace' or 'crimes against humanity' side by side with Soviet representatives of a regime they thought just as culpable.

The conduct of the trials, held at Nuremberg between November 1945 and October 1946, demonstrated two very different approaches to judicial process. The Soviet prosecutors laboured under the disadvantage that confessions had not been wrung from the defendants by weeks of ceaseless torture. They presented a case carefully constructed in Moscow and stuck to it rigidly. There was no mention of the German-Soviet Pact of August 1939 and the division of Poland; no mention of the Soviet-Finnish War. Soviet prosecutors used the language of Communist propaganda as they read out declaratory statements demonstrating the guilt of the 'fascist criminals', about which they were in no doubt. For crimes against humanity the Soviet side contributed lengthy accounts read out from prepared scripts allegedly based on eyewitness testimony. The accounts revealed unspeakable, almost incomprehensible atrocities, and were little questioned, despite the absence of the same witnesses in court. They may well have been entirely fabricated; they were almost certainly (but unnecessarily) embellished in order to demonstrate that the Soviet Union was the victim of greater barbarisms than any other state.[12]

In February 1946 the Soviet team caught their Allied colleagues by surprise by calling to the stand Field Marshal Paulus, who had failed to take Stalingrad, then failed to take his own life. In captivity he chose to support the Free Germany Committee set up in Moscow among German prisoners of war and German Communists, and he became the chief informer against his former comrades in arms. Under cross-examination by General Roman Rudenko, the leading Soviet prosecutor at the Nuremberg Trials, he affirmed that 'beyond doubt' the German Government and armed forces had conspired to attack the Soviet Union and turn it into a colony. The Soviet authorities had no doubt either about the guilt of those arraigned at Nuremberg and wanted them all executed. When Vyshinsky arrived at Nuremberg in November 1945, with the Chief Prosecutor of the Soviet Union, General Konstantin Gorshenin, he raised a toast to the defendants at a dinner in his honour: 'May their paths lead straight from the courthouse to the grave!' British and American judges found themselves in the uncomfortable position of endorsing the death sentence for men they were supposed to be trying in the tradition of judicial impartiality.[13] Although the International Military Tribunal established to try the German war criminals was supposed to be an independent body, arriving at an independent judgment, Vyshinsky was appointed secretly by Stalin to head a 'Commission on the Direction of the Nuremberg Trial', to interfere in the conduct of the Tribunal. Vyshinsky's main task was to ensure that there should be no hint at all at the trial of the Soviet-German agreements made in 1939, nor of any impropriety on the part of the Soviet authorities. Soviet prosecutors were instructed by him to shout down any witnesses whose testimony was 'anti-Soviet'.[14]

The orchestration of the trials from Moscow proved remarkably successful. Only one witness touched, briefly, on the Soviet-Finnish War. The rest of the Soviet story remained unexplored, including the most notorious deception of all, the Katyn forest massacre. The Soviet team insisted on including the atrocity as part of the formal indictment on German war crimes. The other prosecutors argued that there remained so much uncertainty about the circumstances surrounding the murder of the Polish officers that in open court the Soviet Union might be compromised by any discussion. The Soviet prosecutors were unmoved, perhaps anxious that silence might be construed by world opinion as an admission of guilt. The opening of the trial itself was postponed for three days while the indictment was changed from the murder of 925 Polish officers to 11,000. This was approximately the figure given by the German authorities in April 1943 when they announced to the world the discovery of the mass grave in the Katyn forest. The official Soviet line in 1943 was to reject 'Goebbels's slanderers' and 'Hitlerite liars' and to lay the blame on German troops. In September 1943, when the area of Katyn was retaken by the Red Army, the Soviet Government set up a Special Commission for

Ascertaining and Investigating the Circumstances of the Shooting of Polish Officers by the German-Fascist Invaders, thus pre-empting any other conclusion than German responsibility.[15]

The report of this commission was submitted as Soviet 'evidence' at Nuremberg, and Soviet lawyers made crude efforts to prevent any further discussion. The other prosecutors this time refused to co-operate, and three witnesses were heard from each side, giving, as expected, two very different versions of the story. The issue remained unresolved. The tribunal failed to arrive at any conclusion on Katyn. The Soviet authorities refused to countenance anything but their own official report. Indeed some of the Soviet lawyers working at Nuremberg may well have believed that these conclusions, based as they seemed to be on solid forensic evidence, did constitute the truth. Until the collapse of the Soviet Union the files on Katyn remained closed, and German responsibility continued to be the official line. Since the collapse documents have at last been disclosed which prove the responsibility of the NKVD beyond any further questioning. In April 1995 it was publicly admitted by a Russian security spokesman that 21,857 Polish soldiers were murdered at three separate sites by NKVD liquidation squads. In the NKVD files were the names of those decorated for the liquidation of Polish 'nationalists' in the Smolensk area in April 1940.[16]

Katyn was not the only Soviet atrocity blamed on the German invader. In the Kuropaty forest in Belorussia roadworkers excavating a new highway in 1957 uncovered human remains. 'An ancient cemetery' was the explanation given. In 1987 two schoolboys stumbled across a mass grave. What they had discovered was one of an estimated 500 mass burial sites in the forest areas around Minsk, all of them filled with the victims of NKVD terror. They contained, according to the estimates of those who investigated them, between 150,000 and 200,000 bodies. The official position of the Belorussian Government, which authorized a commission of inquiry, was to blame the Germans, and this position was maintained beyond the collapse of the Soviet Communist system, which had kept the lies alive. The evidence from the exhumations damned the NKVD. The bullets were those used in the official-issue Nagan revolver; death was the usual shot through the back of the skull, exactly as at Katyn. There were witnesses who watched the relentless cycle of killing behind the fenced-off area of forest; who saw the forest roads flattened by the constant traffic of trucks coming in full and returning empty; who recalled the timetables of execution: dawn, two o'clock in the afternoon, dusk.[17] To blame the German invader for Katyn was easy in the 1940s, given the unambiguous evidence of German crimes throughout the occupied Soviet area. To sustain the falsehoods for fifty years and to heap on more when the evidence quite literally surfaced in the 1980s is harder to explain. The image of Soviet righteousness, sustained by propaganda after the German invasion, allowed Stalin, and then the entire Soviet system, to erect a curtain of forgetfulness between the pre-war and the post-war world. The post-Stalinist state had no more interest in owning up to atrocities than had Stalin himself. Honesty on such issues was regarded as corrosive.

In addition to the major war criminals who stood trial at Nuremberg, millions of ordinary German soldiers fell into Soviet hands. For years there existed a wide discrepancy between the number that German sources claimed had been taken prisoner and the numbers which gradually made their way back to Germany in the 1940s and 1950s. In 1947 Molotov stated that over one million German prisoners had been repatriated and that a further 900,000 remained in the Soviet Union, but contemporary estimates put the number of German prisoners at three to four million. The not-unreasonable assumption was that most of the one million to two million unaccounted for must have died in Soviet captivity. The official Soviet figures of all prisoners of war taken were finally made available under *glasnost*. They revealed that for once Molotov was telling the truth. The Soviet Union took 2,388,000 German prisoners between 1941 and 1945, most of them in the last eighteen months of the conflict. Of these a total of 356,000 died, leaving a little over two million for repatriation. A further 1,097,000 were captured from the nationalities fighting at Germany's side, mainly Hungarians, Romanians and Austrians, of whom 162,000 died. Approximately 600,000 Japanese prisoners were also taken, of whom 61,855 died in captivity. It has to be assumed that most prisoners died from hunger, disease, cold and exhaustion. Like the unfortunate prisoners of the Japanese who perished building the Burma railway, German prisoners were set to work completing a major rail route from the Volga at Kuibyshev to Lake Baikal in Siberia.[18]

Conditions for German prisoners were poor at first until the authorities established an organization to cope with them, and many of the deaths must have occurred in the early months of neglect. The highest casualty rate among Japanese prisoners came in the first six months of captivity, after which conditions improved. The prisoners were eventually placed in rough camps of tents or huts with few facilities and little medical attention. German prisoners were permitted to keep their uniforms, and camp life was run by German officers. In most other respects they shared the same routine as the prisoners of the Gulag. They worked ten to twelve hours a day. Food consisted of 600 grams of bread daily and three helpings of potato soup; there was little or no meat, animal fats or vegetables. They were supposed to be paid one rouble a day for the work, but payment was said to be irregular. Local camp bosses often wound up with both the money and the food. They were not conditions designed deliberately to exterminate the occupants of the camps, for the labour power of prisoners was needed to rebuild the Soviet economy. Model prisoners, those who took the regular Communist propaganda and recruitment sessions seriously, were given anti-fascist courses and could be returned to the Soviet zone of Germany as Communist educators.[19]

Along with German and other Axis prisoners there came a stream of Soviet citizens. Over five million had been stranded in German-occupied Europe. Some of them were prisoners of war; several million were slave labourers. Others were voluntary exiles – Soviet workers who had helped the German army and moved west as it retreated, or soldiers of the Russian Liberation Army who fought all over Europe on Germany's side. For all of them the costs of repatriation exceeded anything imposed on the defeated Germans, even on those who laboured on the railways. For those who fought against the Red Army the verdict was treason. Thousands were shot where they were caught; others were shot as they returned. For those who survived to feed the relentless demand for labour there were sentences of ten to twenty-five years and the lifelong stigma of betrayal. They were sent to the northernmost camps of the Gulag, to dig out coal and minerals in conditions few prisoners could endure.

Their compulsory repatriation was agreed upon by the Allies at Yalta, and both the British and Americans stuck to the agreement even though they knew that repatriation meant certain death or captivity. The Western states were anxious not to alienate Stalin at a sensitive point in negotiating the post-war settlement of Europe; nor could they be certain that the Soviet Union would return all the former Western prisoners of war or slave labourers who had fallen into their hands in the advance into Germany unless they complied with Soviet demands for repatriation. Both of these were strong political arguments. There were also practical issues. The Soviet soldiers who fought on the German side were enemies and were treated as enemies. Cossack units had fought with a particular harshness against the Soviet population, with whom the British and Americans had been allied only weeks before. They were expensive to feed and hard to discipline, and, in the context of the war's end, the prospect of ridding the Western powers of the burden of supervising them was hard to resist, whatever moral qualms it has aroused since.

Less understandable was the Western willingness to meet the Soviet demand for the return of Russian *émigrés* who had fled the revolution and civil war and had never been Soviet citizens, or the forcible repatriation of Soviet workers and prisoners of war who had been compelled to labour in Germany against their will and were now, sensibly, fearful of what awaited them on their return. Many of the *émigrés* were citizens of other states, where they had settled in the 1920s. Some volunteered to fight against the Red Army, including Cossack generals who had led White forces in the Russian civil war that followed the 1917 Revolution. None wished to return to the Soviet Union; none was technically required to be repatriated under the Yalta agreements. Yet when the Soviet regime requested their return, hundreds were transferred by the British to the mercies of the Red forces from whom they had fled twenty-five years before.

The most notorious of the many cases of forcible repatriation was the return of 50,000 Cossacks, including 11,000 women, children and old men, in May and June of 1945. The Cossack host, led by the veteran

White general, the hetman Peter Krasnow, now age seventy-eight, and the former White general, Andrei Shkuro, had retreated to western Austria, where it had surrendered to the British. Nomads of war, their families followed in their wake. The local British commanders were asked by the Soviet authorities in eastern Germany to hand over the entire group, including the *émigré* generals, who were not Soviet citizens. Who made the final decision to comply is still not known with certainty, although Churchill himself is strongly implicated. The British commanders on the spot were divided. Some knew that the Cossack host contained men, women and children who were not required to be shipped back; others wanted to solve the issue of captive Russians quickly. Rather than screen them all, the British authorities undertook to comply with Soviet demands.

On 27 May 1945 the Cossack officers, including the elderly Krasnow, were told that they were to meet British Field Marshal Alexander for a conference on their fate. The invitation was a hoax, dreamed up by Smersh and communicated to the gullible British commanders. Smersh agents were allowed to enter the British zone to observe the transfer of the Cossack officers and joined in the recapture of the few who tried to flee. On May 29, 1,475 Cossack officers were loaded into trucks and driven, not to a conference with Alexander, but a rendezvous with Smersh and the NKVD. On the way, a number of them committed suicide. The rest were placed in a wire cage at Spittal. The following day they were handed over to the Soviet security forces at Judenburg. They were taken away for interrogation, destined for oblivion or the camps. Krasnow and three other White generals were taken to the Lubyanka for special treatment, together with their families. Krasnow's son and grandson were interviewed by Nikolai Merkulov, Beria's deputy. He greeted them with the words: 'For twenty-five years we've been waiting for this happy meeting with you! Victory is with us, with the Reds. As it was in 1920, so it is now . . .'[20] Both were sent to the camps, where Krasnow's son died. For the aged Krasnow, and for the other Cossack leaders, there was the round of torture and humiliation to endure, the trial and death by hanging.

For the thousands of Cossacks still in British hands the sudden disappearance of their officers caused a growing panic. Some escaped into the hills, where they were hunted down by British and Soviet patrols and shot or recaptured. A few committed suicide, killing also their wives and children, rather than face the horrors of deportation. On June 1 thousands of Cossacks were crammed into the barracks square at Peggetz to attend a religious service, when they were surrounded by British soldiers and forced, screaming and fighting, beaten by rifles and cudgels, into railroad cars. Twenty-seven died in the struggle. When they arrived at the handover point on the river at Graz the Cossacks were forced to cross the bridge to the waiting Smersh guards. One woman darted from the column and leaped onto the parapet of the bridge with her baby. She threw the child in the river; then jumped in herself. Some Cossacks had cut their own throats with knives or razor blades and bled to death on the trains. When they reached the Soviet side of the bridge they were forced into a camp surrounded by barbed wire. Their exact fate remains unexplained but it was almost certainly death for some, slave labour for the rest, state orphanages for the children.[21]

Similar treatment was meted out by the Soviet system to the millions of their citizens who became involuntary prisoners of the German war machine. These were not men and women who had joined with Germany or fought against their fellow citizens. They were men and women captured in battle or rounded up to be labourers in the many sweeps through the occupied territories. They included thousands of Soviet patriots, soldiers who were captured, wounded and helpless, or who fought until further resistance was hopeless. In many cases they were Soviet citizens who had refused every German or renegade entreaty to abandon their country and join the anti-Communist crusade. Unlike the Cossacks or the Vlasov soldiers, these were Soviet people who in many cases wished for repatriation.

Their treatment in practice differed little from the rough justice handed out to those who had deliberately chosen the German side. They were all, in the eyes of the Soviet regime, guilty of treason to the motherland. Order 270, published in 1941, made it clear that all prisoners taken by the enemy were to be regarded *ipso facto* as traitors. The penalty for 'premeditated surrender' was, according to Soviet regulations on military offences, death by firing squad.[22] They were also the victims of an exaggerated and paradoxical socialist xenophobia. Stalin instructed Smersh that every attempt should be made to bring back all the Soviet people stranded in Europe because they were 'undesirable witnesses against Communism', contaminated by nothing more than their mere presence beyond the frontier.[23] Every effort was made to restrict contact with foreign peoples of any kind, however innocent. In an exchange later with the film director Sergei Eisenstein over his film *Ivan the Terrible*, Stalin told him that Ivan's great strength as a leader was that he 'championed the national point of view . . . he safeguarded the country against penetration by foreign influences'.[24]

The millions of Soviet citizens who returned in 1945 were, in Stalin's eyes, unclean, besmirched, potentially traitorous. They were treated accordingly, without welcome. They were placed in camps, sometimes in buildings vacated only recently by the victims of German confinement. They were surrounded by armed guards and isolated from the outside world. Their subsequent fate was eloquently recaptured by one of their number, an army lieutenant, whose manuscript account of his ordeal was written later in the 1940s after his escape to the West. He was taken prisoner at Orel in October 1941, after a bomb tore off three fingers of one hand and his unit had fought to a standstill. He knew what course he should have taken:

How it happened that I, an officer, a candidate for Party membership, failed to shoot myself as instructed and how I let myself be taken prisoner, I cannot explain. Perhaps the acute pain in my hand held me back, or maybe the utter exhaustion after eleven days of uninterrupted fighting had rendered me completely apathetic . . .

He was made to work in mines, then in an armaments firm near Hanover, where he was liberated by American troops in 1945. He was delighted to be returning home. Some of his fellow prisoners opted to stay in the West, but he regarded them as 'absurd, pathological'. He arrived in the Soviet zone with hundreds of other returnees. The disillusionment was immediate. They were lined up, surrounded by armed guards, forced to tear off their epaulettes and subjected to a tirade from an officer who accused the men of treachery and the women of debauching themselves.[25]

The next day the officers were placed in a squalid hut and left without food for forty-eight hours. One by one they were summoned for interrogation. Half were shot out of hand. The other half were forced to change into tattered German uniforms. There followed a forced march for four days with almost no nourishment. They were loaded onto a freight train, over sixty to a car. The doors were opened only to allow the occupants to witness the execution of those who had been caught trying to escape. The trains arrived at a place twenty miles from Omsk. Here they were marched to camps with rows of wooden huts, where they joined the resident population of Gulag labourers and Axis prisoners. Those who could speak foreign languages were used as translators. The army lieutenant with the shattered hand who had waited for liberation with enthusiasm found himself indistinguishable from the enemy, working alongside Germans. They built new factories, filled with German machine tools seized as reparation. This particular project was christened New Germany. The lieutenant was lucky. He met a cousin who arranged false papers and a passage to the Soviet zone of Germany, whence he escaped to the West. Even this carried risks. Not until 1951 did the American Government permit political refugee status for Soviet defectors.[26]

Between 1945 and 1947, when the programme was completed, some 2,272,000 Soviet citizens were returned by the Western Allies to their homeland, many of them from as far afield as prisoner-of-war camps on the American west coast. Altogether, 5,457,856 were repatriated by 1953. Those found guilty of collaboration with the enemy, real or imagined, were sent to the Revolutionary Tribunal in Frankfurt an der Oder, where they were sentenced to be shot or to periods of forced labour. It has been estimated by Soviet historians that around one-fifth of all those who returned were executed or sentenced to the maximum twenty-five years in the Gulag.[27] Others were sent to work with forced-labour units rebuilding the Soviet infrastructure or to exile in Siberia. Around three million men and women were sentenced to terms in the camps. Only about one-fifth of those who came back were allowed to return home, mainly old men, women and children. They were compelled to report regularly to the local NKVD office; those deemed fit for work had to put in two years' reconstruction labour. All those released had the words 'socially dangerous' (*sotsial'no opasnyi*) put on their record. They were denied access to higher education, or to jobs that carried administrative responsibility. They bore the stigma of collaboration or cowardice for years after 1945.

Stalin reserved the most grotesque fate, not for those who had fought against him, nor for those who had fallen into German hands and become 'contaminated' by contact with the outside, but for those he had worked with closely through four years of war, whose contribution to victory was unimpeachable. The victims included the greatest hero of the war, Marshal Zhukov himself. Stalin's motives were rational only in the warped terms of the political system he had fabricated since the 1920s. He wished after the war to restore his personal power, after several years of depending upon the loyalty and competence of others. In his eyes, and in the eyes of other Party bosses, the military leaders constituted a threat to the restoration of an unalloyed Soviet dictatorship. They were popular with the public; they were men of independent mind; theirs was the real victory of 1945. All of these were reason enough for Stalin to return after almost a decade to the crude terrorism of the purge.

Zhukov was the most prominent target in Stalin's sights. Stalin almost certainly respected, perhaps even liked, Zhukov. Towards the end of the war Stalin spoke to him with a disarming and unfamiliar frankness. They spent hours together discussing the war, or Stalin's family, or the future beyond the conflict. It was not personal antipathy that fired Stalin's plot to undo his powerful deputy and confidant, but simple reason of state. As early as 1943 the head of Smersh, Viktor Abakumov, who became in 1946 chief of the NKGB,* was ordered to monitor the telephone calls of all senior generals and marshals. A file was opened on Zhukov, filled up with comments which might later be used to incriminate him. In May 1945, when Zhukov was appointed military administrator of the Soviet zone of occupation in Germany, Beria succeeded in placing his deputy, Ivan Serov, as head

---

* In April 1943 the security service was separated from the Internal Affairs Commissariat (NKVD) and renamed NKGB. In March 1946 NKGB became MGB following the transformation of the commissariats into Ministries.

of the civilian administration. He supplied both Beria and Stalin with a diet of defamatory intelligence on Zhukov, even with rumours that Zhukov was planning a military coup against Stalin himself.[28]

It is true that Zhukov did not help his own cause. He was not a modest man; he basked in the light of his military successes. In June 1945 he gave a press conference on the veranda of his villa at Wannsee in Berlin in which he took the opportunity to remind the wider world that he had played a major part, perhaps the major part, in the Soviet war – at Moscow, Leningrad, Stalingrad, the Ukraine, Warsaw and Berlin. He appended a tribute to Stalin as an afterthought. He did not mention a single one of his military colleagues. Vyshinsky, who was present at the press briefing, interjected with what could only have been mischievous intent: 'Moscow, Leningrad, Stalingrad, Kursk, Warsaw and so on, right on to Berlin – pretty wonderful!'[29] Zhukov seems not to have read the signals. A few months later Beria's case was complete. Zhukov was denounced by Stalin at a Kremlin meeting late in 1945 for claiming that he had won the war. He was summoned back to Moscow in April 1946 following a clash with Abakumov, who had been sent to Berlin to begin a purge of Zhukov's military organization.

Zhukov's reputation saved him. Boastful though he was, he was a figure with enormous prestige both inside and outside the country. Perhaps Stalin, too, had a fondness for Zhukov sufficient to rescue him from death. His downfall was planned with the usual care. One night in April 1946 the head of the Soviet air force, Marshal Aleksandr Novikov, the saviour of Soviet air power during the war, answered the knock on the door to find KGB agents waiting. He was driven away to a vicious interrogation. Stripped, forced like the repatriated Soviet prisoners of war to don a tattered shirt and trousers, he was tortured into confessing his part in sabotaging Soviet aircraft production (a charge even more preposterous than a Zhukov coup). Along the way he incriminated other officers, including Zhukov. Seventy more officers were arrested and interrogated to fill out the accusations. One day in June Zhukov was summoned to appear before the Main Military Council. That same night security men came to search his *dacha* but were turned away by its angry owner. Some days later another group of security police came with an armed guard and searched Zhukov's Moscow apartment looking for valuables allegedly looted from Germany. They took almost everything, including his daughter's doll.

At the meeting of the Council, attended by the Politburo and leading military commanders, Stalin ordered a letter to be read out in which Zhukov was accused of hostility to the Central Committee and the Government. The generals present, except for one, then spoke up in Zhukov's defence. The members of the Politburo all condemned him as a Bonapartist threat to the state. When Zhukov, who sat throughout with a bowed head, was given the floor he rejected the allegations, swore his loyalty to Communism, and agreed that he had out of conceit exaggerated his contribution to victory. The atmosphere of the meeting became tense. It would have been characteristic of Stalin to endorse the accusations, even perhaps to have accepted their truth. Yet according to one recollection Stalin told Zhukov privately that he did not for a moment believe the allegations, but that it would be better for him to leave Moscow for a while. Despite the hostility of the politicians present at the council meeting, Stalin offered Zhukov what amounted to internal exile. He was posted off to be commander of the Odessa Military District; later he was posted to a more obscure command in the Urals.[30]

Zhukov's name disappeared from the press. Stalin became the architect of victory. A film was made on the fall of Berlin which pressed home the message to the point of absurdity. With no staff and no generals, Stalin was pictured attended only by his loyal secretary, directing the great battle. The Soviet system was long practised in the art of writing people out of history. The two standard textbooks on the Second World War, prepared for senior school pupils in 1956, mentioned Zhukov's name only three times (and then in passing), as commander of the Western Front before Moscow and of the First Belorussian Front at Berlin.[31] Other military stars shared the same fate. Chief of Staff Antonov was exiled even further than Zhukov, to command of the Transcaucasian Military District. The names of Rokossovsky, Voronov, Konev, Vatutin and a host of others vanished from the public's eye. The unlucky ones suffered more than Zhukov.

Between 1946 and 1948 senior commanders were executed or imprisoned on trumped-up treason charges. The NKGB continued to pursue the case of the disgraced Zhukov. When General Vladimir Kryukov was interrogated in 1948 on charges of looting luxuries from Germany, he was asked: 'Can you repeat hostile remarks made by Zhukov about the Party or the Government?'[32] Despite the accumulation of further extorted evidence, Zhukov survived, in exile, without further threat. In 1953 he was rehabilitated, but at the end of 1957 was pensioned off by Khrushchev on the grounds once again of excessive self-glorification. History has been a kinder judge.

Stalin turned next to the heroes of Leningrad. The second city of Russia had suffered and overcome the horrors of modern siege warfare. Its defenders were hailed as model Communists. After the war Leningrad threatened to eclipse Moscow, as it had done under Kirov in the early 1930s. Writers, artists and poets established a flourishing and independent cultural life. The city was run by young and enterprising Communists who enjoyed the powerful patronage of Andrei Zhdanov, the former Leningrad Party leader, who in the immediate post-war years became the most influential figure in domestic politics behind Stalin. When Zhdanov died of heart failure in 1948 the Soviet apparatus contained a great many Leningraders, two of whom, Nikolai Voznesensky and Alexander Kuznetsov, were widely tipped as Stalin's successors. Voznesensky had risen, like Zhukov, to giddy heights during the war. He was responsible for planning the Soviet war economy, whose remarkable revival after 1942 played a critical part in the very survival of the state. After the war he began to write a major theoretical outline of the political economy of Communism, a successor to the economic thoughts of Comrade Stalin. By 1948 he was second only to Stalin in the Council of Ministers. Kuznetsov was one of the leaders of the Leningrad siege; like Kirov he was good-looking, energetic, a hard and responsible worker loyal to the Communist ideal. He was second only to Stalin in the Party hierarchy. Their success and popularity, like Zhukov's, was enough to place them in danger, not only from Stalin, but from other contestants in the succession.

During 1949 those rivals, spurred on by Stalin, began a new wave of purges, which were aimed first at Leningrad. On the pretext that the local Party committee was trying to fix elections, Stalin sent Georgi Malenkov, a narrow and ambitious Stalinist, to investigate. It is significant that the Museum of the Defence of Leningrad was closed down, its director arrested and its holdings confiscated. Lest the memory of Leningrad's heroism linger on, wartime newspapers were removed from public access in libraries. Beria and Abakumov supplied the evidence needed to incriminate Kuznetsov and Voznesensky and almost the whole of the Leningrad Party organization. They were all arrested and accused of a catalogue of invented crimes, from espionage for Britain to corruption and debauchery. The show trial was staged in September 1950. Uncharacteristically, and despite repeated beatings, neither Kuznetsov nor Voznesensky was prepared to admit in court to the trumped-up charges. The leading defendants were all found guilty, including Voznesensky's brother, the rector of Leningrad University, and his sister Maria. As the sentences were read KGB men wrapped the prisoners in white shrouds, and carried them bodily from the courtroom; they were shot within the hour (though according to one account Voznesensky was allowed to live another three months before dying in a truck on the way to Moscow). With these deaths, and Zhukov's exile, Stalin was rid of the war's most successful offspring.[33]

No one was free from the fog of suspicion and fear in which Moscow was permanently enveloped. Other wartime leaders were obscured by it. Molotov was sacked as Foreign Minister in 1949; Beria was relieved of his position as head of the NKVD in 1946 and replaced by Sergei Kruglov. Both men remained on the Politburo, but now they relied on Stalin's caprice rather than a power base of their own. In the late 1940s Stalin resurrected the atmosphere of the earlier terror. Peasants were punished for growing rich during the war, though few had. They were forced to meet impossible quotas, which left many on the edge of starvation. Workers were subjected to harsh discipline, long hours and the supervision of the NKVD. Intellectuals were the target of a renewed wave of cultural conformism. With the Leningrad trial the Party itself was opened again to the threat of the purge. The Gulag population began to swell. Between 1944 and 1950 the number of prisoners grew from 1.1 million to more than 2.5 million. Together with deportees, prisoners of war and other categories of slave labourers the overall number of victims may have been as high as 10 million.[34]

During the last, bleak, spiritless years of the dictatorship the regime singled out Soviet Jews as special victims. Their persecution was undertaken in the full knowledge of what had happened to European Jewry under the German occupation. Soviet anti-Semitism flourished unofficially even during the war. It differed from the genocidal imperative of German anti-Semitism only by degree. It was inspired to some extent by traditions of anti-Semitism which re-emerged in the Baltic states, Belorussia and the Ukraine in the wake of German racism. Jews were discriminated against in the armed forces, heir to another anti-Semitic tradition. They were decorated less frequently; they were turned away by some units; their role as partisans was played down by the propaganda apparatus. The word 'Yid' was heard more frequently, although it had been banned after the Revolution. When Jewish refugees and veterans returned home they not only discovered the stark truth about the genocide (only one Jew could be found alive in Kiev when it was liberated in 1943), but found themselves victimized in turn by local populations, which had helped themselves to Jewish possessions, or by local officials hostile to Jewish demands for relief and rehousing.[35] The most crushing blow came with the persistent refusal of the regime to recognize that the German race war had been directed at the Jewish people as such. No references were made to the genocide; officials rebuked those who exaggerated 'Jewish martyrdom' or indulged in 'national egotism'. The report produced in Kiev on Babi Yar talked of the death of 'peaceful Soviet citizens', not of Jews. Jewish efforts to publish a Black Book of anti-Jewish atrocities ended with a blank refusal.[36] Anti-Semitism was sharpened in 1947 with the start of a new public scare directed at 'cosmopolitanism'. The campaign began as a search for scapegoats in the Cold War confrontation with American imperialism. To be cosmopolitan was to be disloyal to the Soviet ideal; it was to be a spy for the capitalist enemy; it was to be the rootless tool of warmongers and chauvinists. While Senator Joseph McCarthy sniffed out America's fifth column of godless Communists, Stalin's policemen invented an insidious conspiracy by bourgeois nationalists and deviationists, paid for in dollars. The

Jewish community, because of their contacts with Jews in the United States during the war and the flow of Jewish aid from abroad, were already suspect. Stalin's habitual distrust of national feeling, even one revived in the face of the Holocaust, sealed the fate of Soviet Jews.

The first victims were those Jewish intellectuals who had set up the Jewish Anti-Fascist Committee during the war. Their chief spokesman was Solomon Mikhoels, a playwright with an international reputation. At Stalin's instigation he was lured to Minsk to discuss a Belorussian play. On 12 January 1948 he was telephoned at his hotel and left in a car. He was driven to the *dacha* of a local Party boss, Lavrenti Tsanava, where he was murdered. His body was dumped by the roadside near the hotel, where it was to be run over by a truck to simulate the accident later given as the official cause of death. He was a popular figure, and Stalin moved cautiously. Further official investigation produced the implausible conclusion that Mikhoels was murdered by the American Secret Service to prevent his exposure of an American spy ring.[37]

Over the following months prominent Jews were sacked or arrested. In October there was a spontaneous demonstration by an estimated 50,000 Soviet Jews outside the Moscow synagogue when the representative of the new state of Israel (and its future Prime Minister), Golda Meir, attended the celebration of Yom Kippur. Stalin was startled by the strength of Jewish feeling and uncertain about what to do. 'I can't swallow them, I can't spit them out,' he is reported to have said. 'They are the only group that is completely unassimilable.'[38] The idea of a Jewish homeland in Birobidzhan on the Pacific coast had been revived after the war, but few settlers arrived there. There is evidence that Stalin thought about another mass deportation. In the end he opted for terror. In November 1948 the activities of the Anti-Fascist Committee were abruptly halted. Its leaders were arrested and another major show trial was prepared. Yiddish schools were closed down; all Jewish literature and newspapers were banned; printer's type in Yiddish was broken up; Jewish libraries were closed and bookshops purged of offending Jewish literature. The cultural and religious life of Soviet Jews was rooted out, and Jewish writers and artists were imprisoned, banished or executed.

The anti-Semitism touched all areas of Jewish existence. Jews were thrown out of high schools and universities; they were removed from any positions of responsibility in the economy or the bureaucratic apparatus. They were denied the right to travel abroad. The anti-Semitic wave was applied with such a remorseless consistency that a number of notorious Jewish interrogators in the Lubyanka, who had played the sadist there for more than a decade, were themselves transferred or liquidated in 1951. The hundreds of Jews awaiting trial were not lacking new jailers or torturers. In their interrogation the current priorities of the regime were revealed. They were accused of Zionist conspiracy, of bourgeois chauvinism, of spying for the West; some, bizarrely, were accused of slandering the Soviet state by suggesting that it was anti-Semitic. Trials began in 1951 and continued up to the time of Stalin's death in March 1953. The main trial of the members of the Anti-Fascist Committee took place in July 1951; only one of the defendants survived the batterings, verbal and physical, with the courage to denounce his persecutors and judges rather than his fellows. All save an elderly doctor, Lina Shtern, were handed the death sentence. Shtern was sent into exile in Kazakhstan.[39]

Soviet Jews expected better of their Government after all they had suffered during the war at the hands of what had been the common enemy. Other nationalists in the Ukraine or the Baltic states had no such illusions. They carried on the fight, begun during the war, to establish independent national states and were as violently opposed to the reconquering Soviet regime as they had been to the German occupiers. Between 1944 and the early 1950s a guerrilla war was waged against the Soviet state. Much of the history of this new civil war is still unwritten. It was waged on a vast scale, and was fought with all the ferocity and passion of that earlier civil war that followed the Revolution. In Lithuania Soviet sources admitted the loss of 20,000 men, fighting a nationalist army estimated at 30,000. In Poland the Home Army revived after the Warsaw rising and was not finally wiped out until 1948; 50,000 Polish nationalists were exiled to Siberia. Thousands of Soviet and Polish troops were tied down trying to root out the irregular forces of the Ukrainian People's Army, which were said to number 20,000 in 1945. The guerrilla war was waged from bases in Poland and Czechoslovakia and was backed by thousands of Ukrainian and Polish peasants hostile to collectivization. The Government resorted to the tactics of the 1930s: mass deportations, the eradication of traditional village life, death or imprisonment for thousands of peasants. Between 1946 and 1950 an estimated 300,000 people were deported or imprisoned from the western Ukraine alone. Only repression on a vast scale could bring the borderlands under Soviet control. By the early 1950s the pacification was largely over. In 1959 the Ukrainian nationalist leader Stepan Bandera was murdered in West Germany by Soviet agents.[40]

This second war of reconquest in eastern Europe kept the Soviet Union fighting long after the war with Germany and Japan was over. The costly and brutal pacification helps to explain the official paranoia about the enemy within and Stalin's own fears for the future security of the new Soviet empire. Soviet leaders were not living in a world of invented danger; they were fighting armed resistance on what was now Soviet soil, in areas where popular hostility to Soviet Communism was widespread. Throughout the states liberated by the Red Army pro-Soviet forces were in the minority. The fragile control over these territories sharpened the conflict with the West, and provoked an almost constant state of alert against the threat of war and internal subversion. The hardening of Soviet attitudes to the West evident from 1946 onwards was a product of Soviet vulnerability as much as of Soviet strength.

The war made the Soviet Union a superpower. Victory secured the survival of Communism as a force in world politics. Only a few years before, with German forces at the gates of Moscow and Leningrad, the Soviet Union and international Communism faced complete eclipse. The turnaround in Soviet fortunes should not obscure the difficulties the Soviet Union faced in maintaining its hard-won position. Stalin did not want to risk another war; nor did he think that the West was either willing or able to attack the Soviet Union. 'A third world war is improbable,' he was reported to have said to a delegation of Chinese Communists, 'if only because no one has the strength to start it.' When the Chinese Communists asked Stalin in 1949 for Soviet help in the conquest of Taiwan, Stalin refused on the grounds that Soviet intervention might, after all, detonate a new world war: 'If we, as leaders, do this, the Russian people will not understand us. More than that. It could dismiss us. For underestimating its wartime and post-war misfortunes and efforts. For thoughtlessness . . .'[41]

The chief source of Soviet vulnerability was the American possession of the atomic bomb. Soviet conventional forces were very large. In 1947, with demobilization complete, the standing army numbered almost three million. Soviet tank, aircraft and artillery deployment dwarfed anything that the West could immediately field in Europe. The nuclear threat was very different. Although Soviet leaders knew that the United States possessed a few atomic bombs and was unlikely to use them unless pushed to the very edge, the fact remained that America could inflict horrific damage on the Soviet Union while the American population remained immune to attack. 'This situation weighed heavily on Stalin,' Khrushchev later recalled. 'He understood that he had to be careful not to be dragged into war.'[42] The paradox arose – the central paradox of the nuclear age – that security from the threat of nuclear destruction could come only through the possession of nuclear weapons.

The Soviet atomic programme began during the war. Nuclear research in the 1930s drew heavily on foreign scientific developments. When research on the possibility of nuclear fission using uranium was published abroad in 1939, few Soviet physicists thought that it would result in practical application for many years. Researchers at the Leningrad Physicotechnical Institute, led by Igor Kurchatov, published in May 1940 the first Soviet paper to suggest that nuclear fission had a military dimension. The German invasion postponed all the atomic research and diverted scientists, including Kurchatov, to other technical projects. In 1941 the British spy John Cairncross supplied Beria with detailed information that Britain was developing an atomic bomb. Late in 1941 the scientist-turned-spy, Klaus Fuchs, began to give a stream of detailed technical information to Beria's organization from his position as a researcher on the British, and later the American, atomic project.[43]

During the summer of 1942 the Government began to explore the possibility of atomic warfare. Senior scientists concluded that the

Soviet Union should begin its own programme to catch up with what was happening in Germany and the West. The decision to start a bomb programme was made by Stalin at some time in the summer, but it was not until November 1942 that Kurchatov was appointed to head Laboratory Number 2 in Moscow, where the Soviet bomb project was to be based. Progress remained slow. Kurchatov lacked a cyclotron, needed for particle separation. The one built before the war in Leningrad was only two miles from the front line of the siege. In March 1943 two scientists were flown to the city to arrange the transfer of the seventy-five-ton machine by rail through the narrow lifeline that had been opened up to the beleaguered defenders. The staff assigned to Soviet atomic research was tiny in comparison with the American Manhattan Project. In 1944 Laboratory Number 2 boasted only twenty-five scientists and forty-nine other personnel. There was almost no uranium. Despite efforts to persuade the United States to provide quantities of the mineral, only one kilogram of poor-quality uranium metal was supplied, together with a larger quantity of uranium powder. Geological exploration in the Soviet Union was conducted half-heartedly. In 1945 most of Kurchatov's supplies came from stocks captured in Germany.

The chief barrier to a more intensive project was the scepticism of the Soviet leadership. Molotov, who was in charge of the overall programme, and Beria, who was in charge of the foreign intelligence on atomic research, were neither of them convinced that the atomic bomb was a feasible weapon, or that the Manhattan Project was close, in 1945, to its first explosion. Stalin and Beria, from habit, half thought that the generous supply of secret scientific intelligence from the United States was part of an elaborate hoax. 'If this is disinformation,' Beria told the Soviet research team, 'I'll put you all in the cellar!'[44] The explosion of an atomic bomb at Hiroshima was thus more of a surprise to Stalin than his calm behaviour at Potsdam suggested. On 20 August 1945, two weeks after the atomic attack, Beria was put in charge of a 'Special Committee for the Atom Bomb'. Stalin ordered unlimited resources to be made available to produce the Soviet bomb. Loyal scientists were promised rewards: their own *dacha*, cars and a generous pay rise. For those of more doubtful loyalty conditions were different. Under Beria, half the workers engaged on the nuclear programme were organized in special prisons known as *sharashi*. In Georgia, close to Beria's own birthplace, a group of German physicists recruited to assist the Soviet programme lived under constant police surveillance in total and demoralizing isolation from the outside world.

The first nuclear reactor was successfully tested on Christmas Day 1946. Beria, who was present, was so excited by the experiment that he had to be dissuaded from entering the radioactive building, though many of those present must have hoped that he would. The first Soviet bomb was exploded less than three years later. The design was based on the American plutonium bomb, details of which had been supplied by Fuchs in June 1945. The test took place on the Kazakhstan steppe, not far from a newly built scientific settlement called Semipalatinsk-21, named after the nearest large town, less than a hundred miles distant. Around the tower that held the bomb were constructed buildings of brick or wood, bridges, tunnels and water towers to allow the scientists to evaluate the impact of the explosion. Tanks, guns and locomotives were distributed throughout the area for the same purpose. Animals were placed in pens and sheds so that studies could be made of the effects of radiation. Kurchatov supervised the whole operation and fixed the test for 29 August 1949, at six o'clock in the morning. The scientists knew that their personal survival depended on the success of the test. Beria turned up a week before, and watched the proceedings every day. On the morning of the 29th, in a small command post built six miles from the bomb tower, sheltered from the effects of blast by a rampart of earth, Kurchatov and Beria gathered with their staff to watch the test. It was cloudy, with a strong north wind. The tower was just visible in the distance. Kurchatov ordered the countdown to begin, and there ensued a wait of thirty nail-biting minutes. Everything worked exactly as planned. On zero an intense bright light shone forth from the top of the tower, illuminating the surrounding country-side. The shock wave reached the command post half a minute later, with a noise 'like the roar of an avalanche'. Smoke and debris rose into the upper sky, and hung there briefly before the wind dispersed them over the distant southern steppe. A converted tank rumbled towards the scene loaded with scientific instruments and the deputy minister of health. The sandy soil had turned to glass and crackled beneath the tracks of the tank. The steel tower had vaporized.[45]

Beria, who had been extremely nervous before the test, embraced and kissed Kurchatov. In his anxiety he wanted to check that the result looked the same as those of American tests and lost valuable time before his triumphant telephone call to Stalin. By the time he called, Stalin had already been informed and had immediately hung up. Beria punched the officer who had informed the Kremlin: 'You have put a spoke in my wheel, traitor. I'll grind you to pulp.'[46] Beria need not have worried. The test pleased Stalin. The scientists were generously rewarded. Kurchatov got a Soviet limousine, a cottage in the Crimea, free education for his children at any school he chose and free travel anywhere in the Soviet Union. The leading scientists all became Heroes of Socialist Labour. For once the accolade was richly deserved. Working under the pressure of the Stalinist state, under the direction of ruthless men who knew no science, Soviet scientists developed a bomb in only a little longer time than it had taken the American team. They were helped by espionage, though not as much as has usually been asserted. Fuchs provided a description of the plutonium bomb but little detailed information on how to reach the state of making the finished product. The main barrier to even faster production was the shortage of uranium.

The Soviet bomb did not alter the strategic balance immediately – by 1950 the United States had 298 bombs and 250 long-range aircraft to deliver them – but it gave Stalin the knowledge that the quantum leap over the technical gap between the two sides (represented by Hiroshima and Nagasaki) had been made. In 1949 he also began a programme of conventional rearmament to match the growing threat from the Western states, which in April 1949 had formed the North Atlantic Treaty Organization (NATO). From then until Stalin's death in 1953 the Soviet face to the West was increasingly uncompromising and defiant. Stalin himself was preoccupied with the threat of war and his own growing infirmity. In 1947 he suffered a minor stroke. On the eve of his seventieth birthday, 21 December 1949, he suffered a serious dizzy spell. He had permanently high blood pressure but would not allow doctors to administer to him, so profound was his distrust of medical experts. He gave up smoking and took longer vacations in the summer months, but otherwise compromised his routine of work very little. His daughter described a man who in his final years lived on his nerves, convinced that he would die a violent death, so many and so deep were the hatreds he had aroused. 'I'm finished,' Khrushchev heard him declare in 1951. 'I trust no one, not even myself.'[47]

This state of mind perhaps explains the more dangerous condition of the confrontation with the West in the early 1950s and the final paroxysm of terror that enveloped the Soviet state in the last years of his rule. Stalin had announced in February 1946 that the real cause of war in 1939, and of any future wars, was the capitalist system itself, which contained the seeds of 'general crisis and warlike clashes'.[48] From 1949 he thought he could once again see the force of that ideological truth: a new world war would, in the long run, be difficult to avoid. In February 1951 *Pravda* published an interview with Stalin in which the new threat of a world war 'organized by the ruling circles of the United States' was the central message. At the 19th Party Congress, held in October 1952, the first since 1939, Malenkov returned again to the theme of a 'third world war'. The day after the congress Stalin addressed the Central Committee. He told them that he was old and would soon die. He wanted them to continue his life's work. According to Konstantin Simonov, a new member, Stalin gave them a warning: 'A difficult struggle with the capitalist camp lay ahead and that the most dangerous thing in this struggle was to flinch, to take fright, to retreat, to capitulate.'[49] The talk in the armed forces was all about war. The mood created among the general public by the fresh war scare could have been little but despondent.

Did Stalin seek a final apocalyptic conflict to stamp his mark on Russian history forever? There is no real evidence to suggest that Stalin thought about war as something immediate, or that he contemplated a pre-emptive strike, although Khrushchev later described the fear the leadership all felt 'that America would invade the Soviet Union'. Stalin, in Khrushchev's account, 'trembled at the prospect . . . was afraid of war' and 'knew his weakness' – a revelation that may also help to explain his desperate efforts to avoid a conflict in 1941.[50] A more likely explanation is that war psychosis was exploited, as it was in the 1920s and 1930s, as a factor in domestic politics. In 1952 ominous signs appeared on all sides that the country was about to be engulfed by a new wave of orchestrated violence. Stalin chose the 19th Congress to launch an unexpectedly sharp attack on some senior ministers, including Molotov, for their failure to face up to the enemy with sufficient toughness. The ministers sat through the tirade ashen-faced and unmoving. Over the two months that followed, the shape of the new terror became visible. A Zionist plot to kill off Soviet politicians and military leaders, backed by the CIA, was unearthed. Anti-Semitism and anti-Americanism were exploited to create a popular hysteria that would give the new purge its shallow justification.

The idea of a Zionist plot has already been remarked upon. Jewish intellectuals arrested since 1949 had been routinely charged with conspiring to undermine the Soviet state while in the pay of American Jews and the CIA. In the summer of 1952 the trial of the Jewish Anti-Fascist Committee was completed. On June 4 a paediatrician at the Kremlin Polyclinic, Yevgenia Lifshits, was arrested, but despite torture and blackmail she refused to incriminate her Jewish colleagues. She was taken to the Serbsky Forensic Psychiatry Clinic for special treatment. The KGB's target was the former chief physician of the Red Army during the war, Meer Vovsi. Evidence was found in the alleged mystery surrounding the death of Andrei Zhdanov in 1948 from heart failure. At the time the electrocardiographer, Lidya Timashuk, a KGB spy, wrote a report for the security ministry accusing the doctors of misdiagnosing Zhdanov's condition. The autopsy exonerated the physicians, but the report was filed away. In the autumn of 1952 it resurfaced – how is not entirely clear – and was used not only to demote the head of the KGB and Stalin's long-serving personal secretary, Aleksandr Poskrebyshev, for lack of vigilance, but also to attack the doctors. Timashuk was hailed as a model citizen, and awarded the Order of Lenin by Stalin himself for what *Pravda* called 'patriotism, resoluteness and courage' in exposing 'the enemies of the Homeland'. The unfortunate Vovsi was arrested on November 11, by which time the security forces had everything they needed to begin a campaign against a number of senior doctors alleged to be at the very heart of the Zionist terrorist conspiracy.[51]

The 'Doctors' Plot' was the last and in many ways the most fantastic of the many conspiracies that were fabricated under Stalin. It is not clear that Stalin was the instigator of the new purge, though his approval was needed for it to proceed. The exact chain of responsibility may never be established with certainty. It may have been orchestrated by Khrushchev as a clumsy attempt to get at Beria and to move one step closer to the succession.[52] The victims caught up in the purge were not only Jewish doctors and intellectuals. Stalin's personal doctor, Vladimir Vinogradov, was arrested on November 7. Stalin is alleged to have discovered Vinogradov's medical notes on him, which suggested 'freedom from all work'. In his fury Stalin called out, 'Put him in leg irons.' Obedient to a fault, and against the usual practice with prisoners, his Lubyanka jailers shackled the elderly professor. Stalin's long-serving bodyguard, Nikolai Vlasik, was first demoted, then in December arrested. Viktor Abakumov, the former head of the KGB, was arrested for failing to detect the conspiracy. The senior doctors at the Kremlin clinic and other leading medical institutions were seized and incarcerated in the Lubyanka or the Lefortovo Prison in Moscow.[53]

On 13 January 1953 the Tass news agency announced the Doctors' Plot to the public. Nine senior doctors were named as the ringleaders; hundreds were now in prison. They were accused of membership of a Zionist terrorist gang. Vovsi, it was claimed, had admitted that he was under orders 'to destroy leading statesmen of the USSR'.[54] Vinogradov, Stalin's personal physician, was discovered to have been a long-standing British agent. The confessions spawned hundreds of new arrests. Jews everywhere were the victims of a sudden wave of spontaneous anti-Semitism. Jewish plots were unearthed against the Moscow Metro and in the Moscow Automobile Plant. The momentum was irresistible. The Jewish-bourgeois-nationalist was the new kulak. The Doctors' Plot thickened. Stalin agreed to, or perhaps instigated, wider plans to deport the Jews to the east.

Deportation was not new either; it was entirely consistent with the habits of the regime since the 1930s. It is hard to refute the evidence assembled by Arkady Vaksberg, who as a young Jew came face to face with the anti-Semitic outrage in the spring of 1953. Extra prison capacity was ordered; railway cars were collected at Moscow stations; wooden huts were hastily constructed in Birobidzhan; lists of Moscow Jews were drawn up and sent to the security police in each Moscow district. In mid-February, while the doctors and their accomplices were being forced to confess to absurd crimes, a plan was hatched with all the hallmarks of Stalinist political guile. Prominent Jewish intellectuals and leaders were invited to sign an open letter to *Pravda* calling on Stalin to save the Jewish people from further persecutions – occasioned by the criminal lapses of a handful of Jewish nationalists – by transporting them to the east, out of harm's way. Most of those asked to sign did so rather than risk their own imprisonment. The trial of the doctors was set for March; the evidence suggests that deportation was intended to follow.[55]

The resurrection of violent Jewish persecution was interrupted, though not entirely suspended, by the death of Stalin. The full details of the dictator's last days were finally published in 1989. He spent what proved to be his final day in his Kremlin office on February 17 and left for his *dacha* at Kuntsevo. On February 27 he attended *Swan Lake*, hidden from view and alone in a box in the Bolshoi Theatre. The following day he watched a film and returned to his *dacha* with Khrushchev, Malenkov, Bulganin and Beria, where they stayed until four o'clock in the morning drinking Georgian wine so weak that Stalin called it 'juice'. When they left, he told his guards, allegedly for the very first time, that they could go to sleep, too, a fact that has allowed unsubstantiated speculation to thrive about what might have happened while they dozed. The following day the guards waited but heard nothing. At six in the evening the light in Stalin's bedroom went on. Nothing more was heard; by ten o'clock in the evening the guards were alarmed enough to risk waking their sleeping boss. He was discovered, barely conscious, on the floor, his arm lifted in mute supplication, his trousers soiled.[56]

He was lifted onto a sofa, and the KGB chief was called. There are a number of versions of what followed. The most plausible testimony was provided by Peter Lozgachev, the deputy commandant of the *dacha*, though he recalled the events long afterwards. The first to arrive, hours after Stalin had been discovered collapsed, were Beria and Malenkov. No doctor was called – most of the senior Kremlin medical staff was in prison. Beria was angry at being disturbed. 'Don't cause a panic ... and don't disturb Comrade Stalin.'[57] Not until the following morning, when Khrushchev appeared, were doctors summoned. Stalin was unattended by doctors for thirteen hours. Whether this was deliberate, an attempt to hasten the end of the tyrant by those who hoped to profit by his death, is beyond proof. It is equally likely that Beria and Malenkov genuinely thought that the sleeping Stalin, snoring lightly, was in less danger than his guards had supposed. Nor is it likely that Stalin could have been saved even if medical help had been on hand during the night. He had suffered a massive cerebral haemorrhage.

Stalin took three days to die. He recovered consciousness at times but never recovered the power of speech. The doctors applied leeches to his head and neck. Their hands trembled as Beria watched and cursed them. Stalin's successors stood and watched, all save Beria, who paced up and down, alternately reviling his master and smothering him with kisses and oaths of loyalty whenever he stirred. His final death agony, on the evening of March 5, was witnessed by his daughter. 'At the last minute,' she wrote, 'he opened his eyes. It was a terrible look – either mad or angry and full of the fear of death.'[58] He raised his left hand in a final gesture and ceased breathing. Beria scrambled out of the room, shouted for his car and drove to the Kremlin to organize the new Government. Three months later he was arrested by his ministerial colleagues and, on a date still unknown, executed. The other witnesses to Stalin's last moments stood gazing at their dead master, then left with greater dignity. The body was taken in a car for embalming. The news was announced to a stunned population. Despite everything that he had inflicted upon them, the Soviet people mourned him in their millions. The body lay in state in the Kremlin while thousands fought outside for a glimpse. People were crushed to death in the throng. He was laid next to Lenin in the Kremlin Mausoleum.

The grief was genuine enough. The cult of personality had done its work. For ordinary Russians Stalin was their protector, teacher, helper. The hindsight that has made Stalin into one of history's monsters was vouchsafed at the time only to those who had lived in his immediate shadow and survived. Stalin was idolized with a literalness that Westerners find hard to comprehend. To the veterans of Russia's war Stalin was the man who led them to a victory unrivalled in Russian history over an historic enemy. There was a truth there, but it was only a partial truth. Victory was won at an extravagant, colossal cost to the victor and the vanquished, a cost that Stalin's people continued to pay until his death. Like the civil war that grew out of the war of 1914–18, the Soviet war lingered on long after silence cloaked the battlefields in 1945.

Epilogue:
Russia's War: Myth and Reality

No one is forgotten, nothing is forgotten . . .
Mikhail Gorbachev, Victory Day, 1990

In February 1956, at a closed meeting of the Central Committee of the Communist Party, Nikita Khrushchev delivered an extraordinary speech. For the first time the myths constructed around the now-dead Stalin were torn aside. Khrushchev did not mince his words. He accused Stalin of cultivating a grotesque tyranny and presented to his amazed audience a grisly catalogue of the leader's crimes. He spoke for several hours, to a largely silent hall. Only when he began to discuss the war did the delegates become animated.

Khrushchev left Stalin's military reputation in tatters. He revealed the incompetence that led to the early German victories; he hinted at Stalin's personal cowardice, the failure to visit the front or the ruined cities; he spoke of hundreds of thousands of needless deaths caused by the obstinacy and wilful blindness of the Supreme Commander; he angrily denounced the public lie that Stalin's genius had saved the Soviet Union. Instead, Khrushchev continued, victory was won by 'the magnificent and heroic deeds of hundreds of millions of people'. It was not Stalin at all, but the Party, the Government, the army, the whole Soviet nation, 'these are the ones who assured victory in the Great Patriotic War'. There followed, according to the stenographic report, 'tempestuous and prolonged applause'.[1] It was a remarkable performance. Although it was officially secret, it was soon leaked by foreign delegates to the meeting and was read out to the Party faithful across the Soviet Union. The effect was immediate, as if a colossal weight had been suddenly lifted from the stooped shoulders of the Soviet people.

Over the next four years much of the Stalin legacy was undone. Over five million prisoners were released from the camps. The thousands of statues and portraits that still cluttered the cities and halls of the Soviet Union were silently removed. Stalingrad, the great symbol of Soviet resistance, became Volgograd. The cult of personality vanished overnight. In October 1961 the Party agreed to the greatest indignity: Stalin's embalmed body was to be removed from the Kremlin Mausoleum and his name erased from its entrance. His body was reburied at night in a grave nearby. Stalin himself had had no illusions about his fate after death. In a speech delivered in April 1941 he surprised his audience with the following morbid reflection:

People have a bad custom – to commend the living . . . but to consign the dead to oblivion, as idols, as was said in olden times, or as leaders, as they say now; to commend, to express sympathy for them as long as they have not died, but when they die, to forget them.[2]

Stalin was not, of course, forgotten, but he did become a fallen idol.

De-Stalinization allowed the Soviet public to look back on the war as their war, not as Stalin's. In the 'year of truth' that followed Khrushchev's speech it proved possible to peel back some of the layers of Stalinist myth that had smothered the reality of the war. Konstantin Simonov, who as an officially approved writer had helped to perpetuate that myth, was scathing about the system's truth. He quoted the official version of the disastrous defeats: 'Various unforeseen circumstances arose.' 'What sort of wording is that?' asked Simonov. 'One can speak thus about a train being late, or about early frosts, but not about the war, the whole course of which from the very outset, to our great misfortune, was an unforeseen circumstance.'[3] Glimpses of the real truth were allowed, even hints of the demoralization and defeatism widespread in 1942, of the damage done by the political officials who stared over every commander's shoulder or the cruel fate of the thousands transported across the Soviet Union to the camps.

The 'year of truth' only briefly allowed painful memories of the suffering and anguish of war to surface. The Party was prepared to use the dead Stalin as a scapegoat but not to overturn the entire history of the war. The war was appropriated by the Party, and a new truth, in many ways little distinguishable from the Stalin version, was established by the official historians and the censors. When Vasily Grossman, who, like Simonov, had written for the war effort, tried in 1960 to publish *Life and Fate*, one of the greatest novels on war in any language and an honest memorial to the reality of the Soviet war effort, the manuscript was rejected. Grossman was told that it could not be published for at least two or three centuries. In February 1961 his apartment was raided and the manuscript, his books, even the typewriter ribbons that carried the offending words, were seized by the KGB. When Anatoli Kuznetsov dared in 1966 to write a novel revealing the truth about Babi Yar and about Stalinist anti-Semitism, it was published only after the censor's pencil had removed everything deemed anti-Soviet. The Soviet version of the war after Stalin was shorn of the cult of personality but remained an arid and distorted truth.[4]

The new story of the war was a simple tale of Communist heroism in the face of fascist treachery. The army was happy to endorse Stalin's personal failure, but it did not want to share the blame for military misfortunes. When the journalist Albert Axell interviewed Marshal Sergei Rudenko, a veteran air force commander, in 1985, he was told that 'everything was done to prepare for the attack' in 1941, and that 'both the Government and the nation managed to be masters of the situation' after the initial German blows.[5] The official version remained the one mocked by Simonov: a few unanticipated complications before the people, united and disciplined by the Party, drove back the invader with the new Communist strategy of the massive counter-offensive. For the Party the official line was important, not for its own sake, but as a means to cement the regime in the years after Stalin. The shared sacrifices and extravagant courage lauded in hundreds of exemplary war stories showed Party workers pointing the way to victory and to the golden path of socialist reconstruction. Victory was appropriated, not as a military triumph, but as a vindication of the historic path now trodden by the Soviet Union and the fraternal states of Eastern Europe.

During the 1960s the memory of the war was observed with an almost religious intensity. May 9, Victory Day, became a public occasion. Solemn meetings were held in offices and factories. 'Victory Day,' recalled one veteran, 'was celebrated in a much more spiritual way than November 7 [the anniversary of the Bolshevik Revolution] or May 1 ... Everyone recalled memories from the war and was amazed to be alive.'[6] Schoolchildren repeated the same liturgy across the Soviet Union: 'The Soviet nation saved mankind from annihilation and enslavement by German fascism, and preserved world civilization.' They could read that the war convinced the whole world of the 'durability and great life force' at the core of socialist society. Victory made possible the 'transformation of socialism into a worldwide system'.[7] The war – the people's war, not Stalin's – was exploited as a foundation myth for the modern Soviet state, eclipsing the Revolution itself, whose architects were now long dead.

So intense was the commitment to the war as a just war, courageously fought and faultlessly executed, that the system could not afford the cost of disillusionment. But with the coming of *glasnost* the floodgates opened. In 1988 *Life and Fate* was finally published in the Soviet Union. The discovery of the truth was painful for generations brought up on the textbook images; even more painful perhaps for the veterans themselves, a shrinking number, who had kept the real war to themselves. Each of the participating states in the Second World War sustained its own version of the conflict, myths and all, but none has been asked to tear up this version almost entirely and to bear witness to the truth as openly and savagely as the Soviet Union and its successor states. The history of the war is no longer a test of socialist loyalty but a symbol of emancipation from the past.

It is too soon for a new history to emerge in the former Soviet Union that can do justice to the experience of war. The reaction to the revelations is recriminatory and demoralizing. A population told for years the mythic version of the war has found the truth despairing. 'I still feel the pain of these memories,' recalled Khrushchev shortly before his death. 'I still experience an ache for the people of Russia.'[8] The literature on the war focuses now on the extravagant capacity of the Russian people to endure suffering and to keep going. War, no longer just a testament to military triumph, has become a crucible of miserable and incomprehensible revelations.

The truth about the Soviet war is more than this. It may not turn out to be true that the 'great exploit' will 'never fade from the memory of a grateful mankind', as generations of Soviet citizens were taught, but the Soviet war effort still remains an incomparable achievement, world-historical in a very real sense. Stalin was right that the conflict was an 'examination for the entire Soviet system', and he knew, better than most, how close the state had come to failing it.[9] The odds against the Soviet Union prevailing over Hitler's Germany were long even before the war broke out, longer still after the first months. The German propaganda machine emphasized the primitiveness of Soviet life. The German army taught its soldiers that the Soviet enemy was 'unsuited for modern warfare' and 'incapable of decisive resistance'.[10] The conventional view of the Soviet Union abroad, beyond the circle of dazzled enthusiasts, was of a system made inert by a stifling bureaucracy and savage repression. Ranged against it were the world's most dangerous armed forces, which had conquered most of Europe in eighteen months. When the news of Barbarossa arrived in Washington, Secretary of War Henry Stimson reported to Roosevelt the almost unanimous view of the American Joint Chiefs of Staff, which he shared: 'Germany will be thoroughly occupied in beating Russia for a minimum of a month and a possible maximum of three months.'[11]

Soviet victory was achieved against almost universal expectation. For all the criticism now levelled in the former Soviet Union against the crass incompetence and meaningless oppression that marked the early years of war, the Soviet system passed its most severe test. This presents historians with a circle difficult to square: the Soviet Union ought by rights to have been defeated in the war, but it prevailed triumphantly and comprehensively. Of course, the Soviet Union was not acting alone. Without the division of German energies prompted by the bombing campaign or the Mediterranean theatre the outcome would have been much less certain, perhaps very different. Nonetheless, the bulk of the damage inflicted on German forces was in the eastern campaign – 80 per cent of their battle casualties – and it was here that the overwhelming weight of the Wehrmacht was concentrated until 1944. Nor can the German dimension be ignored. After the war German generals were quick to argue that Hitler's wayward leadership and shortages of equipment made defeat inevitable: Germany lost the war, the Soviet Union did not win it. This view fits ill with the facts. German generals rode to war in 1941 confident that victory was a matter of weeks (eight to ten at most) against the 'ill-educated, half-Asiatic' Russian fighters, and against Soviet commanders 'even less of a threat than . . . Tsarist Russian generals'.[12] These judgements were almost borne out by events. The defeat of German forces required something German leaders never anticipated: that the Soviet Union would recover its economic strength, reform its armed forces and produce leaders of remarkable quality. Without these, Germany could not have been defeated. The Soviet Union had to *win* its war.

It is more common now to seek the answer deep within the Soviet population, which found reserves of simple patriotism and endurance sufficient to transcend the horrors at home and at the front and to fight. This may well have been a necessary condition for final victory, but it takes little account of the millions who fought or worked under duress, or who could not find it within themselves to share the collective mania for vengeance and self-sacrifice. Nor, in the end, can a righteous enthusiasm alone explain victory in an epic war against a well-armed and disciplined enemy.

At least part of the answer must lie with Stalin and, below him, the political system which ran the Soviet war effort. Stalin supplied more than a capricious despotism. His willingness to bow to the military experts, hard though it must have been to do, showed in the end a sensible awareness of the limits of despotism. The image of Stalin supplied to the public – of a leader who was brave, all-seeing, steadfast – was a necessary one, however distant it was from reality. The contrast between his intervention in the war effort and that of the Tsar thirty years earlier is illuminating: Stalin became a necessary part of the machinery of reconquest; Nicholas remained superfluous to it.

Below Stalin stood the major institutions of state and the Party itself. The post-war Soviet inflation of the Party's role in achieving victory should not blind us to the unpalatable conclusion that the organization of the home front owed its successes, as well as its failures, to the Communist apparatus and the cadres of Communist enthusiasts who spurred on workers, peasants and soldiers with an often raw fanaticism. The mere presence of the NKVD was not enough to explain the modern competence displayed by a system condemned as primitive. Indeed, where the NKVD did intervene the effect was to wound the war effort, not to invigorate it. Soviet planning displayed a flexibility and organizational power which belied its bureaucratic image. It demonstrated, almost accidentally, the qualities needed to mobilize a vast population for a single common purpose. After the war old habits returned. Neither Party nor bureaucracy was able to plan the socialist paradise.

This apparent paradox has at least one explanation. During the war the emergency freed many Soviet officials, managers and soldiers from an atmosphere of passivity and fear of responsibility. After 1941, recalled one veteran army doctor, came a period of 'spontaneous de-Stalinization', when people were forced time after time to 'make their own decisions, to take responsibility for themselves'.[13] In the army that sense of personal responsibility was enhanced when at last, in the autumn of 1942, the political apparatchiks at the front were demoted and officers could act knowing that they were not being checked every hour for political correctness. The novelist and veteran Vyacheslav Kondratyev recalled on Victory Day, 1990, that the war put a great responsibility on every soldier: 'You felt as though you alone held the fate of Russia in your hands.' After the war that heady obligation no longer mattered. 'Whether I exist,' Kondratyev continued, 'whether I do not exist, everything will flow on as usual.'[14] Even on the home front there existed a sense of emancipation brought on by the war. In besieged Leningrad, wrote the poet and survivor Olga Berggolts, there was to be found 'such a tempestuous freedom'. The very immanence of death exalted that freedom, summoned forth a spontaneous resourcefulness, an intensity of living, a baleful stoicism.

Even before the war ended the opportunity to take responsibility, to act on initiative and not wait for orders, began to subside as the apparatus of scrutiny was reimposed. Nevertheless, a greater sense of personal responsibility clearly assisted the fighting power of the Red Army, because it freed so many commanders from the dead weight of political control and allowed them actually to command. It also gave the ordinary soldier much greater confidence in the ability of those he followed, and finally removed the mentality, which could be dated back to 1917 and the notorious Order Number 1 from the Petrograd Soviet, that those in positions of command could be called to account by those they commanded. It can scarcely be coincidental that the great improvement in Soviet fighting power from the late autumn of 1942 followed the demotion of the military commissar.

Soviet success owed something to all these factors: popular patriotism and native endurance; the role of Stalin; the political environment of planning and mobilization; and the temporary flowering of a spirit of initiative and endeavour just powerful enough to transcend the grim climate of fatalistic conformism with which post-purge society had been afflicted. The war effort was not sustained just by the efforts of the people in defiance of the system they inhabited; but neither was it just the product of the Soviet state, its leader and the Party. The two elements operated in an uneasy symbiosis, neither entirely trusting the other, yet bound together by mutual necessity imposed by German aggression. No one doubts that victory could have been bought at a lower price, with less oppression and more humanity, without the countless dead. But that was the tragedy of the Soviet war. The sacrifices of a tormented people brought victory but not emancipation, a moment of bitter-sweet triumph in a long history of loss.

References

Introduction

1. W. J. Spahr, *Zhukov: The Rise and Fall of a Great Captain* (Novato, CA, 1993), pp. xi–xii, 56, 261–3.
2. See the introduction to J. L. Schecter and V. V. Luchkov, eds., *Khrushchev Remembers: The Glasnost Tapes* (New York, 1990).
3. Spahr, *Zhukov*, pp. 103–5.
4. Details in D. Glantz, 'From the Soviet Secret Archives: Newly Published Soviet Works on the Red Army 1918–1991: A Review Essay', *Journal of Slavic Military Studies* 8 (1995), pp. 319–32.
5. See the discussion of figures in B. V. Sokolov, 'The Cost of War: Human Losses of the USSR and Germany, 1939–1945', *Journal of Slavic Military Studies* 9 (1996), pp. 156–71; V. E. Korol, 'The Price of Victory: Myths and Realities', idem., pp. 417–24.
6. Cited in M. P. Gallagher, *The Soviet History of World War II: Myths, Memories, and Realities* (New York, 1963), p. 151.
7. J. Lucas, *War on the Eastern Front: The German Soldier in Russia 1941–1945* (London, 1991), p. 28.
8. I. Ehrenburg, *Men – Years – Life, Volume 5: The War 1941–1945* (London, 1964), p. 16.
9. A. Solzhenitsyn, *The Gulag Archipelago 1918–1956* (London, 1974), p. 605.
10. N. Tumarkin, *The Living and the Dead: The Rise and Fall of the Cult of World War II in Russia* (New York, 1994), p. 81. The quotation is from Aleksandr Tvardovsky's 'A Book about a Soldier'.
11. D. Dallin and B. Nicolaevsky, *Forced Labour in Soviet Russia* (London, 1947), pp. xiii–xiv.
12. Ibid., pp. 300–3.

13. J. Garrard and C. Garrard, eds., *World War 2 and the Soviet People* (London, 1993), p. 17.

Chapter 1

1. For this and other details on the civil war, see O. Figes, *A People's Tragedy: The Russian Revolution, 1891–1924* (London, 1996), pp. 662–74; I. Deutscher, *Stalin* (London, 1966), pp. 191–202; D. Volkogonov, *Stalin* (New York, 1991), pp. 38–45. The best recent history of the Russian Civil War is E. Mawdsley, *The Russian Civil War* (London, 1987).

2. M. von Hagen, *Soldiers in the Proletarian Dictatorship: The Red Army and the Soviet Socialist State, 1917–1930* (Ithaca, 1990), pp. 334–5.

3. On Hitler's views see E. Jäckel, *Hitler's Weltanschauung* (Middletown, Connecticut, 1972); J. P. Stern, *Hitler, the Führer and the People* (London 1976). On the prevailing cultural pessimism see F. Stern, *The Politics of Cultural Despair* (London, 1974).

4. T. J. Uldricks, 'Russia and Europe: Diplomacy, Revolution and Economic Development in the 1920s', *International History Review* 1 (1979), p. 73.

5. J. Stalin, *Problems of Leninism* (Moscow, 1947), p. 160.

6. E. R. Goodman, *The Soviet Design for a World State* (New York, 1960), pp. 30–32.

7. Stalin, *Problems of Leninism*, pp. 157–9, from the pamphlet 'On the Problems of Leninism', January 25, 1926.

8. von Hagen, *Soldiers in the Dictatorship*, pp. 204–5.

9. Ibid., pp. 158–60.

10. Ibid., p. 213, n. 19. See too E. O'Ballance, *The Red Army* (London, 1964), pp. 96–7.

11. von Hagen, *Soldiers in the Dictatorship*, pp. 212–19.

12. Volkogonov, *Stalin*, pp. 64–5.

13. W. A. Harriman and E. Abel, *Special Envoy to Churchill and Stalin, 1941–1946* (London, 1976), p. 266.

14. L. Samuelson, 'Mikhail Tukhachevsky and War-Economic Planning: Reconsiderations on the Pre-War Soviet Military Build-up', *Journal of Slavic Military Studies* 9 (1996), pp. 805–9.

15. Y. Dyakov and T. Bushuyeva, *The Red Army and the Wehrmacht: How the Soviets Militarized Germany, 1922–33* (New York, 1995), pp. 17–18.

16. E. R. Hooton, *Phoenix Triumphant: The Rise and Rise of the Luftwaffe* (London, 1994), pp. 44–9; Dyakov and Bushuyeva, *Red Army*, pp. 20–3.

17. Ibid., p. 25.

18. C. A. Roberts, 'Planning for War: the Red Army and the Catastrophe of 1941', *Europe–Asia Studies* 47 (1995), pp. 1302–4. For the best general history of Soviet operational thinking see D. Glantz, *Soviet Military Operational Art: In Pursuit of Deep Battle* (London, 1991).

19. Samuelson, 'Tukhachevsky', pp. 816–21.

20. Roberts, 'Planning', pp. 1304–7; R. R. Reese, *Stalin's Reluctant Soldiers: A Social History of the Red Army 1925–1941* (Lawrence, Kans., 1996), pp. 52–61.

21. R. Schiness, 'The Conservative Party and Anglo-Soviet Relations 1925–27', *European Studies Review* 7 (1977), pp. 385–8.

22. G. Gorodetsky, *The Precious Truce: Anglo–Soviet Relations 1924–27* (Cambridge, 1977), pp. 222–34; Uldricks, 'Russia and Europe', p. 75.

23. Cited in Deutscher, *Stalin*, p. 276. For Lenin's view see D. Shub, *Lenin* (London, 1966), p. 435.

24. Deutscher, *Stalin*, pp. 22–3.

25. The best evidence we have of Stalin's administrative methods can be gleaned from a recent edition of his political correspondence with Molotov. See L. Lih, O. Naumov and O. Khlevniuk, eds., *Stalin's Letters to Molotov 1925–1936* (New Haven, 1995).

26. Shub, *Lenin*, p. 435. Lenin urged his comrades in his so-called testament, dictated on 25–26 December 1922, to choose a General Secretary who was 'more patient, more loyal, more polite, and more attentive to comrades, less capricious, etc.'.

27. J. Stalin, *Works* (Moscow, 1955), xiii, p. 108, 'Talk with the German author Emil Ludwig, December 13, 1931'.

28. Quoted from interview with D. Volkogonov, Episode 1, 'Russia's War'.

29. A. Amba, *I Was Stalin's Bodyguard* (London, 1952), p. 69.

30. M. Harrison, *Soviet Planning in Peace and War 1938–1945* (Cambridge, 1985), pp. 46–51, 250–53; S. Wheatcroft, R. W. Davies and J. M. Cooper, 'Soviet Industrialisation Reconsidered', *Economic History Review*, 2nd Ser. 39 (1986).

31. Details in L. Siegelbaum, *Stakhanovism and the Politics of Productivity in the USSR, 1935–1941* (Cambridge, 1988), pp. 69–76, 307.

32. Figures from R. W. Davies, 'Soviet Military Expenditure and the Armaments Industry 1929–1933: A Reconsideration', *Europe–Asia Studies*, 45 (1993), pp. 585–601; J. Sapir, 'The Economics of War in the Soviet Union during World War II', in I. Kershaw and M. Lewin, eds., *Stalinism and Nazism: Dictatorships in Comparison* (Cambridge, 1997), p. 213. See too W. S. Dunn, *The Soviet Economy and the Red Army 1930–1945* (London, 1995), Chapters 1–2.

33. Stalin, *Problems of Leninism*, p. 356: speech to the First All-Union Conference of Managers, 4 February 1931.

34. Samuelson, 'Tukhachevsky', pp. 831–9; on the development of Soviet tanks see G. F. Hofmann, 'Doctrine, Tank Technology, and Execution: I. A. Khalepskii and the Red Army's Fulfillment of Deep Offensive Operations', *Journal of Slavic Military Studies* 9 (1996), pp. 283 ff.

35. O'Ballance, *Red Army*, pp. 116–18.

36. For vivid descriptions of OGPU interrogation see V. Brunovsky, *Methods of the OGPU* (London, 1931). On the background of the camp system see E. Bacon, *The Gulag at War: Stalin's Forced Labour System in the Light of the Archives* (London, 1994), pp. 43–7.

37. von Hagen, *Soldiers in the Dictatorship*, pp. 327–8; O'Ballance, *Red Army*, pp. 118–20.

38. Figures can be found in S. Rosefielde, 'Stalinism in Post-Communist Perspective: New Evidence on Killings, Forced Labor and Economic Growth in the 1930s', *Europe–Asia Studies* 48 (1996), pp. 962–3, 975; S. Wheatcroft, 'More Light on the Scale of Repression and Excess Mortality in the Soviet Union in the 1930s', in J. A. Getty and R. T. Manning, eds., *Stalinist Terror: New Perspectives* (Cambridge, 1993), pp. 277–90; A. Nove, 'Victims of Stalinism: How Many?' in Getty and Manning, pp. 270–71; R. J. Rummell, *Lethal Politics: Soviet Genocide and Mass Murder since 1917* (New Brunswick, 1990), pp. 115–16. Rosefielde suggests a range of estimates for famine deaths from 0.7 million to 11.8 million. The demographic evidence, on which the new estimates are based, suggests a death toll on the scale 2.8 to 4.5 million.

39. Nove, 'Victims', pp. 265–7.

40. A. Nove, ed., *The Stalin Phenomenon* (London, 1993), pp. 30–31; Nove, 'Victims', p. 269; R. Thurston, 'The Stakhanovite Movement: Background to the Great Terror in the Factories 1935–38', in Getty and Manning, *Stalinist Terror*, p. 155, who also points out that in 1938 only 18.6 per cent of those in custody had been charged with counter-revolutionary crimes. Many of the remaining camp inmates were ordinary criminals.

41. Details in J. A. Getty, *The Origins of the Great Purges: The Soviet Communist Party Reconsidered* (Cambridge, 1985).

42. Volkogonov, *Stalin*, pp. 208–10. See also R. Conquest, *Stalin and the Kirov Murder* (London, 1989).

43. See the assessment of Stalin's style of military leadership in B. Bonwetsch, 'Stalin, the Red Army and the "Great Patriotic War"', in Kershaw and Lewin, *Stalinism and Nazism*, pp. 202–3.

44. On Vyshinsky see A. Vaksberg, *The Prosecutor and the Prey: Vyshinsky*

and the 1930s Moscow Show Trials (London, 1990), Chapters 3–4; on the executions see Nove, 'Victims', pp. 270–71; Rosefielde suggests a figure for the 1930s of 722,000 for all prison executions ('Stalinism', p. 975). The official NKVD figure for all executions from 1930 to 1950 is given as 786,098, with 3,778,234 condemned at tribunals to death or imprisonment. See R. C. Nation, *Black Earth, Red Star* (Ithaca, 1992), p. 98.

45. C. Andrew and O. Gordievsky, *KGB: The Inside Story* (London, 1990), p. 106; A. C. Brown and C. B. Macdonald, *The Communist International and the Coming of World War II* (New York, 1981), pp. 437–9.

46. Volkogonov, *Stalin*, p. 319.

47. Ibid., pp. 319, 324.

48. Andrew and Gordievsky, *KGB*, p. 106; see also the testimony of W. Krivitsky, *I Was Stalin's Agent* (Cambridge, 1992: first published London, 1939), pp. 239–44. Shpigelglaz, who was liquidated himself in 1938, told Krivitsky that the NKVD had been collecting material on Tukhachevsky and others with former contacts with Germany 'for several years. We've got plenty,' he continued, 'not only on the military but on many others.'

49. A. Bullock, *Hitler and Stalin: Parallel Lives* (London, 1991), pp. 545–6.

50. Volkogonov, *Stalin*, pp. 323–4; E. Radzinsky, *Stalin* (London, 1996), p. 407.

51. Volkogonov, *Stalin*, p. 319.

52. A. Antonov-Ovseyenko, *The Time of Stalin: Portrait of a Tyranny* (New York, 1981), pp. 184–5; Radzinsky, *Stalin*, p. 361.

53. Vaksberg, *Vyshinsky*, pp. 104–5.

54. Volkogonov, *Stalin*, p. 324; Antonov-Ovseyenko, *Time of Stalin*, p. 186, who writes that Yakir's last words as he was executed were 'Long live Comrade Stalin!'

55. Ibid., pp. 188–9; Volkogonov, *Stalin*, pp. 327–8. There are several versions of Blyukher's death. Others suggest that he died of the wounds inflicted during interrogation in his cell, or that he was executed after torture. Further details in B. Bonwetsch, 'The Purge of the Military and the Red Army's Operational Capability during the "Great Patriotic War"', in B. Wegner, ed., *From Peace to War: Germany, Soviet Russia and the World, 1939–1941* (Oxford, 1997), pp. 396–8; R. E. Tarleton, 'What Really Happened to the Stalin Line?' *Journal of Slavic Military History* 6 (1993), pp. 37–8.

56. R. Reese, *Stalin's Reluctant Soldiers*, pp. 134–46.

57. Antonov-Ovseyenko, *Time of Stalin*, p. 186.

58. See Sapir, 'Economics of War', pp. 213–16.

59. Dyakov and Bushuyeva, *Red Army and Wehrmacht*, pp. 287, 290: Report

from German military attaché in Moscow, 27 March 1933; German Intelligence Report on the Red Army, 19 February 1933.

60. O'Ballance, *Red Army*, p. 118; Reese, *Stalin's Reluctant Soldiers*, pp. 140–9. According to S. Bialer, *Stalin and his Generals* (New York, 1969), p. 63, around one-fifth of unit and sub-unit positions were vacant.

61. Reese, *Stalin's Reluctant Soldiers*, pp. 148–9. In addition 78,000 junior officers were given short training courses in 1938 and 1939 to prepare them to command small units in the expanding army.

62. Tarleton, 'Stalin Line', p. 38; Antonov-Ovseyenko, *Time of Stalin*, pp. 118–19; H. Moldenhauer, 'Die Reorganisation der Roten Armee vor der "Grossen Säuberung" bis zum deutschen Angriff auf die UdSSR (1938–1941)', *Militärgeschichtliche Mitteilungen*, 55 (1996), p. 137.

63. A. Werth, *Russia at War* (London, 1964), p. 9. See too Sapir, 'Economics of War', p. 214, who cites the view of Marshal M. Zakharov in the 1960s that the concept of deep operations using tanks and aircraft 'fell into disrepute [and] . . . was even called sabotage'. On lack of military training, Moldenhauer, 'Reorganisation der Roten Armee', p. 145. On political education, Reese, *Stalin's Reluctant Soldiers*, p. 144.

Chapter 2

Epigraph: A. Knight, *Beria: Stalin's First Lieutenant* (London, 1993), p. 109.

1. On the memorandum see A. Kube, *Pour le mérite und Hakenkreuz: Hermann Göring im Dritten Reich* (Munich, 1986), pp. 153–4; E. Fröhlich, ed., *Die Tagebücher von Joseph Goebbels* (4 vols., New York, 1987), iii, pp. 26, 55, for the comments on the conflict of the future.

2. For the text of the memorandum see W. Treue, 'Hitlers Denkschrift zum Vierjahresplan, 1936', *Vierteljahreshefte für Zeitgeschichte* 3 (1955), pp. 184–210. The translation here is from J. Noakes and G. Pridham, *Documents on Nazism* (Exeter, 1980), ii, pp. 281–7.

3. Noakes and Pridham, *Documents on Nazism*, p. 282. On the German military build-up see R. J. Overy, *War and Economy in the Third Reich* (Oxford, 1994), pp. 191–3, 294.

4. G. Roberts, *The Soviet Union and the Origins of the Second World War 1933–1941* (London, 1995), p. 19; J. E. Davies, *Mission to Moscow* (New York, 1941), p. 60, letter from Davies to Cordell Hull, 6 February 1937.

5. J. Hochman, *The Soviet Union and the Failure of Collective Security 1934–1938* (Ithaca, 1984), pp. 29, 32.

6. M. Heller and A. Nekrich, *Utopia in Power: The History of the Soviet*

Union from 1917 to the Present (London, 1982), pp. 310–11; Roberts, *Soviet Union and War*, pp. 43–7.

7. Heller and Nekrich, *Utopia*, pp. 312–13; C. Andrew and O. Gordievsky, *KGB: The Inside Story* (London, 1990), pp. 126–7; W. G. Krivitsky, *I Was Stalin's Agent* (Cambridge, 1992), pp. 244–8.

8. Roberts, *Soviet Union and War*, pp. 50–51.

9. G. Jukes, 'The Red Army and the Munich Crisis', *Journal of Contemporary History* 26 (1991), pp. 196–8; Roberts, *Soviet Union and War*, p. 58.

10. Roberts, *Soviet Union and War*, p. 57.

11. I. Lukes, 'Stalin and Beneš in the Final Days of September 1938', *Slavic Review* 52 (1993), pp. 28–48.

12. Jukes, 'Munich Crisis', p. 199; Hochman, *Collective Security*, pp. 166–7; J. von Herwarth, *Against Two Evils* (London, 1981), pp. 122–3 for evidence from a German eyewitness.

13. Davies, *Mission to Moscow*, p. 194.

14. A. Vaksberg, *Stalin Against the Jews* (New York, 1994), pp. 83–8. Vaksberg argues that Stalin was planning a major trial of Soviet diplomats for 1940, but cancelled it because of the deteriorating international situation. Litvinov died in December 1951 in a car accident, organized, according to Beria's testimony at his own trial, by the security services.

15. Details on Molotov from B. Bromage, *Molotov: The Story of an Era* (London, 1956); on Beria see the excellent biography by A. Knight, *Beria: Stalin's First Lieutenant* (Princeton, 1993), pp. 5, 14–16, 21–8.

16. J. Stalin, *Problems of Leninism* (Moscow, 1947), p. 606: Report to the 18th Congress of the CPSU, 10 March 1939.

17. Details on the *rapprochement* in J. Herman, 'Soviet Peace Efforts on the Eve of World War II: A Review of the Soviet Documents', *Journal of Contemporary History* 15 (1980), pp. 583–4.

18. Stalin, *Problems of Leninism*, p. 602.

19. P. Sudoplatov, *Special Tasks: The Memoirs of an Unwanted Witness – A Soviet Spymaster* (New York, 1994), p. 95; Herman, 'Soviet Peace Efforts', pp. 594, 597.

20. A. Read and D. Fisher, *The Deadly Embrace: Hitler, Stalin and the Nazi-Soviet Pact 1939–1941* (London, 1988), pp. 157–8.

21. Ibid., p. 158.

22. Ibid., p. 160; Stalin's reaction is recorded in L. Namier, *Europe in Decay: A Study in Disintegration* (London, 1950), p. 242.

23. Roberts, *Soviet Union and War*, pp. 73–5.

24. G. Roberts, 'The Soviet Decision for a Pact with Nazi Germany', *Soviet*

Studies 44 (1992), p. 61, citing a report from Astakhov of 12 May 1939.

25. Roberts, *Soviet Union and War*, p. 88.

26. M. Bloch, *Ribbentrop* (London, 1992), p. 247.

27. E. Radzinsky, *Stalin* (London, 1996), p. 428.

28. There are several versions of Hitler's response to the news. This version is cited in D. C. Watt, *How War Came* (London, 1989), p. 462.

29. Namier, *Europe in Decay*, p. 246.

30. J. L. Schecter, ed., *Khrushchev Remembers: The Glasnost Tapes* (Boston, 1990), pp. 46, 53.

31. Soviet statement to Poland, 17 September 1939, in G. Kennan, ed., *Soviet Foreign Policy 1917–1941* (New York, 1960), Document 32, p. 179.

32. J. Gross, *Revolution from Abroad: The Soviet Conquest of Poland's Western Ukraine and Western Belorussia* (Princeton, 1988), pp. 172–4; other details from G. Malcher, *Blank Pages: Soviet Genocide against the Polish People* (Woking, UK, 1993), pp. 7–10; K. Sword, *Deportation and Exile: Poles in the Soviet Union 1939–1948* (London, 1996), pp. 1–12; Esperanto speakers from K. Sword, ed., *The Soviet Takeover of the Polish Eastern Provinces 1939–1941* (London, 1991), Appendix 3c: 'NKVD Instructions Relating to "Anti-Soviet Elements"', p. 307.

33. Sword, *Deportation*, pp. 13–26; Malcher, *Blank Pages*, pp. 8–9. The figure of two million refers to all Poles moved eastward, including prisoners of war. The four deportation actions took between an estimated 1,050,000 and 1,114,000.

34. Details in Malcher, *Blank Pages*, pp. 23–35. Figure for POWs from J. Erickson, 'The Red Army's March into Poland, September 1939', in Sword, *Soviet Takeover*, p. 22.

35. Bloch, *Ribbentrop*, p. 249.

36. Details from Heller and Nekrich, *Utopia*, p. 353; H. Schwendemann, *Die wirtschaftliche Zusammenarbeit zwischen dem Deutschen Reich und der Sowjetunion von 1939 bis 1941* (Berlin, 1993), pp. 373–5. See too W. Birkenfeld, 'Stalin als Wirtschaftsplaner Hitlers', *Vierteljahreshefte für Sozial- und Wirtschaftsgeschichte* 51 (1966).

37. Radzinsky, *Stalin*, p. 429; Molotov speech in R. Medvedev, *Let History Judge: The Origins and Consequences of Stalinism* (London, 1971), p. 442; 800 Communists from Heller and Nekrich, *Utopia*, p. 355.

38. Stalin quotation from V. A. Nevezhin, 'The Pact with Germany and the Idea of an "Offensive War" (1939–1941)', *Journal of Slavic Military History* 8 (1995), p. 811; 'action last' from R. Tucker, *Stalin in Power: The Revolution from above, 1928–1941* (New York, 1990), p. 49; 1934 speech in J. Degras, ed., *Soviet Documents on Foreign Policy* (Oxford, 1953), iii, Report of Stalin

to the 17th Congress of the CPSU, 26 January 1934, p. 68. Molotov talk in Nevezhin, p. 821.

39. C. Roberts, 'Planning for War: The Red Army and the Catastrophe of 1941', *Europe–Asia Studies* 8 (1995), pp. 1308, 1315; R. Tarleton, 'What Really Happened to the Stalin Line? Part II', *Journal of Slavic Military Studies* 6 (1993), p. 30–1, 34–5; J. Sapir, 'The Economics of War in the Soviet Union during World War II', in I. Kershaw and M. Lewin, *Stalinism and Nazism: Dictatorships in Comparison* (London, 1997), pp. 215–17.

40. Tarleton, 'Stalin Line', pp. 37, 39; other details in Heller and Nekrich, *Utopia*, pp. 343–6.

41. W. Spahr, *Zhukov: The Rise and Fall of a Great Captain* (Novato, CA, 1993), pp. 27–30. For a less sanguine view of the battle see R. H. Reese, *Stalin's Reluctant Soldiers*, (Lawrence, Kans., 1996), pp. 169–70.

42. Tarleton, 'Stalin Line', p. 39; Schecter, *Khrushchev*, p. 64.

43. C. Van Dyke, 'The Timoshenko Reforms March–July 1940', *Journal of Slavic Military Studies* 9 (1996), p. 87.

44. Ibid., pp. 89–90; Tarleton, 'Stalin Line', p. 39; Meretskov quotation in S. Bialer, ed., *Stalin and his Generals* (New York, 1969), p. 139: memoir of General M. I. Kazakov. On training see H. Moldenhauer, 'Die Reorganisation der Roten Armee vor der "Grossen Säuberung" bis zum deutschen Angriff auf die UdSSR (1938–1941)', *Militärgeschichtliche Mitteilungen*, 55 (1996), pp. 134–5, 146–7; Reese, *Reluctant Soldiers*, pp. 174–5.

45. Tarleton, 'Stalin Line', p. 29.

46. Schecter, *Khrushchev*, p. 46.

47. Roberts, 'Planning for War', pp. 1311–12.

48. Details in Spahr, *Zhukov*, pp. 33–5 for Zhukov's role in the occupation of Romania; on Latvia see R. J. Rummell, *Lethal Politics: Soviet Genocide and Mass Murder since 1917* (New Brunswick, 1990), p. 133; V. Vardys, 'The Baltic States under Stalin: The First Experiences 1939–1941', in Sword, *Soviet Takeover*, pp. 268–87.

49. F. Taylor, ed., *The Goebbels Diaries 1939–41* (London, 1982), p. 124: entry for 10 August 1940.

50. M. Cooper, *The German Army 1933-1945* (London, 1978), pp. 252–3; J. Toland, *Adolf Hitler* (New York, 1976), pp. 624–5.

51. Ibid., p. 626. There is now a wealth of German literature on planning for Barbarossa. The best introduction is B. Wegner, ed., *From Peace to War: Germany, Soviet Russia and the World, 1939–1941* (Oxford, 1997), especially Chapter 7. But see H. Boog et al., *Der Angriff auf die Sowjetunion* (Stuttgart, 1983).

52. On occupation plans see A. Dallin, *German Rule in Russia, 1941–1945*

(2nd ed., London, 1981); R-D. Müller, *Hitlers Ostkrieg und die deutsche Siedlungspolitik* (Frankfurt-am-Main, 1991).

53. Roberts, *Soviet Union and War*, pp. 126–8; see too B. Pietrow-Ennker, 'Die Sowjetunion und der Beginn des Zweiten Weltkrieges 1939–1941. Ergebnisse einer internationalen Konferenz in Moskau', *Osteuropa* 45 (1995), pp. 855–6. This is an extensive report on a conference of historians in Moscow to mark the fiftieth anniversary of the end of the war. The Russian historians present confirmed that Stalin and Molotov were genuinely seeking a second pact.

54. Roberts, *Soviet Union and War*, pp. 129–31; Bloch, *Ribbentrop*, pp. 313–16.

55. R. G. Reuth, *Goebbels* (London, 1993), p. 282.

56. J. Förster, 'Hitler Turns East – German War Policy in 1940 and 1941', in Wegner, *From Peace to War*, p. 127.

57. Bloch, *Ribbentrop*, p. 317.

58. Tarleton, 'Stalin Line', pp. 43, 48–9.

59. Ibid., pp. 45–6; Roberts, 'Planning for War', pp. 1308–9.

60. Roberts, 'Planning for War', pp. 1315–18.

61. Spahr, *Zhukov*, pp. 35–7; Bialer, *Stalin and his Generals*, pp. 140–41, memoir of General Kazakov.

62. Bialer, *Stalin and his Generals*, pp. 143–5 and 146–8, memoir of Marshal A. Yeremenko.

63. Spahr, *Zhukov*, pp. 42–4; Roberts, 'Planning for War', p. 1307; Reese, *Stalin's Reluctant Soldiers*, pp. 175–85.

64. For a discussion of the nature of the document see Spahr, *Zhukov*, pp. 47–9; Roberts, 'Planning for War', pp. 1315–18. For the argument about Soviet pre-emption see V. Suvorov, 'Who was Planning to Attack Whom in June 1941, Hitler or Stalin?' and comment on the Suvorov thesis of pre-emption in Pietrow-Ennker, 'Sowjetunion', pp. 856–67. Support for the idea of Soviet offensive planning in R. Raack, 'Stalin's Plans for World War II', *Journal of Contemporary History* 26 (1996), pp. 215–27; J. Hoffmann, *Stalins Vernichtungskrieg 1941–1945* (Munich, 1995), Chapters 1–2; E. Topitsch, *Stalins Krieg* (Munich, 1985).

65. Roberts, 'Planning for War', p. 1319; Tarleton, 'Stalin Line', p. 50.

66. Nevezhin, 'Pact with Germany', pp. 832–3.

67. Spahr, *Zhukov*, pp. 51, 59.

68. G. Gorodetsky, 'The Hess Affair and Anglo-Soviet Relations on the Eve of Barbarossa', *English Historical Review* 101 (1986), pp. 405–20; Pietrow-Ennker, 'Sowjetunion', reported the current Russian view that the Hess flight had a profound influence on Stalin's thinking. On intelligence warnings

see Andrew and Gordievsky, *KGB*, pp. 209–13; D. Glantz, *The Role of Intelligence in Soviet Military Strategy in World War II* (Novato, CA, 1990), pp. 15–19.

69. F. W. Deakin and G. A. Storry, *The Case of Richard Sorge* (London, 1966), pp. 227–30; Andrew and Gordievsky, *KGB*, p. 213.

70. Medvedev, *Let History Judge*, p. 450.

71. Andrew and Gordievsky, *KGB*, p. 211; see also Knight, *Beria*, pp. 107–9.

72. Cited in R. McNeal, *Stalin: Man and Ruler* (London, 1992), p. 237.

73. Schecter, *Khrushchev*, p. 56.

74. McNeal, *Stalin*, p. 238.

75. Spahr, *Zhukov*, p. 49; G. K. Zhukov, *Reminiscences and Reflections* (2 vols., Moscow, 1985), i, pp. 217–29.

Chapter 3

1. D. Volkogonov, *Stalin* (London, 1991), p. 402; O. P. Chaney, *Zhukov* (2nd ed., Norman, Oklahoma 1996), p. 110.

2. A. Axell, *Stalin's War through the Eyes of his Commanders* (London, 1997), p. 162.

3. W. J. Spahr, *Zhukov: The Rise and Fall of a Great Captain* (Novato, CA, 1993), p. 49.

4. A. G. Chor'kov, 'The Red Army during the Initial Phase of the Great Patriotic War', in B. Wegner, ed., *From Peace to War: Germany, Soviet Russia and the World, 1939–1941* (Oxford, 1997), pp. 417–18.

5. R. C. Nation, *Black Earth, Red Star* (Ithaca, 1992), p. 106; Dalton reference in M. Kitchen, *British Policy Towards the Soviet Union during the Second World War* (London, 1986), p. 56. See also S. Olsen, ed., *Harold Nicolson: Diaries and Letters 1930–1964* (New York, 1980), p. 213, diary entry for June 24: '80 per cent of the [British] War Office experts think that Russia will be knocked out in ten days.'

6. C. Roberts, 'Planning for War: The Red Army and the Catastrophe of 1941', *Europe–Asia Studies*, 47 (1995), p. 1307; Chor'kov, 'Red Army', p. 416 for airfield figure.

7. R. Stolfi, *Hitler's Panzers East: World War II Reinterpreted* (Norman, Oklahoma, 1991), pp. 88–9.

8. S. Bialer, ed., *Stalin and his Generals* (New York, 1969), pp. 208–9, memoir of Marshal N. Voronov; on the first week see S. J. Main, 'Stalin in June 1941', *Europe–Asia Studies* 48 (1996), pp. 837–9.

9. E. Radzinsky, *Stalin* (London, 1996), pp. 451–2.

10. Ibid., pp. 453–4.

11. S. A. Mikoyan, 'Barbarossa and the Soviet Leadership', in J. Erickson and D. Dilks, eds., *Barbarossa: The Axis and the Allies* (Edinburgh, 1994), pp. 127–8 (a slightly different version of Anastas Mikoyan's memoir is in Volkogonov, *Stalin*, p. 411); Radzinsky, *Stalin*, p. 455 for the Voroshilov quotation.

12. J. Stalin, *The Great Patriotic War of the Soviet Union* (New York, 1945), pp. 9–15, radio broadcast, 3 July 1941. Pravda reference from Nation, *Black Earth*, p. 115.

13. Cited in A. Werth, *Russia at War 1941–1945* (London, 1964), pp. 166–7.

14. J. L. Schecter and V. V. Luchkov, eds., *Khrushchev Remembers: The Glasnost Tapes* (New York, 1990), p. 57; on the militia see J. Barber and M. Harrison, *The Soviet Home Front 1941–1945* (London, 1991), pp. 60, 73–6. An estimated two million volunteers enlisted in the militia during the war.

15. Chor'kov, 'Red Army', pp. 422–3; Barber and Harrison, *Home Front*, pp. 163–4.

16. On Order 270 see A. Sella, *The Value of Human Life in Soviet Warfare* (London, 1992), pp. 100–102. The Yakov story in Volkogonov, *Stalin*, p. 430; Radzinsky, *Stalin*, pp. 461–2.

17. Spahr, *Zhukov*, pp. 59–60; the text of this portion of the tenth edition of Zhukov's memoirs is reproduced in O. P. Chaney, *Zhukov* (rev. ed., Norman, Oklahoma, 1996), pp. 122–3.

18. A. Knight, *Beria: Stalin's First Lieutenant* (Princeton, 1993), pp. 113–14. The July 20 order was for all military units to be 'purged of unreliable elements'.

19. G. C. Malcher, *Blank Pages: Soviet Genocide against the Polish People* (Woking, UK, 1993), pp. 13–14; O. Subtelny, 'The Soviet Occupation of Western Ukraine, 1939–41: An Overview', in Y. Boshyk, *Ukraine during World War II: History and its Aftermath* (Edmonton, 1986), pp. 11–13.

20. B. Krawchenko, 'Soviet Ukraine under Nazi Occupation, 1941 –4' in Boshyk, *Ukraine*, pp. 16–17.

21. Ibid., pp. 19–23; I. Kamenetsky, *Hitler's Occupation of Ukraine (1941–1944): A Study of Totalitarian Imperialism* (Milwaukee, 1956), pp. 52–6.

22. Kamenetsky, *Occupation of Ukraine*, p. 45.

23. J. Förster, 'The Relation between Operation Barbarossa as an Ideological War of Extermination and the Final Solution', in D. Cesarani, ed., *The Final Solution: Origins and Implementation* (London, 1994), pp. 90–5; C. Streit, 'Partisans, Resistance, Prisoners of War', in J. L. Wieczynski, ed., *Operation Barbarossa: The German Attack on the Soviet Union* (Salt Lake City, 1992),

pp. 262–70. Hitler quotation from Kamenetsky, *Occupation of Ukraine*, p. 35.

24. Chor'kov, 'Red Army', pp. 417–26; for an extensive discussion of the opening of the Soviet campaign see D. Glantz and J. House, *When Titans Clashed: How the Red Army Stopped Hitler* (Lawrence, Kansas, 1995), pp. 52–64.

25. M. Cooper, *The German Army* (London, 1978), p. 314.

26. Soviet Embassy, London, *Strategy and Tactics of the Soviet–German War* (London, 1942).

27. J. Lucas, *War on the Eastern Front: The German Soldier in Russia 1941–1945* (London, 1979), pp. 61–2.

28. Ibid., pp. 31–3.

29. M. van Creveld, *Supplying War. Logistics from Wallenstein to Patton* (Cambridge, 1977), pp. 150–3; R. L. di Nardo, *Mechanized Juggernaut or Military Anachronism? Horses and the German Army in World War II* (London, 1991), pp. 37–40.

30. Von Hardesty, 'Roles and Missions: Soviet Tactical Air Power in the Second Period of the Great Patriotic War', in C. Reddel, ed., *Transformations in Russian and Soviet Military History* (Washington, 1990), pp. 154–5.

31. Cited in Barber and Harrison, *Home Front*, p. 67.

32. Glantz and House, *When Titans Clashed*, pp. 76–7; J. Erickson, *The Road to Stalingrad* (London, 1975), pp. 207–10.

33. Werth, *Russia at War*, pp. 785–6.

34. Glantz and House, *When Titans Clashed*, pp. 78–9.

35. Erickson, *Road to Stalingrad*, pp. 216–17.

36. Cooper, *German Army*, p. 312; on armaments see R. J. Overy, 'Mobilization for Total War in Germany 1939–1941', *English Historical Review* 103 (1988), pp. 631–2.

37. J. Toland, *Adolf Hitler* (London, 1976), p. 685.

38. Ibid., p. 684.

39. A. Fredborg, *Behind the Steel Wall: Berlin 1941–3* (London, 1944), pp. 48–9; H. K. Smith, *Last Train from Berlin* (London, 1942), pp. 59–64.

40. Radzinsky, *Stalin*, pp. 465–6.

41. Volkogonov, *Stalin*, pp. 412–13 dates the meeting with Stamenov in July 1941, which seems less plausible than October. See the discussion in J. Barros and R. Gregor, *Double Deception: Stalin, Hitler and the Invasion of Russia* (Dekalb, Illinois, 1995), pp. 219–21; P. Sudaplatov, *Special Tasks: The Memoirs of an Unwanted Witness* (New York, 1994), pp. 146–7, 376–85, 397–401, who maintains that the 'peace feeler' was part of a wider programme of disinformation disseminated on Beria's instructions.

42. I. Ehrenburg, *Men – Years – Life: Vol. 5, The War 1941–45* (London, 1964), pp. 17–18.
43. Werth, *Russia at War*, p. 235.
44. Volkogonov, *Stalin*, pp. 434–5.

Chapter 4

Epigraph: V. Inber, *Leningrad Diary* (London, 1971), p. 38.
1. Details on Zhukov's early life from O. P. Chaney, *Zhukov* (2nd edition, Norman, Oklahoma, 1996), Chapters 1–4.
2. W. J. Spahr, *Zhukov: The Rise and Fall of a Great Captain* (Novato, California, 1993), pp. 270–1. On the persistent post-war hostility to Zhukov shown by former colleagues see Chaney, *Zhukov*, pp. 451–65.
3. C. Andrew and O. Gordievsky, *KGB: The Inside Story* (London, 1990), pp. 220–21; A. Vaksberg, *The Prosecutor and the Prey: Vyshinsky and the 1930s Moscow Show Trials* (London, 1990), pp. 221–4.
4. Chaney, *Zhukov*, pp. 121–3, 125–6.
5. G. Zhukov, *Reminiscences and Reflections* (2 vols., Moscow, 1985), i, pp. 416–17.
6. Ibid., p. 418; Chaney, *Zhukov*, pp. 145–7.
7. J. Erickson, *The Road to Stalingrad* (London, 1974), p. 194.
8. Ibid., p. 192.
9. H. Salisbury, *The 900 Days: The Siege of Leningrad* (London, 1969), p. 206.
10. A. Werth, *Russia at War, 1941–1945* (London, 1964), p. 308.
11. Zhukov, *Reminiscences*, i, p. 453.
12. Erickson, *Road to Stalingrad*, pp. 194–5.
13. A. Werth, *Leningrad* (London, 1944).
14. D. V. Pavlov, *Leningrad 1941: The Blockade* (Chicago, 1965), pp. 56–7; Inber, *Leningrad Diary*, pp. 16–25 on the impact of bombing.
15. Pavlov, *Leningrad*, pp. 75, 79, 84, 88.
16. L. Goure, *The Siege of Leningrad* (Stanford, 1962), pp. 219–20.
17. Ibid., p. 219.
18. Salisbury, *900 Days*, pp. 474–6. Documents have recently been released in St Petersburg which confirm the practice of cannibalism, but its scale cannot be calculated, even from official reports.
19. Zhukov, *Reminiscences*, i, pp. 438–9.
20. Goure, *Leningrad*, p. 233; on the story of the Kirov works, Werth, *Leningrad*, pp. 111–15.

21. L. Nicholas, *The Rape of Europe: The Fate of Europe's Treasures in the Third Reich and the Second World War* (London, 1994), pp. 187–90, 194–6; N. Kislitsyn and V. Zubakov, *Leningrad Does Not Surrender* (Moscow, 1989), p. 138. The Leningrad Symphony was not performed in the city until August. The first concert of Russian music since the siege began was held in March 1942.

22. Pavlov, *Leningrad*, pp. 96–104.

23. Kislitsyn and Zubakov, *Leningrad*, p. 111; Pavlov, *Leningrad*, pp. 136–8; Werth, *Russia at War*, pp. 329–30.

24. Goure, *Leningrad*, pp. 152–3, 204–5.

25. Pavlov, *Leningrad*, pp. 78–9, 145–6; Inber, *Leningrad Diary*, p. 37.

26. Kislitsyn and Zubakov, *Leningrad*, pp. 116–18.

27. Goure, *Leningrad*, pp. 259–61.

28. Werth, *Leningrad*, Chapters 1–3.

29. Goure, *Leningrad*, p. 262.

30. Salisbury, *900 Days*, pp. 515–17.

31. Werth, *Russia at War*, p. 356; on Soviet prisoners of war see C. Streit, *Keine Kamaraden. Die Wehrmacht und die sowjetischen Kriegsgefangenen 1941–1945* (Stuttgart, 1981).

32. Zhukov, *Reminiscences*, ii, pp. 12–19.

33. Werth, *Russia at War*, p. 254.

34. Radzinsky, *Stalin*, pp. 467–8.

35. J. Stalin, *The Great Patriotic War of the Soviet Union* (New York, 1945), pp. 33–4: speech of 6 November 1941; see also Werth, *Russia at War*, pp. 244–9.

36. S. Bialer, *Stalin and his Generals* (New York, 1969), pp. 306–9: memoir of General P. A. Artemyev, and General K. R. Sinilov; on the filmed speech, Radzinsky, *Stalin*, p. 468.

37. R. G. Reuth, *Goebbels* (London, 1993), p. 297.

38. This and subsequent account of the battle from Erickson, *Road to Stalingrad*, pp. 250–66; Zhukov, *Reminiscences*, ii, pp. 33–40.

39. Panfilov story in Werth, *Russia at War*, pp. 154–5.

40. Spahr, *Zhukhov*, pp. 74–5; Zhukov's reply from interview in Programme 4, 'Russia's War'.

41. German figures in *Kriegstagebuch des Oberkommandos der Wehrmacht* (5 vols., Frankfurt am Main, 1961–3), i, pp. 1120–21. Soviet figures calculated from J. Erickson, 'Soviet War Losses', in J. Erickson and D. Dilks, eds., *Barbarossa: The Axis and the Allies* (Edinburgh, 1994), pp. 264–5.

42. *Kriegstagebuch*, i, p. 1120.

43. Bialer, *Stalin and his Generals*, pp. 295–6: memoir of General P. A. Belov.

44. L. Rotundo, 'The Creation of Soviet Reserves and the 1941 Campaign', *Military Affairs*, 65 (1985), pp. 21–7; D. Glantz, *The Military Strategy of the Soviet Union: A History* (London, 1992), Appendix 1, Soviet Mobilization in the Second World War, pp. 308–10.

45. J. Lucas, *War on the Eastern Front: The German Soldier in Russia 1941–1945* (London, 1979), pp. 78–94; Cooper, *German Army*, pp. 233–4. Temperature in Bialer, *Stalin's Generals*, p. 324.

46. Cooper, *German Army*, p. 344.

47. G. Gorodetsky, *Stafford Cripps's Mission to Moscow 1940–42* (Cambridge, 1984), pp. 280–88.

48. Zhukov, *Reminiscences*, ii, pp. 52–3.

49. Erickson, 'Soviet Losses', p. 254.

50. See in particular K. Reinhardt, *Moscow – The Turning Point: The Failure of Hitler's Strategy in the Winter of 1941–42* (Oxford 1992) and R. Stolfi, *Hitler's Panzers East: World War II Reinterpreted* (Norman, Oklahoma, 1991).

51. Erickson, *Road to Stalingrad*, p. 287.

52. Spahr, *Zhukov*, p. 67.

53. N. Tumarkin, *The Living and the Dead: The Rise and Fall of the Cult of World War II in Russia* (New York, 1994), pp. 76–8; Werth, *Russia at War*, p. 273. On the Zoya cult see K. Hodgson, 'Soviet Women's Poetry of World War 2', in J. Garrard and C. Garrard, eds., *World War 2 and the Soviet People* (London, 1993), pp. 80–81.

54. Ehrenberg, *The War*, pp. 27–8, 35.

55. Nicholas, *Rape of Europa*, pp. 193–4.

56. Werth, *Russia at War*, p. 274.

Chapter 5

Epigraph: C. Andreyev, *Vlasov and the Russian Liberation Movement: Soviet Reality and Emigré Theories* (Cambridge, 1987), p. 209.

1. M. Burleigh, *Death and Deliverance: 'Euthanasia' in Germany 1900–1945* (Cambridge, 1994), pp. 230–31.

2. B. Krawchenko, 'Soviet Ukraine under Nazi Occupation', in Y. Boshyk, *Ukraine During World War II* (Edmonton, 1986), p. 17.

3. A. Dallin, *German Rule in Russia* (2nd ed., London, 1981); S. Kudryashov, 'The Hidden Dimension: Wartime Collaboration in the Soviet Union', in J. Erickson and D. Dilks, eds., *Barbarossa: The Axis and the Allies* (Edinburgh, 1994), pp. 240–41.

4. O. Caroe, *Soviet Empire: The Turks of Central Asia and Stalinism* (London, 1967), pp. 247–8.

5. N. Heller and A. Nekrich, *Utopia in Power: The History of the Soviet Union from 1917 to the Present* (London, 1985), pp. 428–9; figures from M. R. Elliott, 'Soviet Military Collaborators during World War II', in Boshyk, *Ukraine*, pp. 92–6.

6. Elliot, 'Military Collaborators', p. 94; S. J. Newland, *Cossacks in the German Army, 1941–1945* (London, 1991), pp. 105–6, 116–17; W. Anders, *Hitler's Defeat in Russia* (Chicago, 1953), pp. 177–9. The figure of 250,000 includes some 50,000 who were incorporated into the Cossack Division (15th SS Cossack Cavalry Corps) and other Cossacks recruited into anti-partisan units, a further twelve reserve regiments and those who served in small numbers in German units, or as non-combatant auxiliaries. The usual figure given for Cossack combatants is from 20,000 to 25,000 in 1943; the larger figure includes all those who fought for or worked for the Germans at some time between 1941 and 1945.

7. Elliot, 'Military Collaborators', p. 93.

8. Kudryashov, 'Hidden Dimension', pp. 243–5; Elliot, 'Military Collaborators', pp. 95–6.

9. Anders, *Hitler's Defeat*, p. 191.

10. Details from Andreyev, *Vlasov*, pp. 19–29; J. Erickson, *The Road to Stalingrad* (London, 1976), pp. 352–3.

11. Andreyev, *Vlasov*, pp. 38–40.

12. Ibid., pp. 210–15, Appendix B, Vlasov's Open Letter, 'Why I Decided to Fight Bolshevism.'

13. Ibid., pp. 206–8, Appendix A, The Smolensk Declaration, 27 December 1942.

14. J. Hoffmann, *Die Geschichte der Wlassow-Armee* (Freiburg, 1984), pp. 205–36.

15. Heller and Nekrich, *Utopia*, pp. 437–8; Hoffmann, *Wlassow-Armee*, p. 244.

16. Andreyev, *Vlasov*, pp. 78–9.

17. On German plans for the East see R-D. Müller, *Hitlers Ostkrieg und die deutsche Siedlungspolitik* (Frankfurt am Main, 1991); M. Burleigh, 'Nazi Europe', in N. Ferguson, ed., *Virtual History* (London, 1997), pp. 317–39; N. Rich, *Hitler's War Aims: The Establishment of the New Order* (London, 1974), pp. 322 ff.

18. Krawchenko, *Soviet Ukraine*, pp. 22–3.

19. Rich, *War Aims*, pp. 359–60.

20. I. Kamenetsky, *Hitler's Occupation of Ukraine, 1941–1944: A Study in Totalitarian Imperialism* (Milwaukee, 1956), p. 35.

21. Ibid., pp. 43–6.

22. On peasant 'intellectuals' see R. Bosworth, *Explaining Auschwitz and Hiroshima: History Writing on the Second World War* (London, 1993), pp. 149–51; Krawchenko, 'Soviet Ukraine', p. 27; O. Zambinsky, 'Collaboration of the Population in Occupied Ukrainian Territory: Some Aspects of the Overall Picture', *Journal of Slavic Military Studies* 10 (1997), p. 149.

23. Krawchenko, pp. 26–7; Zambinsky, 'Collaboration', p. 148 on Kiev rations; T. P. Mulligan, *The Politics of Illusion and Empire: German Occupation Policy in the Soviet Union 1942–1943* (Westport, Conn. 1988), pp. 93–103 for figures on German food supplies from the USSR. Over 10 million tons of grain and almost 2.5 million tons of hay were taken.

24. Out of 2.8 million Ostarbeiter carried off to Germany, 2.3 million came from the Ukraine. See Krawchenko, 'Soviet Ukraine', pp. 27–8; Kamenetsky, *Occupation of Ukraine*, pp. 46–8.

25. J. Förster, 'Jewish Policies of the German Military, 1939–1942', in A. Cohen, ed., *The Shoah and the War* (New York, 1992), pp. 59–61.

26. J. Schecter and V. V. Luchkov, eds. *Khrushchev Remembers: The Glasnost Tapes* (New York, 1990), p. 27. For a recent discussion of Stalin's attitude to the Jews see M. Parrish, *The Lesser Terror: Soviet State Security, 1939–1953* (London, 1996), pp. 197–200.

27. A. Vaksberg, *Stalin Against the Jews* (New York, 1994), pp. 64–6; N. Levin, *The Jews in the Soviet Union since 1917* (2 vols., London, 1990), i, pp. 282–311.

28. Vaksberg, *Stalin Against the Jews*, pp. 82–6.

29. B-C. Pinchuk, *Shtetl Jews under Soviet Rule: Eastern Poland on the Eve of the Holocaust* (London, 1990), pp. 66–70, 104–6, 127–32.

30. Vaksberg, *Stalin Against the Jews*, pp. 105–10; Parrish, *Lesser Terror*, pp. 200–201.

31. Levin, *Jews in the Soviet Union*, pp. 363–4; Parrish, *Lesser Terror*, pp. 200–201.

32. Levin, *Jews in the Soviet Union*, pp. 379–85, 455–6.

33. C. R. Browning, *The Path to Genocide* (Cambridge, 1992), pp. 100–106; Browning, 'Hitler and the Euphoria of Victory: The Path to the Final Solution', in D. Cesarani, ed., *The Final Solution: Origins and Implementation* (London, 1994), pp. 142–5.

34. G. Fleming, *Hitler and the Final Solution* (London, 1985), p. 67.

35. R. Headland, *Messages of Murder: A Study of the Einsatzgruppen of the Security Police and the Security Service 1941–43* (London, 1992), pp. 54–5.

36. Ibid., pp. 59–60.

37. Browning, 'Hitler and Euphoria', pp. 139–40. For the wider context of

race policy the best study is M. Burleigh and W. Wippermann, *The Racial State: Germany 1933–1945* (Cambridge, 1991).

38. G. Reitlinger, *The Final Solution* (London, 1971), pp. 233–4; Levin, *Jews in the Soviet Union*, pp. 404–6. On the killing of Soviet non-Jewish prisoners, V. E. Korol, 'The Price of Victory: Myths and Realities', *Journal of Slavic Military Studies* 9 (1996), p. 419.

39. Reitlinger, *Final Solution*, p. 235.

40. Ibid., pp. 240–41.

41. Headland, *Messages of Murder*, p. 105; Zambinsky, 'Collaboration', pp. 143–4. In Voroshilovgrad the police found 1,000 volunteers in ten days willing to denounce Jews and Communists.

42. On the background see A. A. Maslov, 'Concerning the Role of Partisan Warfare in Soviet Military Doctrine of the 1920s and 1930s', *Journal of Slavic Military Studies* 9 (1996), pp. 891–2; C. Streit, 'Partisans – Resistance – Prisoners of War', in J. L. Wieczynski, ed., *Operation Barbarossa: The German Attack on the Soviet Union, June 22, 1941* (Salt Lake City, 1993), pp. 265–6.

43. J. Stalin, *The Great Patriotic War of the Soviet Union* (New York, 1945), p. 15.

44. J. A. Armstrong, ed., *Soviet Partisans in World War II* (Madison, 1964), p. 662.

45. M. Cooper, *The Phantom War: The German Struggle against Soviet Partisans, 1941–1944* (London, 1979), p. 17.

46. Streit, 'Partisans', p. 271.

47. Ibid., p. 269; see too T. Schulte, *The German Army and Nazi Policies in Occupied Russia* (Oxford, 1989), pp. 317–44, documentary appendix on treatment of partisans and prisoners of war.

48. Streit, 'Partisans', p. 270.

49. Cooper, *Phantom War*, p. 73; on the establishment of a central partisan organization see J. A. Armstrong and K. DeWitt, 'Organisation and Control of the Partisan Movement', in Armstrong, *Soviet Partisans*, pp. 98–103. On the 'Partisan Guide' see A. Werth, *Russia at War 1941–1945* (London, 1964), p. 710.

50. N. Tec, *Defiance: The Bielski Partisans* (Oxford, 1993), pp. 41–4, 74–6, 103–6, 202–3, 207–9.

51. On the Ukraine see Cooper, *Phantom War*, pp. 67–8; Kamenetsky, *Occupation of Ukraine*, pp. 69–82. On total numbers in the partisan movement there is no real agreement. The exact figures are incapable of discovery because of the very nature of partisan activity. See E. Ziemke, 'Composition and Morale of the Partisan Movement', in Armstrong, *Soviet Partisans*,

p. 151; Cooper, *Phantom War*, pp. 66–8; Werth, *Russia at War*, pp. 715, 725 gives higher figures.

52. Cooper, *Phantom War*, p. 59.

53. Armstrong, *Soviet Partisans*, pp. 750–52, Document 73, diary of V. A. Balakin, January–February 1942.

54. Cooper, *Phantom War*, p. 69; Ziemke, 'Composition and Morale', pp. 148–50.

55. Kamenetsky, *Occupation of Ukraine*, pp. 69–73; M. Yurkevich, 'Galician Ukrainians in German Military Formations and in the German Administration', in Boshyk, *Ukraine in World War II*, pp. 71–3.

56. Kamenetsky, *Occupation of Ukraine*, p. 81.

57. Figures in Maslov, 'Partisan Warfare', pp. 892–3.

58. Werth, *Russia at War*, pp. 791–2.

59. Ibid., p. 792.

Chapter 6

Epigraph: A. Werth, *Russia at War 1941–1945* (London, 1964), p. 560.

1. J. Erickson, 'Soviet War Losses', in J. Erickson and D. Dilks, eds., *Barbarossa: The Axis and the Allies* (Edinburgh, 1994), p. 264.

2. On economic losses see W. Moskoff, *The Bread of Affliction: The Food Supply in the USSR during World War II* (Cambridge, 1990), pp. 71–2; A. Nove, *An Economic History of the USSR* (London, 1989), p. 262.

3. H. Trevor-Roper, ed., *Hitler's War Directives* (London, 1964), p. 178.

4. C. Andrew and O. Gordievsky, *KGB: The Inside Story* (London, 1990), p. 224; D. M. Glantz, *The Role of Intelligence in Soviet Military Strategy in World War II* (Novato, California, 1990), pp. 49–51.

5. M. Heller and A. Nekrich, *Utopia in Power: The History of the Soviet Union from 1917 to the Present* (London, 1982), p. 391; D. M. Glantz and J. House, *When Titans Clashed: How the Red Army Stopped Hitler* (London, 1995), p. 121; J. Garrard and C. Garrard, eds., *World War 2 and the Soviet People* (London, 1993), p. 19.

6. A. Sella, *The Value of Human Life in Soviet Warfare* (London, 1992), pp. 158–9; W. Spahr, *Zhukov: The Rise and Fall of a Great Captain* (Novato, California, 1993), p. 147. Zhukov approved the penal units on 26 September 1942. Each army was ordered to establish from five to ten penal companies.

7. Erickson, 'Soviet Losses', p. 262 for figures on penal battalions. Figure for those condemned to death from review by E. Mawdsley in *War in History* 4 (1997), p. 230.

8. Cited in J. Barber and M. Harrison, *The Soviet Home Front: A Social and Economic History of the USSR in World War II* (London, 1991), p. 72.

9. I. Ehrenburg, *Men – Years – Life: The War Years 1941–1945* (London, 1964), p. 123.

10. A. Werth, *Russia at War*, pp. 415–16.

11. R. Bosworth, *Explaining Auschwitz and Hiroshima: History Writing and the Second World War 1945–1990* (London, 1993), p. 153.

12. Heller and Nekrich, *Utopia*, p. 407.

13. Ibid., pp. 408–10; W. P. and Z. Coates, *A History of Anglo-Soviet Relations* (London, 1944), pp. 696–7; on the revival of religion M. Spinka, *The Church in Soviet Russia* (Oxford, 1956), pp. 82–6.

14. Heller and Nekrich, *Utopia*, p. 409.

15. R. Parker, *Moscow Correspondent* (London, 1949), pp. 21–2.

16. Werth, *Russia at War*, p. 417, from the poem 'Kill Him!' published in *Pravda*.

17. Ibid., p. 414.

18. G. Gibian, 'World War 2 in Russian National Consciousness', in Garrard, *World War 2*, p. 155.

19. A. Seaton, *Stalin as Warlord* (London, 1976), p. 39; for a critical account of Stalin's behaviour at Tsaritsyn see A. Antonov-Ovseyenko, *The Time of Stalin: Portrait of a Tyranny* (New York, 1981), pp. 10–14, 20.

20. *Great Patriotic War of the Soviet Union 1941–1945: a general outline* (Moscow, 1970), p. 117.

21. J. Wieder, *Stalingrad und die Verantwortung der Soldaten* (Munich, 1962), p. 45.

22. G. Zhukov, *Reminiscences and Reflections* (Moscow, 1985), ii, pp. 83–4; Werth, *Russia at War*, pp. 448–9; von Hardesty, *Red Phoenix: The Rise of Soviet Air Power 1941–1945* (London, 1982), p. 102.

23. W. Warlimont, *Inside Hitler's Headquarters* (London, 1964), pp. 246–7.

24. Zhukov, *Reminiscences*, ii, pp. 87–8.

25. Ibid., pp. 93–4; Spahr, *Zhukov*, pp. 101–2.

26. Zhukov, *Reminiscences*, ii, p. 96.

27. Maisky quotation in S. M. Miner, *Between Churchill and Stalin: The Soviet Union, Great Britain and the Origins of the Grand Alliance* (Chapel Hill, 1988), p. 158; Lend-Lease figures in M. Harrison, *Soviet Planning in Peace and War, 1938–1945* (Cambridge, 1985), pp. 258–9.

28. V. Berezhkov, *History in the Making: Memoirs of World War II Diplomacy* (Moscow, 1983), p. 195.

29. Ibid., pp. 196–9; W. A. Harriman and E. Abel, *Special Envoy to Churchill and Stalin, 1941–1945* (London, 1975), pp. 152–64.

30. Spahr, *Zhukov*, pp. 103–5.

31. Details in G. A. Kumanev, 'The Soviet Economy and the 1941 Evacuation', in J. L. Wieczynski, ed., *Operation Barbarossa: The German Attack on the Soviet Union, June 22, 1941* (Salt Lake City, 1993), pp. 168–81; F. Kagan, 'The Evacuation of Soviet Industry in the Wake of "Barbarossa": A Key to Soviet Victory', *Journal of Slavic Military Studies* 8 (1995), pp. 389–96.

32. Kumanev, 'Soviet Economy', pp. 191–3; Erickson, 'Soviet Women at War', in Garrard, *World War 2*, p. 54.

33. Figures in Kumanev, 'Soviet Economy', p. 189; Kagan, 'Evacuation', p. 406.

34. Harrison, *Soviet Economy*, pp. 72–9; Kagan, 'Evacuation', p. 396–8.

35. K. Simonov, *Days and Nights* (London, n.d.), p. 134.

36. Werth, *Russia at War*, pp. 559–60; V. I. Chuikov, *The Beginning of the Road: The Story of the Battle of Stalingrad* (London, 1963), pp. 14–27.

37. Chuikov, *Stalingrad*, pp. 78–9.

38. H. C. Cassidy, *Moscow Dateline 1941–1943* (London, 1944), pp. 224–5.

39. Details in Chuikov, *Stalingrad*, pp. 93–102; Werth, *Russia at War*, pp. 452–3; J. Erickson, *The Road to Stalingrad* (London, 1975), pp. 391–3.

40. Rats detail in Cassidy, *Moscow Dateline*, p. 226.

41. Chuikov, *Stalingrad*, p. 191.

42. Figure in J. Erickson, 'Red Army Battlefield Performance, 1941–45: The System and the Soldier', in P. Addison and A. Calder, eds., *Time to Kill: The Soldier's Experience of War in the West 1939–1945* (London, 1997), p. 244.

43. Simonov, *Days and Nights*, p. 6.

44. Werth, *Russia at War*, p. 456.

45. Von Hardesty, *Red Phoenix*, pp. 97–104; *The Soviet Air Force in World War II* (London, 1982 from the Russian original), pp. 114–34; S. Zaloga and J. Gransden, *Soviet Tanks and Combat Vehicles of World War II* (London, 1984), pp. 152–4.

46. Details on Uranus from Erickson, *Road to Stalingrad*, pp. 447–53; Zhukov, *Reminiscences*, pp. 115–17; Glantz and House, *When Titans Clashed*, pp. 133–4.

47. K. Zeitzler, 'Stalingrad', in W. Richardson and S. Frieden, eds., *The Fatal Decisions* (London, 1956), p. 138.

48. Glantz and House, *When Titans Clashed*, p. 134; Erickson, *Road to Stalingrad*, pp. 468–9.

49. F. Paulus, 'Stalingrad: A Brief Survey', in W. Goerlitz, *Paulus and Stalingrad* (London, 1963), p. 283.

50. W. Murray, *Luftwaffe* (London, 1985), pp. 141–4.

51. Details in Goerlitz, *Paulus and Stalingrad*, pp. 4–6, 47–8, 59–60.

52. Wieder, *Stalingrad*, p. 43.

53. J. Erickson, *The Road to Berlin: Stalin's War with Germany* (London, 1983), p. 114.

54. Reported in Cassidy, *Moscow Dateline*, p. 253.

55. On the air blockade see Hardesty, *Red Phoenix*, pp. 110–17; on Koltso see Glantz and House, *When Titans Clashed*, pp. 141–2; Erickson, *Road to Berlin*, pp. 46–50.

56. Werth, *Russia at War*, pp. 540–1.

57. Wieder, *Stalingrad*, p. 327.

58. F. Gilbert, ed., *Hitler Directs his War: The Secret Records of his Daily Military Conferences* (New York, 1950), pp. 18–19.

59. Werth, *Russia at War*, p. 543; Ehrenburg, *Men – Years – Life*, p. 92.

60. Erickson, 'War Losses', p. 264. The figure for the defensive operations at Stalingrad was 323,856 killed; for the offensive operations, 154,885 (with a total of 651,000 wounded).

61. From an interview with Werth in *Russia at War*, p. 531.

Chapter 7

Epigraph: K. Simonov, *Days and Nights* (London, n.d.), p. 59.

1. E. von Manstein, *Verlorene Siege* (Bonn, 1955), p. 508.

2. See J. Erickson, 'Red Army Battlefield Performance, 1941–45: The System and the Soldier', in P. Addison and A. Calder, eds., *Time to Kill: The Soldier's Experience of War in the West, 1941–1945* (London, 1997), pp. 237–41, 247–8 on the declining manpower pool available to Soviet forces, and the myth of 'Russian masses'.

3. B. Bonwetsch, 'Stalin, the Red Army, and the "Great Patriotic War"', in I. Kershaw and M. Lewin, eds., *Stalinism and Nazism: Dictatorships in Comparison* (Cambridge, 1997), pp. 203–4; E. O'Ballance, *The Red Army* (London, 1964), p. 179.

4. S. Bialer, ed., *Stalin and his Generals: Soviet Military Memoirs* (New York, 1969), pp. 350–1 (memoir of Marshal A. Vasilevsky), pp. 352–4 (memoir of S. M. Shtemenko), pp. 367–8 (memoir of Marshal N. Voronov).

5. S. M. Shtemenko, *The Soviet General Staff at War* (Moscow, 1970), pp. 125–7.

6. Ibid., pp. 128–9; Bialer, *Stalin's Generals*, pp. 355–9.

7. J. Sapir, 'The Economics of War in the Soviet Union during World War

II', in Kershaw and Lewin, *Stalinism and Nazism*, pp. 219–21; R. M. Ogorkiewicz, *Armoured Forces: A History of Armoured Forces and their Vehicles* (London, 1970), pp. 123–4; S. J. Zaloga and J. Grandsen, *Soviet Tanks and Combat Vehicles in World War II* (London,1984), pp. 146–9, 160–62.

8. R. J. Overy, *The Air War 1939–1945* (London, 1980), pp. 52–6; Von Hardesty, *Red Phoenix: The Rise of Soviet Air Power 1941–1945* (London, 1982), pp. 83–8.

9. Von Hardesty, 'Roles and Missions: Soviet Tactical Air Power in the Second Period of the Great Patriotic War', in C. Reddel, ed., *Transformations in Russian and Soviet Military History* (Washington, 1990), pp. 163–9; K. Uebe, *Russian Reactions to German Air Power in World War II* (New York, 1964), pp. 29–42.

10. Zaloga and Grandsen, *Soviet Tanks*, pp. 131–7.

11. Ibid., pp. 155–66.

12. H. P. van Tuyll, *Feeding the Bear: American Aid to the Soviet Union 1941–1945* (New York, 1989), pp. 156–7; J. Beaumont, *Comrades in Arms: British Aid to Russia 1941–1945* (London, 1980), pp. 210–12. Britain supplied 247,000 telephones and one million miles of telephone line.

13. D. R. Beachley, 'Soviet Radio-Electronic Combat in World War II', *Military Review* 61 (1981), pp. 67–8.

14. See the discussion in D. M. Glantz, *The Role of Intelligence in Soviet Military Strategy in World War II* (Novato, California, 1990).

15. R. J. Overy *et al.*, 'Co-operation: Trade, Aid and Technology', in D. Reynolds, W. Kimball and A. O. Chubarian, eds., *Allies at War: The Soviet, American and British Experience 1939–1945* (New York, 1994), pp. 207–17.

16. W. A. Harriman and E. Abel, *Special Envoy to Churchill and Stalin, 1941–1945* (London, 1945), pp. 90–91.

17. B. V. Sokolov, 'Lend Lease in Soviet Military Efforts 1941–1945', *Journal of Slavic Military History* 7 (1994), pp. 567–8; Khrushchev in J. L. Schecter and V. V. Luchkov, eds., *Khrushchev Remembers: The Glasnost Tapes* (New York, 1990), p. 84.

18. Van Tuyll, *Feeding the Bear*, pp. 156–7; Zaloga and Grandsen, *Soviet Tanks*, p. 207; V. Vorsin, 'Motor Vehicle Transport Deliveries Through "Lend-Lease" ', *Journey of Slavic Military Studies* 10 (1997), pp. 164, 172–3.

19. Sokolov, 'Lend Lease', pp. 570–81. The figures supplied by Sokolov represent the first attempt by a Russian scholar to place Lend-Lease in the context of the Soviet production record. His conclusion is significant: 'Without the Western supplies, the Soviet Union not only could not have

won the Great Patriotic War, but even could not have resisted German aggression' (p. 581). 'Second fronts' from Werth, *Russia at War*, p. 574.

20. Shtemenko, *Soviet General Staff*, pp. 152–61.

21. W. Spahr, *Zhukov: The Rise and Fall of a Great Captain* (Novato, California, 1993), pp. 119–21 on the arguments about the origins of the plan; Zhukov, *Reminiscences*, ii, pp. 150–60.

22. On the revival of the 'deep battle' strategy see D. Glantz, 'Toward Deep Battle: The Soviet Conduct of Operational Maneuver', in Reddel, *Transformations*, pp. 194–202.

23. Zhukov, *Reminiscences*, ii, pp. 168–79; K. Rokossovsky, *A Soldier's Duty* (Moscow, 1970), pp. 184–90.

24. A. Vasilevsky, 'Strategic Planning of the Battle of Kursk', in *The Battle of Kursk* (Moscow, 1974), p. 73; on the logistical effort, N. Antipenko, 'Logistics', in *Battle of Kursk*, pp. 242, 245–6.

25. Details on the size of the two opposing forces have recently come under critical scrutiny; see N. Zetterling, 'Loss Rates on the Eastern Front during World War II', *Journal of Slavic Military History* 9 (1996), pp. 895–906.

26. T. P. Mulligan, 'Spies, Ciphers, and "Zitadelle": Intelligence and the Battle of Kursk 1943', *Journal of Contemporary History* 22 (1987), pp. 237–8; C. Andrew and O. Gordievsky, *KGB: The Inside Story* (London, 1990), pp. 248–9.

27. Mulligan, 'Spies', pp. 238–41; Andrew and Gordievsky, *KGB*, pp. 248–9; Glantz, *Soviet Intelligence*, pp. 99–100.

28. Zhukov, *Reminiscences*, ii, p. 180.

29. Glantz, *Soviet Intelligence*, pp. 100–103; Zhukov, *Reminiscences*, ii, p. 183.

30. Details in Rokossovsky, *Soldier's Duty*, pp. 195–202.

31. Erickson, *Road to Berlin*, pp. 137–40; Manstein, *Verlorene Siege*, pp. 498–500.

32. C. Sydnor, *Soldiers of Destruction: The SS Death's Head Division, 1933–1945* (Princeton, 1977), pp. 283–8.

33. P. Rotmistrov, 'Tanks against Tanks', in *Main Front: Soviet Leaders Look Back on World War II* (London, 1987), pp. 106–9.

34. Ibid., pp. 109–10.

35. Ibid., pp. 112–13.

36. Ibid., pp, 114–17; Erickson, *Road to Berlin*, pp. 144–6.

37. Sydnor, *Soldiers of Destruction*, pp. 290–91; F. W. von Mellenthin, *Panzer-Schlachten* (Neckargemünd, 1963), pp 163–5; Zaloga and Grandsen, *Soviet Tanks*, p. 166.

38. Rotmistrov, 'Tanks against Tanks', pp. 128–9; Spahr, *Zhukov*, pp. 126–7,

who records Zhukov's later claim that the tank battle was less dramatic and decisive than Rotmistrov's colourful account might suggest.

39. Vasilevsky, 'Strategic Planning', p. 74; Werth, *Russia at War*, p. 684.

40. I. Ehrenburg, *Men – Years – Life: The War 1941–1945* (London, 1964), p. 107.

41. Manstein, *Verlorene Siege*, pp. 501–5, who argued that German forces were on the point of victory, a view hard to reconcile with the course of the next three months of fighting.

42. D. Volkogonov, *Stalin* (London, 1991), p. 481.

43. Ibid., p. 481; English version in S. Richardson, ed., *The Secret History of World War II: The Wartime Cables of Roosevelt, Stalin and Churchill* (New York, 1986), pp. 116–17, 'Secret and Personal Message from Premier J. V. Stalin to President Roosevelt, August 8, 1943'.

44. Werth, *Russia at War*, pp. 684–5.

45. Erickson, 'Soviet Losses', p. 264.

46. On female employment see J. Barber and M. Harrison, *The Soviet Home Front 1941–1945* (London, 1991), pp. 215–19; J. Erickson, 'Soviet Women at War', in J. Garrard and C. Garrard, *World War 2 and the Soviet People* (London, 1993), pp. 53–6.

47. A. Sella, *The Value of Human Life in Soviet Warfare* (London, 1992), pp. 163–4.

48. Ibid., pp. 158–9.

49. Quoted in G. Gibian, 'World War 2 in Russian National Consciousness', in Garrard, *World War 2*, p. 155.

50. Ibid., p. 153, citing Vyacheslav Kondratyev's article published in the Soviet Union on 9 May 1990 to mark the forty-fifth anniversary of the end of the war.

51. Erickson, 'Soviet Losses', pp. 261–2; see also A. A. Maslov, 'Soviet General Officer Corps 1941–1945: Losses in Combat', *Journal of Slavic Military Studies* 8 (1995), pp. 607–8, who records the loss of 235 generals during the war (and one rear admiral).

52. Erickson, 'Battlefield Performance', p. 237.

53. For a discussion of losses see E. Bacon, 'Soviet Military Losses in World War II', *Journal of Slavic Military Studies* 6 (1993), pp. 613–33; V. E. Korol, 'The Price of Victory: Myths and Realities', in *Journal of Slavic Military Studies* 9 (1996), pp. 419–26.

54. Sella, *Value of Life*, p. 72.

55. Ibid., pp. 143–4.

56. Ibid., pp. 144–5.

57. Ehrenburg, *Men – Years – Life*, p. 115.

58. Ibid., p. 81,

59. Ibid., p. 115.

60. M. Glants, 'Images of the War in Painting', in Garrard, *World War 2*, p. 117; see too N. Tumarkin, *The Living and the Dead: The Rise and Fall of the Cult of World War II in Russia* (New York, 1994), pp. 79–84 on popular wartime culture and the attitude of ordinary soldiers.

61. W. Keitel, *Memoirs of Field Marshal Keitel* (London, 1965), p. 188.

62. Glantz and House, *When Titans Clashed*, pp. 171–3; Zhukov, *Reminiscences*, ii, pp. 218–20.

63. Erickson, *Road to Berlin*, pp. 186–8.

64. Werth, *Russia at War*, pp. 752–4.

65. This paragraph and following based on V. Berezhkov, *History in the Making: Memoirs of World War II Diplomacy* (Moscow, 1983), pp. 238–98 and S. Shtemenko, *Soviet General Staff*, pp. 177–95. The best account of the conference is to be found in K. Sainsbury, *The Turning Point* (London, 1986).

66. Berezhkov, *History in the Making*, p. 252.

67. Ibid., p. 256. Another version of the meeting in Harriman and Abel, *Special Envoy*, pp. 25–6.

68. Berezhkov, *History in the Making*, p. 287. Also K. Eubank, *Summit at Teheran* (New York, 1985), pp. 350–1.

69. Zhukov, *Reminiscences*, ii, p. 226.

Chapter 8

1. *Great Patriotic War of the Soviet Union 1941–1945* (Moscow, 1970), pp. 82, 143.

2. Details can be found in L. L. Kerber, *Stalin's Aviation Gulag: A Memoir of Andrei Tupolev and the Purge Era* (Washington, 1996).

3. W. Moskoff, *The Bread of Affliction: The Food Supply in the USSR during World War II* (Cambridge, 1990), p. 63.

4. *Great Patriotic War*, p. 140; J. Barber and M. Harrison, *The Soviet Home Front 1941–1945* (London, 1991), pp. 163 5.

5. Moskoff, *Bread of Affliction*, pp. 136, 148.

6. Ibid., p. 108.

7. Ibid., pp. 108–9, 175; Barber and Harrison, *Home Front*, pp. 79–85.

8. W. L. White, *Report on the Russians* (New York, 1945), pp. 148–50.

9. Moskoff, *Bread of Affliction*, pp. 149–50.

10. M. Harrison, *Soviet Planning in Peace and War, 1938–1945* (Cambridge, 1985), pp. 174–6; F. Kagan, 'The Evacuation of Soviet Industry in the Wake

of "Barbarossa": A Key to Soviet Victory', *Journal of Slavic Military Studies* 8 (1995), pp. 389–403; L. D. Pozdeeva, 'The Soviet Union: Phoenix', in D. Reynolds, W. Kimball and A. O. Chubarian, eds., *Allies at War: The Soviet, American and British Experience, 1939–1945* (New York, 1994), pp. 148–56.

11. Moskoff, *Bread of Affliction*, pp. 142–3.

12. Barber and Harrison, *Home Front*, pp. 169–70.

13. E. Bacon, *The Gulag at War: Stalin's Forced Labour System in the Light of the Archives* (London, 1994), pp. 24–8, 85.

14. A. Nove, 'Victims of Stalinism: How Many?', in J. A. Getty and R. T. Manning, eds., *Stalinist Terror: New Perspectives* (Cambridge, 1994), pp. 269–71; Bacon, *Gulag at War*, pp. 23–38, 122.

15. Bacon, *Gulag*, pp. 167–8.

16. Ibid., p. 149.

17. Ibid., p. 153.

18. Barber and Harrison, *Home Front*, pp. 116–19; R. J. Rummell, *Lethal Politics: Soviet Genocide and Mass Murder since 1917* (New Brunswick, 1990), p. 155.

19. A. Knight, *Beria: Stalin's First Lieutenant* (Princeton, 1993), pp. 117–19; D. Dallin and B. I. Nicolaevsky, *Forced Labour in Russia* (London, 1947), pp. 274–5; Rummell, *Lethal Politics*, p. 156.

20. A. Solzhenitsyn, *A Day in the Life of Ivan Denisovich* (London, 1963), p. 140.

21. D. Panin, *The Notebooks of Sologdin* (New York, 1976), pp. 93–5.

22. Ibid., pp. 138–9, 151–4, 210–12.

23. Bacon, *Gulag at War*, p. 144.

24. V. Tolz, 'New Information about the Deportation of Ethnic Groups in the USSR during World War 2', in J. Garrard and C. Garrard, *World War 2 and the Soviet People* (London, 1993), pp. 161–5; Rummell, *Lethal Politics*, p. 159.

25. Tolz, 'New Information', p. 167. The total was 948,829, including 446,480 Volga Germans. A further 120,192 were deported after the war.

26. Dallin and Nicolaevsky, *Forced Labour*, p. 46.

27. Rummell, *Lethal Politics*, pp. 158–9; M. Heller and A. Nekrich, *Utopia in Power: A History of the Soviet Union since 1917* (London, 1986), pp. 533–4.

28. Rummell, *Lethal Politics*, pp. 159–60; figures on deaths among deportee populations are difficult to reconcile. The figures supplied from official Soviet sources in 1990 suggest a much lower sum, approximately 2 to 8 per cent of the exiled populations dying in transit.

29. M. Parrish, *The Lesser Terror: Soviet State Security 1939–1953* (London,

1996), p. 104, and for other deportations pp. 100–103; Rummell, *Lethal Politics*, p. 159.

30. A. Knight, *Beria: Stalin's First Lieutenant* (Princeton, 1993), p. 147.

31. Details in A. Werth, *Russia at War*, 1941–1945 (London, 1964), pp. 776–83; J. Erickson, *The Road to Berlin* (London, 1985), pp. 234–8.

32. Details on bombing from R. J. Overy, *Why the Allies Won* (New York, 1996), pp. 128–32.

33. On the planning background G. K. Zhukov, *Reminiscences and Reflections* (Moscow, 1985), iii, pp. 259–63, 266–7.

34. Erickson, *Road to Berlin*, p. 253 on secrecy; *Main Front: Soviet Leaders Look Back on World War II* (London, 1987), pp. 177–8; D. M. Glantz, 'The Red Mask: The Nature and Legacy of Soviet Military Deception in the Second World War', in M. Handel, ed., *Strategic and Operational Deception in the Second World War* (London, 1987), pp. 213–17.

35. D. Kahn, *Hitler's Spies: German Military Intelligence in World War II* (New York, 1978), pp. 440–1.

36. D. M. Glantz and J. House, *When Titans Clashed: How the Red Army Stopped Hitler* (London, 1995), pp. 199–201.

37. Glantz, 'Military Deception', pp. 218–19; Zhukov, *Reminiscences*, ii, p. 269.

38. Ibid., pp. 266–7; Erickson, *Road to Berlin*, p. 265.

39. M. Stoler, *The Politics of the Second Front* (Westport, Connecticut, 1977), p. 158.

40. P. Winterton, *Report on Russia* (London, 1945), p. 23 [an 'Old Believer' is a member of a Russian Orthodox sect loyal to the traditional church].

41. Ibid., pp. 24–7; W. A. Harriman and E. Abel, *Special Envoy to Churchill and Stalin, 1941–1945* (London, 1975), p. 314.

42. *Main Front*, p. 192.

43. S. M. Shtemenko, *The Soviet General Staff at War* (Moscow, 1970), p. 44.

44. Details in J. Erickson, 'Soviet Women at War', in Garrard, *World War 2*, pp. 62–9.

45. Erickson, *Road to Berlin*, pp. 288–90; Glantz and House, *When Titans Clashed*, pp. 204–5.

46. Ibid., pp. 205–6.

47. Zhukov, *Reminiscences*, ii, pp. 280–1.

48. Ibid., pp. 282–3.

49. P. Padfield, *Himmler: Reichsführer SS* (London, 1990), pp. 523–7; further details can be found in J. Ciechanowski, *The Warsaw Rising of 1944* (Cambridge, 1974).

50. W. S. Churchill, *The Second World War* (6 vols., London, 1948–55), vi, pp. 124–5.

51. V. Berezhkov, *History in the Making: Memoirs of World War II Diplomacy* (Moscow, 1983), pp. 358–9.

52. G. Kolko, *The Politics of War: The World and United States Foreign Policy, 1943–1945* (New York, 1990), pp. 114–17.

53. Berezhkov, *History in the Making*, pp. 357–8.

54. Werth, *Russia at War*, p. 877.

55. Zhukov, *Reminiscences*, ii, pp. 301–2.

56. For details see M. J. Conversino, *Fighting with the Soviets: The Failure of Operation Frantic, 1944–1945* (Lawrence, Kansas, 1997), pp. 135–7.

57. Glantz and House, *When Titans Clashed*, pp. 213–14; Erickson, *Road to Berlin*, pp. 384–7.

58. M. Djilas, *Conversations with Stalin* (New York, 1962), p. 114.

59. Ibid., p. 115.

60. L. C. Gardner, *Spheres of Influence: The Partition of Europe from Munich to Yalta* (London, 1993), pp. 200–203.

61. Berezhkov, *History in the Making*, pp. 370–72.

62. Harriman and Abel, *Special Envoy*, pp. 388–90.

63. Ibid., pp. 391–3.

64. Andrew and Gordievsky, *KGB*, pp. 273–4.

65. See W. Loth, *The Division of the World 1941–1945* (London, 1988), pp. 69–72; Gardner, *Spheres of Influence*, pp. 226–36.

66. Berezhkov, *History in the Making*, p. 411.

67. Harriman and Abel, *Special Envoy*, p. 419.

68. Berezhkov, *History in the Making*, p. 405.

69. Werth, *Russia at war*, p. 980.

Chapter 9

Epigraph: I. Ehrenburg, *Men – Years – Life: The War 1941–1945* (London, 1964), p. 191.

1. G. K. Zhukov, *Reminiscences and Reflections* (2 vols., Moscow, 1985), ii, p. 346.

2. Ibid., p. 347.

3. The best account of this campaign is C. Duffy, *Red Storm on the Reich* (London, 1993). Details also in R. J. Rummell, *Lethal Politics: Soviet Genocide and Mass Murder since 1917* (New Brunswick, 1990), pp. 160–61.

4. Ehrenburg, *Men – Years – Life*, pp. 116, 138, 163.

5. J. Bridgman, *The End of the Holocaust: The Liberation of the Camps* (London, 1990), p. 19.

6. V. I. Chuikov, *The End of the Third Reich* (London, 1967), p. 41.

7. Bridgman, *End of the Holocaust*, pp. 19–20.

8. Ibid., pp. 25–7.

9. Ibid., pp. 23, 27. See too N. Levin, *The Jews in the Soviet Union since 1917* (2 vols., London, 1990), ii, pp. 424–5. When the Jewish Anti-Fascist Committee leaders asked for details of Jewish deaths they were told that records on German crimes were not 'organized according to the nationality of the victims'.

10. M. Djilas, *Conversations with Stalin* (New York, 1962), p. 111; see too N. Tolstoy, *Stalin's Secret War* (London, 1981), p. 269.

11. A. Solzhenitsyn, *The Gulag Archipelago 1918–1956* (London, 1974), p. 21.

12. J. Erickson, 'Soviet War Losses', in Erickson and D. Dilks, eds., *Barbarossa: The Axis and the Allies* (Edinburgh, 1994), p. 265.

13. Chuikov, *End of the Reich*, pp. 123–9.

14. Ibid., p. 136; Duffy, *Red Storm*, p. 246.

15. Zhukov, *Reminiscences*, ii, pp. 339–40.

16. Ibid., pp. 348–9; I. Konev, *Year of Victory* (Moscow, 1969), pp. 79–80; O. P. Chaney, *Zhukov* (2nd ed., Norman, Oklahoma, 1996), pp. 307–8, 310–11.

17. Konev, *Year of Victory*, p. 84.

18. Zhukov, *Reminiscences*, pp. 358–9.

19. Ibid., pp. 353–5.

20. Chaney, *Zhukov*, pp. 308–9.

21. V. Berezhkov, *History in the Making: Memoirs of World War II Diplomacy* (Moscow, 1983), pp. 421–4.

22. Chuikov, *End of the Reich*, pp. 144–6.

23. Ibid., p. 147; Zhukov, *Reminiscences*, pp. 364–6, who claimed that the searchlights and fog 'troubled no one'. See too Chaney, *Zhukov*, pp. 313–15 and the detailed day-by-day reconstruction in T. Le Tissier, *Zhukov at the Oder: The Decisive Battle for Berlin* (London, 1996).

24. Chaney, *Zhukov*, p. 316; W. Spahr, *Zhukov: The Rise and Fall of a Great Captain* (Novato, California, 1993), pp. 173–5.

25. Spahr, *Zhukov*, p. 177; Chuikov, *End of the Reich*, pp. 169–70.

26. Konev, *Year of Victory*, p. 92.

27. Ibid., pp. 171–2.

28. J. Erickson, *The Road to Berlin: Stalin's War with Germany* (London, 1983), pp. 809–11.

29. J. Toland, *Hitler* (New York, 1976), pp. 865−7.

30. Details in F. Genoud, ed., *The Testament of Adolf Hitler: The Hitler−Bormann Documents February−April 1945* (London, 1961).

31. Toland, *Hitler*, p. 867.

32. Ibid., p. 878.

33. W. Maser, *Hitler's Letters and Notes* (New York, 1974), pp. 357−61.

34. On the circumstances of Hitler's death there is still much disagreement. See H. R. Trevor-Roper, *The Last Days of Hitler* (7th ed., London, 1995), Preface and Chapter 7; H. Thomas, *Doppelgängers: The Truth about the Bodies in the Berlin Bunker* (London, 1995).

35. Zhukov, *Reminiscences*, ii, p. 390.

36. Chuikov, *End of the Reich*, pp. 219−23.

37. Ibid., p. 258.

38. Details in Konev, *Year of Victory*, pp. 193−235; D. Glantz and J. House, *When Titans Clashed: How the Red Army Stopped Hitler* (Lawrence, Kansas, 1995), pp. 272−4.

39. D. M. McKale, *Hitler: The Survival Myth* (New York, 1981), pp. 31−3.

40. Ibid., pp. 182−5. Zhukov was not told of the discovery of Hitler's remains for twenty years (Spahr, *Zhukov*, p. 181).

41. McKale, *Survival Myth*, p. 187, based on the testimony of L. Bezymensky, *The Death of Adolf Hitler* (New York, 1968).

42 Details from *Der Spiegel*, 'Hitlers Höllenfahrt', no. 14, 1995, pp. 170−87, no. 15, 1995, pp. 172−86.

43. H. C. Butcher, *Three Years with Eisenhower: The Personal Diary of Captain Harry C. Butcher* (London, 1946), pp. 691−3, entry for 7 May 1945; J. Deane, *The Strange Alliance: the Story of American Efforts at Wartime Cooperation with Russia* (London, 1947), pp. 164−8.

44. S. M. Shtemenko, *The Last Six Months* (New York, 1977), pp. 410−11; Zhukov, *Reminiscences*, ii, pp. 396−7; Deane, *Strange Alliance*, pp. 172−3.

45. Zhukov, *Reminiscences*, ii, pp. 399−401; details also in Chaney, *Zhukov*, pp. 329−32; Deane, *Strange Alliance*, pp. 177−8.

46. R. Parker, *Moscow Correspondent* (London, 1949), pp. 11−14.

47. Ehrenburg, *Men − Years− Life*, p. 187.

48. Ibid., pp. 188−9.

49. P. Grigorenko, *Memoirs* (London, 1983), p. 139; see also P. Sudoplatov, *Special Tasks: The Memoirs of an Unwanted Witness − A Soviet Spymaster* (New York, 1994), p. 170: 'The end of the war is still vivid in my memory as a glorious event that washed away all my doubts about the wisdom of Stalin's leadership.'

50. Zhukov, *Reminiscences*, ii, pp. 423−4.

51. Werth, *Russia at War*, pp. 1001–3.

52. Zhukov, *Reminiscences*, ii, pp. 441–3.

53. D. Volkogonov, *Stalin* (New York, 1991), pp. 498–9; Berezhkov, *History in the Making*, p. 451.

54. Volkogonov, *Stalin*, p. 501.

55. C. Andrew and O. Gordievsky, *KGB: The Inside Story* (London, 1990), p. 302; F. Radzinsky, *Stalin* (London, 1995), p. 493.

56. W. S. Churchill, *The Second World War* (6 vols., London, 1948–55), vi, pp. 498–9, letter from Churchill to Truman, 12 May 1945.

57. Zhukov, *Reminiscences*, ii, p. 443; G. Kolko, *The Politics of War: The World and United States Foreign Policy, 1943–1945* (New York, 1990), pp. 591–2; G. F. Kennan, *Memoirs, 1925–1950* (London, 1968), p. 258.

58. Stalin to Churchill in M. Heller and A. Nekrich, *Utopia in Power: A History of the Soviet Union from 1917 to the Present* (London, 1986), p. 425; on Truman and Stalin, Berezhkov, *History in the Making*, pp. 468–9.

59. Zhukov, *Reminiscences*, ii, p. 449.

60. Glantz and House, *When Titans Clashed*, pp. 277–82; Heller and Nekrich, *Utopia*, pp. 441–2.

61. Volkogonov, *Stalin*, p. 501; on prisoners see S. I. Kuznetsov, 'The Situation of Japanese Prisoners of War in Soviet Camps', *Journal of Slavic Military Studies* 8 (1995), pp. 612–13.

62 Radzinsky, *Stalin*, p. 499.

63. Figures on losses from Erickson, 'Soviet Losses', pp. 259–68. See too the estimates in E. Bacon, 'Soviet Military Losses in World War II', *Journal of Slavic Military Studies* 6 (1993); B. V. Sokolov, 'The Cost of War: Human Losses of the USSR and Germany, 1939–1945', *Journal of Slavic Military Studies* 9 (1996); V. E. Korol, 'The Price of Victory: Myths and Realities', *Journal of Slavic Military Studies* 9 (1996).

Chapter 10

Epigraph: M. Djilas, *Conversations with Stalin*, New York, 1962, p. 106.

1. W. A. Harriman and E. Abel, *Special Envoy to Churchill and Stalin, 1941–1946* (London, 1976), pp. 535–6.

2. H. S Truman, *Memoirs* (2 vols., New York, 1955), pp. 341–2.

3. A. Bryant, *Triumph in the West: The War Diaries of Field Marshal Viscount Alanbrooke* (London, 1959), p. 77.

4. M. Heller and A. Nekrich, *Utopia in Power: The History of the Soviet Union from 1917 to the Present* (London, 1986), pp. 462–3. These were

official Soviet figures. They mask the damage inflicted by the Soviet scorched-earth policy in the early years of war.

5. A. Nove, *An Economic History of the USSR* (London, 1989), pp. 279, 284.

6. Harriman and Abel, *Special Envoy*, p. 536.

7. J. Stalin, *Works* (Moscow, 1955), xiii, pp. 108, 122, talk with the German author, Emil Ludwig, 13 December 1931.

8. Cited in the review of E. Radzinsky, *Stalin*, in *Europe–Asia Studies* 49 (1997), p. 177.

9. Djilas, *Conversations*, p. 82.

10. Ibid., p. 161.

11. T. Taylor, *The Anatomy of the Nuremberg Trials: A Personal Memoir* (London, 1993), pp. 30–3.

12. Ibid., pp. 311–13.

13. Ibid., p. 211.

14. A. Vaksberg, *The Prosecutor and the Prey: Vyshinsky and the 1930s Moscow Show Trials* (London, 1990), p. 259.

15. E. M. Thompson, 'The Katyn Massacre and the Warsaw Ghetto Uprising in the Soviet–Nazi Propaganda War', in J. Garrard and C. Garrard, eds., *World War 2 and the Soviet People* (London, 1993), p. 220.

16. G. C. Malcher, *Blank Pages: Soviet Genocide against the Polish People* (Woking, UK, 1993), p. 35; E. Radzinsky, *Stalin* (London, 1996), p. 483. The announcement was made in Smolensk by A. Krayushkin.

17. D. Marples, 'Kuropaty: The Investigation of a Stalinist Historical Controversy', *Slavic Review* 53 (1994), pp. 513–16.

18. I am very grateful to James Bacque for letting me see the official figures supplied to him for his work on his book, *Crimes and Mercies* (London, 1997). The figures are drawn from a report of the chief of the Prison Department of the USSR Ministry of Foreign Affairs on 'war prisoners of the former European armies for the period 1941–1945', dated 28 April 1956. On contemporary estimates see D. Dallin and B. Nicolaevsky, *Forced Labour in Soviet Russia* (London, 1948), pp. 277–8. On Japan, S. I. Kuznetsov, 'The Situation of Japanese Prisoners of War in Soviet Camps', *Journal of Slavic Military Studies* 8 (1995).

19. Dallin and Nicolaevsky, *Forced Labour*, pp. 279–80.

20. For this quotation and much of the material used in the discussion of repatriation see N. Tolstoy, *Stalin's Secret War* (London, 1981), Chapter 17. See too Heller and Nekrich, *Utopia in Power*, pp. 450–2, for figures on the number of repatriations; N. Bethell, *The Last Secret: Forcible Repatriation to Russia 1944–1947* (London, 1974), pp. 92–118. A less sensational version

of events is in A. Cowgill *et al.* (eds.), *The Repatriations from Austria in 1945: the Report of an Inquiry* (2 vols., London, 1990).

21. Tolstoy, *Secret War*, pp. 314–15; Dallin and Nicolaevsky, *Forced Labour*, pp. 290–6.

22. Dallin and Nicolaevsky, *Forced Labour*, pp. 282–93; A. Sella, *The Value of Human Life in Soviet Warfare* (London, 1992), pp. 100–101.

23. Tolstoy, *Secret War*, p. 312.

24. R. J. B. Bosworth, *Explaining Auschwitz and Hiroshima: History Writing and the Second World War 1945–1990* (London, 1993), p. 154.

25. Dallin and Nicolaevsky, *Forced Labour*, pp. 284–9. The quotation is from an article entitled 'Judge Me!' reproduced in the Paris-based journal *Free Word (Svobodnoye slovo)*.

26. Heller and Nekrich, *Utopia in Power*, p. 452.

27. Details in Dallin and Nicolaevsky, *Forced Labour*, p. 284; Heller and Nekrich, *Utopia in Power*, pp. 451–2; R. J. Rummell, *Lethal Politics: Soviet Genocide and Mass Murder Since 1917* (London, 1990), pp. 194–5.

28. A. Knight, *Beria: Stalin's First Lieutenant* (London, 1993), p. 124.

29. A. Werth, *Russia at War* (London, 1964), pp. 998–9.

30. Details in R. Medvedev, *Let History Judge: The Origins and Consequences of Stalinism* (Oxford, 1989), pp. 782–3; W. J. Spahr, *Zhukov: The Rise and Fall of a Great Captain* (Novato, California, 1993), pp. 199–200; Radzinsky, *Stalin*, pp. 502–3.

31. N. Tumarkin, *The Living and the Dead: The Rise and Fall of the Cult of World War II in Russia* (New York, 1994), p. 108.

32. Radzinsky, *Stalin*, p. 504; Medvedev, *Let History Judge*, p. 783.

33. Details from D. Volkogonov, *Stalin: Triumph and Tragedy* (London, 1991), pp. 520–23; G. Hosking, *A History of the Soviet Union* (London, 1985), pp. 313–15; Radzinsky, *Stalin*, pp. 517–19; W. G. Hahn, *Postwar Soviet Politics: The Fall of Zhdanov and the Defeat of Moderation* (Ithaca, 1982), pp. 122-35.

34. E. Bacon, *The Gulag at War: Stalin's Forced Labour System in the Light of the Archives* (London, 1994), p. 24; Rummell, *Lethal Politics*, p. 198.

35. N. Levin, *Paradox of Survival: The Jews of the Soviet Union since 1917* (London, 1990), i, pp. 423–4, 428–30.

36. Tumarkin, *Living and Dead*, pp. 120–21; Levin, *Paradox*, pp. 432–5.

37. A. Vaksberg, *Stalin Against the Jews* (New York, 1994), pp. 159–81; Levin, *Paradox*, pp. 393–4.

38. Ibid., pp. 477–9, 484.

39. Details in B. Pinkus, *The Jews of the Soviet Union: The History of a National Minority* (Cambridge, 1993), pp. 142–50, 174–7; Levin, *Paradox*,

pp. 512–24; Y. Rapoport, *The Doctors' Plot: Stalin's Last Crime* (London, 1991), pp. 243–8 for details on Shtern's persecution.

40. Details in Heller and Nekrich, *Utopia in Power*, pp. 453–6; Rummell, *Lethal Politics*, pp. 192–6; K. Sword, *Deportation and Exile: Poles in the Soviet Union, 1939–48* (London, 1996), pp. 164–74.

41. D. Holloway, *Stalin and the Bomb* (New Haven, 1994), pp. 264–5.

42. Ibid., p. 270.

43. R. Rhodes, *The Making of the Atomic Bomb* (New York, 1986), pp. 500–502; C. Andrew and O. Gordievsky, *KGB:The Inside Story* (London, 1990), pp. 254–7; Holloway, *Stalin and the Bomb*, pp. 49–57.

44. This quotation and other details from Holloway, *Stalin and the Bomb*, Chapter 5, and Knight, *Beria*, pp. 132–5.

45. Holloway, *Stalin and the Bomb*, pp. 213–20.

46. Knight, *Beria*, p. 139.

47. Holloway, *Stalin and the Bomb*, p. 273.

48. W. O. McCagg, *Stalin Embattled, 1943–48* (Detroit, 1978), p. 217.

49. Holloway, *Stalin and the Bomb*, p. 291; J. L. Schecter and V. V. Luchkov, eds., *Khrushchev Remembers: The Glasnost Tapes* (New York, 1990), p. 100.

50. Schecter and Luchkov, *Khrushchev*, pp. 100, 102.

51. Vaksberg, *Stalin against the Jews*, pp. 243–5; Radzinsky, *Stalin*, p. 534; Rapoport, *Doctors' Plot*, pp. 77–8; Pinkus, *Jews of the Soviet Union*, pp. 178–81.

52. This is suggested in Knight, *Beria*, pp. 173–5.

53. Vaksberg, *Stalin and the Jews*, pp. 242–3; Knight, *Beria*, pp. 171–2.

54. Cited in full in Rapoport, *Doctors' Plot*, pp. 74–5. Rapoport himself was sacked from his hospital post the day after the Tass announcement and arrested a few weeks later.

55. Vaksberg, *Stalin and the Jews*, pp. 258–66.

56. The first details were revealed by Volkogonov, *Stalin*, pp. 571–2. This initial description was based on the testimony of A. I. Rybin, one of Stalin's former guards at the *dacha*. See Radzinsky, *Stalin*, pp. 449–50, for criticism of the Rybin testimony.

57. Ibid., p. 555; Knight, *Beria*, pp. 177–8. According to Rapoport, *Doctors' Plot*, pp. 151–2, his interrogators at the Lefortovo Prison began one day to ask him detailed questions about Cheyne-Stokes respiration – the condition Stalin suffered after his collapse – because all the country's leading experts were incarcerated.

58. S. Alliluyeva, *20 Letters to a Friend* (London, 1967), p. 17.

Epilogue

1. N. Tumarkin, *The Living and the Dead: The Rise and Fall of the Cult of World War II in Russia* (New York, 1994), p. 107–9.

2. R. H. McNeal, *Stalin: Man and Ruler* (London, 1988), p. 235.

3. M. P. Gallagher, *The Soviet History of World War II: Myths, Memories and Realities* (New York, 1963), pp. 147–8.

4. Tumarkin, *Living and Dead*, pp. 113–15, 120.

5. A. Axell, *Stalin's War through the Eyes of his Commanders* (London, 1997), p. 50. He was told the same by Admiral Gorshkov and General Pavlovsky, interviewed later, in January 1987.

6. A. Weiner, 'The Making of a Dominant Myth: The Second World War and the Construction of Political Identities within the Soviet Polity', *Russian Review* 55 (1996), p. 659.

7. G. Lyons, ed., *The Russian Version of the Second World War* (London, 1976). The quotation is from a translation of a standard Soviet history for senior schoolchildren dating from 1956.

8. J. L. Schecter and V. V. Luchkov, eds., *Khrushchev Remembers: The Glasnost Tapes* (New York, 1990), p. 65.

9. D. Holloway, *The Soviet Union and Atomic Energy 1939–1956* (New Haven, 1994), p. 149. The quotation is from a speech given at the Bolshoi Theatre on 9 February 1946.

10. A. Hillgruber, 'The German Military Leaders' View of Russia prior to the Attack on the Soviet Union', in B. Wegner, ed., *From Peace to War: Germany, Soviet Russia and the World 1939–1941* (Oxford, 1997), p. 180.

11. W. A. Harriman and E. Abel, *Special Envoy to Churchill and Stalin, 1941–1946* (London, 1976), p. 67.

12. Hillgruber, 'German Military Leaders', p. 182; see too the article by J. Förster in the same volume, 'Hitler Turns East German War Policy in 1940 and 1941', p. 129, who cites General Blumentritt in April 1941: 'Even the Imperial Army was no match for the German Command, and Russian commanders today are at an even greater disadvantage . . .'

13. Cited in Tumarkin, *Living and Dead*, p. 64–5 from an interview with Michael Gefter, now a Russian historian.

14. G. Gibian, 'World War 2 in Russian National Consciousness', in J. Garrard and C. Garrard, eds., *World War 2 and the Soviet People* (London, 1993), p. 155.

15. Tumarkin, *Living and Dead*, p. 64.

Bibliography

Acton, E. *Russia: the Tsarist and Soviet Legacy* (2nd ed., London, 1995)

Addison, P., Calder, A. (eds.) *Time to Kill: The Soldier's Experience of War in the West 1939–1945* (London, 1997)

Alliluyeva, S. *20 Letters to a Friend* (London, 1967)

Amba, A. *I Was Stalin's Bodyguard* (London, 1952)

Anders, W. *Hitler's Defeat in Russia* (Chicago, 1953)

Andrew, C., Gordievsky, O. *KGB: the Inside Story* (London, 1990)

Andreyev, C. *Vlasov and the Russian Liberation Movement: Soviet Reality and Emigré Theories* (Cambridge, 1987)

Antonov-Ovseyenko, A. *The Time of Stalin: Portrait of a Tyranny* (New York, 1981)

Armstrong, J. A. (ed.) *Soviet Partisans in World War II* (Madison, 1964).

Armstrong, J. A. *Ukrainian Nationalism* (Englewood, Ca., 3rd ed., 1990)

Armstrong, R. A. 'Stalingrad: Ordeal and Turning Point', *Military Review*, 72 (1992)

Axell, A. *Stalin's War Through the Eyes of his Commanders* (London, 1997)

Bacon, E. T. *The Gulag at War: Stalin's Forced Labour System in the Light of the Archives* (London, 1994)

Bacon, E. T. 'Soviet Military Losses in World War II', *Journal of Slavic Military Studies*, 6 (1993)

Bailes, K. E. *Technology and Society under Lenin and Stalin: Origins of the Soviet Technical Intelligentsia 1917–1941* (Princeton, 1978)

Barber, J., Harrison, M. *The Soviet Home Front, 1941–1945* (London, 1991)

Barbusse, H. *Stalin: a new world seen through one man* (London, 1935)

Barros, J., Gregor, R. *Double Deception: Stalin, Hitler and the Invasion of Russia* (Dekalb, Ill., 1995)

Bartov, O. *The Eastern Front 1941–1945: German Troops and the Barbarization of Warfare* (New York, 1985)

Bartov, O. *Hitler's Army: Soldiers, Nazis and War in the Third Reich* (Oxford, 1991)

Battle of Kursk (Moscow, 1974)

Beachley, D. R. 'Soviet Radio-Electronic Combat in World War II', *Military Review*, 61 (1981)

Beaumont, J. 'The Bombing Offensive as a Second Front', *Journal of Contemporary History*, 22 (1987)

Beaumont, J. *Comrades in Arms: British Aid to Russia 1941–1945* (London, 1980)

Berezhkov, V. *History in the Making: Memoirs of World War II Diplomacy* (Moscow, 1983)

Bergen, D. 'The Nazi Concept of the *Volksgemeinschaft* and the Exacerbation of Anti Semitism in Eastern Europe 1939–1945', *Journal of Contemporary History*, 29 (1994)

Bethell, N. *The Last Secret: Forcible Repatriation to Russia 1944–1947* (London, 1974)

Bezymensky, L. *The Death of Adolf Hitler* (New York, 1968)

Bialer, S. (ed.) *Stalin and his Generals: Soviet Military Memoirs of World War II* (New York, 1969)

Bilainkin, G. *Maisky: Ten Years Ambassador* (London, 1944)

Birkenfeld, W. 'Stalin als Wirtschaftsplaner Hitlers', *Vierteljahreshefte für Sozial- und Wirtschaftsgeschichte*, 51 (1966)

Bischof, G., Ambrose, S. (eds.) *Eisenhower and the German POWs: Facts against Fiction* (Baton Rouge, Ca., 1992)

Bloch, M. *Ribbentrop* (London, 1992)

Bohlen, C. *Witness to History, 1929–1969* (London, 1973)

Bonwetsch, B. 'Stalin, the Red Army and the "Great Patriotic War"', in Kershaw, Lewin, *Stalinism and Nazism*

Boog, H. *et al. Der Angriff auf die Sowjetunion* (Stuttgart, 1983)

Boog, H. (ed.) *The Conduct of Air Warfare in the Second World War: an International Comparison* (Oxford, 1992)

Boshyk, Y. (ed.) *Ukraine During World War II: History and its Aftermath* (Edmonton, 1986)

Bosworth, R. J. *Explaining Auschwitz and Hiroshima: History Writing and the Second World War 1945–90* (London, 1993)

Bradley, J. *Civil War in Russia 1917–1920* (London, 1975)

Bromage, B. *Molotov: the Story of an Era* (London, 1956)

Brown, A., Macdonald, C. *The Communist International and the Coming of World War II* (New York, 1981)

Browning, C. 'Hitler and the Euphoria of Victory: the Path to the Final Solution', in Cesarani, *Final Solution*

Browning, C. *Ordinary Men: Reserve Police Battalion 101 and the Final Solution* (Cambridge, 1992)

Browning, C. *The Path to Genocide: Essays on Launching the Final Solution* (Cambridge, 1992)

Brunovsky, V. *The Methods of the OGPU* (London, 1931)

Bryant, A. *Triumph in the West: the War Diaries of Field Marshal Viscount Alanbrooke* (London, 1959)

Bullock, A. *Hitler and Stalin: Parallel Lives* (London, 1991)

Burdick, C., Jacobsen, H-A. (eds.) *Halder Diary, 1939–1942* (London, 1988)

Burleigh, M. *Death and Deliverance: 'Euthanasia' in Germany 1900–1945* (Cambridge, 1994)

Burleigh, M. *Ethics and Extermination: Reflections on Nazi Genocide* (Cambridge, 1997)

Burleigh M. 'Nazi Europe', in N. Ferguson (ed.), *Virtual History* (London, 1997)

Burleigh, M., Wippermann, W. *The Racial State: Germany 1933–1945* (Cambridge, 1991)

Butcher, H. C. *Three Years with Eisenhower: the Personal Diary of Captain Harry C. Butcher* (London, 1946)

Carell, P. *Hitler's War on Russia* (2 vols., London, 1964)

Carley, M. J. 'End of the "Low, Dishonest Decade": Failure of the Anglo-French-Soviet Alliance in 1939', *Europe–Asia Studies*, 45 (1993)

Caroe, O. *Soviet Empire: the Turks of Central Asia and Stalinism* (London, 1967)

Cassidy, H. *Moscow Dateline 1941–1943* (London, 1944)

Cesarani, D. (ed.) *The Final Solution: Origins and Implementation* (London, 1994)

Chaney, O. P. *Zhukov* (2nd ed., Norman, Okla., 1996)

Chor'kov, A. G. 'The Red Army during the Initial Phase of the Great Patriotic War', in Wegner, *From Peace to War*

Chuikov, V. I. *The Beginning of the Road: the Story of the Battle of Stalingrad* (London, 1963)

Chuikov, V. I. *The End of the Third Reich* (London, 1967)

Churchill, W. S. *The Second World War* (6 vols., London, 1948–55)

Ciechanowski, J. *The Warsaw Rising of 1944* (Cambridge, 1974)

Coates, W. P., Coates, Z. *A History of Anglo-Soviet Relations* (London, 1944)

Cohen, A. (ed.) *The Shoah and the War* (New York, 1992)

Cohen, S. *Rethinking the Soviet Experience: Politics and History since 1917* (Oxford, 1985)

Conquest, R. *The Great Terror* (London, 1971)

Conquest, R. *Stalin: Breaker of Nations* (London, 1991)

Conquest, R. *Stalin and the Kirov Murder* (London, 1989)

Constantini, A. *L'union soviétique en guerre 1941–1945* (Paris, 1968)

Conversino, M. J. *Fighting with the Soviets: the Failure of Operation Frantic, 1944–1945* (Lawrence, Kans., 1997)

Cooper, M. *The German Army 1933–1945* (London, 1978)

Cooper M. *The Phantom War: The German Struggle against Soviet Partisans* (London, 1979)

Crampton, R. *Eastern Europe in the Twentieth Century* (London 1994)

Creveld, M. van. *Supplying War: Logistics from Wallenstein to Patton* (Cambridge, 1977)

Dallin, A. *German Rule in Russia 1941–1945* (2nd ed., London, 1981)

Dallin, D., Nicolaevsky, B. *Forced Labour in Russia* (London, 1947)

Dallin, D. *Soviet Russia's Foreign Policy 1939–1942* (New Haven, 1942)

Davies, J. E. *Mission to Moscow* (London, 1942)

Davies, R. W. 'Soviet Military Expenditure and the Armaments Industry 1929–1933', *Europe–Asia Studies*, 45 (1993)

Davies, S. *Popular Opinion and Stalin's Russia: Terror, Purge and Dissent 1934–1941* (Cambridge, 1997)

Dawson, R. H. *The Decision to Aid Russia, 1941* (Chapel Hill, 1959)

Day, R. B. *The 'Crisis' and the 'Crash': Soviet Studies of the West 1917–1939* (Ithaca, New York, 1984)

Deakin, F. W., Storry, G. *The Case of Richard Sorge* (London, 1966)

Deane, J. R. *The Strange Alliance: the Story of American Efforts at Wartime Cooperation with Russia* (London, 1947)

Degras, J. (ed.) *Soviet Documents on Foreign Policy* (3 vols., Oxford, 1953)

Deutscher, I. *Stalin: a Political Biography* (London, 1966)

Djilas, M. *Conversations with Stalin* (New York, 1962)

Duffy, C. *Red Storm on the Reich* (London, 1993)

Dukes, J. R. 'The Soviet Union and Britain: the Alliance Negotiations of March–August 1939', *Eastern European Quarterly*, 19 (1985)

Dunn, W. S. *The Soviet Economy and the Red Army 1930–1945* (London, 1995)

Dyakov, Y., Bushuyeva, T. *The Red Army and the Wehrmacht: How the Soviets Militarized Germany 1922–1933* (New York, 1995)

Dyke, C. van. *The Soviet Invasion of Finland 1939-1940* (London, 1997)

Dyke, C. van. 'The Timoshenko Reforms March–July 1940', *Journal of Slavic Military Studies*, 9 (1996)

Ehrenburg, I. *Men – Years – Life, Volume 5: the War Years 1941–1945* (London, 1964)

Elleinstein, J. *Staline* (Paris, 1984)

Elliott, M. R. 'Soviet Military Collaborators during World War II', in Boshyk, *Ukraine during World War II*

Erickson, J., Dilks, D. (eds.) *Barbarossa: the Axis and the Allies* (Edinburgh, 1994)

Erickson, J. 'New Thinking about the Eastern Front in World War II', *Journal of Military History*, 56 (1992)

Erickson, J. 'Red Army Battlefield Performance, 1941–1945: the System and the Soldier', in Addison, Calder, *Time to Kill*

Erickson, J. 'The Red Army's March into Poland, September 1939', in Sword, *Soviet Takeover*

Erickson, J. *The Road to Berlin: Stalin's War with Germany* (London, 1983)

Erickson, J. *The Road to Stalingrad* (London, 1975)

Erickson, J. *The Soviet High Command: a Military-Political History 1918–1941* (London, 1962)

Erickson, J. 'Soviet Women at War', in Garrard and Garrard, *World War 2 and the Soviet People*

Eubank, K. *Summit at Teheran* (New York, 1985)

Figes, O. *People's Tragedy: the Russian Revolution 1891–1924* (London, 1996)

Fischer, J. 'Über den Entschluss zur Luftversorgung Stalingrads. Ein Beitrag zur militärischen Führung im Dritten Reich', *Militärgeschichtliche Mitteilungen*, 6 (1969)

Fitzpatrick, S. *The Cultural Front: Power and Culture in Revolutionary Russia* (London, 1992)

Fleischauer, I., Pinkus, B. *The Soviet Germans: Past and Present* (London, 1986)

Fleming, G. *Hitler and the Final Solution* (London, 1985)

Förster, J. 'Hitler Turns East – German War Planning in 1940 and 1941', in Wegner, *From Peace to War*

Förster. J. 'Jewish Policies of the German Military 1939–1942', in Cohen, *Shoah and the War*

Förster, J. 'The Relation between Operation Barbarossa as an Ideological War of Extermination and the Final Solution', in Cesarani, *Final Solution*

Fredborg, A. *Behind the Steel Wall: Berlin 1941–1943* (London, 1944)

Fröhlich, E. (ed.) *Die Tagebücher von Joseph Goebbels* (4 vols., New York, 1987)

Gallagher, M. *The Soviet History of World War II* (New York, 1963)

Gardner, L. C. *Spheres of Influence: The Partition of Europe from Munich to Yalta* (London, 1993)

Garrard, J., Garrard, C. (eds.) *World War 2 and the Soviet People* (London, 1993)

Gebhardt, J. 'World War II: the Soviet Side', *Military Review*, 72 (1992)

Genoud, F. (ed.) *The Testament of Adolf Hitler: the Hitler–Bormann Documents, February–April 1945* (London, 1961)

Getty, J. A. *The Origins of the Great Purges: The Soviet Communist Party Reconsidered 1933–1938* (Cambridge, 1985)

Getty, J. A., Manning, R. (eds.) *Stalinist Terror: New Perspectives* (Cambridge, 1993)

Geyer, D. 'Erblauten und Erinnerungen: Mittel- und Osteuropa fünfzig Jahre nach der deutschen Kapitulation', *Osteuropa*, 45 (1995)

Gibian, G. 'World War 2 in Russian National Consciousness', in Garrard and Garrard, *World War 2 and the Soviet People*

Gilbert, F. (ed.) *Hitler Directs his War: The Secret Records of his Daily Military Conferences* (New York, 1950)

Girault, P. 'L'effort humain de l'arrière pendant la première partie de la grande guerre patriotique (1941–1943)', *Revue d'histoire de la Deuxième Guerre Mondiale*, 17 (1967)

Glants, M. 'Images of War in Painting', in Garrard and Garrard, *World War 2 and the Soviet People*

Glantz, D. M. *From the Don to the Dnepr* (London, 1991)

Glantz, D. M. 'From the Soviet Secret Archives: Newly Published Soviet Works on the Red Army 1918–1991. A Review Essay', *Journal of Slavic Military Studies*, 8 (1995)

Glantz, D. M. *The Military Strategy of the Soviet Union: a History* (London, 1992)

Glantz, D. M. 'The Red Mask: the Nature and Legacy of Soviet Military Deception in the Second World War', in M. Handel (ed.), *Strategic and Operational Deception in the Second World War* (London, 1987)

Glantz, D. M. *The Role of Intelligence in Soviet Military Strategy in World War II* (Novato, Ca., 1990)

Glantz, D. M. *Soviet Military Operational Art: in Pursuit of Deep Battle* (London, 1991)

Glantz, D. M. 'Toward Deep Battle: the Soviet Conduct of Operational Maneuver', in Reddell, *Transformations in Russian Military History*

Glantz, D. M., House, J. *When Titans Clashed: How the Red Army Stopped Hitler* (Lawrence, Kans., 1995)

Goerlitz, W. *Paulus and Stalingrad* (London, 1963)

Goodman, E. R. *The Soviet Design for a World State* (New York, 1960)

Gorodetsky, G. 'The Hess Affair and Anglo-Soviet Relations on the Eve of Barbarossa', *English Historical Review*, 101 (1986)

Gorodetsky, G. *The Precarious Truce: Anglo-Soviet Relations 1924–27* (Cambridge, 1977)

Gorodetsky, G. *Stafford Cripps' Mission to Moscow 1940–1942* (Cambridge, 1984)

Goure, L. *The Siege of Leningrad* (Stanford, 1962)

Great Patriotic War of the Soviet Union 1941–1945: a General Outline (Moscow, 1970)

Grigorenko, P. *Memoirs* (London, 1983)

Gross, J. *Revolution from Abroad: the Soviet Conquest of Poland's Western Ukraine and Western Belorussia* (Princeton, 1988)

Guderian, H. *Erinnerungen eines Soldaten* (Heidelberg, 1951)

Hagen, M. von. *Soldiers in the Proletarian Dictatorship: the Red Army and the Soviet Socialist State 1917–1930* (Ithaca, New York, 1990)

Hahn, W. *Postwar Soviet Politics: the fall of Zhdanov and the Defeat of Moderation 1946–1953* (Ithaca, New York, 1982)

Hardesty, V. *Red Phoenix: the Rise of Soviet Air Power* (London, 1982)

Hardesty, V. 'Roles and Missions: Soviet Tactical Air Power in the Second Period of the Great Patriotic War', in Reddell, *Transformations in Russian Military History*

Harriman, W. A., Abel, E. *Special Envoy to Churchill and Stalin 1941–1946* (London, 1976)

Harrison, M. *Accounting for War: Soviet production, employment and the defence burden 1940–1945* (Cambridge, 1996)

Harrison, M. 'Resource Mobilization for World War II: the USA, UK, USSR and Germany 1938–1945', *Economic History Review*, 2nd Ser., 41 (1988)

Harrison, M., Davies, R. W. 'The Soviet Military-economic Effort during the Second Five Year Plan', *Europe–Asia Studies*, 49 (1997)

Harrison, M. *Soviet Planning in Peace and War 1939–1945* (Cambridge, 1985)

Haslam, J. 'The Soviet Union and the Czech Crisis', *Journal of Contemporary History*, 14 (1979)

Haslam, J. *The Soviet Union and the Struggle for Collective Security 1933–1939* (London, 1984)

Headland, R. *Messages of Murder: A Study of the Einsatzgruppen of the*

Security Police and the Security Service 1941–1943 (London, 1992)

Heller, M., Nekrich, A. *Utopia in Power: The History of the Soviet Union from 1917 to the Present* (London, 1982)

Henri, E. *Hitler Over Russia* (London, 1936)

Herbert, U. *Hitler's Foreign Workers* (Cambridge, 1996)

Herman, J. 'Soviet Peace Efforts on the Eve of World War II: a Review of the Soviet Documents', *Journal of Contemporary History*, 15 (1980)

Herwarth, J. von. *Against Two Evils* (London, 1981)

Herzstein, R. *When Nazi Dreams Come True* (London, 1982)

Hesse, E. *Der Sowjetrussische Partisanenkrieg 1941–1944* (Göttingen, 1969)

Hirschfeld, G. *The Politics of Genocide: Jews and Soviet POWs in Nazi Germany* (London, 1988)

Hochman, J. *The Soviet Union and the Failure of Collective Security 1934–1938* (Ithaca, New York, 1984)

Hodgson, K. 'Soviet Women's Poetry of World War 2', in Garrard and Garrard, *World War 2 and the Soviet People*

Hoffmann, J. *Die Geschichte der Wlassow-Armee* (Freiburg, 1984)

Hoffmann, J. *Stalins Vernichtungskrieg 1941–1945* (Munich, 1995)

Hofmann, G. 'Doctrine, Tank Technology and Execution: I. A. Khalepskii and the Red Army's Fulfillment of Deep Offensive Operations', *Journal of Slavic Military Studies*, 9 (1996)

Holloway, D. *Stalin and the Bomb: The Soviet Union and Atomic Energy 1939–1956* (New Haven, 1994)

Hooton, E. *Phoenix Triumphant: the Rise and Rise of the Luftwaffe* (London, 1994)

Hosking, G. *A History of the Soviet Union* (London, 1985)

Hughes, J. 'Capturing the Russian Peasantry: Stalinist grain procurement policy and the "Urals-Siberian method"', *Slavic Review*, 53 (1994)

Inber, V. *Leningrad Diary* (London, 1971)

Jackel, E. *Hitler's World View: a Blueprint for Power* (Middleton, Conn., 1981)

Jakobsen, M. *Origins of the Gulag: the Soviet Prison Camp System 1917–1934* (London, 1993)

Jukes, G. *The Defence of Moscow* (London, 1969)

Jukes, G. *Hitler's Stalingrad Decisions* (Berkeley, 1985)

Jukes, G. 'The Red Army and the Munich Crisis', *Journal of Contemporary History*, 26 (1991)

Kagan, F. 'The Evacuation of Soviet Industry in the Wake of Barbarossa: a Key to Soviet Victory', *Journal of Slavic Military Studies*, 8 (1995)

Kahn, D. *Hitler's Spies: German Military Intelligence in World War II* (New York, 1978)

Kamenetsky, I. *Hitler's Occupation of Ukraine (1941–1944): a Study of Totalitarian Imperialism* (Milwaukee, 1956)

Keitel, W. *Memoirs of Field Marshal Keitel* (London, 1965)

Kennan, G. F. *Memoirs, 1925–1950* (London, 1968)

Kennan, G. F. *Russia and the West under Lenin and Stalin* (London, 1961)

Kennan, G. F. (ed.) *Soviet Foreign Policy 1917–1941* (New York, 1960)

Kerber, L. L. *Stalin's Aviation Gulag: a Memoir of Andrei Tupolev and the Purge Era* (Washington, 1996)

Kershaw, I., Lewin, M. (eds.) *Stalinism and Nazism: Dictatorships in Comparison* (Cambridge, 1997)

Khrushchov [*sic*], N. S. *Report of the Central Committee to the 20th Congress of the CPSU* (London, Feb. 1956)

Kilmarx, R. *A History of Soviet Air Power* (London, 1962)

Kislitsyn, N., Zubakov, V. *Leningrad Does Not Surrender* (Moscow, 1989)

Kitchen, M. *British Policy towards the Soviet Union during the Second World War* (London, 1986)

Knight, A. *Beria: Stalin's First Lieutenant* (London, 1993)

Knight, A. 'The fate of the KGB Archives', *Slavic Review*, 52 (1993)

Koch, H. 'Operation Barbarossa: the Current State of the Debate', *Historical Journal*, 31 (1988)

Kolko, G. *The Politics of War: the World and United States Foreign Policy 1943–1945* (New York, 1990)

Konev, I. *Year of Victory* (Moscow, 1969)

Korol, V. E. 'The Price of Victory: Myths and Realities', *Journal of Slavic Military Studies*, 9 (1996)

Krawchenko, B. 'Soviet Ukraine under Nazi Occupation 1941–1944', in Boshyk, *Ukraine during World War II*

Kriegstagebuch des Oberkommandos der Wehrmacht (5 vol., Frankfurt-am-Main, 1961–63)

Krivitsky, W. *I Was Stalin's Agent* (2nd ed., Cambridge, 1992)

Kube, A. *Pour le mérite und Hakenkreuz: Hermann Göring im Dritten Reich* (Munich, 1986)

Kudryashov, S. 'The Hidden Dimension: Wartime Collaboration in the Soviet Union', in Erickson, Dilks, *Barbarossa*

Kumanev, G. A. 'The Soviet Economy and the 1941 Evacuation', in Wieczynski, *Operation Barbarossa*

Kuznetsov, S. 'The Situation of Japanese Prisoners of War in Soviet Camps', *Journal of Slavic Military Studies*, 8 (1995)

Laqueur, W. *Russia and Germany: a Century of Conflict* (London, 1965)

Laqueur, W. *Stalin: the Glasnost Revelations* (London, 1990)

Larionov, V. 'Why the Wehrmacht Didn't Win in 1941', in Wieczynski, *Operation Barbarossa*

Lavan, M. 'Le folklore soviètique (1941–1945): arme psychologique et document historique', *Revue d'histoire de la Deuxième Guerre Mondiale*, 17 (1967)

Leach, B. *German Strategy Against Russia* (Oxford, 1973)

Levin, N. *Paradox of Survival: the Jews of the Soviet Union* (2 vols., London, 1990)

Linz, S. (ed.) *The Impact of World War II on the Soviet People* (Totowa, NJ, 1985)

Loth, W. *The Division of the World 1941–1945* (London, 1988)

Lukacs, J. *War on the Eastern Front: the German Soldier in Russia 1941–1945* (London, 1991)

Lukes, I. *Czechoslovakia between Stalin and Hitler* (New York, 1996)

Lukes, I. 'Stalin and Beneš in the Final Days of September 1938', *Slavic Review*, 52 (1993)

Lukes, R. *The Forgotten Holocaust: the Poles under German Occupation 1939–1944* (Lexington, Kty, 1986)

Lumass, V. *Himmler's Auxiliaries: the Volksdeutsche Mittelstelle and the German National Minorities of Europe 1939–1945* (Chapel Hill, 1993)

Lyons, G. (ed.) *The Russian Version of the Second World War* (London, 1976)

Main, S. J. 'Stalin in June 1941', *Europe–Asia Studies*, 48 (1996)

Main Front: Soviet Leaders Look Back on World War II (London, 1987) (introduction by J. Erickson)

Maisky, I. *Journey into the Past* (London, 1962)

Malcher, G. *Blank Pages: Soviet Genocide against the Polish People* (Woking, UK, 1993)

Manstein, E. von. *Verlorene Siege* (Bonn, 1955)

Marples, D. 'Kuropaty: the Investigation of a Stalinist Historical Controversy', *Slavic Review*, 53 (1994)

Marples, D. *Stalinism in the Ukraine in the 1940s* (Cambridge, 1992)

Maser, W. (ed.) *Hitler's Letters and Notes* (New York, 1974)

Maslov, A. A. 'Concerning the Role of Partisan Warfare in Soviet Military Doctrine of the 1920s and 1930s', *Journal of Slavic Military History*, 9 (1996)

Maslov, A. A. 'Soviet General Officer Corps 1941–1945: Losses in Combat', *Journal of Slavic Military Studies*, 8 (1995)

Mawdsley, E. *The Russian Civil War* (London, 1987)

McCagg, W. O. *Stalin Embattled 1943–1948* (Detroit, 1978)

McCauley, M. (ed.) *Communist Power in Europe 1944–1949* (London, 1977)

McKale, D. M. *Hitler: the Survival Myth* (New York, 1981)

McKenzie, K. *Comintern and World Revolution* (New York, 1964)

McKenzie, S. 'The Treatment of POWs in World War II', *Journal of Modern History*, 56 (1994)

McNeal, R. H. *Stalin: Man and Ruler* (London, 1988)

Medvedev, R. *Let History Judge: the Origins and Consequences of Stalinism* (London, 1971)

Mellenthin, F. von *Panzer-Schlachten* (Neckargemünd, 1963)

Mikoyan, A. *Memoirs of Anastas Mikoyan, vol. 1* (Madison, Conn., 1988)

Mikoyan, S. A. 'Barbarossa and the Soviet Leadership', in Erickson, Dilks, *Barbarossa and the Allies*

Millman, B. 'Toward War with Russia: British Naval and Air Planning for Conflict in the Near East 1939–1940', *Journal of Contemporary History*, 29 (1994)

Milward, A. S. *War, Economy and Society 1939–1945* (London, 1987)

Miner, S. M. *Between Churchill and Stalin: the Soviet Union, Great Britain and the Origins of the Grand Alliance* (Chapel Hill, 1988)

Moldenhauer, H. 'Die Reorganisation der Roten Armee vor der "Grossen Säuberung" bis zum deutschen Angriff auf die UdSSR (1938–1941)', *Militärgeschichtliche Mitteilungen*, 55 (1996)

Moskoff, W. *The Bread of Affliction: The Food Supply in the USSR during World War II* (Cambridge, 1990)

Muller, R-D. *Hitlers Ostkrieg und die deutsche Siedlungspolitik* (Frankfurt-am-Main, 1991)

Mulligan, T. P. *The Politics of Illusion and Empire: German Occupation Policy in the Soviet Union 1942–43* (New York, 1988)

Mulligan, T. P. 'Spies, Ciphers and "Zitadelle": Intelligence and the Battle of Kursk, 1943', *Journal of Contemporary History*, 22 (1987)

Naimark, N., Gibianskii, L. (eds.) *The Establishment of Communist Regimes in Eastern Europe 1944–1949* (Boulder, Co., 1997)

Namier, L. *Europe in Decay: a Study in Disintegration* (London, 1950)

Nardo, R. L. di *Mechanized Juggernaut or Military Anachronism? Horses and the German Army in World War II* (London, 1991)

Nation, R. C. *Black Earth, Red Star* (Ithaca, New York, 1992)

Nevezhin, V. A. 'The Pact with Germany and the Idea of an "Offensive War" (1939–1941)', *Journal of Slavic Military Studies*, 8 (1995)

Newland, S. J. *Cossacks in the Red Army 1941–1945* (London, 1996)

Nicholas, L. *The Rape of Europa: The Fate of Europe's Treasures in the Third Reich and the Second World War* (London, 1994)

Nove, A. *An Economic History of the USSR* (3rd ed., London, 1992)

Nove, A. *Stalinism and After* (London, 1975)

Nove, A. (ed.) *The Stalin Phenomenon* (London, 1993)

O'Ballance, E. *The Red Army 1917–1963* (London, 1964)

Ogorkiewicz, R. *Armoured Forces: A History of Armoured Forces and their Vehicles* (London, 1970)

Olsen, S. (ed.) *Harold Nicolson: Diaries and Letters 1930–1964* (New York, 1980)

Orenstein, H. (ed.) *Soviet Documents on the Use of War Experience in World War II* (3 vols., London, 1993)

Overy, R. J. *The Air War 1939–1945* (London, 1980)

Overy, R. J. *Goering: the 'Iron Man'* (London, 1984)

Overy, R. J. 'Mobilization for Total War in Germany 1939 1941', *English Historical Review*, 103 (1988)

Overy, R. J., Ten Cate, J., Otto G. (eds.) *Die Neuordnung Europas: NS-Wirtschaftspolitik in den besetzten Gebieten* (Berlin, 1997)

Overy, R. J. *War and Economy in the Third Reich* (Oxford, 1994)

Overy, R. J. *Why the Allies Won* (London, 1995)

Padfield, P. *Himmler: Reichsführer SS* (London, 1990)

Panin, D. *The Notebooks of Sologdin* (New York, 1976)

Parker, R. A. *Struggle for Survival* (Oxford, 1989)

Parker, R. *Moscow Correspondent* (London, 1949)

Parrish, M. *The Lesser Terror: Soviet State Security 1939 1953* (London, 1996)

Pavlov, D. V. *Leningrad 1941: the Blockade* (Chicago, 1965)

Pietrow-Ennker, B. 'Die Sowjetunion und der Beginn des Zweiten Weltkrieges 1939–1941: Ergebnisse einer internationalen Konferenz in Moskau', *Osteuropa*, 45 (1995)

Pinchuk, B-C. *Shtetl Jews under Soviet Rule: Eastern Poland on the Eve of the Holocaust* (London, 1990)

Pinkus, B. *The Jews of the Soviet Union: the History of a National Minority* (Cambridge, 1993)

Porter, C., Jones, M. *Moscow in World War II* (London, 1987)

Raack, R. C. *Stalin's Drive to the West 1938–1945: the Origins of the Cold War* (Stanford, 1995)

Raack, R. C. 'Stalin's Plans for World War II', *Journal of Contemporary History*, 26 (1991)

Radzinsky, E. *Stalin* (London, 1996)

Rapoport, Y. *The Doctors' Plot: Stalin's Last Crime* (London, 1991)

Rascale, M. 'L'organisation et le rôle de l'état soviétique pendant la guerre', *Revue d'histoire de la Deuxième Guerre Mondiale*, 17 (1967)

Raymond, P. 'Witness and Chronicler of Nazi-Soviet Relations: the Testimony of Evgeny Gnedin', *Russian Review*, 44 (1985)

Read, A., Fisher, D. *The Deadly Embrace: Hitler, Stalin and the Nazi-Soviet Pact 1939–1941* (London, 1988)

Reddell, C. (ed.) *Transformations in Russian and Soviet Military History* (Washington, 1990)

Reese, R. R. *Stalin's Reluctant Soldiers: a Social History of the Red Army 1925–1941* (Lawrence, Kans., 1996)

Reinhardt, K. *Moscow – the Turning Point: the Failure of Hitler's Strategy in the Winter of 1941–1942* (Oxford, 1992)

Reitlinger, G. *The Final Solution* (London, 1971)

Reuth, R. G. *Goebbels* (London, 1993)

Reynolds, D., Kimball, W., Chubarian, A. (eds.) *Allies at War: the Soviet, American and British Experience 1939–1945* (New York, 1994)

Rhodes, R. *The Making of the Atomic Bomb* (New York, 1986)

Rich, N. *Hitler's War Aims* (2 vols., London, 1973–4)

Richardson, C. R. 'French Plans for Allied Attacks on the Caucasus Oilfields, Jan–Apr 1940', *French Historical Studies*, 8 (1973)

Richardson, S. (ed.) *The Secret History of World War II: the Wartime Cables of Roosevelt, Stalin and Churchill* (New York, 1986)

Richardson, W., Frieden, S. (eds.) *The Fatal Decisions* (London, 1956)

Rittersporn, G. *Stalinist Simplifications and Soviet Complications: Social Tensions and Political Conflict in the USSR 1933–1953* (Reading, 1991)

Roberts, C. A. 'Planning for War: the Red Army and the Catastrophe of 1941', *Europe–Asia Studies*, 47 (1995)

Roberts, G. 'The Soviet Decision for a Pact with Nazi Germany', *Soviet Studies*, 44 (1992)

Roberts, G. *The Soviet Union and the Origins of the Second World War 1933–1941* (London, 1995)

Rokossovosky, K. *A Soldier's Duty* (Moscow, 1970)

Rosefielde, S. 'Stalinism in Post-Communist Perspective: New Evidence on Killings, Forced Labor and Economic Growth in the 1930s', *Europe–Asia Studies*, 48 (1996)

Rosenberg, W., Siegelbaum, L. (eds.) *Social Dimensions of Soviet Industrialization* (Bloomington, Ind., 1993)

Rossi, J. *The Gulag Handbook* (New York, 1989)

Rotundo, L. 'The Creation of Soviet Reserves and the 1941 Campaign', *Military Affairs*, 65 (1985)

Rummell, R. *Lethal Politics: Soviet Genocide and Mass Murder since 1917* (New Brunswick, 1990)

Rzheshevsky, O. (ed.) *War and Diplomacy: the Making of the Grand Alliance: from Stalin's Archive* (London, 1996)

Sabrin, B. *Alliance for Murder: the Nazi Ukrainian-Nationalist Partnership in Genocide* (London, 1991)

Sainsbury, K. *The Turning Point* (London, 1986)

Salisbury, H. (ed.) *Marshal Zhukov's Greatest Battles* (London, 1969)

Salisbury, H. *The 900 Days: the Siege of Leningrad* (London, 1969)

Samuelson, L. 'Mikhail Tukhachevsky and War-Economic Planning: Reconsiderations on the Pre-War Soviet Military Build-Up', *Journal of Slavic Military Studies*, 9 (1996)

Sapir, J. 'The Economics of War in the Soviet Union during World War II', in Kershaw, Lewin, *Stalinism and Nazism*

Schecter, J., Luchkov, V. (eds.) *Khrushchev Remembers: the Glasnost Tapes* (New York, 1990)

Schiness, R. 'The Conservative Party and Anglo-Soviet Relations 1925–27', *European Studies Review*, 7 (1977)

Schmider, K. 'No Quiet on the Eastern Front: the Suvorov Debate in the 1990s', *Journal of Slavic Military Studies*, 10 (1997)

Schulte, T. *The German Army and Nazi Policies in Occupied Russia* (Oxford, 1989)

Schwendemann, H. *Die wirtschaftliche Zusammenarbeit zwischen dem Deutschen Reich und der Sowjetunion von 1939 bis 1941* (Berlin, 1993)

Seaton, A. *The Russo-German War 1941–1945* (London, 1971)

Seaton, A. *Stalin as Warlord* (London, 1976)

Sella, A. *The Value of Human Life in Soviet Warfare* (London, 1992)

Serge, V. *Portrait de Staline* (Paris, 1940)

Service, R. *A History of Twentieth-Century Russia* (London, 1997)

Shtemenko, S. M. *The Last Six Months* (New York, 1977)

Shtemenko, S. M. *The Soviet General Staff at War* (Moscow, 1970)

Shub, D. *Lenin* (London, 1966)

Shukman, H. (ed.) *Stalin's Generals* (London, 1993)

Simonov, K. *Days and Nights* (London, n.d.)

Smith, H. K. *Last Train from Berlin* (London, 1942)

Sokolov, B. 'The Cost of War: Human Losses of the USSR and Germany 1939–1945', *Journal of Slavic Military Studies*, 9 (1996)

Sokolov, B. 'Lend Lease in Soviet Military Efforts 1941–1945', *Journal of Slavic Military Studies*, 7 (1994)

Solzhenitsyn, A. *The Gulag Archipelago* (3 vols., London, 1973–8)

Souvarine, B. *Stalin* (London, 1939)

Spahr, W. *Zhukov: the Rise and Fall of a Great Captain* (Novato, Ca., 1993)

Spinka, M. *The Church in Soviet Russia* (Oxford, 1956)

Stalin, J. *The Problem of Leninism* (Moscow, 1947)

Stalin, J. *The Great Patriotic War of the Soviet Union* (New York, 1945)

Steinberg, J. 'The Third Reich Reflected: German Civil Administration in the Occupied Soviet Union 1941–4', *English Historical Review*, 110 (1995)

Stephan, J. J. *The Russian Fascists: Tragedy and Farce in Exile 1925–1945* (London, 1978)

Stern, J. P. *Hitler, the Führer and the People* (London, 1976)

Stoler, M. *The Politics of the Second Front* (Westport, Conn. 1977)

Stolfi, R. *Hitler's Panzers East: World War II Reinterpreted* (Norman, Okl., 1991)

Strategy and Tactics of the Soviet-German War: Lessons of the Operations on the Eastern Front (Soviet Embassy, London, 1941)

Streit, C. *Keine Kameraden. Die Wehrmacht und die sowjetischen Kriegsgefangenen 1941–1945* (Stuttgart, 1981)

Streit, C. 'Partisans, Resistance, Prisoners of War', in Wieczynski, *Operation Barbarossa*

Subtelny, O. 'The Soviet Occupation of Western Ukraine 1939–1941: an Overview', in Boshyk, *Ukraine during World War II*

Sudaplatov, P. *Special Tasks: the Memoirs of an Unwanted Witness – a Soviet Spymaster* (New York, 1994)

Suvorov, V. 'Who Was Planning to Attack Whom in June 1941, Hitler or Stalin?', *Military Affairs*, 69 (1989)

Sword, K. *Deportation and Exile: Poles in the Soviet Union 1939–1948* (London, 1996)

Sword, K. (ed.) *The Soviet Takeover of the Polish Eastern Provinces 1939–1941* (London, 1991)

Sydnor, C. *Soldiers of Destruction: The SS Death's Head Division 1933–1945* (Princeton, 1977)

Tarleton, R. E. 'What Really Happened to the Stalin Line?', *Journal of Slavic Military Studies*, 6 (1993)

Taylor, F. (ed.) *The Goebbels Diaries 1939–1941* (London, 1982)

Taylor T. *The Anatomy of the Nuremberg Trials: a Personal Memoir* (London, 1993)

Tec, N. *Defiance: the Bielski Partisans* (Oxford, 1993)

Thomas, H. *Doppelgängers: The Truth about the Bodies in the Berlin Bunker* (London, 1995)

Thompson, E. 'The Katyn Massacre and the Warsaw Ghetto Uprising in the

Soviet-Nazi Propaganda War', in Garrard and Garrard, *World War 2 and the Soviet People*

Thurston, R. *Life and Terror in Stalin's Russia, 1934–1941* (London, 1996)

Tissier, T. Le *Zhukov at the Oder: the Decisive Battle for Berlin* (London, 1996)

Toland, J. *Adolf Hitler* (New York, 1976)

Tolstoy, N. *Stalin's Secret War* (London, 1981)

Tompsen, W. *Khrushchev* (London, 1994)

Topitsch, E. *Stalins Krieg: die sowjetische Langzeitstrategie gegen den Westen als rationale Machtpolitik* (Munich, 1985)

Tolz, V. 'New Information about the Deportation of Ethnic Groups in the USSR during World War 2', in Garrard and Garrard, *World War 2 and the Soviet People*

Treue, W. 'Hitler's Denkschrift zum Vierjahresplan 1936', *Vierteljahreshefte für Zeitgeschichte*, 3 (1955)

Trevor-Roper, H. (ed.) *Hitler's War Directives* (London, 1964)

Trevor-Roper, H. *The Last Days of Hitler* (7th ed., London, 1995)

Truman, H. S *Memoirs* (2 vols., New York, 1955)

Tucker, R. *Stalin in Power: the Revolution from Above 1928–1941* (London, 1990)

Tumarkin, N. *The Living and the Dead: the Rise and Fall of the Cult of World War II in Russia* (New York, 1994)

Tuyll, H. van *Feeding the Bear: American Aid to the Soviet Union 1941–1945* (New York, 1989)

Uebe, K. *Russian Reactions to German Air Power in World War II* (New York, 1964)

Ulam, A. *Expansion and Coexistence: a History of Soviet Foreign Policy 1917–1967* (London, 1968)

Ulam, A. *Lenin and Bolsheviks* (London, 1965)

Ulam, A. *Stalin: the Man and his Era* (London, 1973)

Uldricks, T. 'Russia and Europe: Diplomacy, Revolution and Economic Development in the 1920s', *International History Review*, 1 (1979)

Vaksberg, A. *The Prosecutor and the Prey: Vyshinsky and the 1930s Moscow Show Trials* (London, 1990)

Vaksberg, A. *Stalin against the Jews* (New York, 1994)

Vardys, V. 'The Baltic States under Stalin: the First Experiences 1939–1941', in K. Sword, *Soviet Takeover*

Volkogonov, D. *Stalin: Triumph and Tragedy* (London, 1991)

Vorsin, V. F. 'Motor Vehicle Transport Deliveries through "Lend-Lease"', *Journal of Slavic Military Studies*, 10 (1997)

Warlimont, W. *Inside Hitler's Headquarters* (London, 1964)

Watt, D. C. *How War Came; the Immediate Origins of the Second World War 1938–1939* (London, 1989)

Wegner, B. (ed.) *From Peace to War: Germany, Soviet Russia and the World 1939–1941* (Providence, RI, 1997)

Weinberg, G. *World in the Balance* (Hanover, New Eng., 1980)

Weinberg, R. 'Purge and Politics on the Periphery: Birobidzhan in 1937', *Slavic Review*, 52 (1993)

Weiner, A. 'The Making of a Dominant Myth: the Second World War and the Construction of Political Identities within the Soviet Polity', *Russian Review*, 55 (1996)

Werth, A. *Leningrad* (London, 1944)

Werth, A. *Moscow '41* (London, 1942)

Werth, A. *Russia at War 1941–1945* (London, 1964)

Wheatcroft, S. 'More Light on the Scale of Repression and Excess Mortality in the Soviet Union in the 1930s', in Getty, Manning, *Stalinist Terror*

White, W. L. *Report on the Russians* (New York, 1945)

Wieczynski, J. (ed.) *Operation Barbarossa: the German Attack on the Soviet Union, June 22 1941* (Salt Lake City, 1993)

Wieder, J. *Stalingrad und die Verantwortung der Soldaten* (Munich, 1962)

Winterton, P. *Report on Russia* (London, 1945)

Yurkevich, M. 'Galician Ukrainians in German Military Formations and in the German Administration', in Boshyk, *Ukraine during World War II*

Zaloga, S. J., Grandsen, J. *Soviet Tanks and Combat Vehicles of World War Two* (London, 1984)

Zambinsky, O. 'Collaboration of the Population in Occupied Ukrainian Territory: Some Aspects of the Overall Picture', *Journal of Slavic Military Studies*, 10 (1997)

Zeidler, M. *Reichswehr und Rote Armee 1920–1933* (Munich, 1993)

Zeitzler, K. 'Stalingrad', in Richardson, Frieden, *Fatal Decisions*

Zetterling, N. 'Loss Ratios on the Eastern Front during World War II', *Journal of Slavic Military Studies*, 9 (1996)

Zhukov, G. K. *Reminiscences and Reflections* (2 vols., Moscow, 1985)

Ziemke, E. 'Composition and Morale of the Partisan Movement', in Armstrong, *Soviet Partisans*

Ziemke, E. *From Stalingrad to Berlin: the German Defeat in the East* (Washington, 1968)

Index